942.02 H 59 22

8407

The Medieval English Economy 1150–1500

D1471285

The medieval English economy
108532

W█████████VN

Non-Fiction   0460112740   941 BOL
Wycliffe College

The
Medieval English Economy
1150–1500

J L BOLTON

Department of History,
Queen Mary College, London

J M Dent & Sons Ltd London

Rowman & Littlefield Totowa, NJ

© J. L. Bolton 1980
All rights reserved
Printed in Great Britain by
Billing & Sons Ltd
Guildford, London, Oxford & Worcester
and bound at the
Aldine Press, Letchworth, Herts for
J. M. Dent & Sons Ltd
Aldine House, Welbeck Street, London
First published in the U.K. (Everyman's Library), 1980
First published in the United States by
Rowman and Littlefield, Totowa, N.J., 1980

This book if bound as a paperback is subject to
the condition that it may not be issued on loan or otherwise
except in its original binding

This book is set in 11 on 13 pt. V.I.P. Baskerville by
Western Printing Services Ltd, Bristol

British Library Cataloguing in Publication Data
Bolton, J L
  The medieval English economy, 1150–1500. –
  (Everyman's university library).
  1. England – Economic conditions
  I. Title   II. Series
  330.9'42   HC254

  ISBN 0–460–10274–5
  ISBN 0–460–11274–0 Pbk

Rowman and Littlefield edition
  ISBN 0–8476–6234–9 (Hardback)
  ISBN 0–8476–6235–7 (Paperback)

Contents

Foreword

This book is intended as an introduction to a complex but fascinating subject, the economy of medieval England. Each chapter is designed to cover one specific theme or period and can be read separately. Consequently there is some repetition in the argument and I hope that this will not cause annoyance to the more general reader. It is not, apart from Chapter 9, a work based on original research but on the labours of countless other historians. My debt to them is great and cannot, alas, be fully acknowledged here. I should, however, like to thank my colleagues at London University, Professor F. R. H. Du Boulay and Dr Sarah Palmer, for kindly reading and commenting on certain chapters; Val Robinson who managed to type parts of an almost illegible manuscript; and Professors R. F. Leslie and G. Williams who arranged a year's leave from the History Department at Queen Mary College for me. Last and most important I must thank Ann for her constant support and for patiently reading, correcting and criticizing all the various stages through which this book has passed.

Queen Mary College,   J. L. Bolton
University of London

Acknowledgments

I should like to thank the following for permission to use their copyright material:

The editors of the *Economic History Review* and the authors for the reproduction of wage tables from W. Beveridge, 'Wages on the Winchester Manors', *Economic History Review* 1st series, vii, 1936 and 'Westminster Wages in the Manorial Era', *Economic History Review* 2nd series, viii, 1955; the grain price tables from D. A. L. Farmer, 'Some Price Fluctuations in Angevin England', *Economic History Review* 2nd series, ix, 1956 and 'Some Price Movements in Thirteenth-Century England', *Economic History Review* 2nd series, x, 1957; maps of the distribution of wealth from R. Schofield, 'The Distribution of Wealth in England 1334–1649', *Economic History Review* 2nd series, xviii, 1965; and the graph showing high and low population estimates from J. Hatcher, *Plague, Population and the English Economy 1348–1530*, Studies in Economic History (London, 1977), p. 71.

The Oxford University Press and Miss O. Coleman for permission to reproduce the graphs of wool and cloth exports from E. M. Carus-Wilson and O. Coleman, *England's Export Trade 1275–1547* (Oxford, 1963).

The Editor of *Economica* for permission to reproduce statistics of builders' wage-rates and the prices of consumables from E. Phelphs Brown and S. V. Hopkins, 'Seven Centuries of the Prices of Consumables Compared with Builders' Wage-Rates', *Economica* 1956.

1 Introduction: Settlement and Society

Every age has its own vision of the past, of how its ancestors conducted their affairs and ordered their lives. Usually that vision is a rosy one; the pressures of modern life produce a nostalgia for the good old days when everything was so much simpler. Those good old days often lie no more than 30 or 40 years distant when summers were long and hot, winters cold and snowy, taxes were lower and the trains ran on time. The further back most men cast their minds the more hazy their ideas, but the notion of well-being persists. Life in the Middle Ages may have been hard but it cannot have been totally bad. After all there were so many fewer people, and even if the lord of the manor was harsh there was always a Robin Hood to protect one, a good King Richard to return from the Crusades and right all wrongs, a Simon de Montfort to create a parliament and a maypole to dance around

> When the merry bells ring round
> And the jocund rebecks sound . . .
> And young and old come forth to play,
> On a sunshine holiday.

The stock response of the professional historian to such dreams is, 'Ah, but it wasn't like that at all.' Unfortunately it is much more difficult to say what it *was* like. In part this is due to the limitations of the evidence. There are records enough, great surveys like Domesday Book or the Hundred Rolls of the late thirteenth century, manorial court rolls from the thirteenth century onwards, estate accounts, agricultural treatises, but all were made for or by lords. For the most part we have to see the peasantry, the mass of the population, through the lord's eyes, and this inevitably gives us a one-sided view. Just as important, the research of the past three-quarters of a century has destroyed the idea of a uniform medieval society, never varying from

9

time to time or place to place. The picture of a land covered with villages nestling in the midst of open fields, of a society where the lord of the manor continually demanded heavy labour services from the peasantry as rent for their land, has been shattered. In its place a mosaic has been pieced together which shows very considerable variations from region to region, within the regions themselves and from century to century as the demands of the economy changed the obligations of society. Generalizations are difficult to make for there was no one economy but a whole series of interrelated regional economies. There was no one society but varying sets of bonds and responsibilities.

To describe that changing pattern of society between the twelfth and fifteenth centuries is the object of this book, but it follows that some point of departure is needed. So, what manner of country was England in the mid-twelfth century and how was it peopled? In broad terms the main physical features were the same as they are today: hills, rivers and streams have altered little over the past 700 years. The fens on the East Coast had yet to be drained. They had been described in the eighth century as stretching from Granchester to the North Sea, with immense marshes, black pools of water, foul running streams and many islands, on one of which stood the Abbey of Ely. More tracts of marshland would have been found in and around Athelney and the Sedgemoor levels, whilst the configuration of the South Coast between Hastings and the North Foreland was very different. Much of Romney Marsh remained to be both formed and drained whilst Sandwich, now far inland, was a flourishing port in the thirteenth and fourteenth centuries.

But one difference would have been immediately obvious – the extent of the forests. The natural covering for most of lowland England is trees or scrub. At the beginning of the Middle Ages England had been virtually covered with woodland. Between Tyne and Tees lay a vast forest, uninhabited except by wild beasts. In the West Midlands the forests of Dean, Wyre, Morfe and Kinver, and in the East Midlands those of Rockingham and Sherwood covered much of the land. Essex was under oak, hornbeam and ash whilst the Weald was supposed to have been 30 miles wide and 120 long from east to west. In Wessex Selwood ran north to south along the western edge of Salisbury Plain and acted as a barrier between Saxon and Celt for over a century.

By 1150 a sustained assault had been made on the woodland. The Anglo-Saxons and later the Danes and Norwegians were great colonizers. Numerous place-name endings in and compounded with 'leigh' or 'ley' or 'hurst', meaning the woodland clearing, bear witness to this. In the Scandinavian north, endings such as 'lundr', 'skogr' or 'viothr' indicate wood, 'scarth' a clearing as in Aysgarth, the open space by the oaks. By 1086 most of the villages we know today were in existence. In the Cherwell valley in Oxfordshire there are 37 parishes and the names of all but five are to be found in Domesday. Some villages were already substantial. Tackley had nearly 150 inhabitants and 1,200 acres under the plough, Somerton 130 people and possibly more arable land than the 1,119½ acres to be found in the parish exactly 800 years later.

England was thus an old land in terms of settlement by the mid-twelfth century. Most of the best sites with adequate supplies of water and land suitable for both arable, meadow and pasture had long been settled. Much of what was left was either high or poor ground or a combination of both. The old county of Middlesex is a good example of this. The light gravel soils in the south of the county were settled early but the intractable clay woodland to the north and north east lay largely deserted. Yet colonization continued, to meet the demands of a growing population. Within most villages there was some uncultivated land – woods, for instance, which provided grazing for pigs, fuel and building material and a reserve of land for future expansion – and all over England sections of forest land were being cleared and brought into arable cultivation or opened up for cattle grazing.

Yet, if the forests and woods provided a vital reserve of land, they also presented a formidable barrier to expansion. The soil was often poor but, more important, since the Conquest large areas of wood, scrub heath and moor had been brought under the forest laws. Over them the king and his courtiers hunted the beast of the chase and by and large agriculture was not permitted within their limits. Private forests also existed, some 70 in all in the thirteenth century, where a lay nobleman had rights similar to the king's. In other places the local lord had the right of warren, the privilege of hunting lesser game, the fox, hare or rabbit over their estates to the detriment of agriculture, whilst private parks were created from woodland to give cover for the deer and hunting for the lord. The extent of the royal forests was indeed a major source of friction between the Crown and its subjects, and of the private forests between lords and their tenants in the thirteenth century. The Charter of the Forest in 1217, which tried to set the limits of royal forests, was regarded by contemporaries as of equal importance to Magna Carta. But the situation was not entirely static. Legally or illegally clearing (assarting) did take place and the king was often prepared to accept a fait accompli in return for a fine. At times, when his needs were greater, he would disafforest a whole area for a price. So the Abbeys of Peterborough and Dore paid John 200 marks (£133.6s.8d.) each for the disafforestation of Nassaburgh Hundred in Northamptonshire and Trivel Forest in Herefordshire. Devon was disafforested in 1205, providing a stimulus to settlement and altogether, between 1250 and 1325, the royal forests were reduced in size by one-third. That still left two-thirds, however, and there was to be no release of this final reserve of land until the seventeenth century.

Much of what has been said applies more to the South and the Midlands than the North, although there were forests there too. In the North, however, the main barrier to settlement was the hills. Crops will not grow easily above the 800 feet contour line. The high hills of the Cheviots and the Border, Bewcastle Fells and the North Pennine scarp were and are sparsely populated, whilst the lowlands and the coastal plain of east Northumberland and Durham were extensively adopted as the favoured site for villages. Indeed geography and geology partly, if not largely, explain the distribution of the population. By the middle of the twelfth century there were probably at least two million people in England. Assuming there had been no major changes since the time of Domesday Book the most densely populated area was East Anglia. In Suffolk and Norfolk there was a density of 15 to the square mile of recorded population (that is, landholders only) with a total density of 50 plus per square mile.[1] There were also heavy concentrations on the fertile coastlines of Kent and Sussex, but as one moves west and north, so the density falls. Nowhere in the Midlands was there a density of over 15 per square mile of recorded population and in the North the figure falls below 5, in some areas to as low as 2.5. But overall figures disguise quite stark local variations. The Sussex coastlands may have been densely populated but the Weald was not and there were low densities in the sandy Bagshot areas in Surrey and north-east Hampshire.

It was almost entirely a rural population, although the economy had moved beyond the purely subsistence stage. Enough surplus food was produced to support towns and supply the limited market. One hundred and eleven places are named as boroughs in Domesday Book, but the name was applied to fortified villages and prosperous commercial centres alike. London, with a population of about 10,000, was the chief city, although it is not mentioned in the Domesday survey. It had extensive trading links with the Continent and was gradually emerging as the centre of government. Winchester, also omitted from Domesday, was the old capital of Wessex and early twelfth-century surveys suggest a population of 6–8,000. The regional centres of York, Lincoln, Norwich and Thetford (then flourishing) had 4–5,000 inhabitants in 1086 whilst county towns such as Bury St Edmunds, Colchester, Dunwich, Exeter, Huntingdon, Oxford, Stamford and Wallingford had at least 2,000. Evidence for other towns is scanty. A twelfth-century Evesham Abbey survey suggests that Gloucester had a population of 3,000 and below this there was a whole variety of settlements calling themselves towns but often with agricultural land attached worked by the inhabitants. Cambridge, for instance, had a population of 1,600 or so in 1086 but lent its plough teams to the sheriff three times a year.

The urban population, then, was small, perhaps little more than 100,000 people in all. Most folk lived in villages, scattered hamlets or berewicks, isolated farmsteads. Housing was primitive. Wood-frame dwellings were made by standing together pairs of crucks – curved wooden beams reaching from the ground to the apex of the roof – to form an arch, which was then joined to another pair of crucks by a ridge pole. Walls were either wattle or layers of mud and straw whilst the roofs were thatched. Houses could be extended by adding further pairs of crucks, but for the most part were small, with one or two rooms for people and animals alike. Most countrymen faced a hard, unrelenting life whose main purpose was to provide enough for their families to eat, to pay their dues and put something by for a rainy day.

But, as has been said, this was not a homogeneous society. There was considerable variation in patterns of settlement and farming, in the layout of the fields and in the power lords exercised over their tenants. Even within a broad geographic area where one type of field system predominated anomalies existed. The Chilterns, for instance, lie within everyone's definition of the open-field area,[2] but they are a hilly, wooded region. The number of fields in a parish ranged from one single large one in the South West to between 10 and 30 in townships such as Berkhamsted or Great Gaddesden. The 'typical' Chiltern farm combined arable held in open fields and enclosed portions, along with a share in the wooded pastures on the upland slopes. Equally, lordship – and the term lord in this setting may mean very different things, a great baron, a modest knight who could later be thought of as a country gentleman, or a corporation like an abbey, a bishop or a college – varied according to time and the lord's needs. A great Benedictine monastery required a constant supply of food delivered to a fixed centre. So, on their estates, heavy labour services were exacted from the peasants to farm the lord's lands. By contrast absentee landlords like the Abbeys of Bec and Caen in Normandy, which had been given English estates after the Conquest, were more interested in money than food and demanded not services but rents. Similarly, a lay lord like Ralph Paynell in the late eleventh century had estates stretching from Devon to Yorkshire and administrative and military duties which kept him continually on the move. He needed a regular cash income and so the peasants on his manors paid rents instead of performing labour services. The type of lordship considerably affected the obligations of the peasantry, although a good general rule is that where the demesne[3] was large and controlled directly by the lord, labour services were likely to be heavy, whilst where the demesne was small or the social structure of the region militated against them, labour services might be minimal.

It is a complex picture and to try to reduce it to uniformity is to distort badly. Nevertheless some broad patterns in farming, field systems and social structure can be observed, always remembering that exceptions to the rule were many. First and best known is the open or common-field manorialized area. Here settlement was concentrated in compact or nucleated villages, which were the true economic unit. Each village's arable land, the most important part of its economy, lay in two or three large open blocks or fields, unenclosed by hedges. The basic unit of ploughing within the fields was the land or selion, which in a perfect world was 22 yards wide by 220 yards long, or approximately one acre in area, a day's ploughing for a horse or ox team. These lands were ploughed in such a fashion as to throw the soil towards the centre, forming the ridge and furrow characteristic of the open field. In practice, where the soil was heavy, the land might be no more than three yards wide to provide frequent drainage furrows, whilst on heavily contoured slopes it might run for no more than a quarter of the ideal 220 yards. So the strip, the basic unit of tenure, might consist of a single land an acre in size or a collection of lands amounting to a half or whole acre. Within the fields the units of ploughing would be grouped together to form furlongs or culturae, subdivisions of the main field. One furlong might run one way, the next another, giving the fields a patchwork appearance. The reason for this is quite simple: practice had shown that each collection of strips was best ploughed in a particular way. At the top and bottom of each land lay an area called the headland which provided room for the cumbersome four or eight ox team to turn.

It might be ploughed lengthways, after the rest of the field was finished, or left as grass for access or for grazing livestock.

Arguments rage as to how such fields emerged. The old view that they were brought over lock, stock and barrel by the Germanic settlers in the fifth and sixth centuries has long since been abandoned. The great students of the whole system, the Orwins, saw them as the result of co-operative efforts in colonization. Selions were long because no ploughman wanted to turn his team more often than necessary, they were narrow because no animal-drawn team could do more work in a day. The plough teams themselves were formed by co-operation between families since few peasants were rich enough to own eight oxen outright. So the land was divided among the families, each contributor to the team receiving a day of its work. In this way each peasant family received a share of good and bad land scattered among the fields. More recent research has suggested a multiplicity of origins and has urged the consequences of partible inheritance, the division of land among all the heirs, the strip being the unit beyond which no further subdivision could take place. Newly cleared lands might at first be held separately in consolidated sections. Then, due to partible inheritance, strips would be created and the land joined to the open fields. Alternatively, communal assarts might have been divided up among those who had done the work and joined to their holdings in the existing fields. The process of creating the open fields was by no means complete, even in the twelfth century, but from a variety of causes their main outlines had clearly emerged.

Here, however, an important distinction must be introduced. There is a difference between open-field and common-field farming. Open fields could be farmed by groups of individuals practising localized rotation systems. Common fields were farmed in common, that is a fully co-operative farming system was practised over the whole of the village's land. Common-field farming, which took place upon the open fields, has various elements of which the first, the arable for growing cereal crops, was the most important. Over all the arable in an open-field village a common three- or later four-course rotation system would be practised. Three courses were the most usual. A portion of the land would be given over to winter wheat or rye, some to spring barley, oats or legumes and the rest left fallow. In the thirteenth century legumes gradually became a separate part of the rotation system, making it four course, or they were substituted for fallow by a procedure known as inhoking, to produce more food. Rotation courses must be distinguished from fields and indeed by the end of the thirteenth century the rotation was often carried out by groups of furlongs rather than whole fields. A three-course rotation could be practised over a two- or three-field system alike. Under a two-field system one half of the land was left fallow each year and the other half divided between spring and winter wheat. In the thirteenth century the three-field system was widely adopted. Its advantages were that only one-third of the land was left fallow every year. Fallow land was always ploughed twice, so the peasant had less work to do and more land to cultivate, with a better balance between autumn and spring sowing and therefore less risk of famine if one failed. But the land was also being used more intensively which had its disadvantages at a time when there were no artificial fertilizers.

Obviously such a rotation pattern would require a high degree of co-operation between the villagers and a reasonably equitable distribution of strips throughout the fields for each man. Co-operation was even more essential for the next element in the system, the common grazing of the animals on the stubble after harvest. This has been described as the basic factor in the common-field system, for the right to graze animals meant that everyone had to harvest at the same time to avoid crops being eaten. The right of common grazing applied to all land, even where a peasant had been fortunate enough to consolidate and enclose a few strips to cultivate them as a whole. It even applied to the lord's demesne unless it was completely consolidated and lay outside the common fields. The third element in the system was meadow and pasture, meadow land being used to grow grass for hay, the winter fodder for the animals, pasture for grazing. Meadow was held in common and divided among the villagers according to the size of each man's share in the arable. A man's arable holding also determined the number of beasts which could be grazed on the rough pasture and waste. At Shillington in Bedfordshire in 1473, for instance, villagers were not to exceed a quota of 30 sheep per virgate allowed by custom on the common pasture. Within most open-field villages except those with access to uplands it was in short supply, especially in the twelfth and thirteenth centuries, and care had to be taken to see that it was not over-grazed.

There is as much argument over the introduction of common-field farming as there is over the origins of the common fields. One historian at least sees it as the product of the rising population in the twelfth and thirteenth centuries. Until then it had been possible to clear land and cultivate it in severalty, that is individually. But as inheritance customs forced the subdivision of land, raising problems of access to strips and the protection of crops, communal enterprise became essential. Other historians disagree, but whatever the truth of the matter it is clear that in the open-common field areas the village was the most important economic unit. Decisions about agriculture had to be taken by all, not just the lord, and enforced by village bye-laws and village officials – haywards, harvest or reap reeves, and woodwards for the woods. It is also clear that the system evolved to meet the needs of the intensive cereal farming to be found on the lowland plains and valleys in all parts of the kingdom. That is why it is virtually impossible to produce a map precisely delineating the limits of the open-field system as H. L. Gray attempted to do in 1915.[4] He believed its origins were ethnic, the fields being the product of the Anglo-Saxon settlers, and that the open-field area ran down the heartland of England from Durham and Yorkshire in the North to the South Coast. Wales and the North West, East Anglia, Kent, the Lower Thames Basin and Devon and Cornwall lay outside it. Since then evidence of open fields has been found virtually everywhere, especially on ecclesiastical estates. But the main proposition of Gray's argument still stands, for the area where open fields lay thickest was the central area he delineated – because it was that area which in the Middle Ages was the most suitable for corn growing.

It was also the area within which manorialism flourished. Open fields and manorialism did not always coincide, as will be seen, but in the central and west Midlands, and the southern parts of the open-field area, manorialism thrived. The manor had many functions. Its court could, in certain circumstances, be the lowest royal court in the land where minor crimes such as assault were punished. When manor and village were coterminous, that is there was only one manor in the village, bye-laws governing the open fields were often made in the court. But at root, in its 'ideal' form, a manor was no more than an agricultural estate, great or small, over which lordship was exercised. There were two parts, the demesne and the tenants' or the customary land. The demesne was the land over which the lord retained direct control: it might be scattered in strips in the open fields or held separately in enclosed fields. It was either farmed to produce food for consumption or for sale, or it was leased out to provide a cash income for the lord.[5] Some of the work on the demesne was carried out by paid estate labourers (the famuli) or skilled hired labour like ploughmen. But a great deal of it was performed by the tenants of the customary land. Essentially they were paying rent for their holdings by their labour and providing capital equipment in the form of ploughs, oxen and other tools. This is the ideal form. There could be manors with large demesnes and few tenants, and vice versa, money payments might be asked in lieu of labour services, but in its classical state about one-third of the land was held in demesne, the other two-thirds occupied by the peasants.

Peasants on such estates go by a bewildering variety of names – villans in Domesday Book, villeins in the thirteenth century, nativi or neifs, serfs, cottars, bordars. Sometimes they are described by the amount of land they held, the virgaters or half virgaters, the acremen. Their holdings and obligations varied from manor to manor, but on a typical estate two main classes can be discerned. The largest group in the twelfth century were those with holdings of substantial and uniform size and who had consequently to provide a substantial amount of labour or its cash equivalent. These were the villeins or virgaters and half virgaters, the former being a corruption of villager, the latter referring to the size of the holding. A virgate or yardland was a quarter of a hide, the unit of taxable land measurement in the area. It was not an absolute measure any longer, but varied according to the quality of the soil, since the better the land the more tax it could bear. In some places the hide was 120 acres, roughly the maximum, in others no more than 60. Since the hide varied in size, so did the virgate. On the Ramsey Abbey estates in the twelfth century, the virgate was 16 acres at Hemingford (Hunts), where there were, perversely, six virgates to the hide, but 30 acres on the uplands of Wistow (Hunts). So the virgater in one village might well hold only as much as the half virgater in another and for this reason it is impossible to talk of a standard holding of one virgate or 30 acres per villein. What matters is that on any given manor villeins had holdings of roughly uniform size comprised of strips scattered in the open fields.

The labour they had, in theory, to provide was onerous, and the more land the peasant held the greater the works. On the manor of Temple Cowley near Oxford in 1185 the virgate had to render the following works: one whole day every week between 15 days before 24 June and 15 days before 29 September. If the task involved carrying the lord's produce to market on Saturday the peasant had to provide his own food. At harvest time three boon or extra works had to be provided reaping the lord's corn and with four men present at each work. The lord did, generously, provide food on the third of these boons. Between

14 September and 9 June two days' work had to be performed every week and each virgate was responsible for ploughing, sowing and harrowing one acre of the demesne at both winter and spring sowings. In addition, the Cowley virgaters had to pay a fixed annual rent (a rent of assize) of 6s. This is a formidable list, requiring both regular week work and extra duties (boons), at harvest time. It was placed on the virgate, not on the man; those holding less land did proportionately less work, and the standard tenant on the Cowley estate was in fact the half virgater.

The second group of customary tenants found on most manors were the cottars or bordars. At Cowley the cottar or cottager held a messuage (dwelling) and a curtilage, a small plot of land probably of about five acres. For this he paid a money rent varying from 9d. to 3s., and gave one day's work a week from 29 September to 1 August and two days from 1 August to 29 September, with the same boon works as the half virgater. This was hard. Cottagers did not usually perform week work. At Great Horwood (Bucks) the cottage holding had to provide a man to do a day's weeding, a day's tossing grain after winnowing, a day's turning and lifting the hay, one man to make a cock of hay and two days' binding in the autumn after reaping. He also had to attend the great boon (reaping the corn) with all his family to bind after the reapers, and find one man for one day to gather nuts.

Such was the basic peasant structure in a manorialized open-field village. Virgaters or half virgaters farmed their own land and the lord's land; cottars, bordars, acremen, with less land of their own probably earned their living by providing the spare labour needed by lord and villein alike. Other men were to be found of course – freemen,[6] specialists such as the miller or the smith – but the majority of the agricultural population were virgaters, half virgaters or cottars, providing the necessary manpower for labour-intensive arable agriculture. Lordship over them brought with it other powers beside the right to demand services. The customary tenant was subject, or over the years became liable, to a whole range of other payments, other disabilities, which in the end were to amount to personal unfreedom. It is best to summarize these when at their fullest, although the peak often came after 1180 and particularly in the thirteenth century. First, there was no ownership in the land at all. The peasant was a tenant, but the tenancy was not severable at will. The peasant and his family were increasingly tied to the holding, which was theoretically indivisible. It descended according to the local custom, decided by the practice of ages. The community as a whole took great trouble to find the right heir and protect the rights of women and young children. In most open-field villages primogeniture (descent to the eldest surviving son), and impartible inheritance were the rule, but in some areas Borough English (inheritance by the youngest son) was practised, to provide support for the most dependent member of the family. When the tenant died the lord took heriot, a death duty, usually the best beast, and the heir had to pay an entry fine before he could have seisin or possession of the land.

Secondly, since the peasant was a tenant, it follows that his tenement could not be bought, sold or sublet without the lord's licence. Indeed, the unfree peasant could not buy freehold land without the lord's licence, lest by doing so he acquire free status. Thirdly, the peasant was tied to the land to ensure that his labour, or a money equivalent, was always available. He could not leave the manor without permission and payment of an annual fine called chevage. Fourthly, his assets were at the lord's disposal. Besides allowing the lord to use his equipment, he might be asked to pay toll on the sale of his animals, he could be tallaged (taxed) at will, and he had to pay a small fine when his daughter married (merchet) or for her immoral conduct (lerywite, childwite). Fifth, he could be compelled to use his lord's oven to bake his bread, the lord's mill to grind his corn, always at a price. Lastly, he was obliged to attend his lord's court and fell under its jurisdiction. The court baron for customary tenants should have been held every three weeks, and there were two great courts every year held in spring and autumn when property transfers were recorded, fines were paid and judgments made. Through the court the lord enforced his authority over his tenants, and particularly over his customary tenants who were unfree in respect of their time and their person and passed this unfreedom on to their families. Unfreedom, then, meant considerable limitations on the peasant's ability to exploit his lands and the liability to a considerable number of compulsory payments which had to be made before he could feed his family or save for emergencies.

The man who held freehold had far less in the way of liabilities. Normally he did not perform the arduous labour services, although sometimes boon work at harvest time was demanded of him. He had to attend a lord's court, for there was no land without seigneur and he might, as at Great Horwood (Bucks), be subject to wardship (the administration of the holding after death if his heir was a minor), relief (the fine paid for seisin of the property) and marriage (permission to marry his sons). But he had personal freedom in respect of his time and his land. He could buy or sell land freely, he had the protection of the royal courts, which by the thirteenth century was denied to unfree men, and his compulsory outgoings were far less than those of the unfree. Freemen were to be found everywhere in the manorial open-field area, whether they went by that name (liberi homines), or were tenants in socage or in serjeanty, that is for non-military service to the lord. Their numbers were not substantial compared with those in other areas, but they were always there, to act as a spur to the unfree.

To generalize is to make sharp distinctions which did not always exist at the time. In the thirteenth century the lines were clearly drawn between freedom and unfreedom and his status before the law was critical to the peasant. Those who performed or whose fathers had performed labour services or who paid merchet or heriot or were liable to tallage were unfree. But this was not necessarily so in the twelfth century. There is no doubt that the manor existed. Indeed its origins are Saxon, not Norman. Some argue that such estates were to be found from the very beginning of the Saxon settlements, others that the Danish raids and the growth of kingship and taxation forced peasants into dependence on a lord for protection. But to be a tenant paying one's rent by labour is very different from being a completely unfree man. There is some evidence to suggest that even in the early part of the twelfth century there was no clear distinction between freedom and unfreedom, that whilst labour services were demanded, heriot, merchet and other payments were not. Merchet and heriot only begin to appear in manorial records at the end of the twelfth century and labour services were not performed in many places, but a money rent was substituted instead. This might be economic dependence, but it was not legal unfreedom. A combination of circumstances at the end of the twelfth century seems to have forced the change. First there was the rapid spread of effective royal justice from Henry II's reign onwards. A whole new range of procedures became available for the protection of property, or rather possessory rights. Who could have recourse to them, all men or only the free? The answer was, only the free, but who were the free? Here economic events acted as the catalyst for change. The rapidly rising prices of the last quarter of the twelfth century forced landlords to reassess the way in which they managed their estates. If they were to prosper they would have to undertake more direct and efficient management and maximize their revenues. They needed both labour and rents from their peasants and in the last decades of the twelfth and the opening decades of the thirteenth centuries, either by

21

the redefinition of existing powers or the imposition of new ones, the mass of the peasantry lost their personal freedom. In this the lords received the clear backing of the royal courts for class supported class. The question of freedom or villeinage was essentially decided in the last twenty years of the twelfth century.

In other parts of England, however, very different field arrangements and social structures prevailed. East Anglia, Norfolk, Suffolk and parts of Cambridgeshire, had a variety of soils ranging from the heavy clays of central Norfolk and Suffolk to sands by the sea coasts. Not all were as yet fully settled. In the Brecklands, the relatively infertile region of South Norfolk and North Suffolk, and on the Fenland borders clearing and colonization were still taking place. On these soils sheep/corn and wood/pastoral husbandry were practised but no one field system predominated. Most of East Anglia was a land of large villages to which were attached one or more sizable open fields. Villagers' lands were not scattered but were compact tenements, often consisting of a number of strips or larger portions of land lying within a limited area. The fields were not divided up into furlongs but precincts, more for locational purposes than anything else. Alongside this system, in areas of clearing like south-east Cambridgeshire large numbers of smaller fields were being created. In 1251 the bishop of Ely possessed 21 fields at Balsham and although some amalgamation into open fields did take place, at the time of enclosure many centuries later, Balsham still contained 13 fields of varying size. Thirdly, in the Brecklands the infield-outfield system was to be found. Part of the cleared land, the infield, was cropped continuously for a number of years. When it began to lose its fertility, it was allowed to revert to pasture and another portion of the outfield was brought into arable cultivation.

Over these fields three- or four-course rotations were practised, either by co-operation between neighbours, so that several rotations might be followed within one or two fields, or groups of fields could be organized to allow for the various courses, or the shift system could be adopted, by which certain sectors of the fields were allocated to one of the courses. Not only were full common-field systems rare, but manorialism was also weak. It is possible to find large manors, especially on ecclesiastical estates. Ramsey Abbey had one at Brancaster in Norfolk, where it held the whole vill. But this was unusual. Manors were for the most part small and often there were several within one village, of differing sizes and with differing seigneurial rights. In many cases they seemed to have been imposed on the countryside after the Norman

Conquest. At Whelnetham in Suffolk there were, in 1086, 12 cottagers and 41 freemen: in the reign of Edward I, Edmund of Whelnetham, one of the lords of the village, possessed in addition to his free tenants an arable demesne of 260 acres and a further 128 acres held by his villeins. The variety of field systems and manors is matched by variety among the peasantry: no standard holding for services existed. In Norfolk pride of place went to the 12 acre tenement and its multiples, whilst in Suffolk there was a trend towards 10, 20 or 30 acre holdings, but in neither county was the virgate at all common.

Nor were villeins the predominant class of peasant. In Norfolk and Suffolk, two classes of peasants, the sokemen and the liberi homines or free men alone formed 40 per cent of the recorded population in 1086, and sokemen were also to be found in the neighbouring counties of Nottinghamshire, Leicestershire, Northamptonshire and Cambridge-shire, and in Essex. The relationship between a sokeman and his lord was very different from that between lord and villein. In part the bond was personal. In pre-Conquest days, for protection, a man often commended himself to a lord, promising to be faithful and true to him. This did not lead to complete subservience. Personal freedom remained and the man had the right to sell his land, 'to go where he would with it'. Many lords had also been granted the right of sac and soke, toll and team and infangentheof. Of these the most important was the right to soke, the right to hold a court, which his men were bound to attend and where he did them justice. The duty of attending the court in origin was, again, probably personal, attached to the man, who remained bound to his lord if he sold his land. Increasingly it became territorialized, that is it always attached to the ownership of certain pieces of land. But, from the point of view of the growth of manorialism, it is important to understand that these territorial sokes were not compact, not confined to one vill. Because they originated from lordship over men, they were often widely scattered. The 119 sokemen appurtenant to the manor of Bergholt (Suffolk) in 1086 were dispersed over several vills, whilst the 10 sokemen at Cawston (Norfolk) were divided among six lords. Although their numbers were considerably depressed after the Conquest, they survived in sufficient strength to militate against the growth of the compact manor. It was difficult to impress the complex systems already described on fields where holdings were individual and could be freely bought and sold. Moreover, few sokemen owed much in the way of services. One early statement of such services from the Abbey of St Benet of Holme shows that they made money payments of various kinds, performed carrying duties and boon works, one day's hoeing in winter, one day's reaping, eight days of other services in the year and two days' digging. There was no week work and no mention of other disabilities such as heriot. The existence of large numbers of free peasants also affected the policies of landlords within the region. They had, in a sense, to bow to the inevitable. Ely Abbey in the twelfth and thirteenth centuries was content to see the creation of substantial numbers of free or semi-free tenants on newly assarted land. In the bishop's hamlet of Elm near Wisbech there were 7,000 acres of cleared land in 1251, of which 1,500 were held by ten free tenants, and 2,400 by censuarii, rent payers performing a few boon and carrying services. The result was that by the thirteenth century manors in East Anglia consisted of a nucleus of demesne and villein land surrounded by a sea of free or semi-free rent-paying peasants of so many kinds that definition is all but impossible.

Needless to say, there is great controversy over the origins of so much personal freedom in East Anglia. Some regard the sokemen as the descendants of the free Danish warriors who settled in the area. Others point out that the number of settlers was small. They see older liberties being preserved as East Anglia was kept out of the grip of the oppressive Wessex monarchy. Yet another theory suggests ethnic origins, in that the original settlers are held to be Frisians who maintained their customs through the Dark Ages. Perhaps so, but some attention should be given to the type of agriculture and inheritance customs. The structure of open-field society was clearly affected by the need for a large, tied labour force. In East Anglia arable husbandry was combined with extensive sheep farming. Peasants grazed their animals on their fields, keeping them out of their neighbours' lands by the use of wattle fences. There was no need to throw the fields open, so the pattern of landholding was stabilized, whilst the wool provided the peasants with a cash income which might help keep them out of the hands of a lord. Freedom was also protected by the practice of partible inheritance, the division of land and especially socage land among all the heirs. This resulted in the disintegration of tenements as division took place, and in the joint holding of land. It also meant that holdings in East Anglia were often smaller than elsewhere, and that there was an active market in land. The first did not necessarily lead to poverty, since there were alternative sources of income in sheep farming or, in the fens, cattle grazing and poultry rearing. And there was land to buy or to rent on an active market in which, eventually, even villein tenures were involved. Given these, it was very difficult to maintain the fixed holding owing a standard amount of service. The land market and partible inheritance promoted the cause of freedom. As Dr Miller remarks, when landlords began to exploit their demesnes intensively in the thirteenth century it proved hard to augment the villein burdens, hard to add to the number of villein tenures and almost impossible to create a villeinage where new settlement was arising. On nearly all the bishop's manors hired labour was to play an important part at all times.[7]

The region of England most akin to East Anglia was Kent, where there was a similar diversity of soil and varied patterns of settlement. The Weald, a heavily wooded area of poor soils was still being colonized, population was low and settlement scattered. The farmers lived near their fields the better to be able to work them when weather conditions made them neither too cracked nor too boggy. Similar settlement patterns are to be found on the heavily wooded clay-with-flint soils on top of the Downs and the London Clay of the Blean region. Elsewhere, on more fertile soils with a greater density of population, the normal pattern was a mixture of villages surrounded by hamlets and isolated farmsteads. The pattern of farming was just as diverse. Arable was important: wheat and barley predominated in the lands north of the chalk escarpment in the thirteenth century, oats in the Weald. East Kent, Thanet and Romney were much given over to sheep whilst the marshes were also important centres of dairying and in particular of cheese production.

The diversity meant that there was no one field system but again, many. On poor soils cleared from woodland, fields were held severally (individually) or by groups of kinsmen living in isolated hamlets. In the arable areas there were large open fields surrounded by smaller enclosures or, as at Westerham, an area of permanent arable (the infield) surrounded by land from which intakes of arable were made for a period of years and then returned to fallow. But, in the open fields, there was no scattering of strips: rather, holdings were consolidated, and this applies to both manorial demesne and to peasant lands. In the thirteenth century the Archbishop of Canterbury's demesnes were often in large blocks fenced off from the peasants' holdings or in separate arable fields, as at Wingham. Older ideas that the land was divided into regular areas, the sulung of 240 acres and its quarter division, the yoke, have had to be abandoned. By the twelfth century the sulung and yoke like the hide and virgate varied from place to place according to the quality and taxable value of the soil. They extended over the ground in the sense that this piece of land belonged to this or that sulung, but in no sense was this a field system. Rather, it was a device for apportioning burdens or their money equivalents. The real field system was more complex. By the thirteenth century it is clear that full common-field practices did not exist. Common grazing was to be found, but by mutual arrangement and not as of right. Completely separate cropping arrangements were practised over the Archbishop of Canterbury's demesnes whilst the nature of farming operations on the peasants' lands is almost completely unknown.

The nature of lordship and manorialism was thus as complex in Kent as in East Anglia. Whilst by the twelfth and thirteenth centuries there were large manorial demesnes, they were not surrounded by a servile or a semi-servile peasantry owing heavy labour services. A final legal decision in 1293 declared that villeinage did not exist in Kent, but that was recognizing fact, not creating precedent. There seem to have been three main classes of tenants – freemen, who owed money rents and suits of court (i.e. obligation to attend a lord's court); the small holders, cotmen, inlanders, who held small parcels of land only; and then, most important, the great mass of gavelkinders, all sorts and conditions of men who had in common that they held by the custom of gavelkind. Personally they were free, to buy and sell their land and in respect of their time. They owed only a small amount of ploughing service (gavelreth) and sowing, harvesting and reaping (gavelrip) per yoke. The burden was negligible. Wingham had over 5,500 acres owing services at the end of the thirteenth century, but the whole gavel ploughing came to only 30 acres out of 1,200 acres of demesne arable. Most of the work had to be done by hired labour.

Nor had the lord much control over the movement of the gavelkinders' lands. Gavelkind was a form of partible inheritance; the holding was divided among all the male heirs at death. If there was a widow, she was to have half the holding and minors were to be under the guardianship of the nearest relatives who could not inherit. This was not the climate in which manorialism could flourish. It was a free society in every sense, and not least in that to counter the effects of gavelkind an active land market had to develop, as in East Anglia. But, as with East Anglia, it is very difficult to explain how this freedom had come about. There are those again who seek ethnic origins and argue that Jutish settlers in the fifth and sixth centuries brought with them Frankish customs which permanently affected Kent's social structure, and that of surrounding areas in Sussex and Surrey. Others look to links with London, the early growth of trade and travellers to and from England's only major town and the pull of the London market. These offered the peasantry alternative sources of income from the sale of their produce and made reliance on a lord, as in the Midland counties, less necessary. It cannot be said that the type of farming affected the structure of society because large arable fields certainly existed. In truth, no thoroughly convincing explanation can be given, but Kentish freedom and wealth were bywords in the Middle Ages.

Further north, in the counties of Leicester, Derby, Rutland, Lincolnshire, Nottinghamshire, Northamptonshire and Yorkshire lay the Danelaw. Unquestionably, apart from the uplands, these counties lay within the open-field area. In Yorkshire such fields were actually being created in the twelfth and thirteenth centuries as the county was resettled after the devastation wrought in crushing the revolt of 1069. In other areas the open fields were of some antiquity. The only immediately discernible difference between these and the other Midland counties is the unit of land measurement. Here it was not the hide but the ploughland or carucate and its subdivision the bovate or oxgang, suggesting communal effort at clearing and ploughing, the bovate being the lot of the man who supplied one beast to the eight-ox team. By the twelfth century like the hide it had become a fiscal unit, varying in size according to the quality of the soil. But a comparison between the Danelaw and the Midland open-field areas reveals some striking differences. Manors and villeinage did exist: at Wigston in Leicestershire there were two manors with 32 villein households in 1086, at Wellingborough (Northamptonshire), 36 half virgaters performing full week work in 1320, whilst twelfth-century tenants on the Peterborough Abbey estates which provided food directly to the monastery owed three days' full services a week. But, at the same time, alongside these villein tenants, there were large numbers of freemen and sokemen. In Domesday Book 30 and 33 per cent respectively of the recorded population of Northamptonshire and Leicestershire were sokemen, there were large numbers of them in Northamptonshire and they formed no less than half the recorded population in Lincolnshire.

In contrast to East Anglia, however, the holdings of individual sokemen were not interspersed in the fields, rendering soke or custom to many different lords. The Danelaw surveys reveal the existence of compact blocks of sokeland, frequently entire vills, subordinate to common manorial centres, but, again, the manor co-terminous with the village was rare. Indeed, there was a great variety of manorial institutions. Few of the manors formed when new monastic institutions were endowed in the twelfth century had either large or consolidated demesnes: their endowment consisted of small parcels of land scattered in many villages. Thus, in Domesday Book, it is possible to find as many as seven manors in one vill. The Normans seem to have tried to force manorialism on the area, and numbers of sokemen fell after the Conquest, but in spite of this manors remained small, the number of freemen rendering only minimal services remained high. The village, not the manor, was the economic unit. In Wigston, with two manors, 33 villeins, 31 sokemen, 12 bordars and cottars and six persons of superior rank, it had to be.

Why was there such a strong element of free peasantry in a region suited to arable husbandry? It is inescapable that this was the area settled by the Danes, however much some modern historians may seek to minimize this fact. Stenton suggested that the geld (tax) was less heavy in the North than in the South, so that peasants would not be forced to submit to a lord in return for payment of their taxes. It is also noticeable that the great Benedictine monasteries were not to be found in the eleventh and twelfth century northern Danelaw. Lordship, in consequence, lay far more lightly on the land. As has been said, the twelfth-century foundations did not have large demesnes with the consequent need for heavy labour services and the Cistercians had granges – compact farms, worked by lay brothers or hired labour. Perhaps a combination of all these factors preserved a much freer society in the North East.

A freer society was also to be found in the South West. Devon and Cornwall form part of the Western Highland Zone. They are lands where wide moorland expanses and high tors alternate abruptly with thickly wooded valleys. Devon was very much a mixed farming area with corn growing and dairy farming intermixed. As far as it is possible to tell before the thirteenth century, convertible husbandry seems to have been quite common, that is cropping one section of the land without fallow for several years, then allowing it to return to grass, whilst another section is brought into cultivation. This is a system suitable for dairy farming combined with corn growing, although much of the product of the arable land went to feeding the beasts. It was also a system which could be practised as well in enclosed farmsteads or bartons as in large open fields which were to be found in only two areas of the county, in the vales of East Devon, a country of fertile valleys, and in South Devon between the edge of Dartmoor and the sea. All that can be said of Devon applies equally to Cornwall. Pastoral farming predominated, but there was sufficient demand for foodstuffs from the non-agrarian sectors of the economy – mining, fishing and seafaring – to encourage arable cultivation. Convertible husbandry and enclosure were the order of the day, however, when information becomes readily available at the end of the thirteenth century. In both counties manorialism, with its villeins and bordars, clearly existed in the twelfth and thirteenth centuries, but there was a considerable amount of personal freedom, which in itself affected manorial structures. There was no week work on the Tavistock Abbey estates for example, even at the height of the thirteenth-century manorial reaction; as in Kent, only boon works were performed.

For once the reasons for this freer society are not difficult to discover. Both counties were areas of colonization in the Middle Ages. There were ample opportunities for the creation of compact holdings, which might be small compared with the 15–32 acres of the customary tenant on the Tavistock estates, but which brought with them freedom. The other great catalyst to freedom was mining. At the end of the thirteenth century when the structure of society in Cornwall becomes clearer, there were again three main classes of peasants, the freemen, the conventionary tenants and the villeins. Most men held by conventionary tenure, seven-year leaseholds at free market rents and no renewal as of right. There were ten times as many conventionary tenants as there were villeins in 1337, and hand in hand with this went an active land market. In part this freedom was due to colonization, but the main reason for its existence was the growth of the tin mining industry. This is dealt with fully below;[8] suffice to say here that as the industry expanded miners were protected by royal charters which gave them the privileges of tenants on the royal demesne. Thus they acquired the status of sokemen and the protection of the royal courts. The Cornish landowners protested in vain: any serf who could stake out a claim automatically acquired free status. Given this, villeinage could barely survive and the leaseholding, free tenant emerged.

Finally there remains the far North outside the Danelaw, the old counties of Cheshire, Lancashire, Highland Yorkshire, Westmorland, Cumberland, Northumberland and Durham. To speak with such territorial precision is in fact anachronistic, since in the twelfth century no one was quite sure where England ended and Scotland began. Through the Middle Ages this region was subjected to raids by the Scots which, in the early fourteenth century, were to prove quite devastating. Nor was it one region, but three, the coastal plains on the West and East and the high Pennines in between. On the coastal plains it is possible to find large open fields, of up to 3,000 acres in some Cumberland townships where arable farming was combined with grazing cattle on the common waste in the hills. Over in Durham there were also open fields which were probably in a transitional stage, not yet having a full common-field system. Villeins existed: in 1183 the bishop of Durham had 22 on his manor in Boldon, holding two oxgangs of 30 acres, paying rent and performing both week and boon works. Conversely, at Carlton 23 farmers held 46 oxgangs for rent and boon work only and this mixture of freedom and unfreedom is to be found widely in the coastal areas. But the highlands of the Pennines cover most of the North – wet, cold, acid lands. Cereals would barely grow there and the main emphasis was on cattle and sheep raising. The typical pattern of settlement was the small vill in the valley with an area of arable where hardy strains like oats were grown, or the isolated farmstead using the infield-outfield system. Meadow was also vital to provide animal fodder, since the real economy of the vills was based on livestock grazed on distant summer pastures in the hills (where temporary shelters were made for the herdsmen), and then brought down into the valleys for the winter.

Here existed an almost entirely different society from that in the rest of England. Even in the thirteenth century the demesne and customary tenure played little part, for cattle raising does not require a large, tied labour force. Nor did lordship weigh heavily on the land. The Normans were only beginning to penetrate the North in the twelfth century. The only great feudal landlords were the bishop of Durham, and the earl of Northumberland who in the twelfth century was either the king of Scotland or the king of England. The monasteries which played such a large part in colonizing the area preferred to create compact granges worked by hired labour. Northern society thus remained much as it had done in the Anglo-Saxon period, partly Celtic, with strong links to Wales, and partly Germanic. The older aristocratic orders of thegn and dreng survived the Conquest to co-exist with the baron and the knight. The thegn was a free man of ministerial rank, that is of the higher servant class, holding a village heritably and paying rent to his superior lord in money or in kind. The dreng was on the fringes of the noble order, holding a small township, and performing both menial and free services; but he was a free man who exercised some lordship over others. Lordship at a higher level was not exercised over the single manor, but over a number of vills, grouped together into a 'shire' and owing services to a particular centre. The peasants in the vills, the husbandmen or molmen, smallholders like the cottars in the South, were liable to two kinds of service, that laid on the vill as a whole and that laid on individual holdings. The latter were often money rents or light services whilst the vill owed payments in kind, in grain and cattle; provided entertainment for the lord and his retinue at certain times and particularly assisted in the chase with dogs, nets and ropes; but most of all paid cornage or horn money (rent) for the use of the vital seasonal pastures. Thus lordship in the highland North was exercised over large and unbroken estates but depended for its revenues not on the direct exploitation of the land but on rent from the peasants. The peasants themselves went by a variety of names, but were taxed not so much as individuals as members of communities whose most valuable asset was access to the communal pastures. It was a freer, but infinitely harder life than that to be found in the manorial South.

So, within England there existed wide variation in the nature of agriculture, patterns of settlement and the burden of lordship. Distinguishing the main regions is slightly artificial since there were many local peculiarities and there were many transitional areas where one system merged into another. In origin the differences were partly ethnic, partly geographical or geological, partly seigneurial. Whatever their cause, they stimulated trade between region and region, and within regions, as corn was exchanged for dairy produce and local inequalities were ironed out. At the same time, vital distinctions, more important in some places than others, were emerging between the free and the unfree, both in respect of standing before the law and of freedom of time and enterprise. The freeman's holding in arable could be, and often was, smaller than that of the customary tenant but he had far less in the way of outgoings and more time to engage in other occupations. It is no coincidence that the number of freemen was greatest where alternative sources of occupation and income were available – alternative, that is, to arable farming. In the Fens fish and fowl were readily available, there were geese to be reared, cattle and sheep to be kept; the forests housed a whole variety of sylvan and other industrial occupations; in Cornwall, Devon, part of Gloucestershire and the North there was mining and metal working; around the coasts fishing and shipping; in the pastoral areas tanning and leather working and wool to be sold. This might not be so crucial in the middle of the twelfth century, but when the land became full of people it was vital.

31

Also vital was the matter of agricultural productivity. In many ways this was the most important problem in agrarian society and two questions need to be answered: what did the land produce, and were there any limits on productivity? The broad distinction can obviously be drawn between arable and pastoral agriculture, although it is artificial in the sense that animals, especially sheep and draught animals, were an integral part of arable husbandry. As has been seen, arable farming was cereal farming – wheat, barley, oats, rye or mixtures thereof, drage (barley and oats) or maslin (wheat and rye), along with leguminous crops, peas, beans and vetches. Cropping patterns were varied: rye was widely grown in Devon but little in the east Midlands, whilst on high or poor soils oats predominated. In general, however, wheat was the cash crop whilst barley and oats provided the bread and ale of our forefathers. Leguminous crops were only introduced slowly. They were valuable in two senses, as food for men and, especially, beasts, and because they fix nitrogen from the atmosphere in nodules on their roots and by decomposition return this valuable fertilizing agent to the soil. But in the thirteenth century they were not grown on some manors at all and on others, like those of Canterbury Cathedral Priory, the percentage of arable sown with legumes was small. It was to increase generally in the later Middle Ages until by the sixteenth century legumes constituted a sizable proportion of the total acreage under crops. As will be seen, that was important in relation to the problem of soil fertility.

By the end of the twelfth century much of the available arable land was already under cultivation. If production was to be increased to feed a rising population then either more land would have to be found or techniques would have to be improved. These were in fact exceedingly primitive. The problem lay chiefly in sowing, reaping and maintaining the fertility of the soil rather than in ploughing. By the twelfth century the heavy plough with iron-tipped share, a coulter in front of it to make the initial cut and mould board to turn the soil over into a furrow was in extensive use. This plough could tackle heavy lands and was drawn by a team of between two and eight oxen or horses. The size of the team depended mainly on the quality of the soil and whilst the use of the horse was spreading the ox remained the supreme draught animal. As the thirteenth century writer Walter of Henley pointed out, oxen were less expensive to feed, stronger on heavy land and could be eaten once their working life was over.

The land ploughed, it was next sown, by the broadcast method, and here lay the first great source of waste. It was scattered by hand, as the sower moved along the furrows. More seed was required than by modern drilling methods and much went to waste, being eaten by the birds or falling upon stony ground. Harrowing pushed the seed down into the soil and after that there was little to be done but pray for good weather and wait for the harvest. First came the hay, the grass crop from the meadow, in June and early July, and then the corn in August. Hay, peas, barley oats and beans were cut by the scythe, but for wheat a reap hook or sickle was used. All the operations were labour intensive: hay had to be turned regularly to allow it to dry, corn required not only reapers but binders and stackers as well. Reaping by hand was wasteful. The corn ears were cut off high on the stalk, leaving the straw standing, and in the process as much was left on the ground as was gathered in. That is why gleaning was so important and seldom left to the poor but regarded as a valuable part of the harvest. Threshing was done by flail and the chaff and the straw were separated from the grain by tossing into the air so that the breeze could blow away the chaff and leave the heavier grains of corn to fall to the ground (winnowing). The chaff and any damaged grain were swept up and used as fodder for the beasts. The grain itself was stored, to make bread and ale and, in desperate circumstances, to be given to the animals.

At each stage, then, there was considerable wastage. Moreover, the whole of arable farming, in which the majority of the population were involved, was at the mercy of the weather. There were no mechanical harvesters to bring the crops in speedily and take advantage of a break in the rain. There were no grain dryers either. A run of two or three bad harvests spelt disaster and the awful consequences can be seen only too clearly in the decade 1315–25. But the chief problem was not so much inefficient techniques as limited productivity and soil fertility. The soil would only give back as much as was put into it. Medieval men understood that, and tried, with the limited resources at their disposal, to tackle the problem, which is why so much of the ground in the open-field system was left fallow. Not that it was left alone. At worst it was allowed to grass over and the grass was then ploughed in to provide some organic content. At best it was dunged or put down to leguminous crops, provided that they were being used to replace nitrogen and not just as extra fodder. The longer the land was left fallow the better, but when demand for food was high the temptation was to use the fallow land more often than was good for it. The only other way to replace goodness was by the use of such fertilizers as were available. In some areas near the coast, sea sand rich with calcium carbonate from pulverized shells and some seaweed could be used, in others there were deposits of marl, a mixture of clay and carbonate of lime, which could be dug out and put on the soil. Rough land could be prepared for sowing and fertilized by beat burning, cutting off the top sward, allowing it to dry, burning it and ploughing in the ashes. Although much is made of these practices, however, their effects must have been limited. Marling was expensive and even the wealthy monks of Canterbury Cathedral Priory used it sparingly. Sea sand and beat burning were not available to the Midland peasant; he had access only to animal manure, the most widely used of all fertilizers.

The critical question, therefore, is whether supplies of dung were sufficient to keep the arable in good heart. There is a common misconception that all that was necessary was to graze the village flocks on the stubble after harvest. This practice had more to do with keeping the flocks alive than anything else: animals only enrich fallow or any ground by dropping on it what they have eaten elsewhere. Moreover, the fertilizing value of such droppings was much decreased by exposure. It was dung gathered in the farmyard, where the potassium and nitrogen in the animal's urine had been absorbed by straw, which was of the greatest value. Again, medieval man understood this. Dung was highly prized, carting dung was a regular week work and closes cropped intensively were kept in good heart by intensive dunging. But the amount of manure depended simply on the number of animals: larger flocks produced more dung but there were severe limitations on the size of flocks and herds. The key factor was not summer grazing, although that became a problem as more and more land was converted into arable, but winter fodder. There were no root crops, no sown meadows to provide abundant hay for overwintering substantial numbers of beasts. If larger flocks were to be kept then they would have to be fed on precious cereals and this was simply not possible. In all, 'unless the animals had some commercial value apart from the value of their dung, the cost of keeping animals for the purpose of restoring the fertility of arable was likely to have imposed an insupportable burden upon the profitability of arable farming'.[9] So it was a vicious circle. Large flocks could not be kept by the majority of tenants, especially when the need to grow corn to feed an expanding population placed a premium on land. But, without large flocks, there was insufficient manure and so yields would remain low.

And, compared with those from present-day farming, low they were.

Some care has to be taken when discussing medieval productivity since the evidence is often confusing and misleading. Yields can be expressed either in ratios to seed sown or in gross or net terms, less tithe and reaping allowances, per acre. Medieval writers and accountants often used ratios. The anonymous author of the thirteenth-century treatise on *Hosebonderie* declared that barley should yield to the eighth grain, that is a ratio of eight harvested to one sown, rye to the seventh, wheat to the fifth, oats to the fourth. The difficulty in transferring these abstracts into practice is that very often modern statistics drawn from medieval records take little heed of sowing ratios or harvest qualities. An eightfold yield from a sowing ratio of two bushels per acre will produce far more than from a rate of one bushel, whilst it was quality which ultimately mattered to lord and peasant alike. Yields per acre are bedevilled by the problem that there are as many variations in the size of the acre as there are in the size of the bushel, making both local and medieval-modern comparisons very difficult. Finally, once more, virtually all our evidence comes from the records of great monastic estates whose lands may have been more productive than those of the 'average' peasant. Professor Postan would argue that they were, that the great lord possessed better land and had superior command over capital equipment, pastures and folds (grazing animals on the stubble). But might not the East Anglian peasant with his separate holdings, and knowledge of the advantages of folding and manuring have produced the same results? Who knows? No one, for the peasants have left no records.

With these reservations in mind, the records show that few great estates consistently produced the yield ratios recommended in the *Hosebonderie*. Yields of wheat on the Kentish estates of Canterbury Cathedral Priory in the thirteenth century were between 1:3 and 1:3.5, barley seldom higher. On the Winchester estates the average yield of wheat per measure of seed between 1200 and 1249 was 3.8, barley 4.4, oats 2.6. Tavistock Abbey did better than this, achieving more than the recommended ratios for wheat, rye and oats on some of its manors in the late Middle Ages, but only because of intensive manuring and the use of sea sand. It would seem that few great estates reached the targets set by the medieval writers, and when comparisons are made with modern yields the results are even more striking. The average gross yield per acre on the Battle Abbey manor Alciston (Sussex) in the late fourteenth century was about 17 bushels of wheat, 26 of barley, 22 of oats. Now Alciston was one of the best-managed and most fertile of all medieval manors, with ample supplies of manure from large flocks of sheep on the Downs and legumes used on the fallow to replace nitrogen. Average yields per acre for Great Britain 1958–68 were 72.6 bushels for wheat, 65.8 for barley and 59.0 for oats.[10] In other words, the modern cereal farmer produces nearly four times as much as the very best of his medieval rivals, using far less labour. Other medieval landlords were likely to have produced much worse results.

The only way to increase arable productivity, then, was to apply more labour to more land. The labour may have been available, but as has been seen there were limitations on the supply of land, and by the beginning of the thirteenth century a delicate balance between land and people seems to have been reached in both arable and pastoral farming. To be sure, we know little enough about pastoral farming except for the running of sheep. Large flocks were kept at all times, especially upon marsh and uplands. They probably increased in size during the thirteenth century as wool exports expanded. They provided a cash crop, wool and essential animal fats in milk and the cheese made from it. But we still wait for a full study of the production and consumption of meat, butter and cheese and of pastoral farming generally. The difficulties are considerable. Most of the animals were bred out in the eighteenth century, so that only guesses can be made as to their quality and productivity. What is clear is that in areas of mixed farming, the limitations on arable production could not be offset by turning to pastoral farming, for the reasons already stated. Indeed, the central problem of the English economy in the thirteenth and early fourteenth centuries was the low productivity of arable agriculture.

Thus far the main emphasis has been on the lowest level, on the ways in which the land was farmed and lordship exercised over the peasantry. That theme of lordship must now be pursued further since it was the lords who exploited the capital resources of the peasantry and profited from their labour and their rents. Clearly lordship could vary as greatly as the countryside itself, both legally and geographically. It ranged from the man with lordship over one manor and the right to hold a court for his tenants, to the men or the institution holding estates the length and breadth of the land with authority over peasants and other nobles alike. In an age when towns were tiny and industry and commerce on a small scale, land equalled wealth. The rich man was the great landlord, land was the source of his riches. Since so much of the economic history of medieval England is studied through the records of great estates, it is necessary to investigate both their composition and their organization, in fact what lordship meant on a larger scale.

Between 1066 and *c.* 1135 there was a tenurial revolution in England, a massive redistribution of land and thus of wealth. As a result of the Norman Conquest some 4–5,000 Anglo-Saxon thegns were replaced by a foreign feudal aristocracy amongst whom wealth, land, was very unevenly distributed. At the top of the pyramidic structure of society lay the king, the legal 'owner' of all the land. He retained a large area of this land, some 25 per cent, as the royal demesne, for his own use, to provide him with food, income and a source of patronage. The rest he granted out to some 1,400 tenants-in-chief, that is men who held directly of the king, but a massive concentration lay in the hands of a few great men and great ecclesiastical institutions, bishoprics and abbeys. The Church had about a quarter of the land, the great lay followers of the Conqueror about half, but the concentration was in fact far greater than this since ten men held half the land in the hands of all the tenants-in-chief. The Conquest settlement saw, in effect, the creation of the great estates.

Much has been made of the way in which these estates were scattered over the length and breadth of England. Only, it is said, along the Marches of England were large, consolidated territorial lordships created for the protection of the frontiers. There is some truth in this, but in most cases great lords held their lands in one main area; William fitz Ansculf, for instance, held an honor (the name for the whole lordship) in twelve counties but the core lay in a group of villages around his castle at Dudley. Similarly, the estates of Ramsey or Peterborough Abbeys lay mainly in the counties surrounding the houses. Nonetheless, although they lay in one area, they were not in contiguous stretches, and this coupled with the fact that outlying estates were often 60 or 100 miles from the centre, was to pose considerable problems of organization and management.

Nor was this the only difficulty. The fact that these estates were held by feudal tenure, that is conditionally by certain customs and in return for the service of so many knights, posed two further problems. The first was long-term insecurity of tenure, especially for lay estates. Feudal custom was not immediately settled at the Conquest – indeed bitter disputes over what it should be dragged on to Magna Carta and beyond. But, in grossly simplified form, the rules were these. When a tenant-in-chief died his lands escheated to the Crown, that is they returned back into the king's hands. They were granted to the male heir on payment of an inheritance duty, a relief. If the heir was under age, the king had the right to wardship of the lands, to administer them himself to his own profit or appoint someone else to do it in his place. If there were no male heirs but an heiress or heiresses, then the king had a say as to whom they should marry. If there were no direct heirs at all, then after provision had been made for the widow, the king could grant out the land again to whom he pleased. The tenant-in-chief could also be asked to aid the king, to pay a form of taxation in certain circumstances. All these feudal incidents were open to abuse. Outrageous reliefs could be demanded for seisin of property, wardships could be granted to men out to make a quick profit who would farm the land to death, the Crown could deliberately interfere with the rules of inheritance and deprive one family of its estates to reward another. As a result lay estates in particular were subject to continual disruption (aside from the basic failure of many families to provide male heirs) – to what Professor Postan has called periodic bouts of disinvestment.

Ecclesiastical estates were not as badly affected. After the Conquest, bishoprics and monasteries held their estates by feudal tenure as well, and when the bishop or abbot died they escheated to the Crown, which might retain them until it appointed a new head of the see or house, with all the consequences described above. But churchmen were astute enough to see that the body of monks was a perpetual corporation which never died and whose estates should not therefore pass back into royal hands. So they divided the lands between the bishop or abbot and the convent. When the bishop or abbot died, only his lands escheated. As a result most ecclesiastical lands enjoyed a security of tenure and a continuity of economic administration unknown on lay estates until the later Middle Ages. That explains why so much of our information comes from their records, and why care should be taken not to take conditions pertaining to them as typical of the country as a whole.

The second problem was that tenants-in-chief did not have economic control over all their lands. The condition of tenure was the provision of a quota of knights 'upon demand', when the king needed them for defence of the realm. In the troubled years immediately after the Conquest it was logical for the knights to live in the lord's household. This was expensive for him and both custom and common sense demanded that they too should be settled on the land, given their own fees in return for service, becoming the lord's tenants over whom he exercised rights similar to those the king exercised over him. Each tenant-in-chief had a different quota of knights and thus subinfeudated a different proportion of his estate. In 1086 the Archbishop of Canterbury had enfeoffed knights on 15 per cent by value of his lands, the bishop of Winchester 20 per cent, Peterborough Abbey a massive 40 per cent whilst Eudo Dapifer, a great royal servant, had subinfeudated 38 per cent of his estates and Ralph Paynell, whose honor stretched from Devon to Yorkshire, one-third of his.

Thus there was a tenurial revolution at two levels in the late eleventh and early twelfth centuries, for beneath the tenants-in-chief a whole new class of sub- or mesne tenants was scattered on the land. The whole process had to be handled with some care by the great landlords. Failure to control it bred disaster. The Archbishop of Canterbury's estates were valued at £2,334 in 1087 and he had to find a quota of 60 knights. In fact he enfeoffed more, for safety's sake and to reward clients, but whilst the knights were allowed a free choice of land (and they chose the best) what they took was carefully supervised to make sure that too much land did not pass out of the lord's hands. Ramsey Abbey owed only four knights from estates valued at £365 but no care was taken to create distinct knights' fees. This was to prove a costly mistake. The Abbey's knights took a multitude of small pieces of land and the extent of the military tenure at Ramsey was out of all proportion to the service actually owed. There were other dangers too. With so much land being redistributed the opportunities for a ruthless local official like the sheriff, or during the breakdown of government in the Anarchy of Stephen's reign (1135–54) for other men, to seize what was not theirs by right, were great. Peterborough Abbey lost the village of Pytchley in this way – and never recovered it.

In all, then, a substantial amount of land was granted away by the tenants-in-chief into the hands of a widely disparate group of sub-tenants. Some sub-tenants held many knights' fees and were lords, mesne barons, in their own right, whilst others, the majority probably, held only a hide or so. On the Canterbury estates the knight had an average of one and a half ploughs working on his demesne and lordship over eight or so substantial village families having two ploughs, which was scarcely a vast landed patrimony. But, great or small, these men were distinguished from the peasantry by the service they gave and their status in society. The Archbishop of Canterbury not only expected his knights to fight, but to serve in his court, to give him advice and to carry the burden of his estate government. They were sufficiently linked by marriage to form a distinct class in society which stood between the Archbishop and his rural tenants.

They also farmed, to their own profit, a substantial amount of land, for the estates granted to them were economically outside their lord's control. It was the sub-tenant who took the demesne and exercised rights over the peasantry. The estate had passed out of the lord's hands permanently unless the line failed and it escheated to him. But no great lord subinfeudated more than half his lands: in most cases it was less than a third. He was therefore left with a very substantial proportion of his estates under his own direct control, in demesne. It was from these estates, along with feudal dues and such tolls and dues as he might receive from towns he owned, that the lord drew his income and his food. The ratio of food to cash income varied from estate to estate. A monastic house, with a fixed centre, would need regular supplies of grain and other foodstuffs and specific manors would be assigned to supplying its needs. Lay nobles were more peripatetic and might be more interested in money rather than food. A small landlord might, like the monks of Bolton Priory in the thirteenth century, consume all the grain the estates produced, but greater monastic and lay lords could not and did not do so. There always remained a balance of manors which had to be managed to provide a cash income to meet the needs of building, taxes, litigation, consumption and the hospitality expected of a great and noble household.

There were two basic ways in which the landlord could mobilize wealth in the form of a cash income from his largely static assets in land. He could farm the demesnes directly, appointing his officers, the bailiffs and the reeves, the latter being chosen from the ranks of the peasantry and responsible for the day-to-day running of the estate, to supervise their working and sell the surplus produce on the open market. The proceeds would thus bring him a money income but one which would fluctuate according to the state of the market. Alternatively the landlord could abandon direct responsibility and lease or farm the demesnes for a money rent and commute or convert the labour services of the peasantry into money payments. By so doing he would secure for himself a regular income not dependent on the state of the market for agricultural produce, but certainly affected by the demand for land. Before 1180, from the Conquest onwards, the latter method prevailed; and indeed, on ecclesiastical estates it was no more than a continuation of Anglo-Saxon practices.

By the twelfth century it was not a haphazard business, an abnegation of responsibility, but a clearly thought-out policy. The lessee took over the demesne for a fixed period, usually for a term of lives, that is for his own life and that of his heir or heirs. Most leases were for stock and land. The tenant would take over not only the land and the crops growing on it but the manorial stock as well, the plough beasts, horses, cows, sheep and pigs. He would have to hand back the demesne in the same condition as when he took it on and pay his rent in money or kind at a specified day or days. A St Paul's Cathedral lease of its estate at Kenesworth (Herts) to Humfrey Boucvinte in 1152 shows the system in operation. Boucvinte agreed to pay a rising rent for the demesne of £5 in the first year, £6 in the next, £7 in the third, £8 in the fourth and then £10 per annum for the rest of his life. When the land was returned it had to be stocked with 24 oxen, 2 harrows each worth 30s. and 120 sheep each worth 4d. and sown with 70 acres of winter wheat and 70 acres spring wheat with 20 acres left fallow. Such specifications were probably essential to prevent the land being returned in a ruined state. This did happen. Abbot Hugh's farming out of the vills of St Edmund's Abbey in Suffolk led to woods being felled and manorial buildings lapsing into ruin. When Abbot Sampson took them into his own hands he found them with little equipment and stock. After all, the rent was fixed and any profit over and above it went to the lessee. The temptation to farm the land to exhaustion was there, and wise landlords took precautions against it.

Such a system provided opportunities for both great and small. Some of the lessees or farmers were manorial officials, others monks – however much the Church might frown on the practice; some might take on one estate, others as many as a smaller tenant-in-chief might have in demesne. Even the peasants might profit. In 1086 the villani held the whole of the St Paul's manor of Willesden (Middlesex), whilst Lympstone (Devon) was leased to the peasants for £8 per annum. Nor was this the only benefit to accrue to the peasantry, since it is clear that hand-in-hand with leasing the demesne in the twelfth century went the commutation of service. Professor Postan first outlined the history of the movement in his classic article, *The Chronology of Labour Services*.[11] Surveys of Glastonbury Abbey in the twelfth century show large bodies of rent-paying peasants in Wiltshire, Dorset and Berkshire, whilst at the other end of the country the Boldon Book of the bishopric of Durham (1183) records a group of 19 manors on which the bulk of the tenants were rent-paying molmen who had once been villans. The same pattern can be seen on the Ramsey Abbey estates and, reading back from a survey of 1222, on the St Paul's Cathedral manors. Commutation was not a sudden process; on the Holy Trinity, Caen, manor of

Minchinhampton, Gloucs, it took the best part of a century. Nor was it universal. On the Peterborough Abbey manors which supplied the house with grain, full services were still exacted in 1125; but increasingly, all over the country, money was being substituted for labour rent. It is not surprising that the twelfth century is singled out as one of these mythical golden ages for the peasantry. Land was available to lease or assart, there was as yet no personal unfreedom and labour services were being replaced by money rents, which is always held to have been to the peasantry's advantage. Whether it was golden or not is hard to tell. It may have been in contrast with the thirteenth century and indeed golden ages are essentially comparative. In the twelfth century as in much of the Middle Ages crop failure and starvation were spectres at every feast.

   The greatest contrast, however, is between the estate management practices of great landlords in the twelfth and thirteenth centuries, between leasing and direct control producing produce for the market. Two explanations have been offered for this phenomenon. Professor Postan sees leasing as a response to unpropitious economic circumstances, and a response which did not work particularly well. Rather it led to a dissolution, a splitting up of the demesne lands as smaller holdings were carved from them to be held at money rents, and to a declining income in real terms for the landlords. To prove his case he relies on evidence from about 25 manors on the Glastonbury Abbey estates where Domesday Book and surveys of c.1135, 1176, 1189 and 1201 allow comparisons to be made. The manors were chosen for their consistency in size in all the surveys and the extent of the demesne was measured by the number of plough teams kept on them, one team equalling 120 acres in terms of a year's work. The comparisons showed a steady contraction in the size of the demesnes and the creation of new holdings, free and customary, from them. There was a decline of approximately 40 per cent in the number of plough teams used over the century, which was not offset by an increasing use of peasant plough teams, since commutation was a parallel movement. Nor was there a switch to pastoral farming to offset arable losses, since numbers of sheep and other livestock also fell. In all, it meant less income from direct exploitation, a decline which was not completely offset by rising revenues from rents and the sale of works. Professor Postan saw as the cause the political instability of the middle years of the century which upset the market and drove lords to turn to leasing in search of a stable income.

Subsequent studies have shown and confirmed the pattern of leasing and diminution of the demesne, but a different explanation has been offered for its causes. The twelfth century, after all, was no more politically disturbed than many others. The Anarchy of Stephen's reign had its counterpart in the civil wars of the mid-thirteenth century, but the latter did not provoke a similar response. It also seems to have been an age of general expansion throughout Europe. Within England it was a period of continued assarting and the division of existing holdings to accommodate more people. Old towns expanded, new ones were created, internal and external trade flourished. It was not, then, economic stagnation which prompted the policy of leasing, the counter-argument suggests, but a combination of inertia and administrative difficulties. Demesne leasing was in fact the age-old method of estate management which had survived the Conquest and which was prolonged as lay and ecclesiastical noblemen faced the problems of consolidating their control over the land. Any decline in their income as a result of accepting fixed rents was offset by the expansion of their resources as a whole as they acquired new tenants and rising revenues from towns. Finally, of course, direct management needs capable managers and it was only in the twelfth century that the spread of education and the development of royal government began to create reserves of trained men available to staff estate bureaucracies. Given these, leasing the demesne was not a council of despair but a policy of common sense.

The two arguments are not really diametrically opposed, but in a way complementary. That there were grave political difficulties in the mid-twelfth century cannot be denied. More important, between 1154 and 1180 what evidence we have suggests that prices were stagnant. Direct farming would not have brought in sufficient returns to cover the high overheads. On the other hand leasing was the age-old response of a not very well organized society to estate management. Nor was it necessarily unprofitable. Between the Conquest and 1135 both Canterbury and Ramsey were able to increase their rent income; indeed, the Normans generally demanded a far higher return from their land than had the Saxons. After that, stagnant prices and political troubles may have brought a downturn in profitability and accelerated the trend to leasing. But it was only an acceleration, not a beginning. Nevertheless, it committed the landlords to long leases and fixed rents. If prices rose rapidly and farming for the market became profitable, then it would be the lessees who reaped the benefit, not the lords.

This, then, was rural England, a land in which at least 90 per cent of the population engaged in or lived on the profits of agriculture. Towns, as has been seen, existed; indeed they were provided for by the surplus product of the rural economy and acted as markets for the surrounding countryside. They helped iron out local and regional inequalities, they supplied countrymen with the goods and the services which they could not provide for themselves, linking them to wider markets regionally, nationally and even internationally. Towns, too, were growing in the twelfth century, becoming independent units free of seigneurial control. Their very existence, along with markets and fairs, suggests that the economy had moved beyond the purely subsistence stage, as does the use of money as a medium of exchange. That money payments could be substituted for labour services shows that it had more than an occasional use. Increasingly, as government developed in the twelfth and thirteenth centuries it began to demand more and more in the way of taxation, which again had to be paid in coin. Wealth static in land could be mobilized by rents or through recourse to Jewish and Christian money lenders. This was by no means a full money economy, however. Offerings were still made in kind in many cases and we simply do not know how much barter went on in the countryside. But it was also a backward, underdeveloped economy, where the main occupation was producing sufficient food for the population to eat. Techniques were limited and the key factor in such a society was the balance between the number of people and the productive resources of the land. If the one expanded, could the other cope with the new demands placed upon it? That is why one of the most important questions that can be asked is, how many people were there in medieval England?

2 Patterns of Demand

The English economy at the end of the twelfth century was unquestionably underdeveloped. Certainly it had moved beyond the purely subsistence level: a sufficient agrarian surplus had been created to allow the development of towns. Money was used as a normal medium of exchange, rents and taxes were paid in cash, labour services were given a monetary value when commuted, goods were bought and sold by money rather than by barter. But the level of technology in farming and in industry was very low, making it impossible to increase aggregate or per capita production substantially, in order that either the same number of people could enjoy increased supplies of food or industrial products or the economy could support a continuously growing population.[1] It follows therefore that one, if not the prime factor, in any economic change that occurred must have been the size of the population. The basic proposition is quite simple. An expansion in the population would cause an increased demand for land to produce the necessary extra supplies of food, since only by bringing more land into cultivation could demand be met. As long as land was available, all would be well. But, if the supply dried up, if the limits of cultivation were reached either naturally or by reason of artificial constraints on land use, and the population continued to increase, then there would be a whole series of consequential reactions. The price of land in terms of its scarcity value would increase, the price of food would rise sharply since supply was inelastic, that is, it could not be increased proportionately to meet demand. Aggregate wealth would increase but those who would benefit most would be those who could supply the market on a large scale. The opportunities for rich pickings might seem sufficiently attractive to force changes in land management. Great lords who had previously secured most of their income by leasing out their lands would take them back into their own hands and set about

45

farming for the market. Profits from this and from the general demand for land would lead to a rapid increase in their income. At the other end of the social scale, the peasants might not fare so well. Whilst their holdings were of a substantial size, they would be able to grow most of their own food. But if, because of the pressure of people on the land, their holdings shrank in size, whilst monetary demands upon them increased, then they might be forced to go to the market both to buy food, and to sell sometimes artificially contrived surpluses to meet their outgoings.[2] Nor would they be able to augment their declining income from one source by hiring out their labour for wages in cash or kind. Wages remained stable in both monetary and real terms (i.e. how much they would buy) as long as demand for labour exceeded supply. If the existence of more people meant that demand could be met, then wage rates would fall, especially in real terms as food prices rose, and opportunities for casual labour would diminish. Economic conditions that were good for some could be very bad for others.

But it would not just be the agrarian sector of the economy which would be affected by an expanding population. Demand for food would lead to interchange on local, regional and even national levels. There would have to be places for that interchange to take place, namely the towns, and the merchants to man them. Old towns would grow, new ones would be founded, families surplus to agricultural requirements would be there to people them. Trade would expand to meet increased demand and, since what happened in England was likely to be repeated elsewhere in Europe, that demand might even come from abroad. The classic case here was the export of wool to supply the burgeoning Flemish textile industry in the twelfth and thirteenth centuries.[3] Production of industrial goods would also increase. More people would need more agricultural implements, more shoes, more clothes, more of everything. Thus population expansion would, or should, affect all sectors of the economy, and the reverse is also true. A sudden, dramatic and sustained fall in the population, by a third or as much as a half, would have considerable economic repercussions. Supply of food would be in considerable excess of demand and so prices would fall. Supply of land would also be in excess of demand, so its price in terms of rent would also fall, whilst supply of labour would be insufficient to meet demand, thus raising wages in both monetary and real terms. Conditions such as these would call into question the whole economics of large-scale farming for the market where overheads were high and profits low. Falling demand might also hit the urban, commercial and industrial sectors of the economy, but not necessarily to the same extent. The fact is that a sharp fall in the population might be to the benefit of the mass of the population. At last there would be more than enough good quality land available to meet their needs. Now, with lower overheads they would be able to farm effectively for the market that still existed, or work for enhanced wages. The pattern of economic expansion was seemingly reversed. But difficult times for the few could well mean good times for the many whose per capita share of the country's wealth automatically increased as the population fell.

Beneath these broader economic movements lie subtler changes in patterns of demand brought about by population movements. For demand must be looked at not only in general but in effective terms. In a period of high population in relation to the productive capacity of the land demand for foodstuffs will concentrate on grain, the staff of life. The majority of the population, with little surplus wealth, will buy cereals in preference to meat or dairy products. Nor will they have much to spend on anything other than food. So trade and industry may well concentrate on the upper end of the market, and produce and supply higher-priced luxury goods. A long period of relatively low population, on the other hand, will bring about changes in farming practices and trade and industry. Demand for grain will become inelastic, in the sense that a family will be able to secure all its needs either from its own holding or, cheaply, on the open market. There will be money left over to spend not on more grain but on other products, such as meat or dairy products. A definite improvement in their standard of living should result and it is interesting to see this happening in the fifteenth century when grain prices fell drastically but those for meat and dairy produce held up.[4] Equally, the family would be likely to have money left over after meeting all its food requirements. They would not spend this on the still expensive luxuries, but on cheaper articles. Here again in the fifteenth century manufactured goods for the mass market played an important part in England's import trade[5] whilst the price of industrial goods fell less than that for grain. In part this was due to increased wage costs, but it might also be the result of continued effective demand.

Thus it is essential to try to establish the size of the English population in the Middle Ages and to define and account for periods of expansion and contraction. That is much easier said than done, for the information is not readily obtainable. There was no census at all until 1801, no comprehensive census until 1811, and no fully effective census till 1841. Medieval man's concept of numbers was very limited. Chroniclers record huge armies fighting battles where pay lists or other records show that only a few thousands were present. Government officials were no better. In 1371 they estimated that there were some 45,002 parishes in England, which was about five times too many. But the truth is that neither governments nor landlords had any interest in counting heads. They only wanted to know how much land they held and the obligations of their tenants, or who had paid their taxes. So the two major sources for the study of medieval population, the records of land tenure and taxation returns, were never intended to be specific records of population at all.

But the records are there, and they are more abundant and more comprehensive than those for any comparable European country. Consequently they have proved irresistibly tempting to those who wish to show the extent and chronology of population change in medieval England by calculating aggregate totals. There are two fixed points at which this can be done, 1086 and 1377, with information respectively from Domesday Book and the first poll tax. In between, a whole variety of records, but especially the 'extents' (detailed descriptions of manors and their tenants), are used to make specific comparisons between a village in 1066 and the mid-thirteenth century; and to make demographic calculations concerning the birth rate, the age of marriage, the life expectancy and age distribution of the population and the aggregate numbers killed in the plagues between 1348 and 1377. The age of marriage, for instance, is a crucial factor. If men and women marry in their late teens or early twenties, then even with an average life expectancy of 40 they have some 20 years in which to produce children, ten of them before the age of 30 when the woman is at her most fertile. The later the marriage, however, the fewer the children. The number of children under 14 is also very important. They seldom or never appear in the records but in modern underdeveloped societies they form a substantial proportion of the population. If it were possible to construct life tables to show age distribution, then they would be a valuable aid in demographic calculations.

It all sounds very simple. In fact nothing has caused more controversy than the calculation of aggregate population totals for medieval England. Trying to pick one's way through the arguments is like walking through a minefield. One false step leads to an explosion of disagreement. The starting point for any discussion must be whether or not the source material is reliable. The three main sets of records used,

Domesday, the 'extents' and the poll tax, are open to considerable criticism. The Domesday survey does not cover the whole of England. The northern counties are omitted along, in whole or part, with the important towns of London, Winchester, Bristol and Southampton. Priests, an important element in medieval society, were recorded in only six counties. It is of course possible to make some intelligent guesses to fill these gaps to add to the total number of people listed in the text. But was everyone on the land or in the towns counted? Did Domesday record undersettles – sub-tenants on other men's land? Were villein holdings occupied by one family only or by several households?

Professor Russell, whose pioneering work on the British medieval population has been the cause of so much controversy, thought that Domesday listed all the land holders in a village, and that there was one family per holding. Other historians are much more uncertain. They believe that holdings had more than one tenant, that undersettles were not recorded, that substantial numbers of poor people in towns escaped the Domesday net. If that were not enough, the very vexed question has to be faced of how to turn lists of landowners into total numbers of people. Demographers construct index figures or multipliers to do this, and their methods are discussed more fully below. Needless to say, there is wide disagreement on the size of the multiplier and from the same basic evidence very different answers are produced. This can best be seen by taking the Oxfordshire village of Hanborough. Domesday records 31 peasant landowners there, 20 villans, 6 bordars, and 5 serfs. Multiply that figure by Professor Russell's suggested index of 3.5 and a total population of 109 for the village is obtained. Use indices of 4.5 or 5, as other historians argue we should, and they give an estimated population for the same village of 140 or 155. Project that degree of difference to the country as a whole and estimates can vary from Professor Russell's 1.1 million (for England alone) in 1086 to 1.4 million, or 1.6 million, differences of nearly 30 and 43 per cent. Some would put the unrecorded numbers of sub-tenants and landless men even higher and postulate a population of between 1.75 and 2.25 million, although this would seem rather on the high side.[6]

Many of the same criticisms can be levelled at the evidence from the extents. These were quite elaborate surveys made of their manors by landlords who wished to know not only how much land they held in demesne but the names and obligations of their tenants and how much it was all worth. The Hundred Rolls are a similar survey initiated on a national level by Edward I in the 1270s. Although they were never completed, they provide valuable information about some Midland villages. Theoretically it should be possible to take a series of villages in 1086 and the 1270s and compare the evidence from Domesday with the evidence from the extents, to show the amount of population increase. At Hanborough, for instance, some 90 tenants are listed in the Hundred Rolls, a seemingly threefold increase in 200 years. Again, it sounds very simple, but is fraught with difficulties. One has to be sure that like is being compared with like. Whilst a manor might be identical with a village in 1086, between then and the thirteenth-century extents there could have been divisions and subdivisions through the workings of the feudal laws of inheritance, so that in the 1270s the manor might be only a portion of the village. As with the Domesday evidence, most manorial historians are by no means convinced that sub-tenants were listed in the extents, and the same difficulties as before exist with the multiplier. Finally, for the most part the extents describe manorial-ized unfree villages. It will be suggested that there was often a very different population growth rate in manorialized and free villages, so that extrapolating evidence of population increase from the extents to cover the whole country is not possible.[7]

The last piece of 'hard' evidence used is the poll tax of 1377. This was a tax of a groat (4d.) on every head, male or female, of 14 years of age or above, and should theoretically list everyone in the country over 14. 'Theoretically' is the right word to use, since the first problem with any tax return is that some people avoided payment. How many? Professor Russell thought that evasion was on a small scale as compared to the later tax of 1381. But collection posed a formidable problem for a primitive administration. Collectors had to visit isolated hamlets and farmsteads, to deal with the floating population with no fixed abode, to know the ages of those who claimed to be under 14. It seems inconceiv-able that evasion ran at less than 5 per cent. Perhaps it was not as high as Professor Postan's 25 per cent, but it must surely be somewhere near that figure. Given this, one has a very different and higher starting point for estimating the population of England even after wave on wave of plague between 1348 and 1375. Then a further calculation has to be made: what proportion of the population were children under 14 in the late fourteenth-century England? Russell used his life tables to suggest that under 14s comprised one-third of the population, and so he multiplied his total for the poll tax by 1.5 to allow for this. Again, this has been much criticized. Basing their arguments on evidence from pre-industrial societies like nineteenth-century Russia and modern underdeveloped countries, other historians suggest that the figure should be somewhere in the region of 40–50 per cent of the population. This substantially increases post-plague numbers and has the immediate effect of raising all estimates of the total population before the arrival of the plague. If one accepts a minimum aggregate mortality from the plague of $33\frac{1}{3}$ per cent, an evasion rate of only 2.5 per cent for the poll tax, and the under 14s as one-third of the total, then one arrives at Professor Russell's estimates of 2.235 million people in England in 1377 and pre-plague 3.7 million. If one uses the higher figures for the under 14s, an evasion rate of 25 per cent for the poll tax, and aggregate mortality of all plagues between 1348 and 1377 of 50 per cent, then the post-plague population rises to 3 million and the pre-plague to 6 million. If one also accepts that the population actually began to decline before the arrival of the plague, then it could have been as high as 7 million in the 1290s and early 1300s.

The sources, therefore, are statistically unreliable, but clearly the major differences as to the number of people in medieval England arise from disputes over the value of the multiplier and the proportion of children under 14. They are interrelated problems, the latter affecting the size of the former. The multiplier is used to convert holdings or tenants into people, and to arrive at its proper value a fair balance has to be struck between the following problems. (1) Was it one household per holding? (2) How many of these households consisted of families, how many were single persons? (3) What was the nature of the family, was it nuclear or extended? (4) How large was the family and what was its age distribution? (5) Should the multiplier always be the same, should it rise and fall in line with population increase and decrease?

There is no real evidence as to the first point until the thirteenth-century. extents and surveys. Looked at objectively such evidence makes one doubt the unity of holding and household assumed by Professor Russell. Manorial surveys list holdings, not tenants. Some tenants often had more than one holding and thus more than one dwelling. A rental of the bishop of Winchester's manor of Waltham (Hants) in 1331–2 lists 705 holdings and 363 tenants of whom 19 held between them some 70 dwellings, cottages or messuages. Such tenants do not represent single households at all. They did not move progressively from one dwelling to the next: rather they sub-let them to other villagers or settled members of their families in them. More important sub-tenants were often completely concealed and only occasionally revealed by accident. A mid-thirteenth century custumal of the Glastonbury Abbey manor of Damerham (Hants) states under one of its subheadings where only virgaters are recorded that 32 cottagers held of the villeins. The weight of evidence in fact suggests that there was often more than one tenant per holding and any multiplier trying to convert tenants into total population must take account of this. If this is the case, then the multiplier must be raised from 3.5.

Secondly, the weight of evidence also suggests that the majority of holdings were occupied by families and that the number of single-person households was very small. Again, this must affect the size of the multiplier. If there were substantial numbers of people living on their own, then the multiplier must be adjusted downwards. Professor Russell thought that the number of single-person households was quite large. He noted, rightly, that on many manors there were many women tenants, some 17.3 per cent of the whole on the surveys he examined. He believed that most of them were widows living on their own in cottages, having moved to them after surrendering their holdings to their sons. He also thought that the number of single women would be matched by a similar number of single men, in the same condition, since death struck at both sexes equally. Thus the proportion of single-person households might be as high as 34 per cent of the whole. In fact, the last point is pure supposition, without supporting evidence, and can be dismissed at once. But there were these women tenants, although the estimate of 17.3 per cent is probably too high. J. Z. Titow, in the best current critique of Professor Russell's theses in the introduction to his *English Rural Society 1200–1350*,[8] suggests on a random sample of 13 manors on the estates of the bishop of Worcester, the bishop of Winchester and the abbot of Glastonbury, that the proportion ranged from 10–15 per cent. Of this sample, the majority were not cottagers: 66.2 per cent had holdings of five acres or more. Presumably they were working them until their sons came of age. Why, in any case, should we assume that widows were settled in separate cottage holdings by their heirs? In most instances widows seem to have stayed within the family when the heir came of age, or had a cottage erected for them out of the existing holding which would not appear on the extents. Of the widows who were cottagers, most were probably supporting households. Death did not strike all classes with equally hurtful consequences. Those with little land were probably badly nourished and died off at a higher rate than those with larger holdings. Since the female of the species is in fact much tougher than the male, it is likely that the women cottagers had families to support. Indeed, the single-person household is a phenomenon of an industrialized, not a peasant society, both in the Middle Ages and the modern world.

That automatically leads to the third point, the nature of the medieval family occupying the holdings. The question is, was the family nuclear or extended, did it consist simply of parents and children unable to provide for themselves, or along with these were there other relatives, aged parents unfit for work, unmarried adult sons with no holdings of their own, indigent uncles or aunts and perhaps servants as well? Deciding whether the family was or was not nuclear obviously makes a substantial difference to the size of the multiplier. Unfortunately there is no real consensus of opinion on this point. Professor Russell, inevitably, argues for the nuclear family. He bases most of his argument on what he believed to be true from the evidence of the extents, that widows and younger sons were provided for by separate cottage holdings, that sons did not have to wait for their inheritances as there were plenty of opportunities for them in the expanding towns, or by the creation of new tenements within the village. In view of this evidence, he felt that the chances of families piling up under one roof were not great. Professor Homans, writing on the thirteenth-century villager, used extensive data to show that it was common for the father to retire and hand his holding over to his son who would provide for him and his wife in their old age within the family. On the other hand, Professor Hallam, using some of, if not the only, direct evidence for medieval population size and structure, from the fens, concluded that the family, whilst much larger than Russell would admit, was still entirely nuclear.[9] The best solution to the problem is probably a compromise, that the family moved naturally from one state to the other. Aged parents and others would live with the family for a time. Then, by a process of death or migration, it would revert to the nuclear condition, until the children took over from their parents. This still means that the multiplier will need upward revision to allow for the changing size of the family.

But how many people were there in the average family? Professor Russell believed that the best evidence for this came from the 1377 poll tax. He thought that this had been collected street by street, house by house, as indeed it seems to have been in the Leicestershire village of Wigston Magna. He would therefore argue that it is possible to estimate from this data the number of persons over the age of 14 to a house, remembering that he believed large households to be balanced by substantial numbers of single-person households. His 'average' is 2.3, which would seem to represent a couple plus one child over 14 for every third couple, or one couple and a servant for every third couple. This average is then multiplied by a figure which will adjust it to allow for the under 14s. The figure itself is derived from his life tables which Russell claims show patterns of life expectancy and thus the age distribution of the population both before and after the plague. The life tables themselves are a very elaborate series of calculations based on evidence from the Inquisitions Post-Mortem, investigations made after the death of feudal tenants to see who their heir was and whether or not he was of age. Obviously, given a series of these for several families, it should be possible to work out life expectancy, age of marriage, surviving children and so on. So, from the life tables, Russell takes the total population aged 15 and above, adds to it one-fifth of the population alive in the age range 10–15 (to allow for the 14-year-olds), then divides this into the total population, to secure the ratio of the group aged 14 and above to the total. For the years 1276 to 1450 he concluded that the ratio was 1:1.5. So, multiply 2.3 by 1.5 to adjust for the under 14s and the index of about 3.5 emerges, which Russell believed should be used constantly through the Middle Ages to convert tenants into total numbers of people.

To this there are very serious objections, both as to the evidence from the poll tax and from the life tables. With regard to the poll tax, as Dr Titow has put it: 'The assumption which Professor Russell has no right to make is that the size of households can be ascertained on the basis of the poll tax returns. There is nothing explicit or implicit in the documents to indicate that the taxpayers listed in them are grouped together in households, or where one household ends and another begins.'[10] Some persons were linked in payment, for husbands would pay for wives and children. But it is unwarranted to assume that persons linked together in payment represent necessarily separate and complete households and persons not visibly linked to anyone equal single-person households. They may or may not have been. The evidence on this problem has already been discussed, both as to the nature of family and the number of single-person households. That, and the unreliability of the poll tax returns must make one call in question the average of 2.3. The allowance of one-third for children under 14 (as that, effectively, is what multiplying by 1.5 does) also seems to be too low. It is derived from demographically and statistically unreliable evidence. The Inquisitions Post-Mortem are the records of the upper classes, better clothed, better fed, better housed than the rest of the population. Their birth and death rates are scarcely representative of a peasant society. Statistically, the sample is very small. The calculations for 1326–48, for instance, are based on a sample of 355 persons, or 0.00096 of the population in 1347 by Russell's own estimate. The mortality rate of the age group 10–14 in 1301–25 is based on two deaths among 67 persons. And, given the disastrous death rates of the period 1348–77, the age distribution of the population in 1377 must have been one of the most unusual the world has ever seen and thus a very uncertain guide to the age distribution of the period as a whole. To base any conclusions on it would be very dangerous.

So Russell's multiplier of 3.5 must be rejected – which alters the whole profile of the population pattern in medieval England. The multiplier must be higher, although by how much it is very difficult to say. The only 'substantial' evidence comes from the already mentioned Spalding serf lists, dating from the late 1260s.[11] These were actual censuses for three manors, giving in two cases complete information on the size of families. Where the father was dead, the lists say so, and what happened to the offspring. The average size of the household (allowing for single persons, etc.) was 4.68, although the evidence may be slightly skewed. It comes from an area of high population density where partible inheritance allowed greater population growth. Nevertheless, it still suggests a multiplier with a value well above 3.5. So does other, less comprehensive evidence from the bishop of Winchester's large Somerset manor of Taunton. There a head penny tax was collected from all males above the age of 12. Between 1209 and 1311 the male population over 12 rose from 612 to 1,448. Modern censuses show that males over 12 formed 34.8 per cent of the population of England in 1851, males over 14, 31.2 per cent of the population of rural Russia in 1894–1912, and males over 15, 30.7 per cent of the total population of India in 1951. The figure for England in 1851 would therefore seem fairly representative of the over 12s in a peasant society and it means that the total population of Taunton in 1248 was about 2,845. There were 660 holdings on the manor, and dividing 2,845 by 660 gives an average of 4.3 per tenancy. In 1311 the average is higher, at 5.9 per tenancy, the number of holdings not having increased in the late thirteenth century.

That in itself points to another danger. Russell believed that the size of the household remained constant. Others argue that it varied,

55

according to the proportion of children, from a minimum of 4.3 in a population with a low proportion of children to over 5.2 in one with a high proportion of children. We might be justified in attaching dates to these figures: 5.2 would be representative of a period of expanding population in the twelfth and thirteenth centuries, 4.3 or less to the period after the plague when families seem to have been smaller. Whichever way one looks at the problem, however, in calculating aggregates a multiplier higher than 3.5 must be used. That means a higher aggregate population throughout. The graph on page 65 shows the possibilities, the present writer believing that the high estimate is more plausible than the low. All are agreed, however, that there was a threefold rise at the least between 1086 and 1300, that the population fell sharply some time after the Black Death by between one-third and a half, and that it remained relatively low in the late fourteenth and the fifteenth centuries. The evidence for post-plague population is different from that for the earlier period and will be discussed fully later in this chapter.[12]

Having calculated the aggregates, the demographer is by no means at the end of his troubles. He has to try to explain (i) What caused the rise up to the end of the thirteenth century? (ii) When did the peak come, and (iii) Did population decline begin before the Black Death? (iv) What were the consequences of bubonic plague? (v) Why did the population not grow again in the fifteenth century? Why did it apparently remain static, if not in a state of slow decline? The honest answer to the first question is probably that we do not know. There are three hypotheses for the growth. The first is that it was cumulative on the compound interest principle. A period of peace and stability from about 1000 onwards coupled with reasonably good harvests would bring about a growth rate of $c.$ 0.15 per cent per annum, till the peak was reached at the end of the thirteenth century. The second hypothesis accepts the steady growth up till 1086, but then a sudden spurt until 1348 with high growth rates of 0.43 or 0.46 per annum over this period. The third sees the rapid upswing coming at the end of the twelfth and beginning of the thirteenth centuries and then continued growth until the peak was reached by the early fourteenth century. Then the population reached the limits of its subsistence, and by the process of Malthusian checks began to decline. (Malthus believed that fertility was constant, and that once the population had reached the limits of its subsistence it would automatically regulate itself or be regulated by pestilence or famine.) Possibly the third hypothesis best fits what hard evidence there is. There was a sudden rise in prices between 1180 and 1220, followed by a sustained period of price rises to the end of the thirteenth century. At Taunton the growth rate in the thirteenth century was very high, 0.85 per annum. Whatever the rate, in physical terms the increase was substantial. Ninety-one households at Spalding in the Fens in 1081 had become 587 in 1287, an increase of 545 per cent, even more than at Taunton; 71 at Weston and Moulton 389 (a 405 per cent increase), 30 tenants rose to 91 at Hanborough, 39 to 146 at Wellingborough (Northants).

If the population did expand suddenly in the late twelfth and early thirteenth centuries, then it is very much harder to explain than a very gradual cumulative increase. The reasons for population change obviously lie in the relationship between birth and death rates. Before the advent of endemic plague the death rate in the Middle Ages was probably constant, running at somewhere between 25 and 30 per thousand per annum. In 1948 it ran at 10.8 per thousand in England and 9.9 per thousand in the USA. The most at risk in modern society are the young and the old. In the USA in 1948 there was a death rate of 32 per thousand in the first year of life, 0.54 per thousand at ten, 1.49 at twenty, 1.96 at thirty, 9.33 at fifty, 45.40 at seventy. In the Middle Ages the death rate per thousand was likely to have been much higher in the first year, and probably in the 40s and 50s, since life expectancy was much lower. The population was, too, always at the mercy of poor harvests and of diseases such as tuberculosis, diphtheria, dysentry.

The vital factor therefore was not so much the death rate as the birth rate. Fertility was not necessarily constant, as Malthus assumed. It altered quite sharply according to the age of marriage, and in an agrarian society that varied considerably according to the availability of land. The difference can clearly be seen in the Fens, where there was land to be colonized, in many villages partible inheritance was practised and a market in free land flourished. It was thus easier to provide young men and younger sons with some sort of holding. Professor Hallam studied two villages, Moulton and Weston, of the same shape and on similar land. In both villages partible inheritance was practised, but much more so in Moulton than Weston. Moulton was much more populous. In Weston marriage was late and there were far fewer children; in Moulton there were many newly married families of young men and women with children. In Weston young women and young men tended to emigrate by marriage or by stealth, whilst in Moulton they stayed at home 'for they had land or the hope of land to make them stay'.[13] It is noticeable that population density was generally higher in areas of partible inheritance. This makes it difficult to project evidence from the Fens to the whole of England, but the interrelationship of land availability and the age of marriage is clearly demonstrated. Thus the demand for land which is so obvious in late twelfth- and early thirteenth-century England might be interpreted both as a sign of population increase and of the availability of land to make early marriage generally possible.

It follows from this that when the supply of land began to dry up, then the population increase should have slowed down. Indeed, on Malthusian lines, the population should have reached the limits of subsistence and begun to decline. Some historians have chosen to see this turning point at the end of the thirteenth and beginning of the fourteenth centuries. There is no question but that in relative terms England was a land full of people. There may not have been Professor Postan's seven million, but there were far more than Professor Russell's 3.7 million (in 1348). The detailed evidence of the extent of colonization and the density of population in certain areas is given below,[14] but land was brought under cultivation that was not again to see the plough until the world wars of the twentieth century. Many peasants had holdings barely sufficient to keep their families and meet their outgoings. There is some evidence that the population was becoming harvest sensitive – that is, that death rates increased markedly in the spring and early summer of the year following a bad harvest. A run of bad harvests would cause disaster and demographic downturn, so it is argued, as yields from the poor lands recently brought into cultivation and from the overworked and longer settled holdings fell. So the Great Famines which hit all Europe in 1315–17 and lingered on until 1325 are seen as a turning point, when the medieval population reached its peak and began to decline. They were indeed a catastrophe. As much as 10 or 15 per cent of the population may have died of starvation and associated diseases although no one can really be certain. Slowly falling prices after 1325 and evidence of a drift from demesne farming and of land being abandoned seem to indicate a declining population, which was further burdened by heavy taxation and the seizure of supplies to provision royal armies.

But it is very difficult to be positive about this. Falling prices can be explained in monetary terms and wages tended to move with them.[15] Had there been a growing shortage of labour, then they ought gradually to have risen. Most great landlords did not abandon demesne farming. They were not to do so until the very different circumstances of the 1360s, 1370s and 1380s. Presumably this was because of a continued demand for food, for the fact is that one great disaster does not necessarily lead to a falling population. The years following such a disaster often see high birth rates. Marriages which had been postponed in a period of crisis were now contracted, restraints on conception by married people were relaxed. The famines were also likely to have hit hardest at the young and old, and the period after them would be one of high birth rates and low death rates. This would explain what is otherwise inexplicable, that after the first wave of plague landlords found no difficulty in filling vacant holdings. England still seems to have been a land full of people and although there was a retreat of settlement, it may have meant reverse migration back to older villages and worse overcrowding. In these circumstances, it is difficult to see a definite turning point before 1348. The famine may have caused only a temporary downturn, from which the population rapidly recovered between 1325 and 1348. Indeed, that year may well have seen a peak not again to be reached for several centuries.

Yet on one point all historians agree: 1348 marks the beginning of a period of serious population decline, with the arrival of the plague. Plague is enzootic or permanently present in the blood-stream of rats in parts of Asia and the Far East. Every so often it spreads outwards in pandemics, as a result of war or movement along trade routes. There have been three such pandemics in recorded history: that which hit the Constantinople of Justinian in the sixth century AD, spread through the Mediterranean world and possibly to England in the seventh century; that which hit Europe in the form of the Black Death and lingered on until the eighteenth century (or in the case of England until 1665–6); and that which began in the East in 1894 but had little impact on Western Europe.

Plague is not one, but several related diseases. Its most common form is bubonic. Here the disease is transmitted from the blood-stream of the temporarily infested epizootic rat or other rodent by the flea. The flea living on the rat becomes blocked, that is so full of the plague organism that it cannot digest any more blood from its host. It leaves the dying rat, then becomes very hungry, attacks humans, bites them, but not being able to digest their blood either, regurgitates the organism which passes into the human blood-stream. The bubonic plague bacillus attacks the lymphatic glands. Its usual symptoms are buboes, or large swellings in the groin or armpit, or near where the flea has bitten, accompanied by a high fever. Usually it is fatal within two to five days. It spreads most effectively where there are high concentrations of people and rats, and in certain climatic conditions. The Asiatic rat flea flourishes in the temperature range 20–25° centigrade, and in dry weather. In England this would coincide with normal summer conditions. If it is too hot, then the life of the flea is shortened and the epidemic is checked. So the plague is at its most virulent in late spring and early summer, and in late summer and autumn. It ends with winter when the Asiatic flea hibernates. The disease is not transmitted directly from man to man, but via the flea. But the fleas are easily transmissible on humans, or in bales of cloth or other goods; the rats in bulk cargoes like grain. If you caught bubonic plague, then you had a 40 per cent chance of survival, for case mortality is about 60 per cent.

The second type, pneumonic plague, is far more deadly. In certain circumstances bubonic plague becomes localized in the lungs and causes symptoms similar to pneumonia. It can easily be transmitted from man to man, by breathing in bacilli coughed out by the infected person. Pneumonic plague is one of the deadliest diseases known to man. Case mortality is 100 per cent. Obviously it flourishes in the winter independent of the rat/flea relationship, but it cannot exist independently of bubonic plague. When it is present, however, death rates are far higher. The third type of plague is septicaemic. The infection of the blood-stream with the plague bacilli themselves is so massive that the buboes have no time to form. The victim dies within a few hours of the onset of the illness. Fortunately, it is relatively rare. All three types of plague can occur in the same outbreak, however. Bubonic plague may rage in the summer, transmute itself into its pneumonic form in the winter, then revert to bubonic in the next summer.

That is what seems to have happened in the first great outbreak of 1348–50, since plague raged through summer and winter. In spite of recent attempts to play down the death rate on the grounds that there were only sufficient concentrations of people and rats in the towns and that villages must have escaped, many people died. Dr Shrewsbury[16] ignores the fact that the countryside was relatively heavily populated and that there were regular contacts between village and town. Wool, cloth and grain, by all of which plague could be transmitted, passed regularly from one to the other. The Great Pestilence was not confined to the South and East of England, where population was densest. Contemporaries record that it spread through the whole of the kingdom, lowland and highland zones alike. Death rates were undoubtedly heavy, but undoubtedly variable, and there is no certainty as to how many the first plague killed. The problem can be looked at in terms of class. Professor Russell estimates a death rate of 27 per cent using a sample of 505 tenants-in-chief who came into their inheritances before the plague and either survived or died from it. That percentage is likely to be too low. The rich could travel to avoid the plague. They lived in stone houses which gave less shelter to the rats, unlike the thatch-roofed wattle-walled huts of the poor. The most reliable national figure is possibly the number of beneficed clergy who died. Calculations from the bishops' registers of the dioceses of Lichfield, Lincoln and York, show death rates of 40 per cent for the year of the plague. This evidence is not entirely reliable, however, because of resignations, men holding more than one living or those who employed a poor priest to do their duties in their absence. The clergy were also better fed and better housed, although their pastoral duties should have brought them into closer contact with the sick. They were also on average older than the rest of the population, so their death rate may have been higher than average. Certainly, in class terms, it was far above that for the feudal tenants.

But when one turns to look at the evidence for specific manors, the picture becomes even more horrifying. Heriot payments suggest that two-thirds of the customary tenants died at Bishop's Waltham (Hants), Downton (Wilts), Witney and Cuxham (Oxon); between 50 and 60 per cent on three Cambridgeshire, two Essex and two east Cornish manors, and one-third of the tenants at Brightwell (Berks). Calculations based on the decline in the number of persons paying customary dues just before and after the plague suggest average death rates of 55 per cent on 22 Glastonbury Abbey manors and 43 per cent on three Essex manors. Again, the figures here have to be treated with some caution. Plague clearly caused a great upheaval. Accurate records were not always kept. Where more than one heriot was received from the same holding because of the death of the heir, it artificially inflates the number of deaths in the population at risk and customary payments could be avoided in the post-plague chaos. So whilst the figures for the feudal tenants-in-chief are too low, those for the peasant mortality are probably too high. Some seek to strike a neat average and say that about one-third of the population died. On the balance of the evidence, the total was probably nearer 40 per cent or more, although it is doubtful whether it was as high as Professor Postan's 50 per cent.

The curious fact is that, although so many people died in this first outbreak, plague initially had few economic consequences. Holdings were soon all filled, landlords continued demesne farming for the market, wages remained relatively low, prices high. This suggests a countryside still full of people, which perhaps also explains why death rates had been so high. Real signs of economic change as a result of plague come only gradually and are not generally evident until the mid-1370s. Then prices began to fall, wages to rise, landlords began again to lease demesnes, holdings began to fall permanently vacant. As with the Great Famines of 1315–25, one disaster does not lead to demographic downturn. But a whole series of disasters will have a cumulative effect and that is precisely what happened. Plague was now endemic, here to stay. There were further national outbreaks in 1361–2, 1369 and 1375. Evidence of mortality in these years is scant, but the death rates seem to have been lower than in 1348–50. In 1361 on the manor of Bishop's Waltham only 13 per cent of the tenants died, which is roughly in line with the 14 per cent of the beneficed clergy in the diocese of York, but below the 23 per cent for feudal tenants-in-chief. The death rate for feudal heirs and heiresses in 1369 fell to 13 per cent, which was the same as the figure for the clergy in the diocese of York. After this, there is no real evidence at all. There are only indirect indications[17] that a long-lasting decline in the total population had occurred, with an aggregate mortality for all the plagues up to 1380 somewhere in the region of 40 per cent.

Mere numbers, however, disguise what is more important, that from the late fourteenth century onwards, plague and other epidemic diseases acted as a brake on the recovery of the population to its former level. For recover it should have done. Fewer people meant more per capita wealth, an improved standard of living for the survivors. Land was now readily available, food was cheap, real wages high, a better diet with greater consumption of meat and dairy products was now possible. This should have encouraged earlier marriage, a rising birth rate and a declining death rate. But the population did not rise. All the indirect evidence suggests that after the major fall in the third quarter of the fourteenth century, the population remained at best static, at worst slowly declining until the last decades of the fifteenth century. Wages remained high, and prices low. It was in the mid-fifteenth century that the desertion of villages was at its height, and that landlords found the greatest difficulty in leasing their demesnes and collecting their rents. It has been argued that plague could not have caused this decline, indeed that the population was slowly but unevenly recovering in the fifteenth century. This argument is based on the nature of the plague in these years. The evidence, it is said, suggests that after the first outbreak it was largely bubonic, which is far less deadly, and became mainly an urban disease. There were frequent visitations, almost yearly, in London for instance, but on a national level outbreaks of epidemic proportions were fewer and more widely spread. There were only twelve national plagues after the first: in 1361–2, 1369, 1375, 1400, 1407, 1413, 1434, 1438–9, 1464, 1471, 1479, 1485. Between 1413 and 1434 there was a gap of 21 years and between 1438–9 and 1464, of 25, both of which would have allowed time for the population to recover. Not all the ills (if ills they were) of the later Middle Ages should, it is argued, be blamed on the plague.

In a recent and stimulating study, Dr J. Hatcher has challenged this thesis.[18] He points out that demographic decline is not necessarily caused by national epidemics, but that the cumulative effects of lesser, local outbreaks could be decisive. Professor Bean had himself noted the number of localized plagues, in and around provincial towns – Newcastle upon Tyne in 1409, Norwich in 1465, Hull in the 1470s. Plague raged at Canterbury in 1412, 1413, 1419, 1420, 1431, 1447; there was plague in Norfolk in 1420, on the St Albans estates in 1431, in Kent in the 1450s, all of which must have hit the local population severely. To national outbreaks of plague there must also be added national epidemics of other diseases. In 1389–93 famine sickness and dysentery were rife, the 1420s saw outbreaks of fatal pulmonary disease of which one in 1427, called 'the mure', was nationwide. Along with plague there was famine in 1438–9 and in 1485 high mortality from the sweating sickness. The occurrence of these diseases we know about; of the effects of typhus, diphtheria, measles, tuberculosis or dysentery, all of which were normal hazards in the Middle Ages, we know little or nothing. From all this Dr Hatcher concludes that the population was failing to replace itself, and there is some admittedly limited evidence to support his case. Calculations can be made of replacement rates of tenants-in-chief from the Inquisitions Post-Mortem, that is of the numbers of sons surviving the death of one or other of their parents, normally the father.[19] More than one indicates increasing population, less than one declining, and between 1341 and 1441 there was consistently less than one. The same strictures apply as before, that evidence from a privileged class should not be applied to the whole population, but the figures are interesting. Other attempts to calculate replacement rates for peasant families from court rolls and wills have so far failed, but one can see something of the death rates of another class from the obituary and ordination lists of Christ Church Priory, Canterbury, from 1394 to 1504. From these it is possible to calculate crude death rates and the age structure of the monastic population. Crude death rates range from as low as the mid-20s per thousand in the healthiest decades to as high as the mid-40s per thousand in the unhealthiest. The high levels were symptomatic of a community experiencing waves of epidemic disease. Again, the sample is small, and uncharacteristic, but the statistics are interesting to say the least.

So it may not just be a case of regular outbreaks of plague acting as a brake on recovery, but of a population failing to replace itself. Why? One answer could be that the size of families was deliberately being limited, that women were either reluctant to have children or were restricting the numbers they bore, so that they might enjoy the fruits of an improved standard of living. But there is no real proof of that, and the solution to the problem probably lies in differing patterns of mortality. Contemporaries noted that plague struck hardest at the young and the old. Callous though it may seem, high death rates among the elderly would have little effect on long-term population trends. It was the young, the most susceptible to all diseases, who mattered most. If they died in large numbers, this would distort the age structure of the population and severely limit its ability to reproduce itself because the future breeding stock was severely reduced. So if child mortality was high, the fertility schedule would be lowered for decades, 'as depleted cohorts reached marriageable and child bearing age'.[20] Not until the end of the fifteenth century was there any glimmer of an upturn, and even then it was a very uncertain beam. The population of England in the mid-fifteenth century was probably between 2 and $2\frac{1}{2}$ million, scarcely half a million more than it had been in 1086.

The population profile can therefore vary greatly according to values given to the basic figures, to the size of the multiplier and the interpretation of the demographic trends. Most historians would agree that Professor Russell's estimates are too low, many feel that Professor Postan's are too high. There is some sort of consensus that towards the end of the thirteenth century there were as many people in England as there were to be for at least another 300 years. Indeed the wapentake[21] of Elloe in the Fens was not again to be as densely populated as it was in 1300 until 1831. There is much less consensus on other matters, and the views given above, that the population was *c.* 5–6 million in 1300, declined slightly as a result of the Famines, recovered before the plague, then fell by an aggregate of at least 40 per cent and remained low for the rest of the Middle Ages, possibly declining even further in the fifteenth century, are only some among many.

Given this, and the fact that quantification seems to lead to error, it is legitimate to ask the question, is there any point in the exercise of calculating aggregates? The answer is yes. The figures on their own have limited meaning: they should be used not in abstract but with other evidence to show the dynamics of change and especially the relationship between the numbers of people and the productive resources of the land in a backward agrarian economy. Thus at the end of the thirteenth century we can ask the vital question whether there was enough land to support all the 5–6 million people, or in the fifteenth century what were the consequences of a population of only 2–2½ million? In the first instance, pressure on the land can be seen not only in terms of aggregate numbers, but in the shrinking size of peasant

Figure 2.1 Possible maximum and minimum population estimates

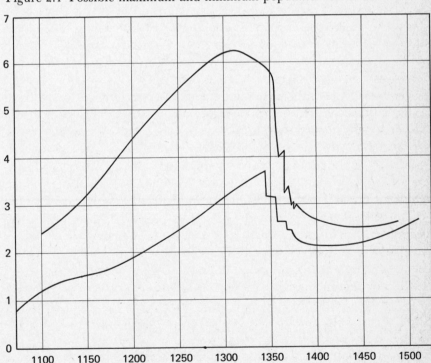

Sources: J.C. Russell, *British Medieval Population* (Albuquerque, 1948), p.280; J. Hatcher, *Plague, Population and the English Economy, 1348–1530* (London, 1977), p.71

holdings. Many villagers in the late eleventh and twelfth centuries held full or half virgates. By the end of the thirteenth century, given at least a threefold increase in the population and in spite of considerable expansion in the area under cultivation, substantial numbers of peasants held less than ten acres, which might have meant overpopulation. Pressure on land can also be seen in the rising level of entry fines and, where they were not fixed by custom, of rents. The importance of the age of marriage has already been discussed although it must be admitted that there is little general evidence of how it rose or fell during the Middle Ages. When, at the end of the thirteenth century, young men in the Sedgemoor levels in Somerset were prepared to jump the inheritance queue by marrying widows with holdings, and paying handsomely for the privilege, then that at least gives some idea of how scarce land had become.[22] Conversely, the whole pattern of settlement and land use in the later Middle Ages points to a declining population. Vacant holdings were to be found on most manors in the fifteenth century, land was falling out of use, arable was reverting to grass, whole villages were being deserted, especially in the Midland grain belt, and some landlords faced falling rents for and incomes from land. Towns, too, were in difficulties as the overall market contracted, and taken together, this all provides good corroborating evidence for sustained population decline in the later Middle Ages.

Such evidence is discussed in detail below, especially in Chapters 3 and 7 and it must not be seen in isolation but against the background of the demographic pattern outlined here. But perhaps the most sensitive indicators of population change and patterns of demand are the movements of wages and prices. Prices are determined by the highly interrelated factors of supply and demand. Theoretically, when the demand for a basic commodity, such as grain, exceeds the supply, then its price will rise. High prices will therefore cure the shortage in two ways. They will cause a reduction in demand, since less is demanded at a higher than at a lower price. They will also stimulate production by making it more profitable, since prices bring the amount demanded into equality with the amount supplied. If, however, demand continues to rise for, say, grain, but production cannot be increased for technical reasons, then prices will continue to rise. Equally, if demand falls, the producers will find surplus stocks building up which can only be disposed of by reducing prices, then such prices must fall. Wages respond to supply and demand in much the same way. If supply outruns demand they will at best remain static, at worst fall: if the reverse is true, then they will rise. Thus, charting the rise and fall in the price of a basic foodstuff such as grain ought to be good evidence of the demand for food and thus of the numbers of people. Similarly the rise and fall of wages ought to be equally good evidence of the supply and demand for labour, and thus, again, of the rise and fall in the population.

Both wage and price tables have their limitations and it is important to understand the way they are constructed. The simplest method, for prices, is to collect as many records as possible of a basic commodity like grain and average them out at national level for each year. This has been done in Table 2.1. The difficulty is that the sample is often very limited, coming mainly from certain estates or from certain geographical areas. Those in Table 2.1 are heavily skewed to the south and east of England. Secondly, they tend to fluctuate rather violently from year to year according to the harvest quality. A bad harvest in one year will affect prices in the next, and so in such tables one should look at the

Table 2.1 Grain price movements in the twelfth, thirteenth and early fourteenth centuries

(a) Twelfth century: wheat per summ (8 bushels)			*(b) Thirteenth century: wheat per quarter*								
Year	*s.*	*d.*	*Year*	*s.*	*d.*	*Year*	*s.*	*d.*	*Year*	*s.*	*d.*
1165	1	9½	1208	2	7½	1265	4	0	1296	4	10
1166	1	9½	1210	3	5¾	1267	3	7	1297	6	4
1167	1	8¼	1211	2	7¼	1268	4	11	1298	5	4¼
1168		11¾	1213	2	3½	1269	5	6¼	1299	5	4
1169	1	5¾	1215	3	3½	1270	6	11½	1300	5	0
1170	1	6	1217	5	0½	1271	7	0	1301	4	10¾
1171	1	7	1218	5	3¾	1272	5	7½	1302	4	7½
1172	2	0	1219	3	8	1273	7	3¼	1303	3	7¾
1173	2	3¾	1220	5	2½	1274	7	4½	1304	5	6
1174	2	0	1223	2	7¼	1275	5	8	1305	5	3
1175	4	0	1224	5	11½	1276	7	0½	1306	4	6
1176	1	2½	1225	4	6½	1277	5	3	1307	5	3½
1177	1	2¾	1226	5	8½	1278	4	2¼	1308	7	0¼
1178	2	2	1231	4	2¾	1279	5	3¾	1309	7	11¾
1179	2	3	1232	3	6¼	1280	5	1	1310	7	11
1184	2	10	1235	3	6	1281	6	3¼	1311	5	0¼
1189	1	10¼	1236	4	0	1282	6	9	1312	4	10¾
1190	1	7½	1244	2	5½	1283	6	10¼	1313	5	6½
1191	1	6	1245	3	4	1284	4	10¼	1314	6	7
1192	1	10	1246	6	5	1285	5	11¼	1315	16	8
1199	4	0	1247	6	3	1286	4	7¾	1316	16	5¾
1201	6	4	1248	3	3¼	1287	2	10½	1317	7	11
1202	7	8¾	1251	3	3	1288	2	11¼	1318	3	11¼
1203	7	7	1252	5	2	1289	4	8¼	1319	4	5
1206	3	11¼	1253	3	5	1290	6	0	1320	6	3½
			1254	2	11¼	1291	5	6½	1321	13	3
			1256	6	6½	1292	6	1¾	1322	8	7
			1257	8	0¾	1293	7	7¼	1323	6	2
			1262	4	0½	1294	8	2½	1324	7	11¼
			1264	4	2¼	1295	9	2¾	1325	5	1¾

Other grains, rye, barley and oats, moved roughly sympathetically with wheat. Figures from D. L. Farmer, 'Some Price Fluctuations in Angevin England', *Economic History Review* 2nd series, ix, 1956; 'Some Grain Price Movements in Thirteenth-Century England'. *Economic History Review* 2nd series, x, 1957.

long- rather than the short-term trend. A way of ironing out such violent fluctuations is to take decennial or moving averages, and to show rises or falls more clearly by expressing them in terms of a base year. This is done in Figures 2.2 and 2.3. In Figure 2.2 the twenty years, 1160–79, are taken as the base. Average grain prices then in terms of grammes of silver are taken as 100. All subsequent prices are expressed as a percentage of that base. In Figure 2.3 the average price of a basket

Figure 2.2 English wheat prices expressed in grams of silver; 1160–79 = 100

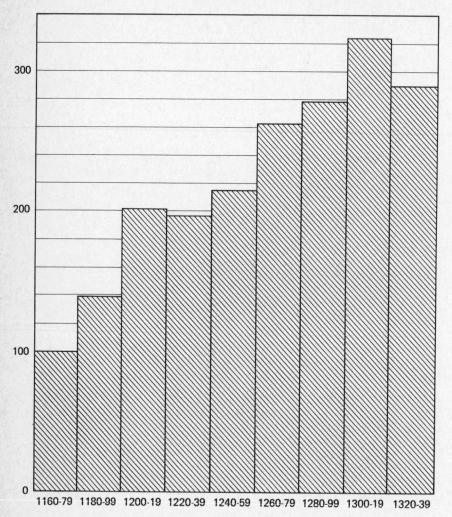

B.H. Slicher van Bath, *The Agrarian History of Western Europe* (London, 1963), p.133

Figure 2.3

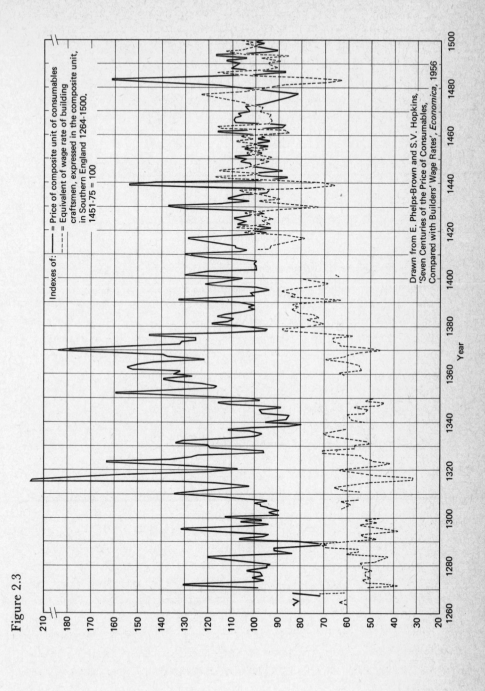

Indexes of:
——— = Price of composite unit of consumables
– – – – = Equivalent of wage rate of building
craftsmen, expressed in the composite unit,
in Southern England 1264-1500.
1451-75 = 100.

Drawn from E. Phelps-Brown and S.V. Hopkins,
'Seven Centuries of the Price of Consumables,
Compared with Builders' Wage Rates', *Economica*, 1956

Year

of consumables in the third quarter of the fifteenth century is taken as the base, and the price of a similar basket is expressed in terms of this from 1264 to 1500. The latter method, taking a basket of consumables, is more sophisticated than simply using grain prices. It takes into account other foods, especially meat, fish, butter and cheese, as well as fuel, light and textiles. Its composition can be varied according to varying patterns of consumption, but the size is always roughly the same. The rise and fall of the price of the basket is then plotted in the form of a graph. There will be annual fluctuations because of bad and good harvests, but taken in the long term, such a graph will show periods of low and high prices. Moving averages are not used in these tables, but they are to be found in other works. They iron out extreme fluctuations, by taking the average price of a commodity in any one year, with a specific number of years on either side of it.

Prices on their own are evidence of general supply and demand. They have to be treated with some caution. Soaring grain prices are not necessarily evidence of mass suffering, since many peasants supplied their own food needs from their holdings. Indeed, it is when prices are compared with wages that they become really interesting. Wage tables are constructed in precisely the same way as those for prices, and have the same limitations. The evidence is often very sparse, often being taken from one or two groups of manors only. Geographical variation can be seen in Table 2.2 where Westminster wages are higher than those on the Winchester manors because of the pull of the London economy. Alternatively, the wage rates could be for highly skilled specialists. Such is the case in Figure 2.3, which uses the wages of well-paid building workers in south-east England. Whether this evidence can be applied to the whole country is a matter of some doubt, but they are at least a good indication of wage trends. More useful, however, are calculations of real wages, what money would actually buy. This is done most comprehensively in Figure 2.3. The wage rate of building craftsmen is experienced in terms of the price of the basket of consumables. The drawback is that no account is taken of important items such as rent, but nonetheless the graph does chart the course of real wages and thus of the standard of living over a long period.

The final danger of such tables is that they can be self-fulfilling, they can be used to confirm what is already believed rather than be treated as impartial evidence in themselves. Bearing this in mind, what do they collectively show?

Table 2.2 Wage Rates on Winchester and Westminster Manors 1201–1460

Decade	Piece rates for threshing and winnowing three rased quarters of grains (wheat, barley and oats)		Daily wage rates of craftsmen and labourers Average of rates on eight Winchester manors			Tiler and helper (4 manors)	General price of wheat per quarter
	Winchester manors d.	Westminster manors d.	Carpenter. Thatcher and helper d.		Labourers d.	d.	s.
1201–10	3.27						
1211–20	2.96						
1221–30	3.51						
1231–40	3.13						
1241–50	3.25						
1251–60	3.30	4.84					4.95
1261–70	3.37	5.84					4.52
1271–80	3.45	6.62			1.63	7.17	6.23
1281–90	3.62	5.62	3.12		1.57	6.40	5.00
1291–1300	3.57	6.75	3.53		1.49	6.19	6.39
1301–10	3.85	6.51	2.82	3.19	1.87	6.44	5.69
1311–20	4.05	8.01	3.41	3.55	1.84	5.91	7.91
1321–30	4.62	6.68	3.39	3.78	1.78	5.73	6.79
1331–40	4.92	7.35	3.18	3.82	1.86	4.70	5.17
1341–50	5.03	7.41	2.96	3.73	2.85	6.25	4.79
1351–60	5.18	13.02	3.92	5.00	3.25	7.01	6.96
1361–70	6.10	12.76	4.29	5.95	3.19	6.89	7.98
1371–80	7.00	12.23	4.32	5.98	3.35	7.54	6.67
1381–90	7.22	10.82	4.40	6.01	3.30	7.36	5.17
1391–1400	7.23	10.44	4.13	5.85	3.53	8.17	5.45
1401–10	7.31	11.00	4.64	6.31	3.69	8.50	6.39
1411–20	7.35	12.40	4.51	6.40	3.83	8.56	5.84
1421–30	7.34	10.00	4.52	6.19	3.87	8.81	5.54
1431–40	7.30	13.00	4.75	6.89	4.11	9.24	7.34
1441–50	7.33	13.00	5.18	8.19			4.86
1451–60	7.25		5.23				

From W. H. Beveridge, 'Wages in the Winchester Manors', *Economic History Review* 1st series, vii, 1936; 'Westminster Wages in the Manorial Era', *Economic History Review* 2nd series, viii, 1955.

(1) A rapid rise in grain prices in the period 1180–1220, a slight fall in the following 20 years, but then a continued rise in the last 40 years of the thirteenth century, to a peak in the famine years of the early fourteenth century. Livestock prices show the same tendencies. There was a rapid inflation between 1180 and 1220. Then they fell back but rose again in the latter part of the century. Between the 1210s and 1310s the purchase price of oxen rose by 120 per cent, the major part of the rise coming after 1265. Horses cost 111 per cent more, cows cost 115 per cent with more of the rise again coming after 1265.

(2) In the thirteenth century wage rates were low and static, so that in real terms wage-earners were worse off at the end of the century than at its beginning.

(3) After the famines of 1315–25 were over, grain prices began to fall in the 20 years before the Black Death. Then, paradoxically they rose in the third quarter of the fourteenth century to the high levels of the late thirteenth and early fourteenth centuries. In the 1370s they began to fall again and in spite of a brief recovery at the beginning of the fifteenth century, they remained low until c.1485. The rise in the 1480s was not sustained. At the end of the fifteenth century prices were far lower than they had been in the late thirteenth century.

(4) Wages moved with prices until the late 1370s. Thereafter they parted company completely. The general trend of wages was up, of grain down. The graph in Figure 2.3 shows dramatically how the purchasing power of wages increased. Building workers were well off in the fifteenth century, indeed better off than they were to be again until the nineteenth century.

All this fits the demographic pattern already established by trying to calculate aggregates. It would suggest that the population rose until the end of the thirteenth century, that the supply of food could not keep pace with demand because of low productivity and perhaps increasing soil infertility through over-use, that labour in the thirteenth century was cheap. At the beginning of the fourteenth century Malthusian checks began to operate, so that the population slowly declined until the Black Death. The first wave of the plague had little economic effect, since prices remained high and wages moved with them. Then in the 1370s came the real turning point as waves of plague led to long-term population decline.

Unfortunately the demographic thesis extrapolated from the price-wage tables makes one assumption: that the value of money remained reasonably constant, a concept which would seem alien in our times. It did not do so, and a monetarist school of historians would argue that we should seek explanation of price movements and thus changes in the economy in terms of changes in the value or supply of money. The basis of their argument is the well-known Fisher equation, $P = \frac{MV}{T}$, where M is the money supply, V is the velocity of circulation per unit, P the index of general price level and T the physical volume of transactions. Since $MV = PT$, changes in PT are limited by M and V. Any change in these will increase or decrease prices and the volume of transactions. So it could be argued that an increase in the money supply and the velocity of circulation, and not a rising population, created the increased prices in the thirteenth century. In fact, little is known about velocity of circulation or the volume of transactions in medieval England, which in itself is a criticism of the use of the Fisher equation to explain economic changes in this period. But there is a considerable body of evidence about M, from the records of mint output, complaints about the shortage of money or bad coin in circulation in the Chronicles and in parliament and the evidence of coin hoards. From this abundance of material monetarist historians have constructed theories to explain price/wage movements at critical points, notably the rapid inflation of 1180–1220 which set off the thirteenth-century boom; the high prices at the beginning of the fourteenth century; falling prices in the 1330s and 1340s; and the general depression of prices in the fifteenth century. To appreciate their arguments fully, it is essential to understand the nature of money in medieval England and how the supply could vary in quantity and value.

The basic unit of currency was the silver penny. There were no gold coins until Henry III's abortive attempts to introduce them in 1257 and Edward III's general issues of such coins in the 1340s. It was the king's absolute right to control the issue of coins. He did this through mints working in London and in certain provincial centres. Both the archbishop of Canterbury and the archbishop of York had mints for example, and in the late fourteenth and early fifteenth centuries there was a mint at Calais.[23] When a general recoinage was ordered, the number of mints was temporarily expanded. But in all cases the dies for striking the coin came from the Crown, and only the Crown could order a general recoinage. The amount of money in circulation was surprisingly small by modern standards, perhaps little more than £1,000,000, sometimes far less. There was also a constant leakage of money out of circulation. Silver wears away quite rapidly, by about 2 per cent per decade. On a coinage of £1,000,000 that would mean a loss of about 7 tons per decade. Also, coins were clipped, losses were sustained by cutting silver pennies into halves and quarters, and throughout the Middle Ages English silver coins tended to drain away abroad. This was simply because they were of a consistently good quality, that is they contained a high proportion of silver. The penny of 1500 contained half the silver of that of 800, a slow debasement over 700 years. By contrast the silver penny of Milan had $\frac{1}{43}$ of its specie content in 1500 and the Venetian silver coinage had been debased even further. Too much credit for this should not be attributed to the far-sighted policies of the Crown. Especially in the fourteenth century, when the temptation to profit from rapid debasement was at its greatest, spirited resistance by nobility and laity alike prevented it. The 1352 Statute of Purveyors made it illegal for the weight of coins to be reduced any further without the consent of parliament. Consequently, English coins tended to drain abroad, to be replaced by poor foreign imitations which caused rising prices, as in the late thirteenth century.

So at regular intervals there had to be recoinages to replace poor and worn coins, and the Crown had to decide how to attract bullion to the mint. This was achieved by ensuring that merchants or others bringing bullion or old coins to the mint to be struck into new coins received more back in face value than they brought in. The Crown could do this because medieval coins had in a sense two values, their face value and the value of gold or silver they contained. Prices tended to adjust to the silver content, in spite of the face value. A reduction in fineness, or bullion content, would eventually lead to rising prices, but in the short term the merchant would make a profit. For example, in 1343–4 the Crown ordered that from the Tower pound of silver (6¼ per cent lighter than Troy) 22s.2d. should be struck. The minters kept 8d. for themselves, the Crown took 6d. seignorage or mint tax, and the merchant who brought in the pound of silver received back 21s.0d. in pennies of 20.3 grams weight. In the next year the market price of silver rose above the mint price. So the mint ratios were adjusted to 22s.4d. from the pound of silver, the weight of the penny being reduced to 20.15 grams. The right price had to be set at the mint, especially if the merchant could get better value from a mint on the Continent. When a bi-metallic coinage, gold and silver, was introduced, the Crown faced a further problem. Edward III issued his gold coins in 1343–4. It was part of a general European movement, beginning in Genoa in 1251 both for reasons of prestige and to offset diminishing supplies of silver, but for England in the 1340s, there were additional reasons for the introduction of gold coins. The most common unit of currency used in international trade was the Florentine gold florin, and Italian merchants were artificially maintaining its value at 3s. when it was worth only 2s.6½d. So Edward III issued his leopards of 108, 54 and 27 grains in weight. They were to pass for 72, 36 and 18 silver pennies of 22⅔ grams each, a ratio of 14.8:1 between gold and silver. Gold at that point was simply not worth 14.8 times its weight in silver on the open market, and the overvalued coins were not accepted. Edward had to restrike the coins at a ratio of 12:1, and that was acceptable. So, mint ratios were important, both to ensure that coins would pass easily into circulation and to encourage merchants and others to bring bullion to the mint.

The Crown, therefore, had the power through the right of coinage to affect prices. If, in the process of a recoinage, a limited quantity of coins with a high specie content was issued, it would depress prices. This happened after Edward I's recoinage of 1279 when only some 500,000 coins of fine quality were reissued. Prices for grain and livestock actually fell for a short time, since the new coins were worth more than those they replaced. By the end of the century, however, much poor coin was in circulation, a great deal of it foreign, so prices rose. Then in 1299 there began a lengthy recoinage, which lasted until 1309. From 1304 to 1309 large quantities of foreign silver were brought to the mint, in all some £608,575 worth. A great deal of the coinage struck from it did not drain abroad, but remained in England. In spite of good harvests, the increased quantity of coin in circulation had the effect of pushing up prices in the first decade of the fourteenth century.

But there were also other ways in which the quality and value of money could be affected, which were partly within and partly outside the Crown's control. One which was the Crown's responsibility was the flow of money abroad to pay for foreign wars. Compared with the total currency in circulation, the amounts could be very substantial. Some £350,000 went abroad to pay allies and troops in Gascony and Flanders in 1294–8. In the opening stages of the Hundred Years' War, between 1337 and 1342, no less than £1 million was spent on armies and allies. That must and, as will be seen, did have a deflationary effect, as the quantity of money in circulation was reduced drastically. Large amounts of gold or silver flowing into or out of the country as a result of

75

a favourable or an adverse balance of trade could also have deflationary or inflationary effects. Finally, the European price for bullion could affect the value of the English coinage. Most silver and gold had to come from abroad, either by way of trade or by merchants bringing bullion to the mints, or by direct purchase. The value of silver in Europe would clearly have effects in England. If there was a glut of silver, for example, it would lessen the value of the silver content of the coin. It would be worth less intrinsically, which would tend to push up prices. Should silver be in short supply, the reverse would be true. The silver value of the coins would rise, with deflationary consequences.

Prices and wages therefore respond not only to population growth or decline but to changes in the quantity and value of money. Were such changes, then, the main determinants of price and wage movements and thus also of the general working of the economy? The first critical point comes with the rapid inflation of 1180–1220 which forced land-lords to change back from leasing to demesne farming for the market and had consequent effects on towns and trade. Professor Harvey has argued in a recent article[24] that prices doubled or trebled between 1180 and 1220, rose only slightly to 1260 and then levelled off. Wages followed a similar pattern: King John had to pay three times as much for his troops as his father had done. Skilled workers in charge of the king's vineyards in Herefordshire and at Windsor were paid 1d. per day at the beginning of Henry II's reign: in 1210–11 carpenters working on the bishop of Winchester's residence at Marwell were paid 1½–2d. per day. By the mid-thirteenth century 2½–3d. per day was the normal rate for this work. Professor Harvey thinks that this inflation was peculiar to England and caused not by population pressure nor by deterioration in the coinage. He thinks, rather, that there was a fall of one-third in the value of the metal due to a massive influx of silver as a result of the wool and cloth trades and grain exports. Thus, monetary change was the main determinant of the pattern of estate management, and of much else, in the thirteenth century.

It is an alluring thesis, but to it there are some very substantial objections. Firstly, as can be seen from the price tables in this chapter and the graph on p. 214 of D. Farmer, 'Some Grain Price Movements in the Thirteenth Century', *Economic History Review* 2nd series, x (1957–8), price movements were erratic, partly in response to harvest fluctua-tions. After 1220, they steadied in the 1230s and 1240s, then began to rise again in the 1250s, reaching a high point in the 1270s when they were double those of 1208. Then they fell back in the 1280s only to rise again in the 1290s when again they were nearly double those of the 1200s. This was not a sustained rise, but by the end of the century prices were far higher than they had been at its beginning. Some, though not all of it, is explicable in monetary terms, as has been seen. Moreover, although evidence as to wage rates is very slight, wages in the thirteenth century do not seem to have risen in either monetary or real terms. The best series is for the Winchester manors. There piece rates for winnowing grain were virtually the same in 1281–90 as they had been in 1201–10. Unreliable though it is to base broad conclusions on one piece of evidence, it does suggest that for the thirteenth century we should still look to the demographic explanation of price/wage movements.

But it could still be true that what set off the inflationary price spiral was rapid monetary inflation. The argument must turn on whether vast quantities of silver did come to and, just as important, stay in England. It seems unlikely that none of the specie gained from the sale of wool or cloth was changed into other goods for import, as it was in the later Middle Ages. German merchants were already finding England a fruitful market for their raw materials and products and at a time of economic expansion it is likely that England would have sucked in imports. Nor do we know how much of the wool trade was in alien hands, ensuring that the best profits went abroad. Much more important, however, is the fact that at the same time as England was supposedly being flooded with silver, coin was also being exported in vast quantities by the Angevins. Boatloads of treasure were shipped abroad to pay for their wars and allies on the Continent, until the final defeat at Bouvines in 1214, to pay for the Third Crusade and part of Richard I's ransom. How much flowed abroad is not known, but the Angevins certainly regarded England as the milch cow of their Empire. It is quite possible that outflows cancelled out a substantial part of the silver inflows. Given this, the notion that monetary inflation caused the price rises of 1180–1220 should be viewed sceptically.

There can be little doubt, however, that the amount and quality of coin in circulation did affect prices in the late thirteenth and early fourteenth centuries. The stabilizing effect of the 1279 recoinage did not last long. By the 1290s much foreign coin of poor quality was in circulation and prices inevitably rose. Similarly between 1304 and 1309 there was an influx of silver, partly from the wool trade, partly because of the attractive mint price the Crown was offering. But this monetary inflation was not the prime economic determinant of price movements. It merely exacerbated an already difficult situation. Those who had to go to the market for grain, especially the poor with small holdings, must have suffered grievously. And what caused prices to shoot sky-high, for grain in 1315–17 and for grain and livestock in the early 1320s, were the famines and cattle murrains of the decade 1315–25, which shows just how precariously balanced in relation to productive resources the population was. Nevertheless, monetary factors should be taken into account when assessing population pressure in the late thirteenth century. The evidence of high prices alone is not reliable.

Where monetary factors are of great importance is in the difficult period twenty years or so before and after the Black Death. There is no question but that the fall in prices in the 1330s and 1340s was due to deflation. Mint output in the years 1322–42 was low. As has been seen, there were large exports of bullion in the opening stages of the Hundred Years' War and the coinage may have shrunk by half. Prices fell but wages tended to move with them. This is extremely valuable evidence against the notion that the population was on the downturn before the Black Death. Had it been, then wages should slowly have risen. Equally the high prices of the two decades after the plague were monetary in origin. Debasement in the 1340s and a sharp fall in the population eased the currency shortage, since there was now more money per head in the country, so prices would rise. Again, wages moved with prices, as one would expect, until the 1370s, when the two parted company as the demographic downturn began to bite.

Thus far, the monetarist explanation of price movements has supplemented rather than seriously challenged the demographic explanation of economic change. In the post-plague period, however, the problem becomes far more complex. If the complaints voiced in Parliament from the 1380s onwards are taken at face-value, then there appears to have been a bullion shortage. It might then be the case that it was not demographic decline which caused low prices and concomitant economic decline, but a shortage of money. Indeed a considerable body of historians believe this to be the case. They argue that the actual production of silver declined in the later Middle Ages as output of silver from Kutna Hora in Bohemia and other Central European mines fell. It was not possible fully to replace losses and scarcity meant a rise in the intrinsic price of silver. The shortage worsened due to the working of what are known as bi-metallic flows, as silver went to the Muslim world and gold came back to the West. This came about because, first, the Muslim world turned from a gold-based to a silver-based currency.

Then from the mid-thirteenth century onwards a gold coinage and thus bi-metallism was introduced in Western Europe. Silver was therefore in demand in the Near East, gold in the West. If merchants exported silver to the Near East, they could bring back a proportionately larger amount of gold; similarly gold taken to the West could buy a proportionately larger amount of silver. Merchants soon grasped this. Silver flowed in vast quantities to the Muslim world in the thirteenth century. An estimated 4,000 metric tons went east (when the total output of the East European mines in 1493–1520 was only 47 metric tons). Although the flow slowed down thereafter trade in silver to the East was still active in the fifteenth century. The famous French merchant, Jacques Coeur, was actively engaged in the silver trade to Syria.

Gold in the Middle Ages was the currency of international trade and traders, of princes and monarchs. Silver was in mass circulation and its continued flow eastwards could have had serious consequences for the prices of ordinary goods. There is no doubt that this hit Southern Europe hard. There had to be continued debasements to keep up with the rising price of silver. The effects were less marked in England where, as has been seen, the quality of the coinage was maintained in the Middle Ages. But to achieve that posed difficulties which were further compounded by bi-metallism. The drain of English silver abroad might be quickened if the Crown did not establish the right mint ratios between gold and silver. Theoretically, if the mint ratio of gold to silver was 10:1 and the ruler decided to debase gold by 20 per cent, the new ratio would be 12.5:1. Merchants could then make a profit by taking gold to that mint, exchanging it for silver and selling the silver on the market or to the foreign mint where the ratio was still 10:1. Bullion tended to flow round Europe and rulers coped with this by frequent recoinages and debasements. But the English Crown could not do this, and was frequently caught with the wrong mint ratios, so that the silver in particular did not flow to the mint. This was clearly seen by a London merchant in 1382 when a commission of inquiry was held into the state of the currency. He argued that the weight of coins should be adjusted regularly, as on the Continent – but his advice was largely ignored.

For both reasons, then, it is argued that English silver tended to move abroad, to be replaced in part by gold. The price of silver was enhanced and the value of silver coins increased accordingly. Commodity prices fell, the more so because the velocity of circulation decreased in line with the declining population. Thus the causes of the fifteenth-century price structure were essentially monetary rather than demographic. Yet it is very hard to accept this argument. Mint output in fifteenth-century England may have been erratic, high in the 1420s, low in the mid-century. But mint output is not a completely reliable guide to total money stock. Money could come in from abroad, to pass into circulation in England. It will be argued below that the English tried to attract bullion by restrictions on its export and by trying to force the terms of trade in England's favour.[25] This led to clashes with the duchy of Burgundy, and it is doubtful whether the government itself could influence the balance of trade. Yet it was mainly favourable; the surpluses were not large, but probably sufficient to meet any outflow. It is also difficult to see how merchants could take coin abroad: regulations on its export were strict and strictly enforced. If there was a major flow of silver abroad, then it may have been to pay for the Hundred Years' War. Between 1337 and 1453 some £8½ million was raised in England by direct and indirect taxation and much of it was spent on the war. Some must have remained in the country, having been spent on armaments or provisions. Much also flowed back to England in the form of wages, ransoms and booty. Quite possibly money exported was balanced by money re-imported.

More important, although stocks had fallen, so had the population. There was a greater amount of money per unit of output and per head than before the plague, and the amount would have increased further as the population continued to decline. Nor, as will be argued later, did the market dry up and the velocity of circulation fall. Rather, since per capita wealth was greater, peasants and artisans were spending more on a whole variety of goods. The velocity of circulation is likely to have increased, offsetting any decline in the total money stock. In any case the increasing use of credit and credit instruments in all walks of economic life greatly helped to ease any shortage of coin. But the most telling of all arguments against monetary deflation is that wages and prices did not move together. Rather, wages continued to push upwards in the middle decades of the fifteenth century when the money shortage was supposed to have been at its height and should have been causing falling demand and unemployment. Quite the reverse: the demand for labour, as shown by wages, remained high – and for all types of labour. Whilst craftsmen's wages on Winchester and Westminster manors rose in the later Middle Ages, those for unskilled labourers rose much faster. The craftsman earned twice as much as the labourer in 1300; by 1400 it was only one and a half times as much, and even less in the mid-fifteenth century. Until some adequate monetary explanation is given for this phenomenon, it can only be seen in terms of a slowly declining population in the fifteenth century.

Variations in the value and supply of money could therefore affect the movement of prices and wages. But, their influence was limited: economic change in the Middle Ages must still be seen in terms of a rising or declining population. Economic change, however, is not quite the same as economic development – improvement in the agrarian sector, for instance, or increased output due to technical advances or investment for capital formation. The latter occurs when a society does not apply the whole of its current productive activities to the immediate needs of consumption but directs part of them to the making of capital goods, tools and instruments, machines and transport facilities, plant and equipment to increase the efficiency of productive effort. In the Middle Ages this would mean investment in tools and equipment by landlords and peasants, on enclosures and drainage to raise agricultural productivity, on roads and bridges to improve transport, on industrial equipment and premises, mills for grinding corn and fulling cloth, on mines and forges, and in building up flocks and herds. Capital was also vital for financing long-distance trade and thus increasing the size of the potential market for raw materials and manufactured goods like cloth and wool.

In the Middle Ages capital was almost always associated with large landowners and especially with merchants living in great cities and engaging in banking and international trade. Obviously, to gauge the extent of economic growth it will be essential to examine both the level of technical expertise and the availability of capital and the level of investment. Indeed it will be argued that lack of capital probably held back development in certain sectors of the English economy. That being the case, the size of the population remained the main determinant of patterns of demand. More people meant a greater need for all forms of goods and services, but increasing poverty for the many. Fewer people meant diminished demand, but not necessarily in ratio to the decline in the population since the majority were undoubtedly better off than they had been or were to be for some centuries.

3 The Overcrowded Island

In the late twelfth and early thirteenth centuries the long process of clearing and cultivating previously unused lands reached its climax. Much had already been achieved, but now more mouths to be fed meant that, somehow, more and more acres would have to be brought under the plough. There were two main ways in which this could be accomplished. Firstly, there was within the boundaries of many existing settlements some spare land, both woodland and waste, a mixture of unimproved pasture and scrub. Previously it had been used as a source of fuel, wood and turf and grazing for sheep, cattle and pigs. Now, by the process of assarting,[1] it was turned into arable. So, in the first half of the thirteenth century over 1,000 acres were added to the bishop of Winchester's manors of Wargrave (Berks) and Witney, where the new land in the tithing of Hailey was still known as the 'Assarts' in the sixteenth century, with a further 680 and 660 acres respectively between 1256 and 1306. Not far from Witney (Oxon) at Hanborough, on the edge of Wychwood Forest, 50 or more new holdings of one or two acres of arable or a cottage and a plot of land had been added to the village between 1086 and the 1270s, whilst further south at Laughton in Sussex some 975 acres were brought into the cultivated area. The expanding population of Wigston Magna (Leics) pushed the village fields to the parish boundaries in the course of the thirteenth century and in Kent and Sussex, on the archbishop of Canterbury's anciently settled manors of Boughton, Wrotham and South Malling new land was continually being cleared from the surrounding woods.

Yet such expansion within the existing framework was not everywhere possible. Often, all the land had already been taken in, as on the Winchester manor of Taunton, or some of the Huntingdonshire villages belonging to Ramsey Abbey. It is this fact that gives the twelfth- and thirteenth-century colonization its peculiar character. For the first time forest, fen, marsh and upland which had not previously been thought worth cultivating were cleared and farmed.[2] The most consistent attack was on the forest and it was undertaken by all classes of landholders from great to small. Although the whole county of Huntingdon was technically under the forest laws,[3] this did not stop Peterborough Abbey or its knights or freeholders taking more and more woodland into cultivation in the period 1175–1225, creating a whole new manor of 600 acres at Paston in these years. Further from the Abbey in the Northamptonshire Forest of Rockingham the woodland was thicker and the movement more spasmodic, but whilst the process of clearing was less advanced by the end of the twelfth century, it continued well into the fourteenth. At Cottingham (Northants), Great Easton (Leics) and especially Oundle (Northants), where the Abbey's largest demesne manor of at least 1,000 acres, Biggin Grange, was formed, the movement was particularly vigorous, so much so that by the middle of the thirteenth century woodland, once so expendable, had become a carefully hoarded commodity. Assarting from the forest brought the neighbouring cathedral chapter of Ely into conflict with the officers of the Crown at the end of the twelfth century, whilst like Peterborough, Ramsey Abbey was attacking the woodland on its South Huntingdonshire Manors. Directly across the country, in Warwickshire, in Stoneleigh Hundred[4] along the south-east margins of the Forest of Arden, some parishes showed between 46 and 759 per cent population increase between 1086 and 1279, whilst lord and peasant alike pressed forward with their flocks and settlements into the Forests of Dean and Feckenham. Everywhere the story is the same. In the Hertfordshire villages on the St Alban's estates the greater part of the arable in the thirteenth century was of comparatively recent creation from the forests. In Blackburnshire, Lancashire, the Forest of Rossendale was opened up for cattle grazing in the thirteenth century, first by the monks of Stanlaw and then by Henry Lacy, earl of Lincoln. The woodlands in Kent not then under the forest laws were being eaten away and in the West, the wooded combes of Devon and Cornwall were being colonized. This extraordinary and little-known story explains why there was so much friction over the extent of the forest in the later twelfth and thirteenth centuries as the Crown sought, with some measure of success, to protect its rights of chase.[5]

Next to the forest, fen, marsh and coastland offered the greatest opportunities. Of these, the fens saw the most reclamation. Some 100 square miles were added to the Wapentake of Elloe (Lincs) but this was only part of a spectacular movement forward into the silt lands of Lincolnshire between Spalding and Boston, Boston and Wainfleet along the northern fen edge in Lindsey, and on the western fen edge in Kesteven between Lincoln and Market Deeping. To the south the fens were flanked by several church estates and all levels of society seized the chances offered. Surviving records suggest that there was more assarting on Ramsey's west fenland manors than on those in the forest in South Huntingdonshire: 100 acres were added to the villeins' land at Ringstead (Norfolk) whilst at Holme (Norfolk) demesne and villein land rose from 485½ to 605½ acres between the twelfth and the mid-thirteenth centuries. The Norfolk fens and Cambridge marshlands were under constant pressure from Ely Abbey, which benefited from the gift of 2,000 acres of new land in Wisbech and its hamlets in the late twelfth century. On the Peterborough estates, however, the movement for reclamation only became vigorous after the decline of forest clearing elsewhere. Part of the reason for this was that Peterborough lay on the western edge of the peat fens, not suitable for ploughing. The reclamation there was mainly for pasture to support poor cottagers; 400 acres were added to Eye which had not existed at all in 1086. These bare facts and figures conceal tremendous efforts of banking and dyking against the sea, such as could only be undertaken by groups of villagers or even villages. Many of the great dykes they built can still be seen, though they are now far inland, stranded by the reclamation of later centuries.

As much land was taken back from the sea in the fens as in all other marsh and coastland areas put together. Even so, extensive efforts were made elsewhere. Further up the East Coast in Holderness, Meaux Abbey drained land to improve pasture, whilst on the South Coast in the Romney Marshes and Pevensey levels various monastic landlords, but particularly the archbishop of Canterbury and the abbot of St Augustine's, Canterbury, were busily engaged in winning new land for sheep pastures. These 'innings' helped in the recovery of 23,000 acres from Romney and Walland marshes by the end of the thirteenth century. A whole custom of the marsh was developed, concerned with water control and the maintenance of sea defences, which received a royal charter in 1252 and was administered by special officers. The monks of Canterbury Cathedral Priory were also active along the Thames estuary in north Kent, where a great deal was spent during Henry of Eastry's priorate (1285–1331) on reclaiming and embanking in the manor of Cliffe, thereby raising an already substantial rent roll of £119 in the early fourteenth century to nearly £140 in 1328. Again, monastic houses were very much involved in draining the Somerset levels both to improve pasture but also, as Glastonbury Abbey did on Sedgemoor, to grow oats.

Lastly there were the uplands, where the relationship between cattle, sheep and clearing is obvious. Best known are the efforts of the new monastic order, the Cistercians, whose houses were concentrated around the fens, in the North Country uplands and in Wales. In Yorkshire they benefited from grants of the right to pasture cattle in private forests and chases consisting mainly of scrub, bog, stands of high timber and rough grazing. So Jervaulx, refounded in 1156, had pasture in the forests of Wensleydale and Richmond-on-Swale before 1170, Fountains had the right to pasture 70 beasts in the Forest of Marsden between 1173 and 1193 and before 1200 Rievaulx could use the Forest of Westerdale on the crest of the North Yorkshire Moors to graze 120 head. Where the right to graze cattle and sheep was given, vaccaries and bercaries,[6] farms with living accommodation attached in lodges, soon followed. Nidderdale was virtually colonized in this way by Byland and Fountains Abbeys at the end of the twelfth century. In South Wales and the Marches sheep were more important and the flocks of Dore, Margam, Neath, Flaxley, Whitland and Tintern were well known to Italian buyers in the late thirteenth century, whilst at Strata Marcella, Valle Crucis and Conway in the North cattle grazing predominated to supply the English garrison towns. The colonization of the Forest of Rossendale and Blackburnshire has already been mentioned. It should be remembered that it was as much part of upland as of forest clearing and that here the lay landlord, the earl of Lincoln, played a more important part than the monastic houses. Yet the uplands were not always cleared for pasture. The monks of Bolton Priory, whose estates were centred around Craven in the West Riding, were forced to cultivate land above the 400 foot contour line for cereal crops, especially the hardy oats. Because of population pressure the chalky uplands of South Wiltshire and Hampshire were also turned into poor, but essential, corn lands.

Colonization, the extension of cultivation, was thus a national, even an international phenomenon in the twelfth and thirteenth centuries. The movement in England has its parallels all over Europe, the most spectacular being the *Urbarmachung*, the expansion of the German peoples into the lands beyond the Elbe and the Oder. The general cause is self-evident – population pressure – but land could be cleared both for different purposes and from different motives. There is a basic and obvious contrast between clearing for arable and for pasture, although all too often the latter had to be used eventually for growing corn. But the distinction also needs to be drawn between the motives of those doing the assarting. In the first instance much of the impetus came from the peasantry, particularly in those areas where partible inheritance[7] was practised. As has been seen, in the fenland villages where impartible inheritance was customary, surplus population had to seek its fortunes elsewhere. The sokemen,[8] practising division of land among heirs, stayed at home and made up for the smallness of their holdings by clearing new lands. Elsewhere the connection between clearing and freedom is equally obvious. In the Stoneleigh woodlands small holding and freedom predominated, at Hanborough as in other villages assarts were freely held at money rents and at Wigston Magna the new lands were freely and often individually held. Clearing in some areas altered the social balance between free and unfree peasants and the motive for bringing new lands into cultivation could have been as much legal as economic.

Yet assarting was not simply a peasant movement, for in the twelfth and thirteenth centuries the lords became increasingly involved. The new monastic orders often led the way, with the Cistercians in the van. The order insisted on isolation and, since most other lands were already occupied, they had to establish their houses in the fens and uplands. Usually they created granges, consolidated farms worked by lay brothers or hired labour, which could lead to depopulation, as in the Vale of York. Bolton Priory and Peterborough Abbey also created granges by carrying out assarting themselves, but depopulation was unusual and landlords benefited from the extension of cultivation in two ways. Firstly, it increased their rent incomes. The rents from certain Ramsey manors rose sharply as smallholdings in wood, waste and fen proliferated, whilst part of the rise in the bishop of Ely's income from £920 in 1171–2 to £1,920 in 1256–7 was due to rents from assarted lands.[9] On the smaller estates, particularly those of the new Augustinian, Premonstratensian and Gilbertine houses founded in the North in the twelfth century, rent income was even more vital. They did not have large, consolidated demesnes, but small parcels of land scattered over many villages. Rents formed a substantial part of their income, and assarting helped them to increase it. This leads to the second main way in which landlords benefited from colonization. New freehold land was brought on to the market, land which would allow them to increase their estates either for direct cultivation or rent income. Such opportunities were only offered on a large scale in certain areas, like the East of England or the North. So Peterborough Abbey created its manor of Paston both by buying land from freeholders and assarting itself, and Bolton Priory deliberately invested in land to expand its rent rolls. At Appletreewick (Yorks) there was an increase in rents from 19s. before 1300 to £21 by 1324–5. What the colonization had created, in fact, was room for movement, room for expansion and above all room into which the burgeoning population, or at least *some* of it, could move.

Colonization, however, was only part of a general expansion in the agrarian economy which was accompanied in the late twelfth and early thirteenth centuries by sharply rising prices.[10] Landlords who had leased out the bulk of their demesnes at fixed rents now found that the lessees were profiting at their expense. Moreover, they faced a general increase in expenditure as the thirteenth century wore on. Royal government demanded more and more in the way of taxation to meet its own rising costs and, at the end of the thirteenth century, the heavy expenses of war in Wales, Scotland and Gascony. As international trade expanded, so more luxury goods became available and the need for a greater cash income became vital. Rents and entry fines[11] could provide some of it, but with rapidly rising prices greater opportunities presented themselves in direct production to supply the market with cereals and, increasingly in the thirteenth century, with wool. The greater landlords' response to changing conditions and new demands is well known and often taken to characterize the whole agrarian history of the period. They returned *en masse* to demesne farming,[12] to feed their households and create a surplus for sale to produce an increased money income. As Professor Du Boulay writes of the archbishop of Canterbury's estates, 'It did not take an advanced knowledge of economics to see during the reign of Henry II that long traditional leases to farming families and middlemen would deprive the chief lord of more and more income as prices rose . . .'[13] Successive popes ordered the archbishops to take back their demesnes and as a result estate policy was reversed. Manors which had produced an average gross rent of £1,560 between 1165 and 1172 were directly exploited by 1205, producing in the 15 months after July of that year £3,428 of which £1,713 came from the sale of produce and £1,423 from rents and other sources. The chronology here is interesting for it was certainly the rapid inflation of 1180–1220 which forced the change in management policy.[14] The archbishop of Canterbury was only one of many lords who drew the same conclusions from prevailing economic conditions. Evidence from royal records shows that on 12 episcopal, 13 monastic and 17 lay estates of large and medium size the demesnes were leased out in the 1170s. By 1184 a clear trend of a return to demesne farming was visible and the change came first, surprisingly, on the lay estates.[15] In every case the revival of direct management meant that a higher percentage of income was drawn from the sale of produce. Of Ely's gross revenues of £3,580 in 1298–9 40 per cent came from the sale of produce, Worcester Cathedral Priory drew 50 per cent of its income in 1312–14 from the sale of grain and wool, Leicester Abbey 27 per cent from grain and 35 per cent from wool in 1297–8 and the Norman Abbey of Bec 43 per cent from grain and 14 per cent from wool from its Wiltshire lands.

The resumption of the demesnes was not always as easy to achieve as it sounds. Older established estates did not find it simple to regain lands once leased. Grants for life hardened into hereditary tenures and with the development of Henry II's possessory assizes[16] the sitting tenant now received a great deal of protection from the law. Ramsey had to fight a running battle in the courts against those, from knight to freeholder, who were reluctant to hand back lands granted to them or their families generations before, and the last long lease on the Canterbury estates did not fall in until the 1290s. Ramsey Abbey, like other lords, found the answer in the purchase of new properties. Abbot William of Godmanchester spent no less than £1,666.13s.4d. on a group of lands comprising mainly Barnwell, Hemington and Crowethorpe manors in Huntingdonshire, £500 for the Le Moigne family holdings in Niddingworth, Holywell and Ramsey, and lesser sums on virgates and half virgates to extend their demesnes elsewhere. Some estates faced other difficulties, such as the dispersal of their endowments in the eleventh and twelfth centuries, or the loss of land to knights at the time of subinfeudation.[17] Peterborough Abbey tried to make up its losses by a policy of active assarting and purchase to create new demesnes like those at Paston and Biggin Grange. The house was doing no more than its lay and ecclesiastical peers in forest and upland areas, forming demesnes for either arable or pastoral farming to provide both for the household and a surplus for sale.

Yet to resume the lands was only the first stage in the return to direct control. There had to be a corresponding managerial revolution, which explains why the wholesale switch to farming for the market on many estates coincided with one particular, energetic man, like Abbot Samson of Bury St Edmunds, Henry of Eastry, Henry Lacy, earl of Lincoln or Prior John of Laund at Bolton. Their object was simple, to maximize revenues for an increased cash income. Its accomplishment was more difficult, for every estate, large or small, had to cope with the fact that its lands were scattered.[18] Two-thirds of Peterborough's estates might be in the Soke immediately around the Abbey, but the other third lay up to 80 miles away in Lincolnshire and Huntingdonshire. Bolton Abbey had one manor 100 miles from the house in Holderness, whilst the bishop of Winchester's estates stretched from Somerset to Sussex. The greater the estate, the greater the problem. Canterbury Cathedral Priory had manors in Kent, Surrey, Oxfordshire, Buckinghamshire, Essex and Norfolk, the vast earldom of Cornwall's lands stretched from Cornwall and Devon to the Thames Valley, East Anglia, Northamptonshire, Rutland, Huntingdonshire, Lincolnshire and Yorkshire. The sheer problems of communication and control, of marketing and policy making, of which crops were to be sown, what livestock to be reared, of whether produce or cash were to be taken from the manors, are obvious. As has been said,[19] different lords had different needs. The monastery needed a regular supply of food sent to a fixed centre and organized its manors accordingly. Lay and ecclesiastical noblemen, busy about their own or the king's business, might need more in the way of cash. Others might choose, literally, to eat their way round their estates. So Robert Grosseteste, bishop of Lincoln, advised the countess of Lincoln in the rules of husbandry he drew up for her: 'Every year at Michaelmas . . . arrange your sojourn for the whole of that year and how many weeks [you will spend] in each place . . .' Inevitably different requirements produced different responses to estate management, but the main object was always the same, to maximize revenues.

The paramount need, therefore, was strong local and central organization to provide food and money or simply money. The recovery of the demesnes, the first stage in the process, was often accompanied by the reimposition or redefinition of labour services[20] to provide the large labour force necessary for intensive arable farming. On the Ramsey estates the services had not only been restored by the mid-thirteenth century but also increased, the villeins being required to provide more plough teams for the lord's demesnes and to perform more work at harvest time. The total amount of work due on the Ely estates increased by an average of 10 per cent between 1222 and 1251 whilst at Glastonbury the Abbey expanded its labour force by the simple process of the subdivision of holdings. The same amount of service was now asked from half the amount of land. These may be taken as typical of a general movement throughout the manorial areas of England, but it would be quite wrong to think that demesne farming and labour services were indivisible. The one could exist without the other and had to in the areas where villeinage was not the norm.[21] Here much hired labour had to be used. On the great central manor of Ely, in the heart of free England, a fulltime staff of 18 had to be employed, receiving part of their wages in money but a great deal in corn. Indeed, almost everywhere the paid estate labourer, the *famulus*,[22] formed the backbone of demesne agriculture, and his usefulness and increasingly his cheapness were not lost on thirteenth-century landlords.

The land and labour secured, the next step was to organize the farming. Here, at the local level, the burden of management was borne by the reeve and the bailiff. The reeve was to be found on arable estates all over England and was usually chosen from amongst the wealthiest customary tenants. Though unfree, he was a man of considerable importance and prestige, responsible for organizing the day-to-day work on the demesne, seeing that labour services were performed and all seigneurial dues and rents were collected. The bailiff or sergeant had the more general task of running a group of two or even more manors, or perhaps one very large and complex one. He was a new type of official, the professional farm manager, a free layman or a clerk in minor orders, who was in part responsible for the managerial revolution of the thirteenth century and in part created by it. Together, as on the Westminster Abbey bailiwick of Todenham (Gloucs), which consisted of the manors of Todenham, Sutton under Brailes and Bourton on the Hill, reeve and bailiff managed the farming of the demesnes and the running of the manors generally. More important, the bailiff linked the scattered manors to the centre. By placing him in charge of the bailiwick, the lord gave him, under his overall supervision, local responsibility for its running. How wide his duties were can best be seen from the oath the archbishop of Canterbury's bailiffs were made to swear. They were bound to hold the courts and leets properly, to become thoroughly acquainted with the property in their charge and put it to profit, to survey repairs and fill vacant tenancies, to supervise the sale of wood, making a special note of the prices, to watch the numbers and health of the livestock, keeping written testimony of disease, to levy debts and uphold the archbishop's tenants against outsiders. A formidable and thorough list, it well emphasizes the essential managerial role these local officials played.

This system of grouping manors together to form larger basic units of management is to be found on most great ecclesiastical estates. Canterbury Cathedral Priory's lands in eight counties had long been organized in this way, for instance. But the method was not confined either to the Church or to arable farming. In 1296–7 the vast lands of the earldom of Cornwall were organized into nine main divisions, each under a steward responsible to the earldom's central administration at Berkhampsted. At roughly the same time on the earl of Lincoln's cattle farms in the Forest of Blackburnshire the chief *instaurator* (stockman) took the place of the bailiff and surveyed the accounts of the stockmen who ran each of the vaccaries. This type of organization could also be adapted to allow for the creation of specialized units within the estate as a whole. Many lords, like the abbot of Crowland in the fens, ran their sheep farming on an extra-manorial basis by the use of such methods. There are plenty of exceptions to the rule of course. A small estate such as Bolton Priory found it more convenient to administer its land around the house directly. Only its distant manors were run by local officials. On the Ramsey estates, the reeve alone was responsible to the central administration, since there were no bailiffs. But these were more variants than totally different methods of estate management. Indeed, Walter of Henley's[23] advice, 'If you choose a bailiff or servant, choose him not by parentage nor comeliness nor otherwise unless he be of good report and well advised', illustrates succinctly how vital the choice of trustworthy officials could be.

But for effective control there had to be some means of linking centre and localities. For the small estate, or those with most demesnes lying near the household, the problem was easily solved. Reeve or bailiff could attend an audit in person and make verbal explanation of his administration in the previous year. For larger estates this was impractical and the thirteenth century saw the emergence of written accounts for each manor, vaccary or bercary. These first appeared on the Winchester estates in 1208–9, much earlier than elsewhere, for it was in the second half of the thirteenth century that they were extensively used by greater landlords. They were very much standardized in their approach to accounting, which is hardly surprising since they show a remarkable resemblance to the yearly returns made by the sheriff for each county to the royal exchequer. Moreover, in the later thirteenth century a number of accounting treatises appeared for use by the clerks who drew up the documents. The aim was to produce a balance sheet for the manor as a whole, to record the financial obligations of the official to the lord. The agricultural year ended after the harvest at Michaelmas (29 September) and the account was drawn up soon after by a scribe working with the local officials, increasingly with the reeve alone as the century progressed. The first part, usually on the face of the roll, dealt with cash transactions, recording receipts from rents, fines, the sale of produce or any other source, disbursements for labour or seed corn, and the sum left which ought to be paid over. Then on the back of the roll very detailed grain and stock returns were made, showing the quantities of crops grown, how they were disposed of, whether to the household or to the market or to another manor to pay servants in kind, the numbers of stock, how many calves or lambs had been born, how many sold and so on. The detail is great and one can only admire the presumably illiterate reeves on whom the burden of collecting the copious information must have fallen.

When the account had been made, it would then be returned, with many others on a large estate, to the central administration, where it would be checked with great care by a body of auditors. On an ecclesiastical estate they were usually a group of senior monks or clergy, on a lay estate the trained administrators. Their task was simple. They had to scrutinize each item, particularly the prices for which the crops were sold – the auditors at St Swithun's Priory, Winchester, seem to have been well informed of market price fluctuations – and the claims for expenses and allowances. If the reeve or bailiff had sold the wheat at too low a price, then he was surcharged for it; if he had hired unnecessary labour, then his expenses were not allowed. The auditors' sole aim was to arrive at and agree a sum either to be paid over or to be owed by reeve or bailiff and carried over into successive accounts until finally settled. If all was well, the money would be handed over and paid into the coffers of the institution concerned. Here there were some differences between monastic and other great estates. An earldom such as that of Cornwall, or a bishopric, would have one central treasury into which the money would be paid and from which disbursements would be made, after the manner of the royal exchequer on which it was modelled. In both Benedictine and Augustine houses, however, which formed the bulk of those in England, there had emerged in the twelfth century separate officers known as obedientiaries. Each was responsible for one aspect of the corporate life. The precentor, for example, looked after the sacred books and the order of services, the sacrist the sacred vessels and vestments, the interior cellarer the general victualling, whilst the general cellarer had overall supervision of the material endowment of the house. These officers were each allocated separate manors or groups of rents to provide the funds necessary for the performance of their duties, but very often inefficiency and corruption had crept in. To rectify this, central treasuries of receipt were established into which all monies would be paid and from which individual allowances would be made to the obedientiaries.

To generalize is to disguise a variety of methods and an uneven rate of progress. In one case, Winchester Cathedral Priory, central auditing emerged in the twelfth century, in others, as at Ely Cathedral Priory, not until the later years of the thirteenth. But on most great estates there were bodies of auditors which served as the nuclei for groups of experts who dictated the economic policy for the lands as a whole. The auditors had all the relevant information at their disposal. The writer of the *Seneschaucy*[24] recommended that they 'should know all the divisions and classes which make up the accounts, in receipts, expenses, and in the corn and stock account' and this gave them the comprehensive knowledge of each part of the estate on which decisions could be made. Associated with them, partly to answer their queries but also to assist in their work, was a professional official, the steward. He acted more or less as the lord's deputy, riding around his lands, holding courts, especially the important twice-yearly leets, and surveying his estates. 'Extend your lands', said Walter of Henley, and this was one piece of advice that was taken. The manorial surveys of the thirteenth century, detailing the extent of the demesne, the number and status of the tenants, the rents they paid and the services they owed exemplify the whole new approach to the management of land in the period.

The stewards were not always laymen. In the priorate of Henry of Eastry at Canterbury Cathedral Priory monk wardens were put in charge of each of the four main estate groups, and a less successful attempt was made to introduce similar officials at Peterborough. But a career was now to be had in this profession for laymen, and one man might serve many masters. Godfrey Russell was steward to Peterborough Abbey between 1250 and 1263. Then he went to serve that great lady Isabella de Fortibus, countess of Aumale and Devon, in 1271, became steward of the Palatinate of Durham and then of the Honor of Wallingford from 1278 to 1281. Expertise was thus spread around, and the administrative bodies at the centre, be they monks or learned councils of laymen, were quite capable of seeing the estate as a whole, administering it as a unit. This is obvious at a local level, where cereals from one manor would be sent to another to pay wages in kind, or breeding stock, cows and ewes, be transferred from one vaccary or bercary to another. Yet such actions were only part of a wider pattern.

93

It was from the centre that the orders came fixing the targets for each manor, the level of production of grain and livestock which had to be reached. These could be varied if it was felt that the land could carry more stock or grow more wheat. It was at the centre that investment decisions were made – to spend heavily on fertilizers or, most important, whether to switch from cultivation to leasing when the latter seemed more profitable. Even more basic was the decision as to which manors should provide the cash income, which supply the household with food, a question in which the estate's nearness to the centre played a major part. However limited the techniques at their disposal, as much respect should be paid to the management which helped provide the wealth to build the great churches of the thirteenth century as is paid to those churches themselves.

For the lands they controlled were indeed extensive. Prior Eastry's survey of Canterbury Cathedral Priory estates in 1321 showed that there were 2,677 demesne acres growing wheat, 367 under rye, 1,434 under barley, 2,385 under oats and 1,510 under legumes, with somewhere between one-third and one-half as much again of that total left fallow. Seventy years earlier the bishop of Ely had 20,000 acres in demesne, allowing for fallow, and at the beginning of the fourteenth century Westminster Abbey possessed 14,500 acres of arable demesne with probably another 2,910 acres of meadow, pasture and woodland. These were the heavyweights. A little further down the scale Peterborough had some 5,000 sown demesne acres in 1300–1 and Bolton Priory 800 of the arable demesne acres available to the house. This gives some idea of the scale of farming, but it is perhaps more useful to compare incomes, since this will both allow a comparison between lay and ecclesiastical estates and focus our attention on the main aim of estate administration, the realization of as great a cash income as possible.

Some care has to be taken in making such comparisons. Often a great estate received in addition to cash a substantial amount of produce. Peterborough Abbey in 1300–1, for instance, received £1,023 in cash and somewhere in the region of an extra £700 worth of grain sent directly to the house. Canterbury Cathedral Priory adopted a more flexible approach and bought most of its grain on the local market, as did Worcester Priory. Comparisons, therefore, are not always of like with like, and show only notional ideas of relative wealth. Secondly, the cash income came not only from the sale of produce but from all sources of manorial profit. Bearing these in mind, and that £20–40 per annum would support a thirteenth-century knight in comfort, whilst royal revenue inclusive of taxation ran at about £60–100,000 per annum in the later part of the century,[25] the comparison can now be made. At the very top, a great earldom like that of Lancaster in the early fourteenth century, had a yearly income of about £10,000. This was in a class by itself, for next to the king the earl was the greatest magnate in the land. Clare of Gloucester or Bigod of Norfolk drew £3–4,000 a year from their lands, whilst the 'average' earl would have had a net income of about £1,600. The archbishop of Canterbury's estates provided him with an average income of £2,128 in the thirteenth century, whilst the bishop of Ely's gross income reached a peak of £3,500 in 1298–9. The smaller estates of the bishopric of Worcester produced revenues of £900 in 1303 and Bolton Priory's some £900–1,000 per annum in cash and kind at the beginning of the fourteenth century. But what matters is the order of magnitude of change. Given that the value of money remained fairly constant in the thirteenth century,[26] then the increase in the bishop of Ely's net income from £920 in 1171–2 to £2,550 in 1298 really does represent a tripling of income, as does the rise on the Peterborough estates from £350 in 1125 to *c*. £1,700 in cash and grain by 1300. Without any doubt, even in an age of rising prices, the return to demesne farming brought a new prosperity to the great landlords.

In that prosperity the sale of grain and wool played a major part. Much of the surplus grain was sold on the local market. Not all estates were as fortunate as Canterbury Cathedral Priory in having the bulk of their lands around the major centre of demand in England, London, but Prior Eastry summed up the attitude of many landlords when he wrote to the Constable of Dover Castle in 1323, 'Know Sir, that one half of our estates lie so far away . . . that it behoves us to sell our corn in those parts and purchase other in the district.' High transport costs for bulk products like grain made production for the local market essential, except where there were readily available river or sea routes. On the Ely manors, as on many others, peasant carrying services provided the link with country towns like Cambridge, Norwich, Bury St Edmunds, Huntingdon, Ipswich and even in the case of some Essex manors, London. Most important of all was Lynn, since it offered the valleys of the Cam and the Great and Little Ouse a way to the sea and thus to markets on the Continent and in the South East. Ramsey, too, required its virgaters to make long trips to London, St Albans and Cambridge whilst the extent of the local trade in the West Midlands can be seen in the existence of 80 chartered markets in addition to the important towns of Bristol (active in the grain trade to Gascony), Gloucester, Worcester, Cirencester, Coventry and Warwick. Further west Tavistock Abbey sold its produce to the flourishing stannary towns[27] of West Devon. Indeed, everywhere a new town was founded or an old one expanded, everywhere in the countryside as the population grew, there was demand to be supplied. If anything broke down the isolation of rural communities in the thirteenth century it was the constant movement of the peasantry back and forth to meet the demands of the market in corn.

Next to corn, and for upland landlords like the Cistercians more important, came wool. By the late thirteenth century some 30,000 sacks per annum, representing the clip of some 8 million sheep, were being exported to the Flemish and Italian cloth industries, besides which there was the home market to be supplied. A lucrative source of income was thus open to the landholder with available pasture on down, upland and marsh. So the bishop of Winchester kept 29,000 sheep in 1259, the Prior of St Swithun's Winchester 20,000 in the early fourteenth century, in 1303 the earl of Lincoln had 13,000, half in Yorkshire, the rest in the South, Peterborough and Crowland Abbeys between them ran some 16,300 sheep on the fenland pastures and Canterbury Cathedral Priory 10,000 on their Kentish estates. To this long list may be added the Bohuns, Berkeleys, Clares, Isabella de Fortibus with her vast Holderness farm and above all the Cistercians, with some 65 houses in England and major interests in sheep rearing. How important wool sales could be for an upland landlord can be seen in the case of Bolton Priory. This Augustinian house with poor corn lands depended on the cash income from wool to buy extra cereals for the household. In 1298–9 sales on their own behalf and for others brought in 60 per cent of their total cash revenues. Their flocks were run extra-manorially, as on so many estates, and between 1287–8 and 1315 production was raised from 6 to 15 sacks of wool, fetching an extra £100 per annum, against costs of £9–16. The canons washed and graded their wool, a practice common also among the Cistercians but not the Benedictines, and so obtained a higher price for it on the export market. Bolton's production was small enough compared with the 50 sacks worth £300 a year sold by Canterbury Cathedral Priory or the 46 sacks from 10,000 sheep on the Gloucester Abbey estates, but it does show how necessary the wool clip was to estate finances. Moreover, monastic involvement in the trade itself, their contact with the great Italian and Flemish exporters, their use of credit sales of their own and other wool they collected as middleman dealers to anticipate revenue, show the extent to which production on the great estate was geared to the market.

Thus demesne farming or high farming emerged as one of the most prominent features of English agriculture in the years 1180–1300. The managerial revolution also inspired a series of treatises on agriculture which demonstrated practically how the job should be done. Walter of Henley's *Husbandry* was primarily intended for the smaller estate holder who was his own manager, whilst the *Seneschaucy* gave the lay official on the greater estate a thorough training in all aspects of his work. Other documents, drawn up for a particular lord like St Peter's Gloucester or Canterbury Cathedral Priory also laid down rules for good management. Yet it is very dangerous to characterize the whole century by its most obvious feature and to build on and from it a glowing picture of great achievement. This, it is said, was an age of large scale capitalist exploitation of land, of increased production due to both increased investment and improved techniques, it was the age of the buoyant demesne. True, it was the one period in English medieval history when great landlords did farm for the market, when profits more than covered costs. But, without in any way denying or minimizing the developments just described, it is now essential, in order to obtain a properly balanced view of the English economy as a whole, to challenge that picture and see demesne farming in two perspectives, that of the estate itself and that of agrarian society at large.

With certain exceptions, a great estate did not consist simply of demesnes but of other lands and property rights, including churches, over which lordship was exercised. Free and unfree tenants owed rents, customary unfree tenements also produced entry fines and heriots,[28] the peasants who held them were liable to a whole range of other payments and to tallage by the lord. Rents were paid for assarted lands, manorial courts brought income from fines, parochial church revenues could also be exploited, towns could be developed to produce substantial incomes,[29] the feudal tenant-in-chief had the same rights of wardship and relief over his sub-tenants as the king had over him. The exercise of secular and spiritual lordship could produce revenues as great as, if not greater than those from demesne production. The proportion of income drawn from the sale of grain and wool at Worcester Cathedral Priory, Leicester Abbey and the English estates of the Abbey of Bec has already been mentioned. They are fairly representative of some of the differing types of landlord and farming regions at the end of the thirteenth century. Worcester was an old Benedictine estate with large manors, Leicester lay in an area with a high proportion of free tenants, Bec was an absentee landlord with highly manorialized lands in Wiltshire. On each estate rents, court fees and aids produced a substantial proportion of the income:

Worcester	1291–2	Rents and aids		45%	Grain	38%	Wool	11%
Leicester	1297–8	Rents		32%	Grain	27%	Wool	35%
Bec	1288–9	Rents, court fees and aids	43%		Grain	43%	Wool	14%

This was reasonably typical. At Ely between 1256–7 and 1298–9 rent income rose from £1,060 to £1,700 whilst that from the sale of produce went from £1,160 to only £1,400. For a smaller Northern monastic house like Bolton Priory rents formed one-third of cash income between 1286 and 1315, and here, as at Peterborough, there was deliberate purchase of land to swell rent rolls.

One has only to look at Kosminsky's study of the Hundred Rolls[30] to realize that in the late thirteenth century more peasants in England paid money rents than performed contractual services, both in the manorialized areas as well as in the North and East. More interesting, perhaps, are the distinct signs on one or two estates of a swing away from demesne production to rents in the second half of the century. This was so at Ely. Up to 1250 the high level of rent income was due to the addition of assarted lands, but the rise after that date was partly because, little by little, the bishops were beginning to lease off portions of the demesne. First to go were the mills, fisheries and grazing rights, then villein holdings at yearly rents often as high as 1s.5d. an acre (compared with an estimated 4½d. to 6½d. an acre on the Buckland (Gloucs) manor of St Peter's, Gloucester), then finally, from 1299 onwards, parts of the demesnes themselves. Similar movements can be seen on the neighbouring Ramsey estates and, further south, on the Winchester manors. The reasons for this will be discussed fully later, in relation to the condition of the peasantry, and it must be emphasized that these were only tenative moves away from demesne farming. For the moment it is essential to grasp that throughout the century rents formed a substantial part of total revenues, a part that was growing as the population increased but land supply did not, a part which in the second half of the century helped as much as the sale of agricultural produce to maintain or even increase the lord's income.

Equally important for Church estates was the appropriation of parish revenues which began to gather pace in the thirteenth century. Briefly, this meant that all or part of a parish church's income was taken from the local incumbent and vested in the religious house. It could produce some very large sums. Worcester Cathedral Priory was assessed on a revenue of £33.6s.8d. from the parish of Bromsgrove and King's Norton for the ecclesiastical taxation of 1291, much more than the agricultural income from any of its manors. This explains why religious houses, especially twelfth-century foundations whose endowments were small, were so eager to appropriate revenues. They produced between a quarter and a fifth of Bolton Priory's income in cash and corn, and when Peterborough Abbey recovered the tithes from their knights in the twelfth century it was a real windfall.

So, agricultural production must be seen in its proper perspective as one, but only one of the elements in estate revenues. Nevertheless, increased income from rents and spiritualities was all part and parcel of the expansion of the economy and particularly of the demand for land in the thirteenth century. It could therefore be argued that the switch to rents on a few estates as demesne production stagnated showed a flexibility of approach, a sophistication of management exploiting the prevailing economic situation to its own advantage. This must raise one of the central economic issues of the period: were the high-farming landlords 'capitalist entrepreneurs', creating opportunities for themselves, or did they simply profit from a situation over which they had little or no control? To answer this it is necessary to examine three interrelated problems, the first being whether increased production resulted from the use of improved techniques or simply the application of more labour to more land. It is a commonplace that many great landlords experimented in order to produce more crops, taking some of the advice given by the writers of the agricultural treatises. Sowing ratios were varied, new crops like peas and beans were introduced, three fields were substituted for two in order to intensify cropping and wheat replaced rye on demesnes. In many areas, like Kent, demesnes were already consolidated[31] and in others, when new lands were brought into cultivation they were farmed in granges with no open fields and no peasant tenants; or, as on the archbishop of Canterbury's estates, they were cropped and fallowed independently of the tenants' lands. Where land was enclosed, as on the Berkeley manor of Cam (Gloucs), it was held to be worth twice as much as land in the open fields, because the latter was subject to common rights and fallow every second or third year. In sheep breeding, wise stewards like Simon of

Senliz, who acted for the bishop of Chichester in the early thirteenth century, went to the masters of the art, the Cistercians, when preparing to stock his lord's lands. It all sounds very impressive but the hard question still remains, how much did all this, of itself, raise production?

The answer seems to be, very little. None of the limitations on agricultural productivity outlined in Chapter 1 were overcome.[32] Yields remained appallingly low by modern standards and there is some evidence, albeit very confusing, that they were falling in the second half of the century when by all accounts they should have been rising. Dr Titow is far less positive than Professor Postan in suggesting that soil fertility was becoming a critical factor yet his comprehensive figures for the Winchester estates show that in the latter part of the century wheat held its own but yields of barley and oats, always grown on the poorest soils, showed a marked downward trend. There also seems to be some sort of connection between this and the fact that the period of greatest expansion on the Winchester demesnes was followed almost immediately by the period of lowest yields. This implies that much of the land brought into cultivation was of low fertility, only worth farming in times of extreme need because of population pressure. Indeed no modern farmer would consider arable culture on the chalk uplands of Wiltshire, the wet highlands of Craven or the sour soil on the fringes of Wychwood into which the villagers of Witney and the surrounding settlements pressed. It was only in times of cheap labour and high prices that the heavy clay lands of Cottingham, Kettering and Irthlingborough were worth cultivating and it was precisely here, as on some of the Winchester manors, that the movement away from demesne cultivation began in the late thirteenth century. Professor Postan would take the argument of marginal lands and soil fertility one stage further and argue that there had been too great an expansion of cereals at the expense of livestock in the arable areas. As corn encroached more and more on pasture, so the problem of manure and soil fertility would become more critical.

These are fascinating hypotheses, but there is not yet sufficient evidence to make a general diagnosis of soil exhaustion. Oat yields may have fallen on marginal lands, but that demesnes were becoming less fertile through over-ploughing and the continual growth of one crop remains to be proved. It does not seem to have been the case on the Ramsey estates where the switch to rents was prompted solely by a desperate need for cash. One thing is certain, however. There was no agricultural revolution in the thirteenth century which raised productivity by technical improvement. Even the substitution of three fields for two meant a more intensive use of the land, and legumes were grown as another crop, not as a fertilizing agent. The real concern of all the agricultural treatises was how to stop servants cheating their lords, not how to grow more crops. Increased production was ultimately due to the expansion of the area of cultivation, therefore. If it proved impossible to continue taking in new lands to meet growing demand, then an extremely serious situation would arise for the mass of the population. At any rate, notions of improving landlords on the eighteenth-century model should be abandoned.

In part this answers the second of the problems: how far was this an age of capital investment in agriculture? There was little in the way of real improvement on which landlords could spend money, and when they did both material and labour were cheap. Nevertheless, it has been powerfully argued that investment rates were too low, less than 5 per cent of gross incomes. Here distinction must be made between investment to create revenue and that intended to form capital by the replacement and improvement of equipment, livestock, buildings and communications.[33] Many landlords, great and small, bought land to increase or create demesnes or to swell rent rolls. For a monastic house with a poor initial endowment, this might bring investment rates above the average, but to balance this it must be recognized that older, better-endowed institutions spent far less. Canterbury Cathedral Priory invested less than 2 per cent of its income at the height of demesne farming under Henry of Eastry, and it is almost impossible to calculate lay expenditure because so much land came from royal patronage or a good marriage, often one and the same thing. But in the strict modern sense of the term more land does not mean capital formation. Where it is possible to isolate this element of investment, it came to less than 1 per cent of income on average. Perhaps more could have been spent on consolidating demesnes but there were severe limitations on increasing the size of flocks and herds, one of the prime ways of capital formation in a primitive society.[34]

The question that should be asked, however, is not whether investment rates were too low but whether they were so low that landlords were actually neglecting their estates and allowing them to run down. The answer seems to be no. Taking the thirteenth century as a whole, the majority of landlords were interested in the expansion of their estate economies to produce cash. There is clear evidence too that some at least were also interested in seeing how much profit, not revenue, each manor produced. As early as 1224–5 Canterbury Cathedral Priory was calculating profit by deducting from all outgoing payments from a manor, such as liveries[35] in cash and kind, expenditure on improvements or sums owed to the lord, all in-going payments such as receipts from other manors or funds from Canterbury. Whatever was left was regarded as profit and in a crude way, so it was. Norwich Cathedral Priory went one stage further and began to isolate the actual profits from demesne arable and contrast them with those that might have been made from alternative methods of exploitation, demesne leasing or the sale of labour services. The same methods of calculating profit were used on the Clare and Bigod estates in East Anglia, but there is scant evidence of the use of such calculations in the determination of estate policy. Nonetheless, the lords knew what their lands were for, to produce cash, and given this, there would be no sense in allowing them to run down.

Yet, if cash was the main aim, then this leads to the third and final problem, how far was the permanent and growing indebtedness of many great landholders in the thirteenth century a sign of their incompetence as managers, and perhaps of the failure of demesne farming to provide a solution to the problems of inflation? The revenues produced by a great estate were clearly for consumption, for providing an adequate and in contemporary terms a high standard of living. Large quantities of cereals, ale, fish and, at least in non-Cistercian households, meat were eaten both by the immediate members of the family or the brethren, and by their officials, servants and hangers-on. The greater the man, the greater his responsibilities and the greater his expenses. Hospitality was, and according to the spirit of the age, had to be, generous. Patrons, friends and potential friends had to be rewarded, visiting bishops, abbots or lay lords with all their retinues had to be fed. Litigation also had to be paid for in both fees and bribes and in 1313–14 the Bolton Priory cellarer spent about £200 on hospitality, bribes, tips, retaining fees and litigation, no small sum compared to the annual income of £900. The tale is the same for other great households and when one adds the cost of 'unproductive' investment, the building or rebuilding of the abbey, castle or cathedral, then it is easy to see why so many religious houses and lay barons contracted heavy debts in the thirteenth century. No less than 60 per cent of the lay baronage owed money to the king in 1230 and most of the 80 or so barons then in debt owed one to six times their annual income. Money was borrowed, at interest, from Jews and Italians or from local landholders or clients who extracted their interest in the form of gifts.[36] Some religious houses were all but ruined by debt. Pipewell Abbey failed to meet forward contracts for wool made with alien merchants whilst the abbot of Meaux in the late thirteenth century left the abbey in debt to the tune of £3,678, of which aliens were owed £2,500.

Yet, compared with annual income and actual assets in property and stock, the debts were not so great. Few, if any, great houses or great men were bankrupt. Prior Henry of Eastry could spend £22,446, mostly on the rebuilding of the priory and heavy taxation, and still leave the house free of debt at his death. The really serious indebtedness of Ramsey Abbey did not come until the very changed circumstances of the fourteenth century. In the thirteenth, in spite of increased demands for taxation, expenses for the abbot attending parliament and hospitality for royal visits, the monks still managed to spend money on estate purchases and restocking manors. Too much should not be made of this permanent indebtedness. The attitude of the age demanded consumption and that demanded cash. Providing some prudence was exercised, then the debts were manageable, repayable and, in the circumstances, intelligible. But one trend is evident, that towards the end of the century the problem was becoming more serious. Taxation, in particular, was hitting some landlords hard. Canterbury Cathedral Priory had to pay £711 to the Crown in 1294, a moiety of its revenues, and a further £1,342 to the papacy for the subsidy of the Holy Land. These were large sums and on this estate and elsewhere, they help to explain the search for new sources of income from rents and appropriations. Income did not seem to be keeping pace with expenditure, in spite of the managerial revolution and the attempts to exploit estates more efficiently. This being the case, should the landlords be categorized as inefficient, able to farm at a profit only when profits were so high as to disguise their ineptitude, or should we acknowledge that, given the techniques available and the attitudes of the age, they were doing the best they could? The latter seems the more acceptable argument. Landlords did all they could to maximize profits but clearly, by the end of the century, the upper limits of production had been reached. Great men were able to survive in these conditions, indeed to live comfortably, and in spite of their inefficiency their achievements in producing vast quantities of grain and wool to supply the market should be recognized. Yet, if there were upper limits to production, then they might be prospering at the expense of other classes, for with an expanding population and no growth, one man's living standards could in the end only be preserved at the expense of another's. Whose?

It is here that a wider perspective must be offered. To see the thirteenth century simply in terms of the great landlord would be absurd. The peasants, after all, farmed 75 per cent of the land, and below the ranks of the great and above those of the unfree there was a whole range of other landholders, many undoubtedly producing for the market and all facing the same problems of inflation. It must also be obvious that most of the evidence so far used comes from the records of great estates, many of them old-established foundations with large manors and substantial demesnes suitable for farming for the market. What is true of them might not be true of the smaller landlord, lay or ecclesiastical. Large ecclesiastical estates also enjoyed a continuity of tenure and administration rare on lay estates. Some great families handed their lands down from generation to generation – Clare, Bigod, Bohun, Lacy, Berkeley, Beauchamp – but accidents of fate and failure to provide male heirs militated against this. On average in the later fourteenth and fifteenth centuries 25 per cent of noble families died out every quarter of a century for this latter reason. Their lands either passed to the heiress, and thus out of the family, or were divided up amongst the co-heiresses, or escheated to the Crown to be doled out again in patronage as it saw fit. The fragmentary tendencies of feudalism, the continual need to create sub-tenancies to reward servants or clients, plus the more scattered nature of their demesnes must have made it more difficult for great lay lords to organize their estates in the way described. Some certainly did. The evidence from the royal records of the early thirteenth century shows demesne farming on the estates of at least 17 lay lords. But it is not surprising to find that at the end of the century the earls of Lincoln and Cornwall drew most of their revenues from rents and feudal dues and not from demesne production.

Below the level of the baronage society was much more fluid, much more complex. There were knights, landed gentlemen, tenants in serjeanty,[37] prosperous and not-so-prosperous freemen. It was no longer largely a military society. Much freehold land had been created in the twelfth and thirteenth century, and there were plenty who no longer held by military service, or who held for only a fraction of a fee. There were men who exercised lordship over many manors, others who held only small estates which in financial terms could not support the status of knighthood. Amongst the peasantry the picture is equally confused. The virgater or half-virgater in the Midlands with his heavy obligations cannot really be compared to the sokeman or the freeman in East Anglia or the fens, which makes general conclusions about the condition of the peasantry difficult. Nor, indeed, do we know anything about the income and expenditure of these classes, outside what the records of the lords, with all their obvious deficiencies, will tell us.

Without extensive information on revenues, costs or farming methods, our picture of the economic performance or well-being of English society below the ranks of the great is therefore both speculative and limited in the extreme. But, clearly, the most important factor both for mere survival or for maintaining one's household in some style was the possession or tenure of land. Medieval society was not static, with each class forever fixed in its allotted station. Some men prospered, others went to the wall and in an agrarian society the key to success or failure was the amount of land one held. Property could be acquired. A market in free land certainly existed in all areas for free men and in some for unfree as well, a market in which both great and small could be involved. But, as has been seen, there were limits on the supply of this most vital commodity. Much land remained under the forest laws whilst in the fens expansion had stopped by the mid-thirteenth century, since the technical problems were too great for even the vigorous free peasantry to overcome. The agrarian economy therefore had to operate within the framework of a fixed upper limit of land supply but increasing demand from a growing population. There was thus not only a rising produce market but what can be called a rising land market. A great estate could exploit both to its own advantage, but they posed difficult problems for other men. Smaller lay and ecclesiastical lords may have consumed the greater part of demesne production and would not have been able to profit from buoyant grain prices. If the evidence from the Midland Hundred Rolls is typical, the estates of these lesser lords were notable for a high proportion of demesne relative to villein and freehold land. Lack of a surplus for sale could not therefore be offset by exploiting the land market through rents.

It is from this reasoning that an argument has been developed which suggests that the great lords profited at the expense of lesser men, and in particular that there was in the thirteenth century a crisis for the middling ranks in society, and especially for the knights. During the century the cost of living rose, not only because of increasing food prices but also because more luxury goods were available as international trade expanded. Warfare, too, became more expensive, as equipment became more costly, so that those with military pretensions faced further difficulties. But income for the knightly class did not keep pace with expenditure. Unable to exploit their lands for the market or for rents, the knights (and others in the middle ranks) tried to maintain their social pretensions by borrowing heavily from the Jews. By the second half of the thirteenth century the burden of those debts had become chronic and the only way out for these men, so the argument runs, was to sell their land. The potential purchasers should be obvious – the greater landlords. Often they had alienated the land in fee to the ancestors of these knights, and were eager to regain it to swell their demesnes. Indeed, as Professor Postan says, 'the records bear witness to the accretions to the estates of lay magnates and of nearly all abbeys at the expense of the smaller landholders'.[38] Dr King has charted the decline and fall of five honorial barons or knightly families on the Peterborough estates and the same was apparently happening at Ely and on the West Midland estates of Worcester Cathedral Priory. The most common reason does seem to have been the weight of Jewish mortgages, and one of the murkier aspects of Edward I's land dealings, described as those of a landowner with capital to spare, was his involvement in these transactions. This leads to the second aspect of the argument. Not only, it is said, did the knights suffer from the prevailing conditions, but they were also oppressed by the greater landlords, hungry for land. Expansion at the top could only be met by contraction and impoverishment in the middle. Professor Postan sees in this exploitation a cause of political grievance which showed itself in the clauses of the Provisions of Westminster in 1259 protecting freeholders from abuse of power by the baronage, in the ending of the ability to create sub-tenancies by the Statute of Quia Emptores in 1290[39] and even in the expulsion of the Jews, since the smaller landholders were their main clients. He would argue that much of the political history of the later thirteenth century, and especially the bringing of knights into parliament, must be seen in the light of the king exploiting the economic grievances of the knightly class to his own ends.

Positive argument has its virtues, but in this case the evidence is such that, at present, no firm conclusion as to the fate of the knights can or should be reached. The first part of the case that, unable to farm for the market, the lesser monastic and lay landlords subsisted in genteel poverty, consuming all they produced, is open to some doubt. Kosminsky, with as much faith but perhaps less evidence than Professor Postan, would argue that, 'the problems of productivity, the extraction of the greatest possible amount of revenue by producing for the market, was bound to play a far greater part on the smaller manor than on the large one. We have reason [not alas given] to suppose that the commodity nature of production developed there earlier and stronger than on the large manor.'[40] Perhaps this is so, although lack of evidence does preclude firm judgment, but a comprehensive study of the fortunes of a smaller monastery not well endowed with favourable lands, shows no signs of genteel poverty. In the latter part of the thirteenth century the monks were able to live very comfortably indeed, even though they were forced to buy cereals on the open market. Moreover, because of their non-arable sources of wealth in wool production, in which many middling landlords must have been engaged, the house was never badly in debt. The small lay landowner, of course, had less resources than Bolton Priory, but he also had fewer obligations in the way of hospitality, litigation, royal and papal taxation, servants and hangers-on. Until some comprehensive and positive evidence has appeared, it would be wise to maintain an open but perhaps sceptical mind on the question of a general fall in the standard of living of the country gentry.

The other evidence for the growing extinction of knightly families is, on the face of it, far more impressive, yet it is also one-sided. It comes mostly from the records of the great estates who were buying the land, or from feudal records which reflect conditions in the mid-twelfth century and take no account of subsequent economic enterprise. These would not have recorded the fortunes of younger sons or daughters, for whom provision was increasingly made from the last quarter of the twelfth century as their tenure was protected by Henry II's new possessory assizes.[41] Nor would they show the small knights holding for a fraction of a fee, or the new non-feudal class of bailiffs and stewards or, most important, those who did *not* succumb to the pressure of the great lords. These reasonable points have been made by Dr King in his study of the Peterborough estates. Alongside his examples mentioned above, he shows how the descendants of a younger son of the Hotot family of Clopton (Northants) were able, by the expenditure of 1,000 marks (£666.13s.4d.) to reassemble the estates the main branch of the family had dissipated, and how a villein family could rise to become substantial freeholders in the thirteenth century, spending money on the rebuilding of the local chapel and on constructing their own manor house. Professor Hilton, in his classic study of the West Midlands, argues that there was a severe social and economic crisis for the knightly class as a whole and that families whose incomes did not match their social pretensions disappeared. But he also notes that in Gloucestershire, Worcestershire and Warwickshire in the last 30 years of Edward I's reign there were at least 200 families from whom knights were dubbed (that is, with an income of over £20 a year), and that the figures hardly bear out the suggestion that there was such a grave shortage of knights that the administration could not be carried on. If they were dying out at the rate suggested, how could this be? Thinly spread on the ground these families may have been, with one to each five villages, but below this élite there were hundreds more freeholders who may or may not have been prospering.

Nor was financial acumen, the trait displayed by Peterborough's Richard Hotot, the only way to rise. Service to the great landlord or to the Crown was equally important. Two of the bishop of Ely's knights demonstrate this admirably. One was Robert Tiptoft whose service to Edward I in the Marches of Wales brought him by the end of the thirteenth century land in six counties and an income of £300 a year. His descendants were to be the earls of Worcester in the fifteenth century. The Lestranges of Knockton followed the same pattern of service and from Henry II's reign they grew in stature as tenants in Shropshire until John Lestrange V, who died in 1309, held land in five counties worth at least £125 per annum. To these should be added the Burnell and Stonor families who rose by ministerial and judicial service to Edward I and similar service to a landlord as bailiff or steward could be equally rewarding. All the Peterborough stewards profited from their office and those, like Godfrey Russell, who served many masters benefited extensively. Certainly, the men who served as the earl of Lincoln's officials in Blackburnshire were persons of consequence who founded landed families and without any doubt similar stories of rising families can be told elsewhere.

So, just as high farming was not the norm on all great estates, the simple story of great men profiting at the expense of the lesser landlord will not do. Undoubtedly there were those families which failed, and this was only to be expected. Great noble families died out and so did some of the country gentry, for society was not static. Yet no firm general pattern can be observed, for the pressure of the great on the less may well have varied in both location and time. Great landlords would be more interested in acquiring lands which lay near the centre of their estates, not many miles away. Nor were they all active in the land market at the same time. In the East Midlands and East Anglia Peterborough Abbey bought extensively in the early thirteenth century, Ramsey much more so in the middle years whilst neither of them was active in the later part when the Clare family, along with others of the great lay nobility, was expanding its lands. Thus there was no unrelenting pressure on the small man throughout the century in all areas. Also there was at least some, if not equal, opportunity for men to prosper as well as to suffer, and perhaps this is as much as can yet be said of the fortunes of the lesser landlords. Equally clearly, if there was prosperity then the key lay in land, in the ability to acquire it and exercise economic and social control over it. In large measure both of these resulted from lordship, whether the lands were exploited directly or indirectly through rents.

It is in this matter of lordship over land and thus the supply of land that the most critical question of the thirteenth century lies, the condition of the peasantry. They formed the mass of the population, farming the major part of the soil, and were the class potentially most exploitable by the lords, great or small. Wherever one looks, their position seems to have been progressively worsening during the period. Some of the evidence which points to the conclusion that there was, relative to productive resources, rural overpopulation in certain areas of England has already been considered, but it can well be reiterated to put it in perspective. Population pressure was pushing up the value of land, to the obvious advantage of those who held it. This can be seen in two main ways, from the rising level of entry fines and of rents for free land. Rents from customary land in the form of money payments were hard to vary. Custom protected them. Services could be increased by redefinition or subdivision of holdings but what the lord wanted was usually more money, not more labour. He could, however, commute services and demand high payments for so doing, but this could produce resistance. A better way was to exploit the only truly flexible element in customary payments, the entry fine. This could be varied in response not only to the quality of the land but also to its scarcity value. Some exceptional levels of entry fines have been discovered. In the Vale of Taunton as much as £40 per virgate was being asked, about one-third of the aggregate value of the crops it would have produced over a period of 20 years. On the newly reclaimed Sedgemoor pastures of Brent and Zowy fines went as high as £60 the virgate, but this was very unusual. Elsewhere the level was much lower but almost everywhere rising towards the end of the century. Fines on the Peterborough estates were a good deal higher in 1300–10 than they had been in 1280–90, but the highest level was £5 and the majority around £3. The whole land or virgate paid between 13s.4d. and 20s. in 1250 on the nearby Ramsey manors; after 1300 it had risen to over £3. The average on the Winchester manors was 24s.4d. a virgate between 1277 and 1348 which sounds relatively low until one compares it with an average of 1s.–1s.8d. in 1219. The serf or neif on the Worcester Priory lands ominously enough was required to pay as much as he was able, whilst at Minchinhampton (Gloucs) the rate had risen from 6s.8d. the virgate in the 1220s to £1 around 1300. These fines were low compared with those at Taunton but, as will be seen, amassing even £1 might well have been a formidable problem for the customary tenant and the prevailing factor in all these cases is the rising trend. It must be taken as evidence of the pressure on land in the Midlands and the South, for in the North fines were much lower, usually less than £1. And, where the evidence is available, there was an equivalent rise in the rent for free land. Both Peterborough Abbey and some of its substantial tenants were exploiting the demand at the end of the century by building cottages for rent on previously underdeveloped land and on the Berkeley manor of Cam free tenures were held at competitive rents even higher per acre than those for the customary yardland where labour rent had been commuted. Nearness to London may have pushed up the rents from small plots on the Bec manor of Ruislip, but it cannot explain the threefold rise on the Ely estates, both from freeholds and from customary tenures converted to money payments.

Rising fines and rents are impressive evidence of pressure on the land, but the best evidence of what this meant in real terms is what happened on the land itself. Colonization had simply not solved the problem of supply. Everywhere holdings seemed to be shrinking in size. The assarts at Hanborough were plots of about an acre or so, some held by customary tenants but most by those without other land. The virgates at Wellingborough had been divided to provide more tenements, and a substantial number of smallholders had emerged. In Kent, in 'yoke after yoke the single tenant or few tenants of former days had given place to a multitude of parceners'[42] and on a dozen or so Ely manors in Cambridgeshire and the Isle of Ely 190 villein tenures in 1086 had been replaced by some 270 full lands divided into halves and quarters. The situation was the same even in the newly colonized areas. The result of rising population and partible inheritance was usually very small holdings. Around Spalding and Wisbech there were nearly as many people in the late thirteenth century as there were to be in 1951, subsisting on one and a half acres per head of enclosed arable, pasture and meadow. Over 70 per cent of men in Sutton and Spalding held five acres and under, and only in the manorialized villages of Weston and Moulton did the predominant class of villagers hold between 5 and 30 acres. There was a very similar situation in the forest lands of Stoneleigh Hundred (Warws) where the half-virgaters and cottagers far outnumbered the peasantry in the more anciently settled and manorialized Kineton Hundred. More important, the evidence of localized studies can be projected to much of South and Central England. Professor Postan's study of 104 manors on the estates of Shaftesbury Abbey, St Paul's Cathedral, the bishopric of Winchester, St Peter's Gloucester, St Swithun's Priory, Winchester, and the bishopric of Worcester show that 45 per cent of all manorial tenants were small holders with half a virgate (10–15 acres) or less. Only 33 per cent corresponded to the so-called 'typical' peasant. Using a non-manorial source, the Hundred Rolls covering the Midland counties,[43] Kosminsky arrived at similar conclusions, that 46 per cent of tenants held a quarter of a virgate and Dr Titow calculated that on the Winchester estates tenants with ten acres or less made up at least 50 per cent of the population. These may well be underestimates, for not all sub-tenants were listed in the manorial extents from which most of the information comes.[44] Indeed it looks as if the equation for the thirteenth century must be more people equals less land per head.

Yet the vital question is not so much the amount of land but whether or not it was sufficient to support a peasant and his family. Was the productive capacity of ten acres or so, along with any income from other sources, sufficient to meet consumption and outgoings and leave any sort of surplus? For the majority of manorial peasants, the bulk of the population in south and central England, which means effectively the bulk of the English population, this seems more and more doubtful. Peasants tended their land diligently. As the major source of food and income it was cultivated with care and villagers would often pay fines for the non-performance of services rather than neglect it. But it cannot be denied that they faced the same agricultural problems as the landlords with far less resources. A landlord could stand the financial strain of one bad harvest. The peasant might be forced to eat his seed corn and unless he could buy more, the next year's planting would inevitably suffer. Other sources of income over and above those from arable cultivation varied enormously from manor to manor and from district to district, but two possibilities were probably widespread, wage labour and the proceeds of pastoral farming. If sons and daughters could earn wages, then this would be a useful bonus, but such evidence as there is suggests that money wage rates, either for piece work such as threshing and winnowing or for day work labouring, were remarkably stable in the thirteenth century.[45] Given the price inflation of the period, then, in real terms they were worth less than they had been in 1200. A large proportion of the wages of both permanent and casual labourers was paid in corn however, and as prices rose this would have increased in value considerably. But landlords were only too well aware of this. As the cost of making payments in kind increased, they either decreased the amount given, or substituted cheaper varieties, or exchanged cash for corn at less than current market prices. It all points to a surplus of labour by 1300 as a result of population growth, low wages and only a limited ability to supplement income from this source. The prospects of a steady flow of cash from the sale of wool should also be viewed with caution. Large flocks must have been kept. The great lay and ecclesiastical landlords between them probably supplied no more than a third of the export market, even with their vast flocks. The rest had to come from sheep kept by middling and lesser men, and particularly by the peasantry. But once again it is a case of to them that hath shall be given. As has been seen, there was a direct connection between the amount of land a peasant held and the number of sheep he could graze.[46] Those who were rich in one were rich in the other and even in the reputedly sheep-farming villages of South Wiltshire the smallholder had very few animals. For them income from pastoral farming was not an alternative to the profits of arable agriculture.

Incomings were therefore limited by the amount of land available and lack of other sources of wealth. Outgoings, by contrast, seem to have been growing for the unfree manorial peasant. The main demand upon them was for labour or its equivalent in money terms, but the renewed commutation of the later thirteenth century brought little or no relief. Pressure on land was great and commutation, whether for a fixed annual sum (ad censum) or the sale of individual works (vendita opera) reflected this. Westminster Abbey was able in this way to extract far higher rents from its customary tenants than it received from other lands. There were also other payments to be made, the customary rent, tithe to the Church, tallage to the lord, taxation to the Crown, fines in the manorial court, as well as money to be found for clothing, equipment and other needs. The half yardlander on the bishop of Worcester's manor of Kempsey (Worcs) faced a formidable set of burdens. Allowing for fallowing in the two-field system he would have had about eight acres under crop. Taking a maximum yield to the third or fourth grain, after feeding himself and his family of three and paying his tithe, he might have had enough grain left to sell for 12s. or 13s. at the average prices then prevailing. Against this his outgoings were 5s.6d. in customary rent and labour services valued at 10s.6d., already in excess of his marketable surplus. Other sources of income were probably small and the inescapable conclusion is that 'he must usually have been on the edge of destitution and must often have reduced his family's subsistence in order to sell more of his produce for the money he needed to pay the lord and others.'[47]

Many peasants must have been in the same plight. By estimating the amount needed by the peasant in terms of corn to meet compulsory outgoings and subsistence requirements, then dividing this by the estimated yield per acre in terms of corn and making an allowance for fallow, Dr Titow has calculated the acreage per head necessary for bare survival – three acres in a two-field system, two and a quarter in a three-field.[48] (More land was needed in the two-field system because half was left fallow each year, against only one-third in the three field.) Multiply these acreages by the average family size of 4.5, and the minimum requirements per household were $13\frac{1}{2}$ acres in the two-field and 10 acres in the three-field system. It must be stressed that this is hypothesis and represents only the bare minimum. Outgoings for the unfree peasant may well have been higher than the 33 per cent of production suggested, no allowance has been made for clothing, repairs, tools, fodder for animals, savings, a bad harvest or anything else. Yet 40–50 per cent of all manorial peasants had only this much land, or less, and must have lived at or even below subsistence level. It would seem that there were not just many people in the countryside but *too* many people.

The problem, which stems entirely from limits on productivity and the availability of land, looks the more serious when seen in relation to the economy as a whole. Urban growth had been able to absorb some of the surplus population in the thirteenth century. But that growth had ceased by 1300. Towns were full and perhaps too numerous for the economy to support in any case. Large-scale industry did not exist, except for the production of cloth, which itself seems to have been in some sort of crisis due to growing Flemish competition.[49] The countryside would have to solve its own problems and there remained one last possible way in which this might have been achieved, through the workings of the land market. Through redistribution, some of the inequalities which had arisen through two centuries of disintegration and proliferation of holdings, or which occurred when a widow or an old man without a family had more acres than he or she wished to cultivate, might have been ironed out. In some areas a market existed for both freehold and customary land. The Carte Nativorum (charters of the villeins or serfs) of Peterborough Abbey record an extensive series of land dealings, mainly by villeins, in the Soke of Peterborough in the late thirteenth and early fourteenth centuries. The Abbey, anxious not to allow its customary tenants to slip out of its hands through the purchase of free land, seized any freeholds they bought and regranted them to hold of the house at will[50] for variable rents. Most of the land involved in the transfers was freehold either of long standing or created by assarting, but here and elsewhere it seems that some villein tenements were also being bought and sold. On both the Ely and Ramsey estates there was in addition to the free market much leasing of villein land, both to create sub-tenancies and to transfer entire holdings both within and without the family. As has been seen, there was an active land market in Kent, whilst on the other side of England on the Glastonbury estates, more than one-third of the sitting tenants had acquired their holdings by various forms of open or disguised purchase, sometimes over the head of the legal heir, whose claims they bought out. So valuable was land, so high the price, that men were tempted to sell long before they were due to retire. Purchase thus became a common method of obtaining a holding.

This land market may not have existed everywhere. It is noticeable that much of the evidence comes from an area where there was a high proportion of free tenures, the East and South East of England. In the heavily manorialized areas there was more incentive for the lord to insist on the impartibility of customary tenures, to ensure that he received all his dues, and a much tighter control on the movement of land resulted. But the question is, whether the existence of a peasant land market solved the problem of overpopulation by the process of redistribution, and the answer seems to be that it did not. The upper limits of cultivation had been reached by the end of the century and competition for land was intense. Great landlords wanted to expand their demesnes or their rent rolls, and they helped diminish the overall availability of the commodity in the market place. More important, the workings of the land market served only to heighten, not to lessen, the inequalities of distribution, since its most common feature everywhere was the emergence of a class of wealthy peasants holding more than a virgate and the multiplication of small holdings and sub-tenancies. On the Peterborough estates a 'kulak' class enriched itself at the expense of a section of the freeholding community. At Boroughbury in the Soke itself a wide range of people were involved in an active land market around 1300. Two generations later five major families, powerful and interrelated, had acquired all the available holdings, and a similar pattern can be seen elsewhere in Eastern England. A class of thriving yeomanry was in the process of formation on the Cambridgeshire manor of Littleport, a manorial aristocracy, and the same phenomenon is to be found the length and breadth of the Ely estates. From 1250 onwards a few energetic, acquisitive or fortunate families at Wigston Magna (Leics) slowly accumulated property. How they realized the capital to do this remains something of a mystery. Perhaps it was borrowed from money lenders, Jew or Christian, perhaps it was raised by leasing or mortgaging parcels of the land to others for fixed terms, at a good profit, or, as with the Peterborough 'kulaks' by building cottages and renting them out to the poor. There was precious little readjustment of resources here. The land market allowed the rich to grow richer and the poor to acquire some land, but in no sense did it provide an answer to the problems of overpopulation.

In the manorialized areas, then, rising population was leading to increasing poverty, to a people living on the brink of subsistence and sensitive in the extreme to harvest failure. This, at least, is the conclusion to be drawn from a study of heriot payments on the Winchester manors in the late thirteenth century. Heriot, the death duty, was taken in kind, the best beast, but if the tenants were too poor to keep animals, a money fine was levied instead. If years of known harvest failure are correlated with such money payments in the second half of the century, then a clear pattern emerges. After a bad harvest there was a sharp rise in money heriots paid in the spring and summer of the following year, as supplies of corn ran out. Village smallholders and labourers seem to have become the harvest-sensitive element in rural society. This was more than poverty, more than could be cured by the remission of court fines or other payments. It was slow, long-term starvation. Such a picture, if it can generally be applied, presents the necessary corrective to the notion of general prosperity which results from looking at the thirteenth century only from the viewpoint of the great landlord. Tenure or lordship over land brought greatly increased incomes, but at the expense of the mass of the manorialized peasantry. Lack of land meant poverty for them on a scale only to be seen in a modern, underdeveloped country.

But what is true of the manorialized peasant is not necessarily true of all peasants, nor should one automatically assume that all smallholders were suffering equally or suffering at all. It was the manorial, unfree peasant who was most at risk, for the freeman faced much less in the way of compulsory outgoings. Those of the half-yardlander whose income was considered above would have been very different had he been a freeman. His money rent would have been only 5s. a year, he would not have had to perform the onerous weekly labour services or pay a money equivalent; nor would he have been liable to tallage and the other dues demanded from the unfree villein. With total compulsory outgoings estimated at only 25 per cent of his income, the freeman might well have been able to live adequately, if not comfortably, on substantially less land than the villein. Indeed, the areas where smallholdings were thickest on the ground were often those where colonization had been at its peak and assarting had created free tenures. In fen and forest acreages per head were small and by all accounts these freemen should have been in a very distressed condition. Their holdings should have been insufficient to support their families and they faced other pressures as both lords and wealthy unfree peasants sought to acquire more land at their expense. But, whilst the fenlanders did have to rely heavily on the uplands for their supplies of bread, they had access to ample supplies of fish and fowl, to extensive pastures for dairy cattle and geese and to salterns for that vital commodity, salt. All this goes a long way to explaining why the fenlander could live on surprisingly little land. They may have faced some difficulties as colonization ceased and land hunger led to an active land market, but it would probably be quite wrong to see them either as starving or being barely on subsistence level. The forests, too, were extensively used as pasture for cattle, pigs and geese, all of which could swell a smallholder's income and help him survive. They were, as well, the home of a whole series of small industries. Not only in the Forest of Dean but also in Cannock Forest, in Inglewood, Knaresborough, Feckenham and elsewhere there were to be found forges and iron works, coal mines, wheelwrights, cartmakers, carpenters, glass makers, charcoal burners, bird trappers and a whole host of other occupations which could be combined with small holdings and free status. There were no signs of serious difficulties in the Stannaries in the West Country where tin mining flourished and villeinage was little known, and in areas like the Cotswolds there was a rural cloth industry.

Personal status and geographical location – who you were and where you lived – thus made a vast difference to the peasant. In those regions where there were alternative sources of income it would be unwise to assume that all smallholders were living at starvation level. Yet this still leaves a very substantial part of England, the corn belt stretching across the centre and the South, where manors were large, discipline was tight and freemen were few. Within villages in this area there was little alternative for the surplus population to squatting on the waste land, working for a wealthy peasant or flight from the manor with all its uncertainties. Holdings grew smaller, sub-tenancies multiplied and it seems possible that there was, relative to resources, rural overpopulation across a large section of the country. It is in these circumstances that resistance by the peasants to their manorial lords becomes more intelligible and more impressive. This was not just a matter of refusal to obey manorial discipline. Court rolls are full of such cases, ranging from non-performance of services, grazing beasts on the lord's pasture to sheltering strangers by night. These are only to be expected, given the complexities of manorial organization, and are not proof of widespread rebellion. All the circumstances were against this, for land was at a premium and all the coercive pressure on the lord's side. Yet, throughout the thirteenth century there were peasants acting as individuals or in groups who were willing to challenge the lord's right either to exact labour services or to treat them as unfree in respect of their land and thus liable to labour services and all the incidents of villeinage. This might be attempted in several ways: by showing that ancestors had paid money rents and not performed services; by proving title to free land with charters; or by showing that as tenants of ancient demesne of the Crown (i.e. lands held directly by the king in 1086) they had rights as sokemen and not villeins. Such cases were heard in the royal courts, generally in the Curia Regis, and involved the peasants in much time and trouble. Professor Hilton sees them as the reaction to growing concepts of unfreedom which went hand-in-hand with the re-imposition of labour services in the later twelfth century. Freedom meant essentially that such services would not have to be performed, but it also meant considerably less in the way of compulsory outgoings and behind a social movement there may have been good economic sense.

Whatever the reasons, however, the resistance could be long and bitter. The complaint of the villagers of Mintey, part of the manor of Cirencester, that Cirencester Abbey had demanded services of them beyond those which they owed when the king was the lord was made before the royal justices at Gloucester in 1241. The king had not been lord since 1155, and for nearly 100 years on the manor of Cirencester the tenants had been waging a complicated case in and out of various courts to prove that they were not villeins. They lost. It was finally established in 1225 that they were unfree and because they were unfree so were the villeins of Mintey. There had been a slow erosion of their personal status and an increase in their services as a result of joint pressure by the lord's and the king's courts. What was true at Cirencester was also true at Halesowen (Worcs), on the Ramsey estates, where opposition to the burden of payments for commuted services flared up in the second half of the century, on the Darnhall manor of Vale Royal Abbey, Cheshire, on various St Alban's manors in the late thirteenth century and on the Bec manor of Ogbourne St George (Wilts) in the early fourteenth. Many more instances of communal refusal to perform increased or new services or make money payments in lieu of them could be added to the list. All are impressive evidence of the communal spirit of thirteenth-century villagers – and the conditions which made such resistance essential.

But for the most part it was in vain. It might have set precedents for the future, but the thirteenth century was the century of the lord, not the peasant, and most of all not the unfree peasant. For the great lord times were good, profits were fat, his income was high and his standard of living rose. His part in creating the opportunities which made this possible must neither be overemphasized nor minimized and it must be seen in perspective, against the background of considerable and growing rural overpopulation and poverty in manorial England. Given the limitations on land supply and poor agricultural techniques it is now clear that the landlords prospered at least in part, and perhaps a major part, at the expense of the mass of the peasantry, whose insatiable appetite for land they were able to exploit. If this was 'Merrie England', then by the year 1300 the failure to raise food production and the increasing problems of marginal lands, overcultivation and possibly soil exhaustion, meant that for the majority of the population it was an overcrowded and perhaps starving isle, an isle whose problems could only be solved in a radical and fearful way – by depopulation.

4 The Growth of the Market

The needs of an expanding economy had created a growing demand for agricultural and other products. There were more mouths to be fed, feet to be shod, backs to be clothed, more tools and consumer goods of all kinds to be manufactured. Wool had to be gathered for export, imports had to be distributed but most important, most fundamental of all, local and regional inequalities in food supply needed to be ironed out. In short, organized markets, with merchants to run them, were vital to the workings of the thirteenth-century economy. To some extent the countryside found the answer to the problem from within its own resources, by the creation of regular weekly markets in villages. Sometimes these were prescriptive or customary, held because there had long been a market on that particular day in that particular village. Increasingly, in the thirteenth century, however, the Crown began to insist that all such markets be held by virtue of a royal charter. In part the motives were financial, because income could be raised from granting and regranting the franchise, but there was also a desire to establish enforceable standards of good trading.

Between 1198 and 1483 some 2,800 grants of market were made by the Crown, and of these over half came in the first three-quarters of the thirteenth century. Some, of course, were held in towns, but the majority were to be found in the countryside. In the west Midlands some 75–80 charters had been bought by lords anxious to profit from the tolls trade would bring. It was the towns which benefited in the Severn and Avon valleys and the Cotswolds, the villages in the less advanced countryside to the west of the River Severn in the Forest of Dean and the Tame valley and in northern Worcestershire and Warwickshire. The pattern was the same in the North East. In the late thirteenth century markets flourished, as one would expect, at Newcastle upon Tyne and Durham, but also at Wark on Tweed, Wooler, Chatton,

Embleton, Alnmouth, Warkworth and Harbottle, which were scarcely more than villages. Devon, too, was covered by a whole variety of small towns. Some, like Plymouth, Barnstaple and Dartmouth were to flourish. Others – Plympton, Dodbrooke, Modbury – were no more than villages holding regular markets and providing an essential service to the surrounding countryside. Seasonal fairs, held in both towns and villages, could perform the same service. Merchants and traders came to such fairs from far afield, bringing with them goods not easily come by locally, whilst local men used the occasion for trading in livestock and horses. The fairs connected the countryside to the outside world and in most counties there was a regular succession of them running from spring to autumn. A Bedfordshire man might attend the fairs at Elstow and Leighton Buzzard in May, Arlesey in June, Potton in July, Luton and Biggleswade in August, Shefford in September and Ampthill in November.

But the fairs were seasonal, the village markets limited in scope to trade mainly in agricultural products. As the economy expanded so did the need for regular weekly or bi-weekly markets held in centres of production which could supply the goods and services an increasingly preoccupied countryside could not. In large parts of rural England the demands of agriculture became all-pervasive. Men were bound to the soil, both by their status and the ever-pressing demands for food. Trade and industry flourished best in centres of population freed from such restraints, in towns. The years between Domesday Book and the last quarter of the thirteenth century saw the rapid expansion of urban England. Some 111 places with urban characteristics were mentioned in the Domesday Survey. Among them were old-established military and administrative centres like York, Lincoln and Chester, county towns such as Warwick and Worcester, the Danish boroughs of Leicester and Nottingham and the Anglo-Saxon burhs (fortified places) like Southampton and Oxford. Almost without exception these towns developed in the propitious circumstances of the late twelfth and early thirteenth centuries. York's population doubled from 4–5,000 in 1086 to about 8,000 by the first quarter of the fourteenth, Gloucester's rose in much the same way to *c.* 3,000 with suburbs being created on the north side of the town. Unfortunately, the only large town in England by European standards, London, was not mentioned in Domesday, and its population can only be a matter of conjecture. The signs of expansion are all there. The city was built and rebuilt as the inhabitants spilled over into suburbs outside the walls. The port became a centre of international trade and by the early fourteenth century the population, which had probably doubled over a century, could scarcely have been less than 40,000.

Urban development did not simply consist of the expansion of existing towns, however. The striking feature of the twelfth and thirteenth centuries is the addition of towns to the existing stock. Some were created by seigneurs from long-settled and advantageously situated villages. Robert fitz Hamon, lord of the Honor of Gloucester, made a town of his village of Burford (Oxon) in this way, giving to it all the free privileges of the borough of Oxford. Others were plantations, towns laid out where none had been before. New Salisbury was created in this way in the thirteenth century by Bishop Poore, and on the East Coast the ports of Hull, Lynn and Boston were developed as trade to the Continent, particularly exports of raw wool to Flanders, expanded. The result was that by the first quarter of the fourteenth century the number of towns in England had doubled. The taxation returns between 1296 and 1336 treated some 226 places as boroughs, whose inhabitants paid a higher rate of taxation than men in the surrounding countryside. To these must be added towns in Cheshire and Durham, and the Cinque Ports, which were not covered by the general assessments, making a grand total of about 240 for the kingdom as a whole, of which 46 were plantations. In addition to these, the collectors in 1334 treated a further 66 plantations not as boroughs but as vills, so there were probably around 300 places with urban characteristics in early fourteenth century England. Impressive though this was, it must, of course, be seen in perspective. Precisely the same phenomenon was occurring all over Europe. In South-West France bastides, fortified townships, were being built by the kings of England and France along the Gascon frontier. Along the Baltic littoral new seaports were springing up as the Germans pushed eastwards into the Slav lands. Europe is littered with Neuvevilles and Neustadts, new towns. The expansion of existing urban centres was equally rapid and, as has been said, by Continental standards England had only one town of any size, London. Florence probably had 90,000 inhabitants by the early fourteenth century, Milan 75,000, Venice 90,000, Padua, Bologna, Lucca and Verona over 25,000. In North-West Europe a whole cluster of clothing towns in Flanders had 10–25,000 inhabitants and in Germany Frankfurt, Augsburg, Breslau, Ulm, Lübeck, Danzig, Nuremberg, Strasbourg, Hamburg, Bremen, Rostock all fell into this category. Urban expansion in England, with one or two exceptions, was essentially geared not to international trade or large-scale industrial production but to serving the needs of an agrarian economy seeking outlets for its surpluses.

The first problem, however, lies in defining what made a collection of people into a town, for there are differing legal–constitutional and economic definitions. It is essential to understand that most towns in the early twelfth century were not the self-governing entities they were later to become. They belonged to a lord, to the king or to a lay or ecclesiastical nobleman, and were valuable pieces of property. They brought him rents from burgage tenures, tolls from the market, fines from the court, tax or tallage from the inhabitants. The earl of Devon was lord of the little Devon borough of Tiverton. In 1286–7 it brought him an income of £14.11s.9¼d., made up of £4.1s.0d. from rents, £3.12.8d. from fines and the perquisites of the borough court, £1.5s.1¾d. in tolls from the fair held there every year and £5.13s.0d. from taxes. This income was one of the main incentives for the foundation of towns. If the lord had an area of poor but well-sited land he could build a town thereon and attract settlers from the surplus population of the surrounding countryside and the younger sons of merchants and artisans from other boroughs seeking their fortune. Neither Boston nor New Windsor was on good land, but both flourished. The best example of the profit to be made, however, is Ravenserrod, built on a large sandbank at the mouth of the Humber. In the decade beginning 1260 it yielded £6 per annum, in 1270 £12, in 1271 £26, in 1287 £39, in 1291 £48 and in 1307 £68, all pure profit for no agricultural land was lost.

Other towns brought in lesser rewards which at first sight do not seem to compare with those from the manors on which they were created. The bishop of Winchester's borough of Downton, founded *c*.1208, brought him about £10 per annum compared with the £140 from the manor in 1208–9. New Alresford provided him with about £20 income in the mid-thirteenth century when the manor brought him a cash revenue five times greater. But the manorial revenue required a great deal of effort to raise. Elizabeth de Burgh's manor of Clare had a value of £113 per annum in the early fourteenth century. To obtain it 550–650 acres of land had to be sown every year, the work supervised, and the sheep looked after. To obtain the £16 Clare borough brought in Elizabeth's officials simply had to collect the rents (£4), organize the court (£6) and receive the £6 the inhabitants had agreed to pay in lieu of all other revenues and tolls. The greater the town, then the greater were the rewards. London's farm (the sum it had agreed with the Crown that it should pay in lieu of all revenues) was fixed at £300 in 1086 and was raised from court fees, local tolls such as scavage on imports, harbour and market tolls at the various quays and marts and from rents. Lincoln paid £100 farm in 1086, a sharp rise from the £30 in Edward the Confessor's day, Norwich £90, Chester £76 and Oxford £60. Finally, a well-sited town could bring profits in other ways. It has been estimated that a town of 3,000 inhabitants consumed at least 1,000 tons of grain per annum, the produce of some 4,500 acres of land or, allowing for fallowing, 9,000 acres in a two-field and 7,500 acres in a three field-system. Few new towns grew to that size, but some did, New Salisbury, Lynn, Boston or Newcastle upon Tyne, for instance. The expansion of old towns and the foundation of new ones had profound effects on the surrounding countryside, from which the lord with large demesnes could benefit.

Towns, then, were worth the having, a fact which their lords knew well. They were anxious to encourage their growth by granting them charters of privileges. But what the townsmen wanted more than anything else was freedom to run their own affairs, freedom from the prying eyes of the lord's officials, be they the royal sheriff or the seigneurial bailiff. The struggle for local self-government – and often it was indeed a struggle – was a long one. It has often been argued that the reason why it was so long was royal hostility to urban freedom. On the Continent independent towns proved a thorn in the flesh for local rulers and the kings of England, it is said, were determined not to let that happen here. But there is no real evidence to support such an argument. The period immediately after the Conquest was one of urban expansion in England. There was urban growth around new castles and revived monasteries and Norwich, Lincoln, Northampton and Nottingham all expanded. New town customs were introduced when those of the little Norman town of Breteuil were bestowed on Hereford by William fitz Osbern, whence they spread to other rising boroughs along the Welsh borders. London received its first charter of liberties from Henry I whilst York's liberties were well established before the grant of its charter between 1154 and 1158. The civil war brought as much confusion to the towns as it did to the rest of the country, but when strong rule was restored it might seem that the movement towards town independence was stifled. Such was not the case. London may have lost its charter and its right to elect its own officials and its farm may have been raised, but what London lost, York gained, as did the citizens of Oxford whose charter of 1155 ironically gave them the customs of London. Gloucester's attempt to establish a fully self-governing commune in 1169–70 was a failure, admittedly, but it was in Henry II's reign that the town gained the right to pay a fixed annual sum, the farm, in lieu of all its revenues. Southampton, too gained the right of farm, and had it reduced from £300 to a more realistic £200. The years 1154–89 were in fact an era in which the solid foundations of urban liberty were laid. Towns were well placed to grasp the opportunities offered by the rapid economic expansion of 1180–1220 and the reigns of two kings, Richard I and John, who, desperate for money, were prepared to sell liberty at a price.

But it was always liberty on a tight rein. It is wrong to see the Crown happily creating in independent towns a non-feudal counterbalance to the power of the landed nobility. Kings were as wary of towns, and particularly of London, as they were of the magnates. Ten times between 1239 and 1259 the government of the city of London was taken back into the king's hands on the pretext of abuses of power, which explains in no small way London's support for the baronial cause in 1258–65. Liberty was regained on payment of a fine of 20,000 marks (£13,333.13s.4d.) – but by 1272 internal quarrels again led to royal intervention. Thus began 27 years of conflict between city and Crown during which city government was in royal hands between 1284 and 1297. London's experience was not unique. Lincoln suffered from supporting the wrong side in the civil war of 1216–17 and was fined heavily for attacks on the Jews and involvement in the barons' wars of 1258–67. Non-payment of the fine led to suspension of the town's liberties but the more serious clash with the Crown came, as at London, at the end of the century.[1] Again, the cause was internal divisions in the town and between 1290 and 1301 Lincoln was governed by a royal official. The Crown took Southampton back into its own hands in 1251, 1274 and 1292–3, and York in the 1290s.

Relations between towns and lay and ecclesiastical lords were often no better, especially when the lord was resident in the town. At Bury St Edmunds there was a running battle between the town and the abbey in the thirteenth century, since the sacrist and the cellarer enjoyed oppressive rights and supervised the town's courts. The quarrel's roots were also partly economic. The abbey regarded the town as a milch cow whilst the citizens wanted freedom from the financial burdens imposed by the convent. This they did not achieve. Although forced to grant a charter of privileges allowing self-government and a gild merchant in 1327, the abbot had no intention of keeping his word and all the liberties were eventually suppressed. Warwick suffered from the presence of a powerful earl, Cirencester, Evesham and Winchcombe from great abbeys, Coventry from the division of the town between the earl of Chester and the prior of Coventry. Discontent with the prior reached such a level in the early fourteenth century that the citizens, it was alleged, paid a sorcerer to try to remove him. In Tavistock the abbot continued to appoint the chief local official, his steward presided at the borough court, he took a percentage of corn ground at the town mill, collected relief on inheritance and exacted watching and carrying services from the burgesses. These were all seigneurial boroughs, but Chester and Norwich had royal charters. Nevertheless, they both suffered from the presence of a powerful lord. The abbey at Chester occupied a quarter of the area within the walls, which was outside the jurisdiction of the mayor and corporation. It had also been granted the right to a three-day annual fair on 24 June each year, during which traders were forbidden to buy or sell elsewhere within the town. Serious conflict arose between abbot and citizens which was not resolved until a compromise was agreed in 1288. Norwich was essentially divided into three, the borough, the castle fee and the cathedral precincts. The citizens had their charter from Richard I but it took them until 1345 to gain control of the castle fee – and the cathedral precincts remained outside their grasp. Serious friction arose over trading rights and after a brawl at the Trinity fair in 1271 the citizens made a full-scale attack on the Cathedral priory.

The plain fact is that lords were reluctant to let their towns go or to cease exercising valuable judicial or economic rights within them. Fully autonomous, self-governing towns did not develop in England. They had to fit into a framework of strong monarchy and lordship and what they achieved was really local self-government at the lord's will. When it suited him, liberties could be, and were, suspended. Where a lord had important privileges for himself or his servants, he clung to them, and nearly every town had its military or ecclesiastical enclave. But, that being said, most towns did have local self-government by the late thirteenth and early fourteenth centuries, a series of liberties or privileges which distinguished them from the surrounding countryside and brought important economic benefits. These privileges were embodied in a charter or a series of charters from successive lords in which they were either specified one by one or copied en bloc from those of another town. The most fundamental were the right to a free borough and burgage tenure.

Free borough is an all-embracing term, probably used to establish the separation of the town from the surrounding 'unfree' countryside. Freedom before the common law applied to all inhabitants; as the charter of Haverfordwest put it, anyone living within the borough for a year and a day without being challenged by a lord would become a free man.[2] Burgage tenure was a more important but more limited right. It consisted of the tenure of a specific burgage plot within the town for a fixed annual rent. These plots differed in size from town to town, and as in the countryside, pressure on land often led to subdivision. At Southampton burgage tenements fronting on the streets where the main markets were held were long and narrow, whilst the 162 original burgage plots at Banbury had become 230 by the early thirteenth century. But the most vital features of burgage tenures were that they were free and held at a fixed rent, often one shilling per annum or a fraction of that where subdivision had occurred. The holder was free to do as he willed with his plot. He could sell all or a portion of it, he could mortgage it to raise liquid capital, he could leave it to whom he wished. He was also a burgess, with the right to full participation in all the privileges given to and responsibilities placed upon the town. That right was worth having. Compared to that for arable land, the rent may have been high, but burgage tenure brought favoured terms in the borough market, preferential treatment and political privileges, a share in town government. Those who held it were the favoured few, traders or manufacturers who could pay the heavier rent, or outsiders who bought their way into the franchise or held tenements in the countryside regarded by long-established custom as rural burgages of the borough. Any man not falling into one of these categories, but still wishing to enjoy the liberties and customs of the town, had to pay for it. As was the case at Hull, he had to be prepared to be at geld and scot with the burgesses, to be liable to all the taxes and payments that they were. Burgage tenure was thus an important privilege. Its holder was free in respect of his time, to engage in trade and industry, his compulsory outgoings were relatively limited compared to those of the unfree tenant, and he had a leading part to play in town affairs. In towns of divided lordship, burgage rights were often granted to some tenants but not others, a source of grievance which, as at Hereford, could lead to frequent disputes.

The next test for a borough was whether or not the town had its own court separate from the shire, hundred and manor courts in the surrounding countryside and from any seigneurial court within the town. Provided this borough court was held independently, by the burgesses themselves and presided over by some person or persons chosen by them, and provided the burgesses were given the extra privilege of not being impleaded elsewhere, except in matters touching the Crown, then they had acquired very considerable protection for themselves and their town. If they could not be called into question before other courts, neither could the town's privileges nor their free status. They could be sure that cases concerning debts or weights and measures, breaches of market or other commercial regulations would be heard before a court where they were on equal terms with their accusers and in which commercial matters and technical terms were clearly understood. This might be described as legal self-interest and so it was. But, in a world where jurisdictions clashed and no man was without a lord, that self-interest was vital.

The court had many other functions besides protecting merchants, however. As self-government was gradually acquired in the twelfth and thirteenth centuries, it became the vehicle for the enforcement of all manner of rules and regulations concerning the life of the town. By 1223 Norwich was a hundred in its own right, divided into four leets, each presided over by a bailiff. They exercised minor powers in the king's name and once a year held a long session to deal with all matters concerning hundredal jurisdiction and offences against the custom of the city. Serious crime, such as murder or manslaughter, was beyond the court's competence. But it could deal with cases of theft, assault and the raising of the hue and cry in pursuit of criminals. Almost the first entry on the leet roll of 1297–8 concerns an attack on a stranger who had had two of his fingers cut off. The hue and cry had been raised and the criminal brought to justice. Such cases formed a staple part of the court's business, for medieval urban society was nothing if not violent. Equally regular were cases concerning buildings encroaching on the highway, the removing of boundaries between properties, the altering of watercourses and the removal of nuisances such as a muck heap on which a butcher in 1298–9 had been burning the offal of beasts, with stinking results.

It made little difference who controlled the court which rectified offences such as these. In other matters it did, for the court had wide powers which could affect the trading life and economy of the town generally. Infringements of regulations concerning weights and measures and the selling of unsound food were punished there. The right of the assize of bread and ale gave the town control over the price, quality and weight or quantity of these two staples. The Norwich court was particularly concerned with stamping out forestalling (buying up goods before they reached the open market), and preventing anyone trading within the city who was not entitled to do so, especially 'foreigners' or outsiders. The custom of the city also forbade the establishment of private gilds for individual crafts or trades. It was held that full citizenship meant the full freedom to exercise any sort of trade and in the late thirteenth century cobblers, saddlers and fullers were all fined for having such illegal associations.[3]

One town court differed very little from another. The larger the settlement, the greater the business, but the only major difference between the Norwich and Leicester courts, for instance, was that the latter seemed more obsessed with keeping out the stranger than the former. What is obvious is that such courts could interfere in virtually every aspect of the town's life, and thus it was essential for the towns to control them. Without such control, without the separation from the surrounding countryside and from seigneurial jurisdiction, royal or otherwise, towns had little or no real freedom to manage their own affairs. But, just as important, there had to be financial as well as juridical independence, so that no seigneurial official could ask awkward questions concerning the town's wealth and the conduct of its affairs. So, the next important step for a borough would be for the citizens to hold the town at farm, or better still at fee farm from their lord.

Put at its simplest, this meant in the first instance that the citizens would agree with their lord to pay him a fixed sum of money every year in lieu of the revenues he normally received from rents, tolls and the profits of justice. The lord still had the right to vary the farm, however, and complete independence was not achieved until the borough had managed to come to a final agreement to pay a fixed sum every year called the fee farm, which would not vary from year to year or decade to decade. Such rights were not easily achieved and the experience of Lincoln in this respect is little different from that of other towns, great or small. By the time of Domesday it had to pay £100 to the king, but this was collected by the sheriff and the tales of his oppression in the late eleventh and twelfth centuries (for he kept everything he raised over and above the £100) were numerous. By the time of the first full royal accounts in the pipe roll of 1130 London and Lincoln had moved one stage further on. The men of London offered 100 marks (£66.13s.4d.) to be allowed to elect their own sheriffs, whilst the citizens of Lincoln offered 200 marks of silver and four of gold that they might hold in chief (directly) of the king. Effectively this would have made the citizens responsible for collecting all the Crown's revenues, a considerable step forward in self-government. They managed to cling to the right during both the Anarchy and Henry II's reign, although the farm was raised to £140. The privilege was precariously held. Other towns were granted the right to farm, only to have it revoked. Lincoln, too, was to discover how easily the right could be lost. As punishment for attacks on the Jews in 1190 the citizens were deprived of the farm of the city and when they bought back their charter from a needy king, it was raised to £180. By the charter the citizens held their privileges of the king and his heirs, so the £180 was effectively a fee farm. But there was no guarantee of perpetual liberties. As has been seen, the king could and did take the city back into his own hands and confirmation of the privileges had to be bought from successive rulers. Nonetheless, by the early thirteenth century the citizens were responsible for collecting and paying over a fixed farm to the Crown.

Obviously they thought it worthwhile to keep out the sheriff's prying nose. More than that, the need to administer the revenues – for officials would have to be appointed to collect and answer for them – was to provide, in many cases, a nucleus around which town government could grow. So did another important institution confirmed by charter to many, but not all, towns, the gild merchant. This was no more than a body of traders who had joined together to regulate the town's trade. Often, as at Southampton, its origins were religious and social, a banding together of men to celebrate saints' days, to give alms, see to the burial of the dead, and to provide each other with mutual insurance against natural or political disasters. Southampton's gild, with its entrance fees, regular hierarchy of officials and bi-annual meetings, long preceded its charter, and membership was a valuable asset. Gildsmen shared with all members of the franchise exemptions from local tolls and customs and were privileged before all others to bargain for goods brought for sale in the town. Non-gildsmen could not buy honey, salt herring, any kind of oil, mill stones, fresh hides or skins, nor keep a tavern for wine, nor sell cloth retail except on market and fair days, nor keep above four quarters of corn in their granary to sell retail. Breaches of rules were punishable by fines and the gild had its own court to punish offenders.

It is small wonder that an institution with its own officials, court and funds should prove another of the nuclei of town government in the twelfth and thirteenth centuries. Such was the case at Southampton where the borough court was controlled by the king's reeve. In the mid-thirteenth century the citizens requested that the office of mayor be allowed to lapse and the alderman of the gild governed the town for 50 years or so. Leicester was firmly under seigneurial control and the gild was virtually the only independent body in the town. The earliest mention of its alderman comes in 1209, 50 years before that of the mayor and by 1251 the alderman was the town's chief officer, the gild's court the town court. Bury St Edmunds and Reading were both under the shadow of a great abbey and in both cases the gild acted as a focus of opposition to the lord and emerged as the town's governing body. Not all towns had gilds merchant. London did not, but its government was already well developed by 1066. Its own body of law and custom was expressly confirmed by William I. The citizens enjoyed freedom of alienation and bequest of property and they could not be compelled to plead outside the city walls, except in the most serious of cases. They held their own general assembly, the Folkmoot, and a weekly court, the Hustings. The city was divided into 24 administrative wards, each with its own alderman, 'a traditional and select group of lawmen, to whose authority even the numerous sokes or private franchises were largely subjected'.[4] In other towns the gild merchant developed in the power vacuum of the twelfth century, but in London no such vacuum existed. The city was already well and truly governed, although its battle for complete independence from the Crown was to last for two centuries or more.

The final group of privileges granted by charters was specifically economic. The first has already been mentioned, the essential right to regular weekly markets and fairs. None the less valuable was freedom of toll. Tolls formed a major element in town incomes. They were levied, for the use of the market, on the sale of certain goods, for the right to have a stall at the market (stallage), for the use of warehouses (seldage) and, where a specific grant had been made by the Crown, towards the cost of building and maintaining walls (murage), bridges (pontage) and roads (pavage). Exemption from tolls was a prized right, but it only conferred that right in other towns held by the same lord. If that lord was the king, then the town had freedom of toll in every other town on the royal demesne. Not unnaturally, disputes were frequent. Southampton kept a careful record of some 40 towns whose burgesses had freedom of toll in the borough, ranging from Newcastle in the North, Yarmouth in the East and Shrewsbury and Bristol in the West. Where the town was a seigneurial borough the exemptions were more limited.

Durham's rights existed only in other of the bishop's boroughs, such as Gateshead, Wearmouth (Sunderland) and Darlington, for instance. Nevertheless, the existence of so many royal boroughs enjoying the right of freedom of toll helped create a 'free trade' area within England. Formidable toll barriers did not develop as they did on the Continent, with the result that trade flowed more freely within England than within other European countries.

A combination of some or all of these privileges could make a town into a borough as far as the legal or constitutional historian is concerned. It is self-evident that many of the customs or privileges were economically important. They separated town from countryside, gave its inhabitants protection under their own kind of law, the right to manage their own affairs, pay their own taxes, dispose of their property, for which they payed only a relatively low fixed rent and no services, as they wished. They allowed them to band together with their fellows to regulate the trade of the town and charge outsiders for the use of its markets and fairs. This was only reasonable, for the town both provided a service and relied on tolls to help pay its farm. But no amount of privileges could, by themselves, make a town flourish economically. For that, it had to have a sound geographic and economic basis, and inevitably some old towns declined whilst other new plantations prospered. Contemporaries recognized this. Both taxation assessments and the list of towns returning burgesses to parliament were regularly revised. The small Oxfordshire town of Witney had no extensive franchises, but, thanks to the strength of its cloth industry, it still returned burgesses to some of Edward I's parliaments. Certainly it was economic strength which inspired the townsmen's quest for privileges, but franchises alone could not make a town economically successful. The classic example of this is the neighbouring towns of Warwick and Coventry. Warwick was a borough by Domesday and shortly after 1086 was granted a charter by its earl. Partly due to the dead hand of the lord, but much more to its economic backwardness, the town failed to develop corporate organs of government. Its trade rested solely on the needs of the castle, since it lay off all the important routes in the county. Neighbouring Coventry suffered the even greater disadvantage of being divided between two lords and had only limited powers of self-government. Yet in the thirteenth century Coventry developed as a major centre of trade and industry. It stood at a confluence of routes and was provided with regular markets and fairs. By 1300 cloth making was the main occupation, but there were also flourishing metal working and leather industries, whilst its merchants were active in the wool export trade. From a small village in 1086 Coventry had developed into a flourishing urban centre of some 5,000 souls, returning representatives to parliament. But, it had at that time no proper charter.

What, then, helped towns develop? Much depended, by accident or design, on fortunate siting. The majority of towns in England were small market centres. Their distribution was in part due to the distribution of the population itself. The most urbanized part of the West Midlands was the Southern Cotswolds, where population density was higher than in other parts of the region whilst, naturally enough, there were few towns in the central upland areas of Derbyshire. Location also depended on the distribution of large estates. The proliferation of markets in north Northumberland reflects the sprawl of estates held by such great families as the Umfravilles of Redesdale, the Prudhoes or the Vesceys of Alnwick. Conversely Durham in 1293 had only four market centres, each controlled by a major lord, the bishop (two), the Balliols of Barnard Castle and the Brusa of Hartlepool. Trade in such centres was mainly local. Banbury acted as the market centre for north Oxfordshire for agricultural products, cattle and horses. Grain and livestock were the staples of towns in the North East, like Berwick, Newbiggin, Hartlepool, Northallerton and Richmond, but there were plenty of other goods available on their markets – fish, salt, butter, cheese, wool, cloth, hemp flax, iron, lead, leather, hay, and sometimes more exotic groceries – pepper, cinnamon and almonds. Most of these small market towns were surrounded by flourishing agricultural villages or villages whose inhabitants needed to dispose of surpluses, real or created. They also had to have connections to larger towns, which could supply a greater range of goods than a small market could carry, and to ports for imports like wine. In Derbyshire Derby and Chesterfield performed these functions, in the North East Newcastle upon Tyne.

But there were dangers. A link to a big town was important but it could also be lethal. Along the Severn Valley the rapid growth of Gloucester and Worcester, connected by river to Bristol, stifled the growth of smaller centres. Between Gloucester and Bristol there were only two market towns, Berkeley and Thornbury; north of Gloucester Tewkesbury stood at the confluence of the Severn and Avon and between there and Worcester there was only a small market at Hanley Castle. The larger towns drew trade to them and there was no room for smaller rivals. It was also important that markets should not be too close together. In the mid-thirteenth century the celebrated lawyer Bracton declared that no market should be created within a radius of six and two-third miles of an existing market held on the same day. This was the practical distance for a day's journey on foot from the village to and from the market. Like many another legal dictum in medieval England it was not always obeyed. In Lancashire one market at North Meols was suppressed on the grounds that it was injurious to others in the neighbourhood, although the nearest rival was 13 miles away. But the abbot of Furness complained bitterly, and to no avail, about the establishment of a new market at Ulverston only five miles from his own at Dalton. The dictum in fact made good sense. The growth of Tavistock led to the decay of nearby Lydford and Okehampton and the rapid development of Dartmouth damaged the prosperity of Totnes. Several new towns were created in Bedfordshire in the twelfth and thirteenth centuries, among them Dunstable and Toddington. Dunstable was well sited, as in the south of the parish Watling Street crossed the ancient track, the Icknield Way, and the presence of the priory stimulated local trade. It grew rapidly and by its growth completely overshadowed Toddington which never developed economically into a town.

It was indeed geography which went a long way to dictating both the location and the success of a town. Situation at the crossing of a river or at a major crossroads often contributed to growth. Banbury stood at the gateway from the Thames Basin to the Midland Plain. North of the town an easy road through Fenny Compton or Warmington six or seven miles away crossed the limestone ridge that runs from Lincolnshire to the Cotswolds, a track of great antiquity. To the south lay Oxford, to the north Coventry. The town may have been developed as an administrative centre for the bishop of Lincoln's hundred in North Oxfordshire, but it owed its economic well-being to its position on a juncture of routes. When the bishop of Worcester determined to found a new town in West Warwickshire at the end of the twelfth century, he chose to develop a site on his manor of Stratford, where the road striking off the Fosse Way to Alcester and Droitwich crossed the river route between Evesham and Warwick. He chose well, for the town was an almost instant economic success. Elsewhere crossroads, bridges, fords and ferries acted as focal points for town formation. The ferry crossing from Devon to Cornwall at Saltash caused delay to travellers in the loading and unloading of boats. A small town grew up there to meet travellers' needs, needs which survived until the recent building of the road bridge. Bridges themselves caused delays because of tolls charged, and when a new bridge was built and a route diverted a new town could be created. The bishop of London built a new bridge on the London to Colchester road and brought a new town into being at Chelmsford by leading the road straight into a large, triangular market place.

The more important the route, the larger and more successful the town was likely to be. Lincoln owed a great deal of its importance to its position at the junction of two old Roman roads, Ermine Street, running from London to York, and the Fosse Way from Exeter via Bath and Cirencester to Lincoln. Although Ermine Street had been replaced in the fourteenth century by the Old North Road via Stamford, Grantham and Doncaster, Lincoln was still easily accessible from it via the Fosse Way through Newark. More important, the town was linked to the sea by a system of waterways. The volume of road traffic in the Middle Ages should not be underestimated but wherever possible cheaper water transport was preferred. Lincoln had an outlet to the Trent and thus to the Humber and the Yorkshire Ouse via the Fossdyke, and to Boston and the Wash via the River Witham. The importance of this to the town can be seen in the tax levied on merchants in 1202–4. London, naturally, paid most (£837) but Boston was second with £780 and Lincoln fourth with £657, and between them the merchants of the other Humber ports paid well over £550.

The confluence of major road and river routes bred large towns. Gloucester was the first place above its mouth where the Severn could easily be crossed by the road from London to South Wales and of course there was easy access up the river to Worcester and down to Bristol. York commanded the route to the North and was connected to the Humber estuary via the Ouse. Chester stood at the last practical crossing of the navigable River Dee and at the crossroads of routes to the Midlands and North Wales. Reading gained great advantage from its position on the main route to the West, whilst the growth of New Salisbury demonstrates the coincidence of a number of propitious circumstances. The site for the new town had been well chosen at the focus of five river valleys. Along these for 20 miles or more in either direction lay villages with sheep/corn economies, and the chalk ridges provided hard roads to within a mile of the town centre. That ensured the town's success as a local market. What made it into an important commercial centre was the building of a bridge at Harnham in 1244 which diverted the routes from Southampton to Bristol and London to the West Country into the town and away from neighbouring Wilton. From that moment Salisbury prospered, Wilton declined.

Where the major route connected differing geographic regions, so much the better. Cirencester already stood at the junction of the Fosse Way and the London to Gloucester road. What made it the capital of the Cotswolds, however, with a tax assessment in 1334 half that of Gloucester's, was its location between varying regions. To the south-east lay the corn growing Thames Valley, to the north the wool producing Cotswolds, to the west the Severn Valley, which made it peculiarly suited as a centre of trade. The development of Cirencester itself stimulated a whole series of satellite markets and towns, Fairford and Lechlade, Minchinhampton and Tetbury, Chipping Sodbury and Northleach, all linking Cirencester to its region. In the Cotswolds themselves a group of nascent urban centres connected wolds to lowlands. Some were no more than villages but others, like Winchcombe, Chipping Campden and Cheltenham became thriving small boroughs. Precisely the same phenomenon is found in Derbyshire where Castleton and Bakewell stood at the head of valleys connecting the moors to the lowlands.

Inevitably, many of the towns which stood on major road or river routes also became important military or administrative centres, whilst others were the seats of bishoprics or large monastic houses. That, as has been seen, had its problems, but it cannot be denied that the demand created by a castle or abbey, or, in the case of London, the royal household, stimulated urban growth. Finally, there were the seaports, a natural development when England's foreign and coastal trade was expanding. From Alnwick to New Winchelsea new ports were being created and old ones expanded. Not all flourished, however. Hull's growth on the Humber killed off its rivals, Hedon and Ravenserodd, and Hull grew, like other ports, because of its connections via Trent and Ouse to its hinterland. Such connections were essential. Southampton owed its early growth to its links with Salisbury, Winchester and the wool-growing hinterland, Boston and Lynn theirs to the fact that behind them lay some of the wealthiest counties in thirteenth-century England. Lynn had been made into a borough by the bishop of Norwich at the end of the eleventh century. It lay at a point where road and river met sea, opening up to the port the cornlands of West Norfolk and the fertile eastern and southern fens, as well as Ely, Cambridgeshire, Huntingdon and Bedfordshire via the Great Ouse, and Peterborough and Northamptonshire via the Nene. Boston

135

lay on the Witham which joined it to Lincoln and thus to Stamford and the Midlands by the Welland. From these ports in the thirteenth century flowed vast quantities of grain from the new lands of the fens, and later wool to Flanders. Back came wood and furs from the Baltic, wine from Gascony and dyestuffs, all to be redistributed through the river and road systems to Midland England. Neither town was a Domesday borough, but by the early fourteenth century Boston ranked second to London as a port and Lynn was not far behind.

For any town to grow beyond a certain size involvement by its merchants in international trade was essential. Boston and Lynn tended to be mere ports, through which trade passed in the hands of non-townsmen. London was different. By the eleventh century it already had extensive links with continental Europe. Regulations for the Lorraine wine fleet from the Rhine, with its wine and its goods from Regensburg, Mainz, Novgorod, Persia and Byzantium are amongst the earliest city records. During the course of the twelfth and thirteenth centuries new commercial axes were to be created to Gascony, Spain, the Baltic and the Mediterranean. Although much of this trade was in the hands of aliens, Londoners still benefited considerably from the redistributive trade. It helped make London unique among English towns, able to stand on equal terms with rivals such as Bruges, Toulouse, Bordeaux and Lübeck.

And so, by the end of the thirteenth century England was covered by a whole network of markets, fairs and towns which supplied and lived off the local countryside. The importance of the market can be seen by the way in which settlement in any town, new or old, intensified around the market place. The main market at Norwich became so crowded that subsidiary markets developed in surrounding streets and horses were sold in St Stephen's churchyard. This was a feature of larger markets, where specialization was bound to occur. Stratford upon Avon had markets for corn, hay and livestock in the thirteenth century and possibly for poultry and dairy produce as well. Eventually three separate market crosses were erected and on the Thursday market day almost every corner of the borough was full of activity. For smaller towns one general market would suffice, often a single street broadening into a V-shaped market, as at Market Harborough. Not only did markets expand, but so did towns themselves, siphoning off some of the surplus population from the countryside and throwing out suburbs beyond the town boundaries. Communities of merchants, artisans, urban property owners and workers had become a powerful element in English society, supplying essential goods and services to the countryside. But they were more than mere appendages to rural society. Each was a community in its own right, often by the late thirteenth century self-governing, with the ability to implement and enforce social and economic policies – or perhaps, better, its own rules and regulations. Urban dwellers, or at least the chief amongst them, did have clearly discernible attitudes, both to the town as a corporate body, to other citizens and to the town's economic role and well-being.

The last of these is probably the most observable in the surviving records, and the most intelligible to economic historians. Its aim was simply to secure for the town and its inhabitants the best terms of trade possible. To accomplish this vigorous and sustained action was needed on several levels. Where, in order to further growth, a town had been given a territorial monopoly of certain types of or of all trade, it had to be jealously defended for as long as possible. Lincoln fought, to the end of the thirteenth century, to maintain the right granted by Henry I that all foreign merchants trading in Lincolnshire must go to the city to pay their tolls. That was bound to attract trade to the town, a factor which was taken into account when its farm was assessed. In similar fashion Henry I confined all trade within Cambridgeshire to Cambridge whilst the same king's charter to Nottingham obliged the men of Nottinghamshire and Derbyshire to come to the town's market on Fridays and Saturdays. Nottingham's weavers, like those of London and Winchester had a monopoly of working dyed cloth within ten leucae[5] of the town. These privileges granted in an earlier age were not easy to sustain in the thirteenth century, as Lincoln's disputes with Boston testify, and in the end the monopolies could not be maintained. That towns thought it worth trying is good evidence of how concerned they were with their economic well-being. Indeed, the price of survival was eternal vigilance to see that rivals, internal and external, did not damage that well-being. Nottingham was continually at odds with the nearby Cluniac priory of Lenton whose fair rivalled its own Martinmas fair on 11 November. Southampton faced a formidable rival in the bishop of Winchester whose great St Giles Fair the borough's merchants were compelled to attend. In the 1250s they refused to go, but were eventually forced to agree that whilst the fair was in progress only victuals could be sold at Southampton. Rivalries between towns were just as intense. Wilton tried desperately to stop trade going to New

Salisbury, blocking the roads to its more successful neighbour on occasion, and Lydford struggled unsuccessfully to prevent the rise of Tavistock. Throughout the thirteenth and early fourteenth centuries the citizens of Exeter were locked in a bitter dispute with successive earls of Devon who were trying to build a weir across the river Exe and divert trade to their town at Topsham. Exeter was finally to win the struggle, but even in the 1320s the citizens were still complaining that the earl was compelling merchants to sell their goods at Topsham and refusing to allow them to come to the city.

The first plank of any town's policy then, was to ensure a regular flow of trade to its market. Once there, every effort was made to put the townsmen at an advantage and the outsider at a disadvantage in buying and selling. The most comprehensive records of regulation of the market are those of the Leicester gild merchant in the thirteenth century. To trade one had to be a gildsman. The privilege was mainly inherited, but could be bought, and the rates for outsiders were much higher than those for townsmen. The advantages of membership were very considerable. Gildsmen escaped in full or part the tolls strangers had to pay and, since the wool trade was vital to the town's economy, were provided with an official guide to the wool suppliers in the surrounding countryside. Any Leicester man who taught strangers the way of the country was banished from the town for a year and a day. Having brought the wool within the town, gildsmen could have it weighed free, whilst strangers had to pay, there was an official broker (middleman) to help them arrange its sale and they could sell freely to whom they wished. Strangers, however, could only sell to gildsmen and were not allowed to buy raw wool within the town. In fact, as much as possible was done to ensure that the wool trade of the surrounding region was in the hands of Leicester's merchants. But restriction did not end there. The retail sale of cloth, wax, fish and meat by non-gildsmen was forbidden and the hours and places where outsiders were allowed to sell their goods were strictly regulated so that gildsmen might be present whenever or wherever trading was going on. Illicit partnerships between gildsmen and strangers to evade these regulations were, of course, strictly forbidden and the impression from the records is that these rules were not only made but rigidly enforced.

But, by their very nature, townsmen were not only traders but consumers. They needed substantial amounts of grain, fish, meat and fuel. For a great city like London supplies came from far afield, from the Home Counties, East Anglia and, by the thirteenth century coals were coming from Newcastle and wine from Gascony. Towns also needed raw materials for industry. The range could be very considerable. There were over 130 trades and occupations in thirteenth-century Norwich, some very specialized like the glass painters and manuscript illuminators who worked for the churches and some of the wealthy merchants, others more prosaic and to be found in most towns of any size, leather workers, weavers, masons, carpenters and joiners, smiths, cobblers, candlemakers, saddlers, tailors, mercers, haberdashers, needlemakers and a host of others, all of whom needed a constant supply of raw materials. Herein then lay the second of a town's main objectives, to ensure that regular supply, and a fair distribution of foodstuffs and raw materials. Supply was not too difficult. Frequent and well regulated markets were bound to attract trade, and most of the goods needed could be readily provided either by England's own economy or through imports. The real problem was to ensure that, once within the town, essential commodities were fairly distributed and here lay an area of clear conflict between the town as a body and the merchants as individuals. The latter, naturally, wanted to create monopolies, to corner the market. This could be done by buying up supplies before they reached the market (forestalling) and then holding them back in the short or long term to push up prices (regrating or engrossing). Towns were vehemently opposed to such practices. Manipulation of food prices could and did cause social unrest and any interruption in the flow of raw materials would damage industry. The Norwich leet records of the late thirteenth century show continued attempts to stop forestalling of all manner of goods and the gild at Leicester had a particular objection to middlemen. Butchers' wives were forbidden to buy meat to sell again the same day, unless they had cooked it first. Meat dealers had to be butchers or cooks who prepared meat for immediate use. Both at Leicester and Norwich the intention was honourable but whether the regulations were completely effective is another matter.[6] Fishmongers and poulterers were presented so regularly for buying up meat and fish 'to heighten the Norwich market' that the fines look more like annual licenses than deterrents.

Once on the market, in the shops or stalls of the butchers and bakers, in the alehouses and workshops, raw materials and finished goods were inspected to make sure they were of sound quality. A privilege held by many towns was the assize of bread and ale. This gave them the right, enforceable in their courts, to see that the bread baked and the ale brewed was fit for consumption and sold at standard measures and prices. In addition the town could make its own regulations concerning weights and measures used and the quality of food offered for sale. It is difficult to generalize about enforcement of such legislation, since each town had different customs and different ways. There was also, again, a difference between intention and action. At the Norwich leet there were regular presentments for selling ale by the wrong measure, but no action seems to have been taken over fraudulent loaves. Indeed, the regular amercements of bakers for breaking the assize again seem more like an excise duty than punitive fines. Other rules and regulations were taken more seriously. There were frequent presentments for selling meat, sausages and pies that were unfit for human consumption. Plain fraud was also punished, such as selling one kind of oil for another or the use of false weights and measures so that a man bought at a greater weight and sold at a less. All this took up a great deal of the court's time although it is difficult to match the level of presentments to the total volume of trade in Norwich. Probably the proportion was small, but the evidence does suggest that, in spite of difficulties of inspection and enforcement, the town authorities at least tried to control the quality of food offered for sale.

As in consumption, so in production, for the town had a reputation to maintain. If the goods its artisans produced were shoddy, men would not come to market to buy them. Towns felt they had a duty to search out and prosecute inferior or fraudulent work. The leather industry was important to Norwich and there were fines at the leet court for inferior workmanship in hides which had been tanned with ash instead of oak bark.[7] At Leicester all gildsmen were obliged to submit their goods for examination for inferior workmanship. Particular attention was paid to cloth, the town's staple industry, to ensure that only yarn of good quality was used in weaving. A favourite trick was to use good yarn at the end of a bolt and poor quality in the middle where it would not at first be seen. Stringent regulations governed the dyeing industry. It was 'against the gild' to take wool already dyed in woad (blue) and put it in madder and bran to make it darker. In 1263 it was ruled that perse cloth (bluish-grey in colour) could only be made from wool dyed with woad and crude tartar and not from a mixture of black or grey wool treated with madder and alum. Nor was quality control limited to the inspection of goods. Working conditions were strictly supervised. Working at night was forbidden, since in the ill-lit workshops it could only lead to bad craftsmanship. Leicester weavers were made to swear that they would not work at night and that they would have no infidelity in their work. Insistence on quality control was one of the reasons why town governments were so anxious to keep a firm grip on the craft gilds which were beginning to emerge at the end of the thirteenth century. Some gilds had been royally licensed in the twelfth, the London weavers by Henry I for instance and the Oxford cordwainers and corvesors (shoe and bootmakers), whilst Canterbury had a gild of smiths by 1216. But both at Norwich and at Leicester the pressure for separate craft gilds of cobblers and saddlers in one case and weavers and fullers in the other really began in the later thirteenth century. Boroughs were not keen to see any independent bodies within their walls. They were anxious that there should be no rival courts and that all rules and regulations be enforced in their own. That is understandable but jealousy was not solely explicable in terms of power rivalries. There also seems to have been a feeling that independent bodies, solely representative of one craft, might not have the same allegedly disinterested attitude to quality control that the town had.[8]

Consumer and customer protection inspired the two most coherent sets of town policies. The third and last arose from the fact that towns were communities living within a confined space and becoming increasingly crowded in the thirteenth century. They were noisome, dirty places. Only the houses of the rich were built of stone, like St John's House and Canute's Palace which still stand in Southampton, with warehouses or workshops below and living quarters above. In London – and elsewhere – overcrowding was becoming a problem. Wooden frame houses were built upwards and outwards, storey by storey. The streets were overhung with dwellings and civic regulations had to demand that the projection of the first floor must begin not less than nine feet above ground level, so that a horseman might ride beneath it. The frontage of such houses was small; they were long and narrow, stretching back from the street to provide workshops and living accommodation. The majority of the people lived in nothing so grand. Their dwellings consisted of little more than one all-purpose room with sleeping quarters partitioned off by a screen or curtain. Both London and York suffered from the problem of encroachment on the street by frontagers, to build shops or booths, often blocking the way completely.

Town governments had to grapple with problems of public health and safety, therefore, but, it must be admitted, with little success. Fire was a constant hazard and many towns forbade the use of the highly inflammable thatch as roof covering. Streets were foul, and noxious trades such as tanning and butchering made matters worse by dumping on them the remains of animals. Late thirteenth-century London tried to solve its difficulties by banishing offensive trades to the suburbs and appointing a regular corps of scavengers. Their duty was to gather the filth from the streets and cart it either to the banks of the Thames, where dung boats could carry it downriver, or outside the city walls. The success of the operation must be doubted. The streets may have been a little cleaner, but open sewers remained and the Walbrook and Fleet were used as dumping grounds for rubbish. As important as sanitation was a supply of clear, fresh water. By the mid-thirteenth century the need at London had become acute, with the Thames polluted and the number of wells diminishing. In 1237 the city took over the wells at Tyburn (near modern Marble Arch) and piped the water to a great conduit in the Cheap, controlled by a marshal or warden who secured funds for its upkeep. It was the newly arrived Friars who provided Southampton's water supply, bringing it from springs beyond the town's boundaries. Smaller towns probably had to rely on local rivers and streams, however. Few can have been as lucky as New Salisbury which had a system of canals running through the streets.

Another major charge on town revenues was the upkeep of streets and walls. If it was lucky the town had the right to levy pavage and murage, special tolls designed to meet that need. Otherwise, attempts were made to force frontagers to pay. Like sanitation, the maintenance of good roads seems to have been an impossible task. Rubbish accumulated on them so that new surfaces were continually being placed over old. Walls were an even more burdensome strain on finances. It is a mistake to think that English towns were not walled. Those towards the Marches of Wales and Scotland had to be and, as Southampton was to discover in the opening stages of the Hundred Years War, it was also advisable for seaports. No fewer than 108 towns in England and Wales, mainly royal boroughs, acquired fortifications of their own, replacing earth with stone. The cost was great. Coventry, for reasons of prestige, thought walling the town worthwhile, but it took 200 years and absorbed most of the town's surplus revenue.

For all their faults, for all that they were dirty, unhealthy and often violent places, towns were a vigorous element in twelfth- and thirteenth-century English society. They had expanded, in many cases won their freedom and created a society based on wealth from trade and industry, radically different from that of rural England. This society was also, on aggregate, much wealthier. In 1327 a tax of one-twentieth was levied on all produce of the land, cattle and crops, rents and ready money and the goods of merchants and tradesmen. Three hundred and niney-five tax payers in Cosford Hundred in Suffolk paid together £33.14s.7½d. whilst 364 men at Bury and Ipswich paid £53.8s.2¼d.; the contrast is even greater if the towns are compared to Blything Hundred where over 1,000 taxpayers paid only £76.12s.0d. This pattern is repeated elsewhere, yet in a very real sense the figures are misleading. What they conceal is the very great extremes of wealth within the towns. At London this was striking. Between 1292 and 1332 the tax returns reflect a society in which inequality was deeply rooted. Only two wards, Bridge and Bishopgate, had a fair sprinkling of middle-class fishmongers. In the rest the contrast was between the few like Alderman John Warde, with a great house built round a square with a grand hall, wings to the street and rear and warehouses to complete the pattern, and the countless Londoners of whom it was recorded in the coroner's rolls, 'goods and chattels had he none'. This was at the end of the thirteenth century, but precisely the same extremes can be seen at York in 1204. A tallage levied in that year raised £373, of which 32 men only paid no less than £212. So, too at Bristol in 1327, 347 taxpayers paid £80.12s.10d. for the subsidy in that year; most contributed only a few shillings, but 27 men paid 10–20s., 9 men 20–30s., and 2 men over 40s. Even more significant were the large numbers of men, nearly 600, who do not appear to have contributed to the subsidy at all because they were too poor. As might be expected, property was also very unevenly distributed. A survey of Stratford upon Avon in 1251–2 shows that one man alone held five full burgage tenements, eight half-burgages and five shops, whilst at the other end of the scale there were men with only a quarter burgage, a shop or a stall.

Not surprisingly, it was the wealthy who ran the town. There was nothing new in this; the development of oligarchic urban government was not a thirteenth-century phenomenon. From the twelfth century onwards it was the wealthy few who controlled town affairs, and their wealth came as much from the ownership of property as from trade and industry. London was governed by the aldermen of the 24 wards. In essence they were lawmen who gave judgment and whose presence was required at every court. Inevitably, in the early part of the thirteenth century the office fell to rich men of known character and ability, to members of the great civic dynasties. Richard Renger became mayor in 1222 and held office until 1229. Within two years he was succeeded by Andrew Bukerel who remained mayor until his death in 1237. Both were heirs of families of long standing. The Bukerels were descendants of an Italian pepper merchant who settled in London after the Conquest. The family produced aldermen in every generation from about 1100 onwards. Renger's family, the fitz Reiners, were equally prominent and both men were buttressed by great inherited wealth. Bukerel's property was very considerable, a combination of manors in Kent and Middlesex and holdings around Guildhall and in Cripplegate. Renger fell heir to large estates in Hertfordshire, Middlesex and Suffolk and, within the city, property in Vintry and Bridge, including the cellars used by the Lorraine wine fleet. With property and wealth went establishment at court and in the royal household, which was a feature of London's governing class in the early thirteenth century. Both men were also more than simply landed proprietors, for they committed their fortunes to trade, mortgaging land to Jews and Cahorsins to give them the liquid wealth they needed.

These men were representative of the ruling class in London in the first half of the thirteenth century, a highly interrelated group of some 16 or so families. Nor, for once, was London atypical. At Southampton the fortunes of the main families were made in service to the Crown, especially in supplying wine. Again, as at London, they were a close-knit, propertied group, although there was a tendency for sons not to follow father in trade but to become landed gentlemen. It was endowment in town and country property which brought stability to the ruling class of thirteenth-century York. The Selby family made its money from commerce, but they invested in land. For 17 years there were Selbys in office as mayor, and they were typical of others. Lincoln was dominated by a small wealthy group who repeatedly served in the office of bailiff, Bristol and Gloucester by wealthy property-holding merchants, although the association of property and office cannot be clearly established at either Coventry or Worcester.

It is easy to view these oligarchies with modern democratic eyes and disapprove of them. Medieval men had no such notions. It was the duty of the wealthy to bear the weight of town government, but it was also held that they had a responsibility to govern fairly. This, it seems, many of them were not doing, for in the thirteenth century there was a growing volume of complaints about fiscal and judicial corruption. Lincoln's story seems fairly representative. The city had been heavily involved in the civil war of the mid-thirteenth century on the wrong side, and for that, and attacks on the Jews, was fined £1,000. Of this, £300 still remained unpaid in 1267 and the king took the city back into his own hands. Royal commissioners were appointed to empanel a jury to inquire who were the persons in the city who had been against the king in the recent disturbances; how much of the £1,000 had actually been raised and if more than £1,000 had been raised who had received it; and had there been unfair assessment. There had been. The inquiry revealed that some citizens were being made to pay unjustly for privileges, especially those who were seeking to live in the city for a year and a day. City pleas were supposed to be held weekly, on Mondays, and the fines paid given to the bailiffs towards the farm of the city. But the persons appointed to hold the pleas were failing to do so from month to month. A grant of £10 per annum had been made to a great nobleman, Peter of Savoy, from monies which belonged by right to the commonalty. There had been misappropriation of rents of stalls near the bridge, taxes had been levied but no account made of them, some of the rich had failed to contribute to the fine to the king. The inquiry solved nothing. Self-government was soon re-established, but complaints rumbled on. They are to be heard again in the Hundred Rolls of 1275, about the grant to Peter of Savoy and the freedom of toll given to the merchants of Beverley simply because the mayor had married a Beverley woman. The grievances came to a head in 1290. Rich citizens were indicted by a jury of 24 for divers offences. They were charged with selling the tronage of the city (the toll for the use of the weighing beam) without the consent of the poor, of distraining the poor for 200 marks (£133.13s.4d.) paid to the king as the value of the goods of condemned Jews, and unfairly assessing and collecting tallages from the poor. The king had to appoint a commission of oyer and terminer to appease discord between rich and poor, the city's liberties were forfeited and Lincoln was put into the hands of royal keepers until 1301.

All the evidence points to serious friction in Lincoln as the rich exploited their control of government to feather their own nests. It was a state of affairs to be found elsewhere. There was complaint at Gloucester in the 1290s that the 'potentes' tallaged the community immoderately whilst at Bristol thieves fell out. Disputes arose within the dominant office-holding group over favourable tax assessments given to some but not others. At York, the poorer citizens were made to bear the cost of the tallage levied from time to time by the Crown. The sums involved were large – 300 marks (£200) in 1230, £100 in 1254, 350 marks in 1261. This helped embitter social relationships and in 1267 the commonalty of the city complained that lesser folks paid tallages, fines and amercements out of all proportion to their means.

The greater the wealth, the greater chance for corruption, and nowhere was this more true than in London. Edward I decided to curb the city's independent power, partly again as punishment for taking the rebel cause in the civil wars of his father's reign. An inquiry into city government in 1274 let forth a storm of rage. Some of it was inspired by malice, but many of the charges have the unmistakable ring of truth. There had been fraud. Tallages had been levied from which the greater citizens were exempted, the places of collection had been altered, no true accounts were kept. No one knew what had happened to the money and greater citizens had even purchased exemptions from royal taxation. Differential taxation caused bitter discontent in all great European towns, but it was not the only cause of complaint in London. The common citizens were also enraged by the way in which the houses of the rich encroached on the streets and the ease with which the oligarchs enclosed public land without permission. In the 1250s and 1260s at least 20 public ways had been stopped up. As at Lincoln, the inquiry provided no remedy. Royal denunciations of lax administration grew more frequent. Between 1277 and 1281 there were constant complaints that the Hustings court was sheltering delinquent aldermen. Criminals were escaping, feuds between great men went unpunished and there were professional 'bully boys' from good families on the streets. The king's answer was to take the city into his own hands, and in so doing he broke the power of the old patrician families. They were replaced by a new ruling class whose wealth was based on trade more than on property, but in truth one set of oligarchs was simply changed for another.

There is no doubt that in most large towns complaints increased in the later thirteenth century and the question is, why? Here one must be careful about the amount and nature of the evidence. It comes from the major towns whose history has been fully studied. We cannot be sure that the same degree of peculation obtained in the smaller towns. It did at Bury St Edmunds, but what of the Market Harboroughs, Caernarvons and Ludlows of thirteenth-century England? The answer is we do not yet know. We must also be careful how we read the evidence. It might be that the complaints are symptomatic of the very expansion of the thirteenth century creating a new merchant–craftsman class pressing for a share in town government. Yet the increasing volume of complaints does suggest that urban society was in a state of turmoil, even approaching some sort of crisis. There are, too, other signs of strain, economic in nature, which may help explain the social tensions.

First, if there were too many people in the countryside, there may also have been overprovision of towns. Towns cannot be divorced from the rest of the economy. By the end of the century increasing poverty can only have limited general purchasing power, to the detriment of urban prosperity. As has been seen, England was covered by a whole network of towns, many within close distance of each other. There may not have been room for all of them. It is very difficult to judge when urban decline begins for it is a long-term process whose roots may well lie in the thirteenth or the early fourteenth century. But as far as new towns are concerned, there was a marked slowing down in their foundation after 1240, except for the 'military' towns created by Edward I's conquest of Wales. The reason for this is easily seen. Late thirteenth-century plantations were hard put to it to find a suitable catchment area. In East Yorkshire, of all the new boroughs only Pucklington had an unchallenged hinterland. When markets and fairs are taken into account, East Yorkshire was absolutely saturated with towns. The situation was the same in the West Midlands and neither Moreton-in-Marsh, Bretford nor Broadway, all created between 1220 and 1250, succeeded. After 1240 the failure rate of new towns rose generally and it is noticeable that those which developed into full urban centres were, like Newcastle upon Tyne, founded early, in the twelfth century.

Perhaps this was no more than a sign that there were enough towns for the economy to support in good times. What if times became hard, however? Cloth production was the single most important industry in most English towns of any size, manufacturing both for home consumption and for an important export trade. In the thirteenth century it had to face sustained competition from the highly urbanized and capitalized Flemish industry, and it could not meet the challenge.[9] England turned from being an exporter of finished goods to an exporter of raw materials, and in return imported large quantities of Flemish cloth. English towns therefore faced a considerable threat to their trade in cloth and their industry, which could not be entirely offset by the expansion of wool exports since aliens dominated that branch of commerce. Their response, or rather the response of the merchant oligarchs who played such an important part in town and gild government, was to wield their power in their own interests. It is significant that town records begin to appear in large quantities in the later thirteenth century. In part this is sheer accident, but it is also due to the more rigorous enforcement of rules and regulations on trading and manufacturing, many of which were also being made at about this time. One might expect that in more difficult times there would be more discrimination against the foreigner and the alien. This was especially so at Leicester in the second half of the century where the increasing volume of cases points more to rigid enforcement of rules than to an increasing volume of trade.

But there are also signs of a more general illiberality in urban society which went beyond the only-to-be-expected defence of trading interests. Where there was a gild merchant it had been granted to all the citizens and was open to all. It was not simply an association of merchants but of anyone with trading interests, even outsiders if they were willing to submit to mutual taxation. The Leicester and Shrewsbury gild rolls of the early thirteenth century show a membership open to others than the merchant class. Weavers, coopers, carters, carpenters and masons are found alongside butchers, bakers, dyers, mercers and other merchants. But by the late thirteenth century that liberality had vanished. In particular, no weavers could become members of the gild unless they forswore their craft, thus ensuring that trade in cloth remained in the merchants' hands. The days of reasonably free trade had gone and monopolies were tolerated by towns in the interests of the few. The poor men of Norwich complained in 1304 that the rich bought up the food and other goods before they reached the market, despite all the laws against forestalling. It was not difficult for merchants to defy town policy in their own interests, for they played a considerable part in town government.

Interestingly enough, the main weight of attacks on artisans fell on those working in the textile industry. At York no weavers were admitted to the freedom of the city (i.e. giving them full rights to trade) in the reign of Edward I and weavers and fullers were excluded from the franchise at Winchester, Marlborough, Oxford and Beverley. It has already been seen that towns could control working conditions. They could also regulate wages, as at Leicester, and were hostile to the existence of independent craft gilds. Some of the reasons for that hostility have already been discussed, but to them must be added the crisis in the cloth industry. The problem for employers was how to meet foreign competition. One answer was to use cheaper country labour, but that could only lead to the decline of the urban industry, something to be resisted as far as possible. If cheap country labour was not to be used, then every effort would have to be made to ensure that urban costs were kept down and that meant either the destruction of the craft gilds or strict supervision of their workings to keep wages down. This did not only apply to weavers and fullers. Leather working was important at Norwich and the town's oligarchs fought hard to prevent craft organization there.

It would not be entirely wrong to talk of class warfare in late thirteenth-century towns. Contemporaries certainly saw it as such, with the poor commons ranked economically and politically against the excesses of the potentiores. In mid-thirteenth century Bury it was the maiores (the great) against the minores (the lesser) which sums up an attitude to be found generally elsewhere. However, strife and violence never reached the same level in England as they did on the Continent, where fiscal and mercantile exploitation provoked not riots but rebellions. This was partly due to the fact that, London apart, most English towns were dwarfed by their European contemporaries. Nevertheless, the tension was there. English towns entered the fourteenth century under economic and social stress. That century was to offer them new opportunities as the cloth industry revived and new challenges as plague and demographic decline led to a contraction in the size of the market they served.

5 Supplying the Market

In the modern sense there was no growth in the thirteenth-century English economy. That it expanded is nevertheless surely beyond doubt, which meant an increased demand for goods and services at all levels. Urban development was both a response and a stimulus to rising consumption, whilst the general opening up of European trade offered both new markets for English merchants and a whole new range of imports, from raw materials to costly silks and spices. Demand for industrial products could no longer be met from purely local resources. There were areas where industry and agriculture were combined, sometimes on quite a large scale, but, at this stage, production was at its most efficient when concentrated in towns. Townsmen had the capital to invest, the time to organize the purchase of raw materials, to supervise the work force and to sell the finished goods. Both trade and handicraft production increasingly became the prerogative of the towns in the thirteenth century – until, that is, the lure of cheap labour in the countryside overcame its other disadvantages.

How adequately was this new demand met? The thirteenth century has been called the century of both industrial and commercial revolution. If either were the case, then the argument previously advanced that there were no real changes in the fundamental structure of the English economy would have to be substantially modified. But to justify either term one would need a considerable amount of information which does not, alas, exist. There are no figures for the gross national product in these centuries – although some reasonable estimates can be made about the productivity and profitability of the agrarian sector of the economy, thanks to the survival of the records of lay and ecclesiastical estates. There are no account books of Southampton wine importers or Forest of Dean iron makers or, rather, they have not survived. Pardoxically, we know more of the methods and profits of

Italian than of English merchants, and the discovery of one or two sets of accounts of an English trader or craftsman might well revolutionize our ideas on their operations and their commercial competence. Even the magnificent series of customs' accounts, unparalleled elsewhere in Europe, only begin towards the end of the thirteenth century and will tell us little at this stage about anything except raw wool exports. The evidence has to be taken obliquely from sources never intended to provide information for economic analysis, but rather to list how much cloth the king's household bought and whence it came; to record the gathering of taxes and the settlement of disputes between party and party or the enactment of urban bye-laws. Unsatisfactory it may be, uneven in coverage, but it will at least allow us to see some broad outlines of the way in which industry and trade met the demands made on them.

One myth at least can be rapidly dispelled, that commercial and industrial expansion were severely hampered by inadequacies in transport and communications. There are no signs at all that this was the case. By the thirteenth century England's road system was well established, with London at its centre. Main routes led to Exeter, Bristol, St David's in South Wales and to Carlisle in the North. From them other roads ran to connect York, Lincoln, Norwich, Leicester and Chester both to London and to each other. The growth of trade through the Channel Ports and Southampton meant the development of new roads from them to London and, in the case of Southampton, to the Midlands, whilst around each town there existed local roads connecting it to the surrounding villages. Along these roads passed a whole variety of traffic, on pack horses or, more often, in two-wheeled carts. Cattle and grain were sent to market, wine in great barrels of up to 252 gallons was distributed to the royal and other households, wool was sent from the West Midlands to the East Coast ports for export to Flanders and lead from Derbyshire to Boston. The royal household and royal officials passed ceaselessly over these roads in all weathers and an energetic rider could travel from London to York in five days. Of course they were poor by modern standards, but the roads were capable of bearing a relatively heavy volume of traffic. Nor was land transport quite as expensive as is often made out. In 1278 the royal household's baggage had to be moved from Rhuddlan to Macclesfield via Chester, about 70 miles in all. It was carried in carts drawn by two horses at the rate of 6d. per day per cart. In other cases 3d.–4d. per day was charged, and where goods were sent by common carrier the cost was about 3½d.

151

per ton mile, the carrier taking legal responsibility for the goods and their loading and unloading. At these rates, in the mid-fourteenth century wool could be carried over a distance of 50 miles at about 1.5 per cent of the value of the cargo and grain at about 15 per cent. This was by no means prohibitive, although it did mean that any goods manufactured for sale either nationally or for export would have to be of sufficient value to bear the freight costs.

Wherever possible water transport was used, however, because it was so much cheaper for bulk cargoes. Indeed, good river communications could bring economic success to a town. More and more goods were being moved long and short distances up and down rivers and across the sea. It was in the thirteenth century that the trade in sea coal from Newcastle and wine from Bordeaux to London expanded rapidly. Costs were not great. Roomy, single-masted ships called cogs, high-sided and rounded at stem and stern, could carry up to about 100 tuns of wine (252 gallons each) from Bordeaux to Hull or Ireland for about 18s. per tun, or slightly less than 10 per cent of the freight-on-board price at Bordeaux. It was as cheap in the South East to import timber from the Baltic as it was to bring it from the North West and the Midlands. Perhaps the greatest step forward in the thirteenth century was the opening up of the sea route from the Mediterranean to northern waters. Flanders was at first the chief goal but by the 1270s and 1280s Genoese galleys were calling at London and Sandwich, exchanging cargoes of alum for wool. The real significance of this development might lie in the future, but the linking of northern and southern Europe by sea is symptomatic of the general improvement in communications in the thirteenth century. Had there been large-scale industrial growth, then transport might not have been able to meet the demands placed upon it without significant advances. But all the evidence suggests that road, river and sea transport were more than able to cope in terms of cost and capacity.

If there were restraints on industrial production, then, they were caused by factors other than transport. Before discussing them, however, it is necessary to establish the nature of industry in thirteenth-century England. For the purposes of argument only it is convenient to consider manufacturing under two headings, large- and small-scale, that is, industries which were large either in scale or unit of production or in geographical distribution, and those handicraft occupations which, although widely spread, were organized in small units of production. The distinction is modern and artificial. Nowhere in the

Middle Ages were the lines of demarcation sharply drawn. At one and the same time in one and the same town it is possible to find in the cloth industry large-scale capitalist entrepreneurs working alongside artisan weavers making and selling one or two pieces of cloth a year. They might regard themselves as equals, but to our eyes they appear very different in both social status and economic organization and are treated as such here.

There were probably five large-scale industries, the manufacture of cloth, building in stone, the extraction of metallic and non-metallic ores and metal working, salt production and sea fishing. Of these, the most highly organized, to the extent that they might be called capitalist in nature, were cloth making, building and certain sections of the mining industry. Cloth making was to be found everywhere in the medieval world, in town and country alike. Certain areas, such as the Flemish towns, had specialized in the industry from the eleventh century onwards. At the beginning of the thirteenth century the English industry seemed to be developing along similar lines. Supplies of the essential raw materials – wool, fuller's earth and teasels – abounded and cloth manufacture was widespread. Its centre lay in the towns of the East Anglian plain specializing in fine quality cloths, Beverley, Lincoln, Stamford and Northampton. Cloth of lesser quality was made at York, Louth and Leicester, and every town of any size from Oxford to Exeter, London to Gloucester had its own branch of the industry. There were country cloth workers too. Newcastle merchants in the reign of Henry I and Shrewsbury merchants in the reign of Henry II were able to buy country cloth for dyeing. Not only was the home market supplied by these towns but fine quality cloths were exported in some quantities. English 'Stamfords' were well known in Genoa by 1200 and from there went to places as far distant as Sicily, whilst some Spanish merchants were robbed by pirates off the coast of Norfolk of cloths of scarlet and other cloths from Stamford, Beverley, York, Lincoln, Northampton and Louth.

The widespread production of cloth was due in part to growing demand, national and international, but also to the fact that by its very nature the industry could be organized on a large scale. In no other medieval product were so many different processes, carried on by different people in different places, involved. First the wool was sorted into various grades, cleansed of all foreign matter, washed to remove the grease and beaten to open up its texture to improve its felting properties. These basic preparatory processes were often carried out in

153

the countryside and washed wool fetched a higher price than unwashed. The wool was next made ready for spinning into yarn by carding or combing. Combs were wooden instruments with long metal teeth, cards wooden boards with short wire hooks. Both produced a fluffy mass which could then be turned into yarn, but combing was held to produce the stronger thread suitable for the warp yarn. Spinning was invariably done by women, using the distaff and spindle. The wool was first oiled, then placed on the distaff and from there drawn and twisted into a continuous thread. Although the spinning wheel was introduced in the thirteenth century, its use did not apparently become widespread until the later Middle Ages. It was more productive than the distaff and spindle, but the latter method could be combined with other tasks. If the wool was to be dyed in the yarn, it then went to the dyers. Otherwise it passed to the next group of workers, the weavers. The weft thread was wound on to the shuttle, whilst the warp thread, doubled up for extra strength, was attached to the warp beam of the loom.

The looms themselves deserve careful attention. It was their introduction which allowed the production of long pieces of tightly woven cloth and considerably increased the productivity of manpower. The loom of classical antiquity was simply an upright frame from which the warp threads hung down, weighted by stones or other heavy objects. It produced a cloth of poor quality and open weave and only as big as the frame itself. By the thirteenth century the flat bed loom was in widespread use in Western Europe. It consisted of a horizontal frame, supported on four uprights. At one end there was the warp beam, a cylinder around which the stronger warp threads were wound. At the other, in front of the weaver, was another roller on which the cloth was wound as the weaver finished each section. Pedals beneath the loom worked the shed mechanism which raised and lowered alternative warp threads, whilst the weaver passed the shuttle with the weft threads from side to side. On this loom a whole variety of cloths could be woven. Width could be varied. The standard English broadcloth was approximately 24 yards long by $1\frac{1}{2}$–2 yards wide, but half-size cloths, streits, were also made. Different qualities of cloth could be woven, according to the fineness and tightness of the weave. The loom was very flexible and its existence made volume production possible.

Once woven, the cloth was washed again and then fulled – placed in troughs filled with water and fuller's earth or alum and either pounded by the feet of the fullers or beaten with water-powered paddles, in order to thicken and felt the cloth. It was then rinsed again, dried and finished. A nap was raised on the cloth by brushing it with spiky teasel heads and shorn with large shears to produce a smooth finish. The more times it was sheared, the finer the finish. This is why the highest quality cloths were known as scarlets, not because of their red colour, but because they had been well sheared (eskalata). The cloth, which had certainly shrunk in the course of all these processes, was pulled back into shape by being stretched on a wall frame lined with tenterhooks. It could then be sold or sent for dyeing in a whole variety of colours using many different substances. Dyeing was a skilled job. The cloth had to be soaked in large vats which were constantly stirred with long poles. It was almost invariably a male occupation. Once dried the cloth was ready for sale and, because of its relatively high value, could be sold in distant markets at sufficient price to cover transport costs.

The later history of the industry suggests that it was possible for a family concern to undertake most of the processes, except perhaps the finishing, without using many looms but by keeping one or two in continuous production.[1] A considerable amount of working capital would have to be employed, tied up in stocks of wool and yarn, cloth on the looms, at the finishers and at the market or in the warehouse waiting to be sold. But quite clearly, by the thirteenth century a widespread division of labour had taken place. The urban industry seems to have been controlled by the merchant entrepreneur, who employed capital by supplying various groups of specialists with raw materials and semi-finished cloth. They worked for him, usually at piece rates, spinning, weaving and finishing, passing back to him the finished broadcloth, which he then sold. This allowed much larger-scale production, which helped keep down costs. These capitalist entrepreneurs seem to have emerged at Leicester from the ranks of the dyers, for they had to be not only highly skilled artisans, but merchants as well. They had to buy the dyestuffs and that meant extensive dealings with alien merchants, for most of the vegetable and animal substances used came from abroad. Woad, the basic blue dye also used as a foundation for other colours, did grow in this country. But, by the twelfth century there were considerable imports from northern France. By 1237 Picard woad merchants had secured privileges which allowed them to warehouse their goods in London, to sell there to strangers or citizens and carry their woad out of the city to such parts of the country as they pleased. Madder, too, producing one of the many shades of red, was both grown in this country and imported from other parts of Western Europe. Other dyes came from further afield. Brasil was made

155

from the bark of the East Indian Sappan tree, vermilion, a crystalline substance, was found on the shores of the Red Sea, and the richest and most expensive dyestuff of all, grain, yielding a deep scarlet colour, was made from the dried bodies of an insect found on the Spanish oak. Not only the dyestuffs came from abroad, so did the mordants for fixing them. Most commonly used was potash, or ashes produced from wood fires. These could be had in England but more and more were imported from the Baltic. For the finest scarlets alum was required. This mineral substance, a sulphate of aluminium and potassium, came mostly from the shores of the Black Sea and increasingly from the late thirteenth century, from the Genoese mines of Phocea in the Gulf of Smyrna.

The dyers, then, had to deal with aliens for their raw materials and their mercantile status is reflected at Leicester and in other towns by their membership of the gild merchant, from which artisans were increasingly excluded. Indeed, partly in self protection, one suspects, weavers and to a lesser extent fullers, tried to form their own gilds. Close royal control over towns in the twelfth century allowed the weavers and fullers to ignore civic authorities and buy privileges from the king. In 1130 a gild of fullers existed at Winchester and there were weavers' gilds at London, Lincoln, Oxford, Winchester and Huntingdon. Weavers' gilds also appeared later in the twelfth century at York and Nottingham, and at Leicester attempts were made to form one throughout the thirteenth century. These gilds may have given the artisans some protection, most notably the sole right of members to engage in the craft within the town. But this was small relief when they were increasingly excluded from the town's retail trade. They would be forced more and more into dependence on the merchant dyers, members of the gild merchant and the town's ruling class. The Leicester evidence is quite clear. By the mid-thirteenth century the court rolls show that there had emerged, probably from the dyers, a class of entrepreneurs. They employed the artisan weavers and fullers, controlled the whole production of cloth and sold the finished or semi-finished bolts at the East Anglian fairs of Boston and St Ives.

At the beginning of the thirteenth century this urban industry flourished. By its end it appeared to be in very considerable difficulties. The signs are obvious and start early in the century. By 1202 the York weavers were finding it difficult to pay their annual farm of £10 to the king for their privileges and by 1214 they were £60 in arrears. The Winchester weavers also defaulted in 1198 and 1202, perhaps because they had been compelled by Henry II to double their farm. As the century progressed, so the urban industry's difficulties increased. It would be wrong to overstate the case. Cloth was still being bought for Henry III's household from London, Beverley, York and Leicester, scarlets from Stamford were still being exported. But weavers were finding life in towns more and more difficult. By 1309 the York gild owed the Crown £790 and the farm of the Oxford gild was cut in 1275 because the number of weavers had fallen from 60 to 15. By 1290 there were only 7, by 1323 it was alleged that all were dead and without successors. The number of looms in London had fallen from 380 to 80 in 1321, there were no fullers in Leicester by 1322, the Lincoln weavers had ceased to pay their farm by 1321 and disappeared completely in the following decade. At the same time there is increasing evidence of the strength of rural industry. The royal household began to buy cloth from smaller centres like Cricklade, High Wycombe and Totnes. Whilst the York industry declined, cloth was being made in a whole series of surrounding villages, Otley, Leeds, Pickering, Shipton, Alton, North-allerton, Knaresborough, Guisborough and Whitby. Before the end of the century rural cloth making was to be found in Kent, Oxfordshire, East Anglia, Gloucestershire and Lancashire. The country seemed to be prospering at the expense of the town.

Why? It used to be argued that the growth of the rural industry was simply the result of a massive relocation from town to countryside.[2] The catalyst was supposed to be the widespread introduction of the water-powered fulling mill, which, it was said, stimulated an industrial revolution in the thirteenth century. Introduced to England at some time in the late eleventh or the twelfth century, the fulling mill was a mechanized device whereby a waterwheel drove paddles or hammers to beat cloths lying in the troughs filled with water and fuller's earth. Foot power was now replaced by water and costs were reduced since mechanical effort was substituted for human labour. As a result there was a relocation of industry to areas where water power was abundant, to 'the clear swift streams of the North and West, in remote valleys far beyond the bounds of the ancient chartered cities of the plain'. Around the new mills grew up colonies of weavers and by the end of the century the industry was carried on at the rural mill rather than in the urban home. It was dependent as never before on considerable capital equip-ment and was passing out of the system of gild control.

This is a simple, seductive theory, almost syren-like in its emphasis on the virtues of water power. Unfortunately there are almost as many objections to it as there were fulling mills in thirteenth-century England. In the first place rural industry was to be found everywhere, not simply in the North and West with their swift clear waters, but in East Anglia, for example, where fast streams scarcely abound. Fulling mills could be built in towns, at Salisbury for instance or by the castle at Oxford. Most towns had their own corn mills and the water used to drive the one could as well be used to drive the other. It may well be that only great lords like the bishop of Winchester, the Templars or the abbot of St Albans had the capital necessary for investment in such mills. If so, then they were likely to site them on manors where weavers already existed, as the bishop of Winchester did at Witney and Taunton. It was not, then, a case of taking men from the town, but of setting up in direct competition to it. One may be sure, too, that landlords who had sunk capital into mills expected a reasonable return from them and in some cases compelled their tenants to use them as part of their manorial monopoly. Given this, the savings from the use of mechanical fulling were not likely to have been very great. In any case, later evidence suggests that fulling accounted for only 7–12 per cent of manufacturing costs, compared with at least 30–40 per cent for weaving and spinning.

Yet the evidence still suggests an active, if not flourishing, rural industry whilst that in the towns declined. Indeed, urban entrepreneurs both used and encouraged country cloth making. Weavers at work in Banbury, Cowley and Islip around Oxford in 1275 asserted that their looms had been delivered to them by a little group of Oxford notables. Leicester merchants were alleged to have fulling mills outside the town in 1260, Lincoln merchants were buying country cloth for dyeing in 1300 and there was trouble at London over the use of fulling mills at Enfield and Stratford in 1298 and 1310. At the same time as they were using the rural industry, the urban capitalists were fighting the artisan gilds in the towns, trying to break their hold over wages and working conditions.[3] In early fourteenth-century London the employers accused the weavers of restricting output by reducing hours of work and the number of looms in use and using their gild to enforce these monopolies. The attacks on gilds at Leicester and Norwich have already been noted, and at Winchester in Edward I's reign the city government fixed weavers' wages. Taken together this evidence suggests that in an attempt to keep down costs the merchant entrepreneurs were engaged in a twofold policy of breaking artisan combinations in towns and using cheaper rural labour, not just for fulling but for spinning and weaving.

If this is so, then it presupposes that the manufacturers were facing increased competition and could only survive by slashing costs. That competition came, without any doubt, from the great Flemish industry which reached its zenith in the thirteenth century. Based on the towns of Bruges, Ghent, Arras and Cambrai and their numerous satellites, forming an urban complex far greater than anything in England and heavily capitalized, the industry drew its supplies of the main raw material, wool, from England. By the late thirteenth century England was exporting some 30,000 sacks of wool per annum to Flanders. In return, although statistical evidence is lacking, Flanders seems to have sent back large quantities of finished cloth. As early as the 1230s the royal household was purchasing substantial amounts of Flemish cloth, and from the 1240s the merchants of Ypres and Douai were leading suppliers to the Crown. By the time records of imports begin at the start of the fourteenth century aliens alone were importing 12,000 cloths a year. If the imports of English merchants could be calculated, the total would certainly be far higher. More cheaply produced Flemish cloth was swamping the home market and to survive the English manufacturer had to try in all ways possible to cut costs. The simplest way was to use the cheap, unregulated labour increasingly available in the countryside. But the decline of the industry in so many English towns by the end of the thirteenth century suggests that it was in a parlous condition, a fact to be remembered in any assessment of the thirteenth-century economy.

In sharp contrast, the stone building industry experienced two centuries of almost unbroken boom. The majority of buildings in the Middle Ages were timber framed, infilled with wattle and daub. Only the houses of the rich were built of stone, along with parish churches and in towns perhaps the gild or market hall and, where they existed, the walls. A small force of masons would be all that was required for such work, even on town walls which usually took many years to complete. The masons' main source of employment was in the building and rebuilding of the multitude of cathedrals, monasteries and castles to be found all over the country. There were in England and Wales between 900 and 1,000 monastic establishments and collegiate churches, most of which were built of stone. Continually through the Middle Ages they were improved, expanded, taken down and re-erected. The abbey church at Meaux (Holderness) was built anew three times in 50 years in the late twelfth and early thirteenth centuries and there were three Salisbury Cathedrals between 1075 and the erection of the present building which began in 1220. Sometimes the rebuilding was necessary because the previous structure had collapsed. It is too easily forgotten that what survives today is the best and strongest. Then as now there were poor architects and bad workmen, and not everything was built to last. The west tower of Gloucester Abbey collapsed at the end of the twelfth century 'through default of foundation' as did the central tower of Winchester in 1107 for like cause. Such occurrences were not uncommon and they all provided work for the masons. So did castle building which went on almost ceaselessly between the Norman Conquest and the Welsh and Scottish wars of Edward I. When not building castle or cathedral, there were always the parish churches or the local bridge to be enlarged or improved.

These building operations absorbed a great deal of time and money and, on occasion, a very large labour force which required a high degree of organization. By contemporary standards capital inputs were high. The construction of Vale Royal Abbey (Cheshire) cost £1,500 in the three years 1278–80 and the king spent £14,000 in 1291 on the building of Caernarvon, Conway and Harlech castles. Caernarvon Castle cost in all £20,000 to build whilst by 1330 £14,400 had been spent on the great castle at Beaumaris on the Isle of Anglesey which was never completed. The numbers of men required for these enterprises are equally impressive. At one point 400 masons, 30 smiths and carpenters and 1,000 unskilled workers were employed in the construction of Beaumaris. Admittedly this was during a period of exceptional activity. Military needs were pressing, the building season in North Wales was short (April–November) and large numbers of men were required because of the relatively simple gear and tackle used in lifting and handling stone. Nevertheless, there were as many men working on Beaumaris as there were people in a small English country town in the period.

Such building operations required skilful organization and there were basically two ways in which this might be achieved. Where construction of a cathedral, abbey or other building proceeded only slowly, a small, semi-permanent labour force would be employed, a more or less regular staff of artisans under the direction of a master mason and a master carpenter. Financial control was in the hands of a monastic or collegiate official, usually the sacrist or the custos fabricae. To him would be assigned the revenues of specific estates to pay for the works. But construction of large buildings usually fluctuated between periods of quiescence and vigorous activity, which would require many more men than the permanent staff could provide. On such occasions they might be replaced or supplemented by the second method, the ad hoc organization set up for the erection of a specific building or a part of it. In charge of the financial side there would be a master or clerk of the works, whose duties included the payment of wages and the provision of workmen and materials. The actual works would be directed by the master mason, who may also have been the architect. Such men might be in charge of one building only. The king's works were probably exceptional in that there were at any one time many of them and there was a need for one man to have a general oversight. By the mid-thirteenth century some form of centralized control was emerging, under the direction of the king's mason. The first was Master Henry, from 1243 onwards, succeeded by Master John of Gloucester (1254–61) and Master Robert of Beverley (1262–80), whilst in the 1290s the Savoyard, Master James of St George, had general supervision of the building of Edward I's Welsh castles. Under these men, on each site, there would be a master mason, either drawing up or following the plans given him. He would control the work force, which was made up of a bewildering variety of masons and labourers employed at either day wage or piece rates.

The most skilled were the free masons who cut and set the intricate free stone mouldings for arches and windows. Other free masons of lesser skill would cut the straight mouldings and prepare the ordinary square ashlar stones, quadrangular blocks laid in regular double courses which were infilled with rubble. There was in fact little difference between the bottom ranks of the free masons and the top ranks of the next group, the rough masons. They both worked up some of the rougher stone, partly cut in the quarries, and placed in position the stones worked by the free masons. On the bottom rung were the rough layers or hard hewers who undertook the rough shaping of the blocks and were often found working in the quarries which both supplied the semi-finished stones and served as a training ground for masons. Beneath them were the labourers, totally unskilled and usually recruited locally.

The variety of skills is reflected in the variety of rates of pay. Generalization is very difficult. At Caernarvon Castle in October 1316 the highest-paid mason received 33d. per week, the lowest layer 14d. Wages also varied from winter to summer, since on average $8\frac{3}{4}$ hours per day were worked in the former compared to $12\frac{1}{2}$ in the latter, allowing time for meal breaks and a rest in the afternoon. Holidays (literally Holy Days, Saints' Days) were frequent. There were 27 at Vale Royal in 1279 and 22 in 1280 but they were a mixed blessing since the masons received no wages on those days. On remote sites and even on major works within towns, working and living accommodation had to be provided. Lodges were erected which sometimes served both purposes, sometimes acted only as workshops, with separate buildings for sleeping. The basic tools were also provided, but the masons were generally expected to use their own trowels, squares, plumbs, rules and axes.

Masons were consistently amongst the highest paid of all artisans, earning far more than the agricultural labourer. Their life was hard, however. Employment fluctuated; as today, when one job finished the man moved on to the next. It was probably essential to combine the craft with a small, free agricultural holding, to support the family in slack periods and long absences. The very mobility of the industry and the constantly fluctuating labour force militated against any form of gild organization or apprenticeships. Training seems to have been on the job, with the man moving from one grade to another as his skills progressed. Supply of masons, although it expanded in the thirteenth century, never quite kept up with the voracious demand. So, when the Crown wanted a job done quickly, it simply ordered the impressment of masons who might be sent from one end of the country to the other. Much as today, high pay was combined with uncertainty of employment and, voluntarily or involuntarily, long periods away from home.

The erection of a large building had economic implications far beyond the employment of masons, however. The workers had to be fed, for instance, and the effects of that on a town like Salisbury must have been considerable. More than that, a whole range of raw materials had to be obtained. Stone is the most obvious. There were certain areas where quarrying became a specialized industry; Barnack in Northamptonshire was one, supplying stone to Crowland, Ramsey, Peterborough and other East Anglian houses. Purbeck specialized in a type of limestone 'marble' and considerable amounts of stone were imported from Caen in Normandy, especially for the building of St Alban's Abbey and St Paul's. Transport costs were high. Winning stone from the quarry cost about 2d. a cubic foot (about 155 lb in weight). Carriage at the rate of 2d. per ton mile meant that for a distance of about twelve miles transport costs would be about equivalent to the cost of the stone itself. Small wonder then that wherever possible local quarries were used or new ones opened up, like those which supplied Chester with its soft red sandstone. Little capital was required, since tools were primitive, consisting mainly of bars, wedges and axes for splitting and shaping the stone. It was often hewed roughly to size before being sent to the site, and the nearer the quarry to the building the better. Even so, carting the stone frequently required large numbers of men at no little expense. Between 30 and 40 men were employed at Vale Royal from 1278 to 1280 to cart 35,000 loads of stone a distance of 4–5 miles. The quarriers who cut the stone in those years were paid £104 in all, the carters £347.

In addition to stone, timber was needed in large quantities for scaffolding and roofs, lime had to be burnt for mortar, sand supplied, glass made for windows, iron purchased for cramps, nails, locks and door fittings, smiths employed to work the iron and sharpen the masons' tools. If any industry was organized on a capitalist basis in the Middle Ages, surely it was stone building. Large sums of money were involved, there was a high degree of division of labour and specialization and the industry stimulated a host of other trades and occupations. And yet one can doubt whether its development was entirely beneficial to medieval society. No new techniques appeared. Stones were still laboriously split by hand in the quarries and worked up on the site. There are some signs of the emergence of standard sizes and patterns for mouldings, but little else. More than that, the diversion of so much money into building must have caused a shortage of capital elsewhere, with potentially serious consequences for the medieval economy.

Mining and metal working were almost as widespread as building in stone. Before considering the organization of the industry, it is necessary to establish what was mined and where. Best known of all was tin, in the Stannaries of Devon and Cornwall. It had been mined there since antiquity. At the beginning of the thirteenth century production was concentrated on west Devon but during the century there was a rapid shift to east Cornwall. In 1220 the Devon Stannaries were farmed for 200 marks (£133.13s.4d.) by the Crown, those of Cornwall for 1,000, a lead which was never again lost. Tin was used extensively in the manufacture of pewter, becoming increasingly popular in the thirteenth century, in founding bells, where it was mixed with copper, in building for soldering lead plumbing and guttering and in jewellery. A great deal went for export, to pewter manufacturers in Germany and France and to the Mediterranean world, the Italians being particularly prominent exporters. In the early fourteenth century 560–817,000 lbs were being presented annually for coinage, that is for taxation.[4]

Iron was more widely mined, and used in all forms of tools and agricultural implements, nails, hinges, bars and locks and, when further worked up into steel, for weapons. Although mining was widespread, certain principal areas can be defined. First there was the Forest of Dean and Gloucestershire, probably the most productive area of all. In AD 1188 Giraldus Cambrensis described the forest as abounding in iron and deer. There were large royal forges at work in Henry II's reign. Technically there could be no forge without royal licence, both so that the Crown might profit from the industry and also to preserve woodland. Between 40 and 60 forges were working in the forest in the 1270s and 1280s and the industry had also spread into other parts of Gloucestershire and Wales, particularly Glamorgan. In the North mining and smelting were carried on extensively. Between Sheffield and Bingley and Leeds the clay ironstone of the coal measures was mined. It had more impurities than the brown haematite of Dean, but its manganese content made a harder iron. Iron working had long been established here, but the real expansion came in the later twelfth century, being particularly associated with the arrival of the new monastic orders. On the other side of the Pennines in Cumberland and Lancashire there were extensive workings of red haematite, a rich ore, especially around Carlisle and in Furness. Again, monastic houses were heavily involved. Back in the North East there were iron workings in the Forest of Pickering and the Cleveland Hills and in Northumberland around Alnwick. Finally, there was the South East. The Sussex Weald is probably the best known of all iron mining areas but surprisingly there is little evidence of the industry in the thirteenth century. It does, however, seem to have been growing rapidly. Wealden iron was sent to the Tower from 1253 onwards and by 1300 it had won a footing in the London market, for we hear of the London ironmongers complaining that the rods brought to the city by Wealden smiths were too short.

Lead was mined as extensively as tin, and used for similar purposes in pewter manufacture and for roofs, gutters and pipes. It was found in three main areas, the Mendips, the High Peak in Derbyshire and Alston Moor in Cumberland. In the Mendips mining was controlled by the bishop of Bath and Wells, in the High Peak and Alston Moor by the Crown which leased out the workings. A great deal also went for export, especially to France where it was used in the construction of great cathedrals. Lead was found elsewhere but usually, as at Alston Moor, as a by-product of silver. The most important silver mines were at Bere Alston in Devon. They were owned by the Crown and seem to have been discovered in the late thirteenth century. Between 1292 and 1297 they produced silver worth £4,041 and lead worth £360. Clearly, for a short time, they were a major source of precious metal.

Finally, there was coal. Without doubt there was an increase in coal production in the thirteenth century. It was used both for domestic fuel and for some industrial purposes, for limeburning and for drying and smoking fish. London was a major market, most coal being brought by sea from Newcastle, hence the name, sea coal. By the late thirteenth century there were many complaints about coal smoke corrupting the atmosphere, but sea coal was here to stay. Another reason for its name was that it was at first simply collected from the sea shore, where it had been deposited by river or sea. As demand grew, so mining developed, especially around Newcastle, Gateshead and Wickham. Coal was also dug in the West Riding of Yorkshire, in Nottinghamshire and Derbyshire and of course in the Forest of Dean where the digging was undertaken in a sporadic and small-scale way by peasant miners.

The real problem is in discovering not so much what was mined as the extent of production and the nature of the industry's organization. About tin we know a great deal and it is clear that there were strong elements of capitalism in the industry. At the lowest level the mining was undertaken by free miners who had been given rights by the Crown similar to those granted to the miners of Dean, the Peak and Alston Moor. In each case Crown demesnes and royal forests were extensive and the Crown had to choose the best way of exploiting its mineral rights. They could be leased out, but in the areas cited above it was decided that it would be more profitable to tax production and encourage it by protecting the rights of the free miners against those of the lords. The Stannaries are the best example of this. By the late twelfth century mining was already widespread, but the miners were not far removed from villein status, being subject to customary payments and services. Mining and agriculture were combined, but certain rights had grown up by custom, giving protection to miners, smelters and dealers. The most important of these rights was that of bounding, of searching for tin on any land, regardless of ownership. Effectively this meant that mineral rights did not go with the land. In 1198 the Crown began the formation of the Stannary organization and during the course of the thirteenth century there emerged an elaborate machinery of government with its own courts and officials separate from those of the county. The tinners (miners) were protected, they were removed from pleas of villein and they were exempt from normal taxation. In return the Crown took a tax on all tin produced. From 1198 a duty was paid at both the first rough and the second final smelting which had to be undertaken either at Exeter or Bodmin or other market towns specified by the warden of the Stannaries from year to year. Vastly increased income resulted. The Stannaries had been farmed for £100 in 1194: in 1198–9 the tin duty raised £601. The method of collecting the duty changed when new refining processes were introduced which allowed one smelting instead of two.[5] Block tin now had to be taken to specified towns on specified days. It would then be weighed and assayed by cutting off a corner (coign) hence the name given to the tax, coinage. The tinner was then issued with a certificate showing the weight of the block and coinage due, after which he could deliver the tin to the waiting merchants. Similarly in Dean, the High Peak and Alston Moor the king and other lords gave like privileges to miners in return for a fixed share of the proceeds.

In the Stannaries the basic unit of production might be small, the free tinner working on his own or with one or two others. The method of mining also seems to suggest that little was required in the way of capital. Essentially placer or surface deposits were exploited. The tinner would locate these and determine their quality and extent by sinking a series of trial shafts. A water course would be procured, to carry the water and the waste away from the workings. Water was crucial to this 'streaming'. It was sometimes used to remove the stones and earth lying over the deposits, always for sifting the heavier lumps of ore from the lighter waste. The ore could then be crushed for smelting. Finding a water course could, in fact, be expensive and as the surface deposits were exhausted, the tinners were forced to go deeper. Substantial works were involved and many labourers needed. Most of all, tin prospecting was a risky business, with no return on outlay until the tin was actually sold. Not unnaturally, the smaller tinners often ran short of money. A credit system rapidly emerged, stretching from the free tinner to the London and alien merchants who bought the tin. The latter advanced money to the merchant tinners, usually men of substance from the South West. They in turn loaned money on security of tin to the labouring tinners, nearly always at interest. In return the working tinner delivered black ore, crushed and ready for smelting, to the merchant tinner and he in turn supplied smelted tin, coinage paid, to the merchants. Merchant tinners had a tight grip on the industry. Between one- and two-thirds of all tin presented for coinage in Cornwall in the first decades of the fourteenth century was in the hands of only ten persons per annum. These men bought their way into associations of tinners, either as sleeping partners or through a tinner defaulting on his loan. Alternatively one partner in an association might gain exemption from working by making money payments or by hiring a deputy to labour for him. Consequently, by the early fourteenth century some substantial mining organizations had developed, controlled by merchant tinners owning shares in them, with access to mercantile capital, rather in the same way that the clothiers controlled the cloth industry.

Our knowledge of the working of other branches of mining and smelting is far more hazy. At first sight it would seem that little fixed capital was required. Most mining was to a shallow depth only. Surface beds of iron, lead or coal were worked either open cast or at the most by bell pits. These had a very narrow mouth, about five feet in diameter, and opened outwards beneath the surface where the ore or coal was cut away to a diameter of about 12 feet at the bottom. When drainage became a problem the pit was abandoned and a new one started. Mine workings were dangerous areas and the approach to Newcastle after dark was said in 1256 to be perilous because of abandoned coal pits. Occasionally shafts were driven into the side of hills, with connecting tunnels to lead the water away. But deep mines, which posed formidable problems of drainage and ventilation, were rare. Smelting took place near where the ore was mined. Moving heavy ore in bulk would have been expensive and most mines were in forest areas where there was a plentiful supply of the fuel needed, charcoal. In iron production, and probably for other metals, the most common form of forge or smelting hearth was the bloomery. The ore was mixed with charcoal and covered with more fuel held in position by layers of stones. The hearth was usually sited on a slope against the prevailing wind, so that a draught could be introduced by a duct to increase the heat at the centre of the molten mass. Alternatively hand bellows could produce a forced draught. The mass of ore, or bloom, was worked or moved during smelting by iron bars. This brought closer contact between the ore and the incandescent charcoal, helped the bloom to coalesce and kept the blast hole open. The bloom of metal so produced by the first smelting then had to be reworked on a similar type of furnace, sometimes called a stringhearth, both to consolidate it and to remove the slag. In iron working it was split at the end of the process, to test the quality of the metal, and then sold to the smiths for working up.

167

It was a crude process which required little in the way of capital costs. When ore deposits or fuel supplies were exhausted the miner/smelter simply moved on. But output was low. An itinerant bloomery in Cumberland, working not seasonally, as was common, but throughout the year, produced 1 ton 14 cwt of iron from $14\frac{1}{2}$ tons of ore. Where forges were fixed and more substantial output was a little better, $2\frac{1}{2}$ tons a year at Tudeley in Kent in the early fifteenth century, for example. The only real way in which output could be increased was by the use of more advanced technology – water-driven bellows. These produced a fiercer draught and a single smelting. A bellows forge at Byrkeknott (Weardale) produced 18 tons 8 cwt in 1408–9, a clear indication of what limited technical advance could achieve. But it required capital, for water wheels were expensive. Was it forthcoming? Evidence is scant but it would seem not. In the North at least, great landlords, especially ecclesiastical landlords, did have mining interests. The abbeys of Jervaulx, Rievaulx, Fountains and Byland all had working forges in the twelfth century. They could either operate them themselves or lease them out at what look like attractive rents. An ironmaster paid £25 rent for a smelting forge at Blubberhouses for the year 1258–9. In the same year another master paid £10 for a forge at Henkstank which was only in blast for 20 weeks and a third £17.18s.0d. for a forge which worked for only $13\frac{1}{2}$ weeks. Furness Abbey drew no less than one-sixth of its temporalities from mining revenues in 1292, which was probably exceptional. But this is not to say that landlords invested heavily in new and expensive forges. Income was for consumption, not investment, and it is likely that there was only a small spread of water power in thirteenth-century iron making.

The consequence was that total production was low. There were probably something like 350 iron works in Britain in the thirteenth century. Allowing an output of two to three tons per annum on average, annual production was in the range of 900–1,000 tons. The more efficient iron hearths in Styria produced 2,000 tons a year in the early fourteenth century. Yet there are no obvious signs of an iron shortage in the thirteenth century. Imports of superior grade iron ore from Spain, Normandy and Sweden were not great before 1300, although there do seem to have been imports of steel from Westphalia and France. It would seem that the English economy did not suffer as a result of limited production, but only because it was itself limited. In tin alone does there seem to have been large-scale capital investment, but that was more circulating than fixed, in order to improve productivity. The rise of Western capitalism was much tied up with the development of mining and metallurgy but at this stage there seems to have been very limited capital investment in the English mining industry. Metal working itself seems to have been organized on a handicraft basis. There were smiths to be found in the Forest of Dean, where there was a notable armaments industry. Dean also supplied a considerable industry at Gloucester and Coventry, where metal working was more important than textile production at this point. There were smiths who did the rough shaping of iron, locksmiths, needlers, lorimers (makers of bits and spurs), marshalls (shoesmiths) and makers of cards and combs for the woollen industry. In both the Durham area and the Weald there were substantial metal working industries, supplying horseshoe nails, arrowheads, bars and anchors for royal ships, spades, picks and hatchets. Indeed smiths were to be found in most towns of any size, but we have little information on output or capital investment except that the latter does not seem to have been extensive. No really great metal working complexes emerged to rival those of the Rhineland or Westphalia.

Two other industries were widely distributed geographically, the manufacture of salt and sea fishing. Salt was a vital element in the medieval diet and was used both in cooking and in the preservation of meat, fish, cheese and butter. Salterns were to be found all round the coast between Lincolnshire and Cornwall, producing salt by evaporation from sea water, with heavy concentrations in Kent, Sussex, Lincolnshire and Norfolk. By the early fourteenth century the East Coast predominated, supplying the home market and probably providing nearly all of the considerable exports of salt in these years, Lincolnshire taking first place. This was possibly due to the expansion of the East Coast fishing industry, which both stimulated the production of salt and led to the concentration on Lincolnshire: Norfolk salters were unable to withstand the competition of fishing interests for rights over the foreshore to stretch and dry nets and migrated to the neighbouring county. But there were other major salt producing areas. At Droitwich (Worcs) and Nantwich, Middlewich and Northwich in Cheshire brine from natural springs was boiled down to produce salt. The scale of the industry can be seen by the fact that Droitwich, created a borough in 1215, had a farm of no less than £100, the brine pits being communally managed by the burgesses. The salt was distributed at markets and fairs and along the ancient salt ways to Birmingham, to Wellington (Shropshire), Leominster (Herefordshire), Lechlade (Gloucs), south-eastward to Prince's Risborough and eastward to Coventry, Stratford and Prior's Marston.

Also very important, was sea fishing, about which almost equally little is known. Fish was a staple of medieval diet. Every river had its weirs and traps for all manner of fish and eels. In Domesday Book renders of herrings in tens of thousands point to a substantial industry on the East Coast in Suffolk, and in Sussex. Yarmouth is not mentioned, but sea fishing was clearly important there. By the thirteenth century the town was locked in combat with ships from the Cinque Ports over rights to dry nets on the shore and control of the great herring fair. A 'herring war' broke out, which led to both loss of life and damage to the rival fleets. Investment in the fishing industry seems to have been quite heavy: the Sussex ports alone spent £2,000 a year fitting out ships to participate in it. Elsewhere there was deep-sea cod fishing at Scarborough and Grimsby, extensive salmon fishing in Cumberland and everywhere along the coast mackerel, plaice, conger, turbot, dory and sole were caught. Even in London great nets of two inch might be used west of London Bridge all year and east of the Bridge between 2 February and 25 March. But, on balance, it is a pity that we know so little about the financing of and capital investment in sea fishing in the thirteenth century.

Such then were England's major industries. In many ways it is not a very encouraging picture. Cloth was in decline, metal production limited. Only building boomed and perhaps diverted capital from elsewhere. Was this necessarily bad? Industry does seem to have been able to cope with demand generally, but that merely reinforces the picture of an English economy failing to grow. Nor does capital seem to have been heavily employed in industry. There are as many views on the good or evil of capitalism as there are gods in the pantheon, but it does help to rationalize and increase production, thereby supplying more and cheaper goods. It seems reasonable to argue that greater capital investment might have preserved the English cloth industry and the jobs that went with it. It was not to England's greatest benefit to be an exporter of raw materials rather than finished goods. By the later thirteenth century large-scale investment might have pushed up iron production and stimulated industrial development in metal working, for instance. These are entirely speculative arguments, but it remains true that the English economy in the thirteenth century failed to develop large-scale industries and large towns. One caveat must be made, however. The information given here is selective and deals only with the best-known industries. Our knowledge of the diversity, structure and output of a whole range of both rural and urban handicrafts is very poor for the thirteenth century. Industry, for example, abounded in forest areas where raw materials were plentiful and pastoral agriculture and personal freedom allowed combination of occupations. Not only was there metal working, but a whole range of wood-based crafts, carpenters, coopers, fletchers, bowyers, wheelers and sawyers. Large numbers of trees were felled every year in the Forest of Dean; 935 oaks were cut and sold between 1275 and 1277, besides other trees. Glass making on a small scale was also found in Needwood and Inglewood Forests and the Weald, and there was also rope making from bark, and tanning for which oak bark was vital. But the extent to which these industries supplied anything more than local demand remains unknown.

Nor is our information on urban industry much better. Many lists of occupations exist, drawn from charters and other records. They show the diversity of employment and whether or not a town specialized in one particular branch of industry. These lists can help correct the notion that cloth necessarily reigned supreme. In many towns tanning and leather working were very important. Tanning was a noisome industry in which two different processes were employed. Ox, cow and calf hides were tanned by immersion, for up to a year, in a decoction of oak bark which contains tanin. Deer, sheep and horse skins were tawed in a solution of alum and salt. The two trades were kept firmly apart, each being forbidden to work the other's skins. Tanning required a quite heavy capital investment. The hides were easily acquired from the butchers, but fixed equipment – the large vats needed to soak the hides – was expensive and money was tied up in hides in the course of preparation and whilst waiting to be sold. Both tanning and tawing stimulated a whole range of other industries, shoemakers, saddlers, harness makers, leather clothing, gloves, purses and girdles, and this explains why, collectively, they were often more important than cloth. At York in Edward I's reign roughly 30 per cent of the admissions to freedom where occupations are given were of men in the leather trades, compared with 29 per cent in the food trades and 17 per cent in metal working. At the other end of the scale, in the new town of Stratford upon Avon, some of the occupations of the burgesses can be identified in the survey of 1251–2. Six were tanners, among them one of the wealthiest men in the town in terms of property, and there were also shoemakers, glovers and other leather workers. Leather production was probably never as great in volume as cloth, but it is worthy of more attention than it is often given.

For the rest, the lists of occupations show that a town like Gloucester specialized in textiles and metal working while in another, Worcester, there was no particular specialization at all. The textile industry was small and served only local needs. As was to be expected in a town with a large clerical and administrative population, service industries abounded – butchers and other victuallers, tailors and girdlers, parchment makers and so on. Enough has already been said about general occupations in towns to confirm the overwhelming impression that industry mostly served local needs. Beyond that it is not possible to go. Very little is known, either, about the size of the unit of production. Later evidence suggests that it consisted of the master craftsman, working with journeymen (qualified day wage workers) and apprentices serving variable terms. At this stage, however, most craft producers were not organized into highly structured craft gilds. The gild merchant remained the most important body in most towns since it conferred the right of freedom to trade. Only in London, with its vast range of occupations, did individual trade and craft (manufacturing) gilds begin to appear. The years 1263–1307 saw the rise of the companies in London, the fishmongers, skinners, cordwainers, corders, butchers, mercers, goldsmiths, wool packers, joiners, and Edward I used these men in his attack on the old patricians. By the early fourteenth century they were replacing them and themselves becoming the patrician class. This is not to say that elsewhere craft producers did not work under control. They did, but to standards laid down by the town as a body, not by a single craft. Formal gild regulation of urban industry was very much a feature of the later Middle Ages.

What was made or imported had to be distributed and this was the function of towns and markets, as has already been seen. Most trade was strictly local, most traders, whatever they called themselves, were general dealers rather than specialists. But in thirteenth-century England the long-range trade in three particular commodities, grain, wine and wool, developed or expanded rapidly. The grain trade has two aspects, the purely local which has already been discussed, and the national and international. Grain now began to be moved over long distances, by boat down the Severn for instance, by the Great and Little Ouse to Lynn and thence to London or to Berwick, Scotland, Flanders Zeeland and Brabant, to Gascony which had begun to concentrate on viticulture in exchange for corn and to Norway, whose people lived by fishing and forestry. Specialist merchants began to emerge, the corn-mongers who engaged in the regular day-to-day trade in grain, mostly over short distances, and the corn brokers who arranged deals between merchants. Some were drawn from the countryside, disposing of the surplus crops of the local villages, but increasingly they came from the towns. The best evidence comes from the biggest market, London. By the thirteenth century London's demand for corn had led to the development of a class of middlemen wholesale dealers, supplying not only the capital but Gascony and other areas. In 1300 there were at least 38 men operating in the wholesale trade. These cornmongers or bladers were members of substantial families, often those who had moved into London from East Anglia. They traded on a large scale, victualling both the royal household and the royal armies. That was a major enterprise, particularly in the latter part of the century during Edward I's wars with Wales, France and Scotland. Vast quantities of wheat and oats had to be purveyed (that is, taken by the Crown with a promise of future payment) and shipped abroad or to the North. In the spring of 1296 13,500 quarters of wheat and 13,000 quarters of oats were sent to France and in the next year there were substantial shipments to Gascony and from 1297 to 1307 to the armies in Scotland. Supplying the royal household was one of the ways country merchants were drawn into London. Similarly, Londoners who had connections with the East Coast ports were drawn into the grain trade. Thus it was that the fishmongers, with extensive contacts at Yarmouth and Lynn, came to dominate the London grain trade and prospered from it greatly.

The wine trade, too, produced its specialists. It has already been seen that wine was distributed chiefly through London, Boston, Hull, Bristol, Chester and Southampton, which virtually lived off the trade at this point. Naturally enough, a class of merchants, the vintners, soon evolved to handle the distributive side of the trade. That was only to be expected at London, given the presence of the royal and other great households, and wine imports were substantial. In 1300–1, a bad year, the city handled 3,600 tuns of Gascon wine, twice as much as Boston, Bristol or Sandwich and three times as much as Southampton. On average, in the early fourteenth century, a quarter of the country's annual imports of 20,000 tuns came through London, but the main importers at this stage were Gascons rather than Englishmen. This was also true outside London. Alien merchants dominated the trade through Southampton, although some room was left for native merchants like the Fleming family who used their own ships in ventures to Gascony. The north of the country was supplied through Hull, where the trade was evenly divided between Gascons and men from Hull itself. The distributive trade was, of course, almost entirely in English hands and vintners were to be found as early as the twelfth century in towns like York and Reading where there were important households.

The trade in corn and wine was clearly important and considerable sums of money were involved. But they begin to show a pattern in English trade that was not altogether healthy for what was supposed to be a developing economy. Exports were very much primary products and a large share of English foreign trade was in alien hands. The history of the wool trade in the twelfth and thirteenth centuries shows how true this analysis is. The main market lay in Flanders. Here there was a great urban industry, based on large towns where industrial production could be concentrated and easily controlled. Population expansion also forced the pace of industrialization for local food supplies were soon unable to meet urban demands and cloth had to be exchanged for grain. The industry began to need high quality wool to make the high quality cloth which would bear the cost of transportation. By the 1180s wool exports from England were expanding. English wool had become so essential to the Flemish industry that both King Richard and King John were able to use it as a diplomatic lever in their struggles with France, for Flanders was a French fief. Although Flemish merchants gained important privileges in England, there were frequent interruptions in the trade because of disputes with France until a commercial treaty was finally signed in 1236. This opened a new era of trade between Flanders and England. We have no figures, but it is likely that there was a major expansion in exports, mostly handled by the Flemings themselves. Indeed Flemish domination of the wool trade was not broken until the 1270s. Their eclipse after that was due in part to an increasing concentration of their energy and capital in the industry itself but mostly to protracted disputes between England and Flanders. These caused interruptions in the trade, during which the Flemings lost valuable contacts which they could not recover in time of peace. Flanders remained the main market but the trade passed into other hands. Thanks to the disputes, however, it is possible to determine for the first time the pattern of the trade. Licences were needed for wool exports in these years and in 1275 the first regular customs duty was imposed on wool, the Great and Ancient Custom of 6s.8d. a sack (364 lb), giving us export figures. The English seem to have handled between 30 and 35 per cent of the trade. The other 70 per cent was in alien hands, the most prominent exporters being the Italians with about 25 per cent of the trade, followed by merchants from Cahors and Montpellier, Brabanters with 11 per cent and other Germans with 4 per cent.

The English were therefore the immediate beneficiaries of the Flemish withdrawal. The middlemen who had formerly sold wool to the Flemings and merchants who had dealt with them now became exporters. They were based mainly on London, Southampton and Sandwich and the East Coast ports. But in the long run it was the Italians who gained the most. Italians had been resident in England from the early thirteenth century onwards. Florentines predominated and they were not petty merchants but members of substantial firms, the Pulci-Rimbertini, Willelmi, Bardi and Cerchi. Their large reserves of liquid capital from banking and international trade allowed them to lend money to the Crown and to great lay and monastic lords who demanded cash in advance for their wool clip. Although they were frequently expelled for practising usury, they were ready in the 1270s to take over the wool trade and take it over they did, exporting directly to Flanders and supplying their own industry in Florence and other towns.

Between 1279 and 1290 exports ran at an average of 26,750 sacks per annum, the variation being 24–31,000 sacks. This was possibly slightly less than earlier since inflation in England had pushed up prices and sheep scab led to poor quality wool. Boston was the leading export port, followed by London, Hull and Southampton, Lynn, Newcastle, Ipswich and Sandwich. Most Italian exports went through Hull and Boston. The leading firms took out hundreds of sacks a year, something which few Englishmen could match. Florentine companies dominated the trade, their only rivals being the Riccardi of Lucca, the king's bankers. However, in the mid-1290s the wool trade took a severe knock. Relations with Flanders again became strained as England drifted into war with France and at home into prolonged conflict with Scotland. Desperate for money Edward I saw further taxation of wool exports as the most obvious and lucrative source. His first plan in 1294 was to seize all the wool as a forced loan and sell it in the Crown's name. At the request of the merchants he abandoned this scheme and substituted an extra export duty of £3.6s.8d. on each sack of good wool and £2 on other wool. A standard rate of £2 replaced this in November 1294 but there was a return to the dual rate in 1295. This *maltote* was immensely profitable to the Crown, for between 1294 and 1297 it raised no less than £110,000. But this was at the expense of wool exports, which fell by a half. The closure of the Flemish and Florentine markets was partly responsible, coupled with confusion among the Italian merchants as the king's bankers, the Riccardi, went bankrupt. The chief reason, however, was the passing back of the export tax by the merchants to the growers in the form of lower prices, at which they were not prepared to sell. The trade was further interrupted by the king's second attempt to take a forced loan in wool and not until the last years of the century did wool exports again reach the levels of the early 1290s at around 30,000 sacks per annum.

Two questions, closely interrelated, need to be asked about the wool trade in the second half of the thirteenth century: why did the Italians handle so much of it, and how was the wool collected for export and sold? The answer to the first has already been given. The Italians had large reserves of liquid capital from trade and banking and from the collection of papal taxes which had to be transmitted to Rome. Their role as bankers and tax gatherers brought them into contact with the great monastic houses who were anxious to sell their wool in bulk, both the current clip and for years in advance. One contract might involve many sacks. So Abbot Robert of Meaux in the 1280s sold 120 sacks of wool at one time to merchants from Lucca for £800 and the monks of Canterbury Cathedral Priory 100 sacks to a Florentine firm. Virtually all monastic houses owed money to the Italians as did many lay noblemen – Roger Bigod, earl of Norfolk owed the Riccardi of Lucca no less than £1,000 in the late thirteenth century. The best security for such loans was the wool clip. Concealed interest was probably charged by the delivery of wool of greater value than the money originally loaned. Such borrowing could bring disaster. That same Abbot Robert of Meaux died leaving the house indebted to the tune of £3,678, of which alien merchants were owed £2,500. And, of course, if forward contracts were entered into and in the relevant year the clip failed because of murrain or scab, then like Pipewell Abbey in the early fourteenth century the house could be ruined.

To trade this freely, travelling the length and breadth of England, exporting through Newcastle, Boston and Lynn as well as London, the Italians needed protection, for the English did not like foreigners. That protection they acquired partly by utility but chiefly because of the Crown's attitude to them. In the thirteenth century the Crown began to rely heavily on the Italians for the credit financing of government as well in peace as in war. Henry III borrowed at least £54,000 from

Siennese merchants for his Sicilian adventure in the late 1250s and Edward I used Italian bankers extensively, especially the Riccardi of Lucca. In the first seven years of his reign the Company paid out over £200,000 on his behalf, of which all but £28,000 was repaid from taxes and other sources of revenue. They financed Edward's Welsh wars, collected the taxation in 1275 and acted as agents for other loans. The Crown's aggregate debt to the Riccardi and others between 1272 and 1294 was no less than £392,000, which itself explains why they were allowed freedom of trade, export licences, exemption from duties and other royal favours. This is not to say that one or two Englishmen could not export on equal terms with them. As might be expected there were some Londoners who grew fat on the wool trade. William de Combe Martin was buying wool consignments at £500 from Bardney (Lincs), Thomas de Basing had licences to export 160 and 200 sacks of wool in 1273–4 and another Basing, Robert, made enough money as a wool exporter in the 1290s to add manors in Essex to his already considerable patrimony in 14 London parishes. The greatest of all English wool merchants at this time were the Shropshire brothers, Nicholas and Laurence of Ludlow. Nicholas sold to the mint silver earned through wool exports worth £900 per annum in the 1270s and Laurence bought the entire clip of the Warenne estates in Surrey in 1288 for £400. But these were the exception, not the rule. In general English merchants did not have the liquid capital to operate at this level. Not many exported more than 30 sacks, most a few only.

Wool exports of 30,000 sacks a year could not be supplied exclusively by the great lay and ecclesiastical landlords. At best they may have contributed one-third of the total. The other two-thirds had to come from the flocks of middling men and wealthy peasants. Somehow it all had to be collected together and offered for sale, for individual contracts with farmers providing one sack alone were impractical. In part the great landlords undertook the task, acting as middlemen. The wool they gathered together was known as *collecta*, and as with their own clip they entered into forward contracts for the sale of this also. Certain towns acted as major markets for wool. Bristol certainly did and the merchants of Leicester bought up the wool from the surrounding villages to sell at Boston and St Ives fairs. It was at this level that English merchants profited from the wool trade, in towns and villages alike, gathering the wool chiefly for export by aliens who were free to sell it where they would on the Continent, for there was as yet no staple, no fixed point of sale.

177

England was in a real sense being treated as a partially developed colony in the export trade, with aliens taking a major share in the export of raw materials rather than manufactured goods. The same is true for imports. Here, apart from alum, dyestuffs, spices and luxury goods the Italians were less important, for the direct sea route to the Mediterranean was only just being opened up. Substantial amounts of woad came from Picardy, cloth of course from Flanders and wine from Gascony, but probably the most important development of the thirteenth century was the growth of the Baltic trade. From the northern lands flowed herring, furs in vast quantities, wood for housing, masts, spars and oars, wax for candles, pitch, tar and ashes. They came in through London and the East Coast ports rivalling and perhaps outstripping the older axis of German trade through the Rhineland and Cologne. It has been argued that in London a whole new range of interests drew nourishment from the Baltic trade, skinners, fishmongers, corders, thus stimulating the capital's economy. Perhaps this is so, but the real point to be noted is this, that the trade itself was not in English hands. It was in the thirteenth century that the Hanse became firmly established in England. There had long been trading links between England and Germany. As early as 1157 Cologne merchants had their own gild hall in Upper Thames Street in London. Gradually the eastward expansion of the Germans brought in merchants from Lübeck and the other Baltic towns. In 1237 Henry III granted the merchants of the association of Gotland his safe conduct and exemption from all taxes on merchandise bought and sold. The traffic of the Easterlings grew so much that 30 years later Henry III accorded them equality with the Cologners. The merchants of Hamburg and Lübeck were given the right to form a Hanse, or association, like that of Cologne. Finally in 1281 after disputes between the east and west, one Hanse of Almain emerged, comprising all German merchants. They were to have their gild hall in London at a rent of 40s. a year and their own independent government under an alderman. Commercial privileges were conferred on them by the *Carta Mercatoria* of 1303. In return for duties on wool and hides exported, they were exempted from all other taxes and levies and were allowed to trade freely within the realm. What had been created in London, and was mirrored in one or two East Coast ports, was a self-governing enclave, one of the four great Kontors of the Hanse, the others being at Bruges, Novgorod in Russia and Bergen in Norway.

So both across the North Sea, to the Baltic, to Gascony and to the

Mediterranean the majority of English trade was not in English hands. Where there are details it is noticeable that much of the shipping used was from either Flemish, Dutch or north French ports. England might have been one of the axes of North European trade but much of the profit from it was going into foreign hands. Why were English merchants as yet unable to compete? Again the answer seems to be lack of liquid capital, lack of capitalism. In both trade and to a lesser extent industry there was expansion in the thirteenth century, but from the English point of view the economy had to operate within the constraints of inadequate access to capital. Consequently neither trade nor industry could offer a major alternative source of employment to the growing mass of peasants living on the brink of subsistence. At the very most perhaps 10 per cent of population were engaged in non-agrarian occupations. The remainder worked on the land to produce their daily bread.

6   Towards a Crisis

The half-century before the advent of plague in 1348 is one of the most enigmatic periods in English history, political and economic. Down to about 1300 the trend is clear, expansion in most sectors of the economy. The area under cultivation was much enlarged and more rigorously exploited by lord and peasant alike. Old towns flourished, new ones were planted. England's contacts with Europe were widened as goods from the Baltic and Mediterranean flowed in, along with great quantities of Gascon wine, whilst thousands of sacks of English wool went to the Flemish and Italian cloth industries. The reverse of the coin is less bright. There were too many people and not enough land to feed them all except in good years, too much of English trade was in alien hands, too much capital flowed into grandiose building, ostentatious luxury and taxation and not enough into industry – except of course for building itself. Towns were increasingly controlled by oligarchs who, as the limits of consumption were reached, used their political power to foster their own economic ends. There had been expansion without growth. That expansion brought better living standards for some, but for a fair number of Englishmen it brought no material improvement in their condition at all.

An air of malaise hangs over the last decades of the thirteenth century. Throughout the land there was grumbling which was in part a reflection of the political situation. The last years of the thirteenth and the opening decades of the fourteenth century saw a series of major political crises brought about by a combination of war against Scotland and France, the heavy burden of taxation to pay for the campaigns and the characters of the kings themselves. It is difficult now to see Edward I as anything but an autocrat whose grandiose schemes for feudal control of the whole British Isles were to lead to a war with the Scots beginning in the 1290s and dragging on through most of the fourteenth century. His son, Edward II, inherited in 1307 a bankrupt government, a discontented baronage and a war in the North that could not be won. Edward II was personally unfit to be king. This unstable character heaped lands and offices on his favourites to the disgust and financial loss of the baronage. No soldier, he was unable throughout his reign to protect the North from the Scots. Consequently, the years between 1308 and 1326 were marked by bitter political disputes, open warfare and lawlessness far beyond the level to be expected even in those violent times. The reign of Edward III, beginning effectively in 1330, brought to the throne a competent, even a great king. But it also brought renewed conflict with Scotland and then, in 1337, a war with France which was to last until 1453 and affect the whole political history of later medieval England.

Political problems were accompanied by natural disasters, the great famines of 1315–25, caused by widespread crop failures, and cattle-pest. More than that, politics impinged on the country in subtler ways. Wars cost money. By modern standards vast sums were spent on the Scottish and French campaigns. Between 1294 and 1350 personal taxation was continuous and heavy and imposed a particularly serious burden on the peasantry. They were also liable to have crops and animals seized to provision the armies as the Crown exercised its right of purveyance – of taking supplies which might later be paid for, often at ridiculously low prices. Service in the army was also demanded of them and those chosen had to be provided with arms at the village's expense. Finally, the tremendous outflow of silver to pay allies and troops abroad led to monetary deflation, low prices and profits, whilst rents and entry fines remained high. The wool export duty, imposed to raise money for the war, was also passed back to the growers in the form of low prices, so that falling income from arable agriculture could not be offset by rising profits from pastoral. Taken together, these phenomena are held to have produced 'a crisis of the early fourteenth century' whose main features were the return to demesne leasing by the great landlords, the contraction of cultivation as marginal lands were abandoned, and the further impoverishment of the peasantry, leading to falling population, supposedly witnessed by gradually rising wages in the 1340s. The Black Death would thus appear only to have accelerated existing trends and not to have been their prime cause.

Much of the demographic evidence has already been discussed, but the problems of the famines, taxation, low prices and rising wages and the retreat of cultivation need further examination to determine whether there were any basic changes in the agrarian economy. There is no question but that the famines were severe. In a society which was becoming increasingly harvest sensitive, a bad harvest was a calamity, partial or total failure a catastrophe. But, that is what happened between 1315 and 1325. A run of bad harvests from 1310 to 1314 was followed by serious harvest failure in 1315 due to terrible weather. By the spring and early summer of 1316 wheat had risen to 26s.8d. a quarter, compared to the already inflated price of 8s.4d. a quarter in 1315. Prices went even higher in parts of the Midlands, salt, a vital commodity in the medieval diet, was very scarce due to the lack of solar heat for distillation, meat and dairy produce were in short supply. Clearly there were famine conditions in the first half of 1316, accompanied by a virulent and widespread enteric epidemic which may have killed up to 10 per cent of the population. Only a good harvest could save the situation, but that of 1316 brought no relief at all. There was heavy rain, a harvest failure and a desperate situation now became critical. On the Winchester estates yields were little more than half their normal level in 1315 and those of 1316 were even worse. In the North, gross yields at Bolton Priory fell as low as 19 per cent of the early fourteenth century average; only the hardy oats showed any resilience, answering for 64 per cent of average in 1315 and 80 per cent in 1316. These are extremes of north and south. In between there was considerable local variation. Light sandy soils fared much better than the heavy clays in valley bottoms and Cornwall seems to have escaped the famines altogether. The general picture is grim, however. The famines were Europe-wide, so there was little hope of alleviating distress by grain imports. Lords either could not or would not help the peasants. No alms were given on the Winchester estates in these years and no payments in kind were made to estate labourers because corn was too dear. Relief did not come until the improved harvest of 1317 brought a 50 per cent fall in corn prices and the plentiful harvest of 1318 produced prices as low as those in any year since 1288. But the respite was only temporary. There was another mediocre grain crop in 1321 with prices again approaching those in 1315–17. This time the culprit was prolonged drought, not torrential rain. After that conditions improved for most of the country in 1322, except for the South East where droughts in 1325–6 and serious flooding in 1327 brought localized problems. The whole decade 1315–25, not just the years 1315–17, must be regarded as a disaster for arable farming. The effects on a harvest-sensitive population can best be seen by the fact that a 50 per cent drop in production brought a 400 per cent increase in prices.

Yet it was not just a crisis for arable agriculture but for pastoral farming as well. Cattle rearing was regionally important in the upland North and sheep provided a vital cash crop, wool, for lord and peasant alike. The famine years were accompanied by widespread sheep murrains, more serious than any previous outbreaks of the disease, especially among lambs and yearlings. At Inkpen (Berks) there were only 137 sheep in 1317 compared with 468 in 1313. Half the entire flock died on the royal stock farm of Clipstone in Sherwood, one-fifth of the sheep and half the lambs at Crawley (Sussex) and 28 per cent of the flock of 3,000 sheep on the Crowland estates. Peasant flocks must have been as badly hit, with more far-reaching consequences, since they needed the cash more than the lords. The drop in wool production can partly be seen in the decline of exports through Lynn and Hull, although fraud by the customs officials has distorted the figures. The sheep murrain was followed in 1319–21 by cattle pest, probably rinderpest. Although cattle rearing was only a part of the whole agrarian economy, it did have one vital function, the supply of draught oxen, the universal plough beast. Thus the rinderpest struck at the heart of arable production. The Winchester demesne herds were reduced from 1,088 oxen in 1319–20 to 500 in 1320–1. Ramsey herds suffered a similar fate. In 1319 the abbot complained of losses so severe that the abbey no longer had the means of tilling its lands. Thirty years were to elapse before stock totals reached those of the pre-famine period and the peasants in certain areas were still complaining of shortages of plough beasts in the 1340s.

The famines on their own were a serious enough problem, but they were accompanied by continual and heavy taxation and purveyance. War with Scotland led to direct taxation on a scale unknown before 1294. Edward II reigned for less than 20 years, but during that time he collected seven lay subsidies, totalling over £260,000 and a variety of clerical grants and other mandatory taxes provided him with another £200,000. In the first decade of Edward III's reign four lay subsidies yielded £130,000 and clerical taxes another £100,000. That was before the outbreak of war with France 'drove government expenditure and what was extracted from the country to figures which were astronomical in medieval terms'.[1] Not all the consequences of heavy taxation were bad. It will be seen that the wool duties helped stimulate the revival of the English cloth industry. But it has been argued that the

183

way in which taxes were levied made a return to demesne leasing seem attractive to many great landlords. They were assessed on the value of goods offered for sale, not those intended for domestic use. Obviously the landlord who produced large quantities of corn or wool for the market ought to have been badly hit, but as rents were not touched the lord who gave up demesne production and switched to renting would, in theory, reduce his liability to the subsidy.

Whether or not this was the case will be considered later. For the moment it is as well to observe that through bribery and the purchase of exemptions the rich managed to avoid taxes quite successfully. In 1296 the earl of Cornwall paid only £10 taxes on a total income of £4,700. In the same year the Fellows of Merton College, Oxford, managed to 'persuade' the assessors to lower the valuation of their manor of Cuxham from £6.2s.2d. to £1.1s.6d. The cost was high. They had to expend £1.2s.8¼d. on entertainment and give the assessors 101 bushels of wheat, a pig, ten hens and two cheeses. It was worth it, because the low assessment was to be the starting point for haggling over taxation in future years. Bolton Priory's total bill for royal and papal taxes for the years 1291–1315 came to about 3–4½ per cent of expenditure and Canterbury Cathedral Priory spent about £160 a year on taxation in the 37 years of Henry of Eastry's priorate. Frankly, these were burdens which could be borne, like it or not. They may have equalled investment in lands but it has already been seen how low that was. Some middling folk simply refused to pay. Sir Stephen Bassingbourne of Hertfordshire simply beat up the sub-taxers of the fifteenth in 1339 so that they dare not levy the tax. And, since middling men were frequently the assessors or collectors of the taxes, they often charged themselves and their relatives little or nothing.

It was the poor who had to pay. Until 1334 those with goods worth less than 10s. were exempted. That gave protection to none but the very poorest, for 10s. represented the value of only two quarters of wheat, four to six sheep or a cow. Certainly goods were undervalued by the assessors, often by as much as 50 per cent, and rent often came to more than taxes. But the taxes had to be paid on top of rent and other compulsory outgoings, which, for the unfree peasant, could amount to half his income. Nor was the actual tax the only problem. There were frequent complaints of extortion and peculation by the gatherers, who took far more than was due. If, on top of all this, the peasant's crops and animals were seized by the purveyors or his wool taken in forced loans, then he might be in dire straits. The money taken out of the countryside also meant that there were fewer buyers and sellers, which only made matters worse. As the fourteenth-century rhymer put it, 'Now the fifteenth (lay taxation) runs in England year after year . . . the common folk must sell their cows, their utensils, even their clothing . . . Still more hard on simple folk is the wool collection; commonly it makes them sell their possessions. At market buyers are so few that in fact a man can do no business . . . because so many are destitute.' On top of all this there was military service. True, there were plenty of spare men who could go to the wars but the village community still had to find the money for their increasingly expensive arms. Given the continuation of smallholding, these burdens, it is argued, may well have pushed a substantial number of peasants below the poverty line, leading, with the effects of the famines, to demographic downturn.

The final element in this trilogy of disaster is the low prices coupled with supposedly rising wage rates in the period after 1331. Until then prices had been uniformly high. Now they fell, but unevenly. The prices of animals and hides, dairy produce, poultry and eggs and iron all held their ground. This may have been due to the cattle plagues and to slow restocking and, in the case of iron, to a crisis in production. But the prices of the staple products of the demesne, grain, wool and some sheep fell sharply. Wheat for instance was 2s. a quarter in London in 1339, about the same as it had been before the inflation of the late twelfth century. In part this was the result of good harvests and, of course, monetary deflation but the important element in this argument is that low prices were evidence of falling demand and were matched by rising wages. Only in periods of high prices and low costs was demesne farming viable, as the later fourteenth century was to prove.[2] The answer to the problem for the greater landlords, it is said, was for them to become rentiers for, paradoxically, rents fell hardly at all. We thus have a picture of an agrarian economy in the process of rapid change in the decades before the Black Death. Demesne farming was on the wane, the peasantry was increasingly impoverished by the burdens of taxation and purveyance, and perhaps the best evidence of all of a demographic downturn is the increasing amount of land being left uncultivated.

This, then is the theory; how well do the facts fit it? It must be acknowledged that on some great estates the trend towards leasing was quite marked. Rent had always been an important part of the bishop of Ely's income, much of it coming from assarted land in fen and forest. In the second half of the thirteenth century the bishop's demesnes grew no further. By the early fourteenth century leasehold tenures were being created from them and some villein services were being commuted for money rents. The bishop had become a rentier, because, given the pressure on land, he found it more profitable. On the neighbouring Peterborough Abbey estates there was a clear contraction in direct farming as demesnes on poor soils with falling yields were abandoned. The same is true of the Winchester estates but elsewhere demesne farming flourished. Indeed it reached its peak in the early fourteenth century on the Canterbury Cathedral Priory estates in the South and the Bolton Priory manors in the North. It was thus on a high farming agrarian economy that the famines and the era of low prices fell. In the short term the results were mixed. There was tremendous dislocation, of course, since the harvest failures and cattle pests struck at all sectors of agricultural enterprise. Some smaller monastic houses were certainly ruined by the famines. For Bolton Priory they brought disaster. Rinderpest reduced herds of 500 head of cattle and 250 oxen to 53 oxen and 20 other cattle and an already difficult situation was worsened by destructive Scottish raids. These devastated large parts of the North, so much so that the Vale of York and the western half of the Vale of Pickering had their tax assessments reduced by half. Not only the North suffered, however. The chronicler of Louth Park (Cistercian, Lincs) complained that crop failures and murrains had ruined all the substance of the house and that what was left had been taken by the king's officers at the time of the Lincoln parliament in 1316. Prittlewell Priory in Essex was in a state of poverty and miserable indebtedness and the Augustinian canons of Rocester Abbey were sent out to solicit sustenance from friends and neighbours. On the other hand, the high prices in these years brought the bishopric of Winchester to a high point in its income. In 1315–16 the proceeds from the sale of produce were 23 per cent higher than in the previous year and the next year, 1316–17, was financially one of the best in the whole Middle Ages, with a gross income of £6,406.

Such success was short-lived. Winchester, just as much as Louth Park or Prittlewell, had to face the formidable problems of restocking and then of low prices. Clearly some could not or would not accept the challenge. At Ely the famines and low prices accelerated the existing trend. There was a catastrophic fall in agrarian profits in the second quarter of the fourteenth century, coupled with a pronounced turn away from demesne farming. The depression was severe. At Great Shelford (Cambs) agricultural income from the manor averaged about

£80 per annum between 1319 and 1323. It fell by over half in 1325–33 and averaged only £10 per annum between 1333 and 1346. Only 50 acres of the demesne were leased off and it would seem that the fall in income was due to the fall in prices. The declining profitability of demesne farming forced alterations in the running of the estates. More produce had to be sent to the household rather than offered for sale and capital investment fell. More and more income came from rents and the sale of works. Here there is something of a conundrum, for rents did not fall at all, in line with a supposedly declining population. Rather, they remained at the high levels of the late thirteenth century. At Great Shelford the rent of a demesne acre was 1s.; in 1251 it might have been had for between 2d. and 4d. There was no slackening of rents at all before the Black Death and with falling prices demesne farming seemed less and less attractive to the bishop of Ely. His neighbour, the abbot of Ramsey, adopted much the same policy. The famines and murrains marked a turning point in demesne production. The abbey was heavily in debt and could not restock its manors. Falling income from the sale of agricultural produce was offset by a switch to rents and the same phenomenon of continuing peasant demand for land can be seen. At the same time the Winchester demesnes were shrinking rapidly. Unprofitable, perhaps exhausted land was going out of production and profits were falling substantially. The years 1325 to 1347 were years of considerable difficulty for this estate, as they were for a lesser landlord, Titchfield Abbey. This house had 15 manors in more than 60 villages and hamlets, mainly in Hampshire and at Inkpen in south-west Berkshire. After the famines the abbey was very reluctant to run its demesnes for arable agriculture. Rather, they were converted into permanent pasture for sheep, but on the one manor for which there are complete records, Inkpen, flocks did not reach their pre-murrain level until 1347–8 and cereal production did not recover at all. Not only was arable allowed to return to pasture but land was left fallow for two or three years at a time.

Hard cases, it is said, make bad law. Taking three or four well-known examples of the switch away from demesne farming and extrapolating from them a model for the early fourteenth-century agrarian economy makes bad history. The fact is that on many estates the famines and murrains brought temporary difficulties but no collapse of demesne farming. The pastoral side of Canterbury Cathedral Priory's farming enterprises received a shock from which it never fully recovered, but the arable side scarcely seems to have flagged. The Priory did not begin to

187

lease its demesnes in these years. Rather it continued to cultivate them, using to the full all available sources of compulsory labour, until the 1390s. Income from their manors was only £200 lower in 1390 than it had been in 1314–15. In the extreme south-west of England, in Cornwall, there was no real crisis at all but a sustained boom right up to 1348. Demesne farming was admittedly limited, most landlords drawing their income from rents. The earldom and subsequently the duchy of Cornwall went through a thoroughgoing reorganization between 1317 and the late 1330s as it passed into the hands first of Queen Isabella, then John of Eltham (1333) and then finally of the young Prince Edward in 1337. These years saw the final emergence of the seven-year leasehold for free and unfree tenants. At the end of the term, the lands were put more or less on the open market, going to the highest bidder. A more efficient administration certainly helped increase duchy revenues, but they could not have maintained at a high level without continuing demand for land. Tin mining flourished,[3] stimulating the demand for food. At the renewal of leases in 1333 high rents were obtained and they remained high at the assessions of 1340 and 1347. The profitability of the 17 duchy manors increased by 70 per cent in these years. Only in 1347 were there the faintest glimmerings of a downturn in the Cornish economy.

Perhaps Cornwall was lucky, yet the famines seem to have had remarkably little long-term effect on other estates in south and central England. In spite of one or two short-lived attempts at leasing, demesne cultivation continued on the Westminster and Crowland Abbey estates. Merton College was able to replace its livestock on the manors of Cheddington and Cuxham within two years and high farming was in full swing, scarcely interrupted by the famines, on the estates of Chertsey Abbey. Whilst there was a retreat of cultivation on Battle Abbey's manor of Barnhorn, the abbey's demesnes were still in hand in 1346–7, providing its food and its money income. Nor were there any signs of real crisis on the great lay estates of the Clares in East Anglia and Wales. The overwhelming weight of evidence suggests that the main switch from demesne farming to leasing on great estates came in the period after 1370.[4] There were until then no compelling reasons to make the change. The landlords were certainly inherently conservative but in any case the choice in the 1330s and 1340s was by no means a clear one. Many may have felt that in a deflationary age it was better to take income in kind rather than in money which might or might not have been paid. Moreover, the economics of demesne farming may not have been quite as black as they have been painted. Prices may have fallen, but in real terms wages moved with them. As far as one can tell from the evidence available, there was no rapid wage rise, as Table 2.2 shows. Indeed, the wages for a carpenter with helper and tilers were actually lower on the Winchester estates in 1340–8 than they had been in 1260–1309, whilst labourers were paid only 0.23 per diem more in 1341–50 than in 1291–1300. That is not a wages explosion. Not until the 1370s do wages and prices finally part company in a way that made demesne farming unprofitable. Until then it was probably the best way of managing the estates, supplemented as it was by income from continuing high rents.

Our information on the fate of lesser landlords is very limited. Many must have been hit by the slump in wool prices, since their flocks and those of the richer peasants provided much of the wool that went for export. One man, however, probably typical of other knights, squires and gentlemen in the early fourteenth century, was Lionel de Bradenham – and he certainly prospered. He held the manor of Langenhoe, four miles south of Colchester, bounded by the Colne estuary and the Pyefleet Channel which separates Mersea Island from the mainland. There was marshland for sheep grazing and a demesne of 250 acres of arable with large areas of pasture. Between 1325 and 1348 Bradenham's income from the rents of land, leases of fishing privileges and court dues rose sharply. His household received some of the grain from the demesne but the bulk of the surplus went to Colchester to feed the townsmen. Far from the demesne arable contracting, it was used to the fullest and new, marginal land was brought into cultivation for oats. Bradenham benefited from both increasing sales of cereals and increasing rents, as leaseholds were substituted for customary tenures.

But whilst no great or lesser lord starved to death, many peasants did during the famines. This can be seen from the numbers of holdings changing hands as survivors replaced the dead or the impoverished. At Hindolveston, Norfolk, a manor of Norwich Cathedral Priory, there were three times as many land transactions as normal in the famine years. The dearth and pestilence seem to have had a more profound effect than the Black Death at Sherington, Bucks. Smallholders with scattered strips were particularly hard hit. There were a considerable number of sales and exchanges of holdings in 1315–17 with some, more fortunate, among the peasants taking the opportunity to enlarge their holdings. This is a story which can be repeated elsewhere. On three St

Albans manors, Park, Codicote and Barnet (Herts) and the Barnwell Priory manor of Chesterton (Cambs) surrenders of holdings reached a peak in the crisis years 1315–17 and 1321–2. Some were family transfers from father to son, there were rich peasants enlarging their holdings, but the majority of smallholdings were taken up by persons with no apparent connection with the surrendering party.

This was the almost inevitable immediate reaction to the agrarian crisis. For real signs of a steadily declining population, weakened by famines and impoverished by taxation, there would have to be evidence of land falling out of use on a large scale. On first sight it seems to exist. There were considerable rent deficits and what looks like a retreat of cultivation on Titchfield Abbey's manor of Inkpen on poor soil in south-west Berkshire. At Langley in Leafield, again on marginal land on the edge of Wychwood Forest, Oxfordshire, there were 18 holdings in 1279; by 1316 only 4 tenants were left. Rents fell by 30 per cent on the Derbyshire manors of the honor of Tutbury between 1313–14 and 1321–2. On a sample of 15 of the manors, 58 bovates and 3,000 acres of land lay vacant. The reasons given were poverty, land too poor to be cultivated or a shortage of stock because of the murrains. Similar complaints of poverty and lack of animals preventing tenants taking up holdings were heard in Hertfordshire, Wiltshire and especially in the North where the Scottish raids piled Pelion upon Ossa. Again this was only to be expected in the crisis years, but was there a long-term retreat of settlement? In 1342 Edward III was granted a tax of one-ninth of the value of corn, wool and lambs after tithe had been taken. In fact the tax should have been identical to the tithe of corn, wool and lambs. So, to help them in their work the assessors were given details of the assessment of all clerical incomes (including tithe) for the papal taxation in 1291. Where discrepancies existed between the assessment of 1291 and that of 1342 (on the 1341 harvest) they had to be explained. The explanations make interesting reading. Even allowing for the inconsistencies and inaccuracies found in all tax returns, arable land seems to have been abandoned on quite a large scale in four main areas. First there was the North Riding of Yorkshire, which had suffered badly from the Scottish raids. Next, land had gone out of use in over 50 vills in Shropshire, mostly on the uplands west of the Severn. Thirdly in Sussex 5,600 acres of arable lay untilled, with perhaps a further 3,500 lost to the sea, making some 10,000 acres of land abandoned, and once again the chief reasons given were sterility of the soil and poverty of the tenants. Finally land was left uncultivated in a group of counties to the north and west of London, in and around the Chilterns, in the Oxford clay vale and in Bedfordshire, Buckinghamshire and Cambridgeshire. More than two-fifths of the villages in Bedfordshire had a lower valuation in 1341 than in 1291 because land had been abandoned. There were 4,870 untilled acres in Cambridgeshire and uncultivated lands in 101 of the 176 identified parishes in Buckinghamshire. The lands going out of cultivation were on a variety of soils but in all three counties the contraction was more marked on uplands than the lowlands. The reasons given were impoverished and shrinking population, shortage of seed corn and the weight of taxation.

This was long-term retreat of settlement. It is scarcely stretching the point too far to believe that much of it was less populated marginal land whose tenants had not been able to recover from the famines nor bear the weight of constant taxation. But need we necessarily assume that this points to a declining population? Where did the erstwhile tenants of these lands go? Did they simply die – or did they return to the more fertile lands in the older villages? There is a good deal to suggest that the latter was the case. The continuing demand for land and high rents has already been noted in Cornwall and on the Ely and Ramsey estates. There were few permanent vacancies of the St Alban's manors as a result of the famines and often large tenements were being split up to provide small holdings. That could point to poverty, but also to the pressure of people on land that was so marked a feature of the late thirteenth century. At Cottenham in Cambridgeshire there were 27 tenements in 1280. These had increased to 32 by 1346, all of them held by ten-acre men. The rental of 1341 shows that free tenures on the Leicester Abbey estates had been split up and the same was probably happening on customary land. Inkpen apart, there are clear signs of the demand for land on the Titchfield Abbey estates. There was a growth in the number of land transactions, which reached its height in 1332–7, and levels remained high between 1337 and 1347. Holdings were being broken up, 32-acre tenements being split up into 16-, 8- and 4- acre lots. The proliferation of small holdings was also occurring on some Westminster Abbey manors. In the 1330s the abbot had 160–170 tenants at Pyrford, Surrey, more than 70 of them with cottages or small holdings of less than five acres. Yet by all accounts this should not have been happening. Holdings should have been growing larger and rents falling, but in central, eastern, southern and south-western England this does not seem to have been the case. Retreat from marginal land there may have been but many of the older established English villages were still full of men. The first plague was to show how full, for there were plenty of apparently landless men waiting to take over dead men's holdings.

Thus in the decades before the Black Death there were no fundamental changes in the agrarian economy. In spite of the famines and the poverty caused by the weight of royal taxation and purveyance, there had yet to be a significant demographic downturn. Retreat of settlement was regional and there were few long-term vacancies in the older, longer settled villages on better land. Although the aggregate wealth of the country had increased in the thirteenth century and armies were small, providing for them does seem to have been a burden for substantial numbers of the poor. It was to take the far greater catastrophe of the arrival of endemic plague to bring, paradoxically, a happy solution to the problem of overpopulation. But in other sectors of the economy signs of change and decay are more distinct, those of change being perhaps more obvious and explicable than those of decay. The contrasting fortunes of the tin and iron industries are a case in point. The output of tin rose sharply after a crisis of overproduction in Europe had reduced it to 279 tons in 1301, half the 1214 level. Almost 400 tons were produced in 1324 and a record 734 in 1332. Between then and the plague production contracted slightly to about 550 tons per annum. The increased output was due to increased demand for pewter both abroad and at home. An English pewter industry developed rapidly to supply ecclesiastical, noble and middle-class households with the pewter vessels which were fast replacing the copper and clay utensils previously used. By 1348–9 a craft of pewterers had emerged in London, with ordinances and statutes to regulate standards and the admission of members. A pewterer is recorded at York in 1348, another was at work in Norfolk by 1340 and there was a considerable if illegal industry in Cornwall itself, using uncoined tin.

By contrast the iron industry seems to have been running into some sort of difficulty. Production in the North was severely disrupted by the Scottish raids but the decline in iron-working seems to have been quite widespread. The combined effects of clearing for agriculture and the large amounts of wood used for fuel may have caused a depletion of wood resources. In parts of the North the thoroughness of Cistercian agricultural enterprise, combined with their investment in iron working had caused timber shortages. East and west of Leeds in the Forest of Knaresborough there were only two forges left in 1304–5, of which only one was in operation. Two years later the iron industry in the forest was confined to six small nail smithies. In the parks of Rothwell and Roundhay near Leeds, the industry flourished in 1320 but the consumption of wood was so great that it was almost extinct by 1341. There were similar depredations in the woodlands around Wakefield in the Forest of Shipton and the situation was at its most serious where both lead and iron were mined, as in Derbyshire and Durham. Woodland resources seem to have been better managed in Dean, however. To protect the woodlands a system of coppicing was introduced, securing the replacement of felled trees by natural growth. Stretches of woodland were enclosed to prevent cattle and wild animals destroying the young growth and to prevent the cutting of undergrowth. The effects of wood shortages are difficult to assess. There were areas in the North, in the Forest of Pickering and the North Riding of Yorkshire, where production continued uninterrupted. The Forest of Dean industry suffered only sporadic interruption and demand for iron generally seems to have continued unabated. Indeed, in the opening stages of the Hundred Years War it must have increased, for a great deal of steel was needed for weapons. Much had to be imported, but both Dean, Yorkshire, Shropshire and Staffordshire supplied steel-tipped arrowheads in 1341, by far the greatest quantity coming from the old-established industry in Dean. Increased production of steel may have offset any decline in iron production – indeed we have no means of knowing whether or not the total quantity of iron produced did decline in these years. The best that can be said is that either because of a fuel crisis or because local ore supplies ran out, iron working ceased in certain areas of the North.

The signs of change are far clearer in the wool export trade and the cloth industry. The first half of the fourteenth century saw the triumph of the English in the wool trade as they ousted the Italians and Germans and became the chief exporter. The century opened with a boom in exports. Following peace with France in 1305 they reached a peak of 47,574 sacks in 1306–7, although they fell after that. The Flemish industry could not sustain the high levels of production of the opening years of the century and renewed conflict between England and France led to interruptions in exports. But profound change was under way in the organization of the trade. The years between 1300 and the outbreak of war in 1337 were to see the gradual emergence of the Staple, a fixed point or points at home or abroad through which all wool had to be exported and of a company of English merchants who dominated the trade. Prior to 1310 English merchants trading to the Low Countries had adopted a more or less corporate organization and had taken steps to fix a Staple abroad which moved from town to town as it suited their purposes. The company was not at this point purely a society of wool merchants, nor was there yet any legal compulsion to follow the Staple. That came first in 1313 when a compulsory Staple was fixed at St Omer. Continuing friction between England and Flanders made it unsafe for English merchants to go to the Low Countries lest their goods were seized as a reprisal for attacks on Flemings in England. Aliens, of course, could go to Flanders freely and the English were in danger of losing the grip on the wool trade they had recently won. An extra duty, the New Custom of 3s.4d. on every sack of wool exported by aliens between 1303 and 1311, had pushed the terms of trade in favour of the English, and the aliens' share of exports had fallen to only 35 per cent of the total. The removal of the 3s.4d. duty in 1311 put them on level terms again, but the English were determined to cling to their lead. A compulsory Staple on neutral ground seemed to be the answer. All would have to trade through it, much to the dislike of the aliens who preferred to go directly to Flanders.

Apart from temporary moves to Antwerp in 1315 and Bruges in 1325 the Staple remained at St Omer until 1326. Then home Staples were established at London, Newcastle, York, Lincoln, Norwich, Westminster, Exeter, Bristol, Shrewsbury, Carmarthen, Cardiff and three towns in Ireland. All wool intended for export had to pass through a staple town and remain there for at least 40 days. The purpose was to deny aliens direct access to large producers, much to the benefit of the English middleman dealers and the cloth producers who were not obliged to buy wool at the Staples. Free export was allowed, however, to the advantage of the aliens who could now trade directly to Flanders. The experiment lasted only a year, although it was repeated again in 1333, again for a year. In 1333 there was also a reimposition of differential duties for Englishmen and aliens. Natives had to pay 6s.8d. a sack on top of the Ancient Custom of 6s.8d. and aliens 10s. on top of the Ancient Custom and the New Custom of 3s.4d. which had been reimposed in 1322. This gave the English a substantial advantage, although it was counterbalanced by freedom of trade in all years between 1327 and 1337 except 1333.

By the outbreak of war, then, the idea of a fixed point through which all exports to Northern Europe were to be channelled (direct export to Italy was still allowed) had taken a firm hold. Even when the Staple was at home, the company of merchants, headed by a mayor, was kept in being. And the English merchants now dominated the trade. There had been a spate of bankruptcies among Italian firms, especially the Florentines, in the late thirteenth and early fourteenth centuries, and one of the major companies, the Frescobaldi, was expelled from England in 1311. Firms such as the Bardi and Peruzzi were still active and large exporters, but they now sent wool mainly to Italy. At first they were replaced in the northern trade by the Germans, by old-established families such as the Clippings, Revels, Spicenayls, Suddermanns and Mundepennyngs: Hansards exported 57 per cent of all wool through Hull in 1304–5 but this was the high point of their trade. By the 1320s they had lost their lead, as a consequence of staple policy. They were reluctant to follow an English-dominated staple where they would be treated as second-class citizens.

The English were triumphant. London had become their chief wool export port, increasing its share in the 1310s and 1320s to half of the total trade, but after that the provincial ports regained some ground. Boston ranked second and although Hull had lost its Italian trade to the south coast ports, with direct shipment to Italy, its denizen trade expanded rapidly. This was due to the rise of a dynamic group of Yorkshire merchants, especially from York and Beverley. Three of the four merchants who exported more than 1,000 sacks of wool through Hull between 1298 and 1305 were from Beverley. At Boston it was men from Lincoln, Spalding and Grantham who dominated the trade and at London, merchants who before had acted as middlemen selling to aliens now became exporters in their own right. The capital now became the main outlet for the wool of central England, the Cotswolds and the Welsh Marches. In this story of triumph there is, indeed, only one sour note. Exports were beginning to fall. Between 1311 and 1313 they averaged 38,000 sacks a year, then fell to 21,000 sacks during the war between France and Flanders and were below 30,000 sacks in each of the next three years. The demand for wool was uncertain and civil strife in Flanders meant that on average 24,000 sacks a year were exported between 1323 and 1329. As soon as peace was restored exports picked up, but there is no denying that in these years the underlying trend was downwards.

With the outbreak of war in 1337 the wool trade was thrown into chaos. It is very difficult to follow the intricate manoeuvering between Crown, parliament and native and alien merchants in these years.[5] Each had a different interest. The Crown's needs were very simple – money to fight a war. The ordinary revenue would not suffice and even grants of lay and clerical taxation would not cover the vast sums paid out to Continental allies. Edward III borrowed more in a shorter time between 1337 and 1340 than any other medieval English king. In October 1339 it was estimated that he owed £300,000. The Bardi and Peruzzi alone had lent him £125,000 and the greatest English merchant, William de la Pole of Hull raised £100,000 for the king from his own resources and by borrowing from other Englishmen and foreigners in the Netherlands. Loans could only be made on security, however, and in return for privileges. What better security than the wool trade, what better way to repay interest on loans than by grants of the right to export wool when there was a general embargo on exports. The king could also use the trade as a diplomatic lever, to force the Flemish towns into alliance with him against the French.

The king's interest is simple, parliament's more complicated. First there was the question of who should grant the subsidy, the export duty on wool. At the beginning of the war it was generally agreed that customs duties could not be increased without the consent of the merchant community. With the prospect of a permanently enhanced rate of duty this consent came to be regarded as insufficient. High duties meant lower prices for the growers who were well represented in both Lords and Commons. The consent of the Commons in parliament now came to be regarded as essential for wool taxation but the king refused to concede the point and a lengthy constitutional battle ensued. Thirdly, the English merchants were split into two groups. The greater capitalists, the de la Poles, Melchebournes, Chiritons and Swanlands, wanted monopoly control of the trade in return for raising loans for the king. The main body of merchants objected to this. They felt squeezed out of the trade by the capitalists and thought that the trade should be controlled through the staple to put them at an advantage vis à vis the aliens. Finally, all the aliens wanted was free trade – although that seemed less and less likely.

From this welter of interests there finally emerged a Staple policy, but up to 1350 the history of the wool trade is still very confused, with the Staple now at Bruges, now at Antwerp, now at Dordrecht as the diplomatic, military and financial needs of the Crown dictated. Between 1337 and 1342 the king tried to exploit the trade by taking loans of and taxes on and in wool. The aim at first was to create a royal wool monopoly, for all other exports were banned, so as to enhance the price of wool abroad and sell at a profit. The king also required groups of financiers, Italian and English, to handle the trade for him in return for licences to export. The merchants as a whole found it difficult to refuse the king's requests. It was not so much that they disliked the alternative to loans in wool, the heavy export duty, but because they feared the king's most effective weapon, the right to stop all trade. Admittedly that weapon was double edged. Lengthy embargoes meant no customs duties, but a small merchant might well be ruined by a six- or twelve-month prohibition on trade to Flanders. Reluctantly they acquiesced and in 1337–8, 1340 and 1341 the king took loans of wool and taxes in kind. The whole venture was not a success; indeed, it may be typified by the notorious affair of the Dordrecht bonds. Ten thousand sacks of wool, the first instalment of a loan of 30,000 sacks, were dispatched to Dordrecht in 1337 but the wool remained unsold. Disputes between the king and the merchants who were supposed to handle the sale led to its seizure by the Crown. Edward issued the 317 owners of the wool with bonds for the repayment of its value. It was all fairly done with the wool being valued by the merchants themselves. The real disgrace came when the king thereafter persistently refused to honour the bonds, forcing many of the lesser merchants to sell them at discount to syndicates of monopolists. It left a nasty taste in the mouths of many merchants and was continually being discussed in parliament.

Edward found that trading in wool on his own account simply did not meet his financial needs, partly because of depressed prices on the Continent. It also caused an imbalance in trade because much of the silver paid for the wool was spent abroad on troops and allies. He therefore abandoned the attempt at a state wool monopoly and decided to leave the trade to the merchants, taking high export duties instead. As has been said, that raised constitutional issues and there remained the problem of who were to make him the loans against the security of the tax. His Italian bankers were sliding into bankruptcy, thanks in part to the huge loans they had made him. One or two German syndicates lent him money, but the answer was that native merchants would have to be his main financial prop. In 1343 a compromise was reached whereby the king was granted his export duty of 40s. a sack on top of the Ancient Custom, provided the Dordrecht bond holders received a rebate of 20s. a sack for a year and then 6s.8d. a sack for a further two months. All wool was to be exported through the Staple at Bruges, under the direction of the mayor and Company of the Staple. Finally the farm of the customs duties, hitherto in alien hands, was to be taken over by a group of 33 English merchants who were at first representatives of the Company of the Staple. They were to pay the

Crown 1,000 marks (£666.13s.4d.) cash every month, to account for the balance every quarter and pay a further 10,000 marks (£6,666.13s.4d.) a year above all issues.

There were compelling reasons why they should have entered into this agreement, which was otherwise disadvantageous to them. To counteract a shortage of coin in England merchants had been required to deposit two marks of silver at the mint for each sack of wool exported in the early 1340s. This on top of the duty was an intolerable burden and the merchants hoped that by controlling the customs they could obtain both a lowering of the duty and the removal of the bullion regulations.[6] They certainly achieved the latter, but parliamentary grant or no, the king continued to levy the *maltote*, the export duty. Moreover, although the syndicate started off as representative of the whole community of wool merchants, it soon came to be merely a group of monopolists anxious to exploit the trade to their own advantage. This and subsequent syndicates were led by men like William de la Pole of Hull, Walter Chiriton and Thomas Swanland of London, John Goldbeter and a group of northern merchants, the brothers Melchebourne and John de Wesenham from the East Anglian ports. With the exception of de la Pole and one or two others, these men did not have the large initial capital resources of the Italians. Their capacity to raise loans depended entirely on the special privileges they were given, and the syndicates themselves borrowed at home and abroad to meet the king's needs. If the wool market collapsed, because of strife in the Flemish towns, or was interrupted in any way, the syndicates were ruined. That is precisely what happened. On the eve of the Black Death the king was still without a satisfactory mechanism for raising loans against the security of the wool export duty. Parliament, joined by the lesser merchants, was bitterly opposed to monopolist control of the trade and there was still a long way to go before a compromise based on the Staple was to be reached. Yet the wool trade was now firmly in English hands. Although there are no export figures for the years 1343–51 Italians and Hansards were in a minority. The English were now in control of the most important branch of their overseas trade.

High export duties and constant interruptions in the wool trade were also having profound repercussions elsewhere in the English and Flemish economies. The price of wool abroad was increased to as much as the market would bear and the Flemings were now in competition with Italians and Brabanters for English wool. Flemish costs therefore rose, and at a time when there was great unrest in the towns. Externally there were wars with France and internally a series of revolts aimed at giving the textile crafts a greater share in urban government and improved standards of living. That meant higher wages – and again, higher costs. The immediate beneficiaries were the cloth workers of Brabant, but in the years before the Black Death the depressed English industry also began to show signs of revival. If the price of the basic raw material, wool, was high abroad, at home the effect of the heavy export duty was to depress prices paid to the growers. The merchants effectively passed the tax back to the growers. This had been noted in 1294–7 and is confirmed by William de la Pole's wool accounts in the late 1330s. They suggest that the only way merchants could make a clear profit was to pay lower prices to the growers. Because of unrest and falling production in Flanders, wool prices had been held down for a number of years. In 1337 transport and other costs added about £2 per sack to the English cost price of de la Pole's best Lindsey and Shropshire wool, bringing it to a Netherlands cost price of about £8.8s.9d. per sack. Wool of similar quality was sold by the king's agent, Paul de Monte Florum, at about £10 the sack in 1339. At that price, the profit per sack would have been about £1.10s.0d. That was on best wool; profits were less on the lower grades and from them the custom and subsidy had to be paid. This could be managed when the duty was 6s.8d. but scarcely when it was 33s. or 40s. The duty had to be passed back to the growers and the abbot of Meaux, a great wool producing house, was certainly right when he wrote at the end of the fourteenth century, 'After that time the price of English wool was brought down lower than ever before. And so it is those who own the wool who pay the tax to the king, and not the merchants who appeared to make the grant to him; for wools are sold at a lesser price the greater the tax payable to the king for them.'

Interruptions in supplies of cloth from abroad, a virtual tariff barrier pushing down the price of wool at home, demand for cloth to equip soldiers and sailors at the start of a great war – there could scarcely have been a better set of circumstances for stimulating an already reviving English cloth industry. The first signs of a limited revival come in fact in the early fourteenth century. The records of the petty custom, levied after 1303, show that cloth was being exported as well as imported through Southampton, Sandwich, Lynn and Hull. In the 1320s imports of foreign cloth were still considerable, but in the 1330s they fell rapidly and by 1340 had virtually ceased. Significantly, in the mid-fourteenth century 15–20 per cent of English exports were worsteds, medium-priced cloths which began to appear early in the century

199

among the purchases of the royal wardrobe, along with kerseys, traditional London burel and cheap russets, streits (narrow cloth) from Cornwall. There were no expensive Lincoln scarlets, however, which suggests that the first platform for the English industry's recovery was the cheaper fabrics, slump products playing something of the same role that the new draperies played in the sixteenth century. As the century wore on and the cost advantage began to tell, broadcloths reappear, first recapturing the home market, then moving into the export trade. By 1348 the revival of the cloth industry was well under way.

This is not to say, of course, that cloth exports were anywhere near as valuable as wool exports by the mid-century. They were not to outstrip wool until the third decade of the fifteenth century, in fact. None the less it was economically more beneficial for the English industry both to supply the home market and send its products abroad. More people were employed in making cloth than exporting wool. Industrial employment gave them greater spending power, and in spending they quickened the general velocity of circulation, stimulating economic activity generally. Made-up cloth was also worth more than raw wool because of the added value of labour and brought more wealth back to the country. Lastly, the very revival of the cloth industry ought to have brought renewed vitality to the towns, whose economies were beginning to show signs of strain by the end of the thirteenth century. Was this the case?

Once again, the evidence is contradictory. When the industry revived, it did so in both town and countryside and its potential growing points were widely spread. They included old-established centres like Norwich, Beverley and Bristol; that west country port was again exporting cloth by the first quarter of the fourteenth century. Some of it undoubtedly came from Ireland and from Bristol's rural hinterland, but some was also made within the town itself. There are signs of renewed activity at York where the industry had been in crisis: four weavers were admitted to the freedom in 1319 and cloth manufacturing grew so rapidly that by the second half of the century 17 per cent of York's citizens were engaged in the cloth trade. At Lincoln the fullers' ordinances were promulgated again in 1337. By 1348 there were complaints that citizens were employing weavers who were not members of the gild whilst other Lincoln weavers were refusing to contribute to the gild's royal farm. But the town no longer held the prominent place it once had. By the mid-century it was a producer of the second rank only. Salisbury, Bristol, London and Winchester were ahead of it, York and Gloucester behind it.

But there were towns where the industry did not revive at all. Oxford was one, Leicester another. By the early fourteenth century there are signs of the industry migrating from Leicester to the surrounding countryside. The inquest of 1322 into the oppressive rule of Thomas, earl of Lancaster, stated that there was only one fuller in the town, and he a poor person. Admissions to the gild merchant in the early fourteenth century confirm this picture of decline. Only 10 known dyers were admitted between 1300 and 1351, which scarcely suggests a thriving cloth industry or even a finishing trade. There was no revival either at Northampton, Stamford or Nottingham, where in 1348 the weavers' gild was complaining of reduced membership. By contrast, even in the first decades of the fourteenth century there is some evidence that the industry was active in the countryside. Cloth exported from Ipswich in those years was purchased in the town itself, at the old-established centres of Colchester and Sudbury and at new semi-rural centres like Coggeshall and Maldon, which were to be the focus of a very important industry on the Essex–Suffolk borders in the later fourteenth and in the fifteenth century. In 1327 men whose names suggest involvement in cloth making are to be found in some 40 Suffolk villages and towns and especially at Long Melford, Lavenham, Clare and Kersey. At this point they were producing a light, cheap cloth which like Norfolk worsted took its name, kersey, from a village where it was made. The Norfolk and Suffolk industry fed both the East Coast export trade and the London market with these cheaper cloths. But, when the time came, and the cost advantage told, the switch to broadcloths would be easy. There was also development in the North, in the West Riding villages, and in Wiltshire around Salisbury, both of which were to become major cloth-producing regions in the later Middle Ages.

So both town and countryside benefited from the renewed vigour of the cloth industry. But, as far as the towns were concerned, it would be a serious mistake to think that the benefits were evenly distributed, bringing universal prosperity. Within the same region different fortunes awaited different towns. As has been seen, Leicester was in considerable difficulties. As part of the earldom of Lancaster it had profited from the great state kept at Earl Thomas's residence there in the early fourteenth century. In one year alone he spent no less than £7,000 on hospitality. Yet he lived beyond his means and to raise money his officers resorted to oppression, especially in the famine years. Extra duties were imposed on cloth offered for sale, butchers were forced to pay a levy, heavy ransoms were charged for goods liable to toll and burgesses were impleaded in the castle court in suits which should have been heard in their own courts. Then, in the 1320s, the town suffered great damage during the earl's final rebellion and during the overthrow of Edward II. Its economy stagnated and yet, not 25 miles away, Coventry was prospering. The latter town at last achieved full self-government in the early fourteenth century as conflicts with the prior were resolved and various charters of liberties were granted by Queen Isabella in 1330, by Edward III and by Edward the Black Prince. In 1345 the townsmen received a charter which granted them the right to elect their own mayor and bailiffs and cognizance of all pleas and finally, in the tripartite indenture of 1355, the prior surrendered most of his claims to rights and privileges within the town. As self-government was achieved, so the town's economy, based on active cloth-making and metal-working industries, expanded. Coventry was, of course, dominated by the merchants, who in the 1340s were forming themselves into a series of gilds: St Mary's in 1340, St John the Baptist in 1342 and St Katherine in 1343. Three wool merchants from the town were summoned to discuss affairs with the king at York in 1322 and eight had their wool seized by the Crown at Dordrecht. Birmingham, too, began to develop as a non-chartered urban settlement. It acted as the centre for the South Staffordshire iron and coal industries and in 1327 and 1332 the town's assessment to the subsidy was greater than that of the majority of neighbouring settlements. By 1340 it ranked third, with Stratford, amongst Warwickshire towns in the contributions of merchants to a levy on goods, a very rapid rise indeed.

Thus, within the Midlands, one town prospered, another sank into decline, and this is a pattern which can be seen elsewhere. In the North East, York gained greatly not only from the revival of the cloth industry but from the Scottish wars. For a time the town became the capital of England and centre of government, as the royal court resided there. A wide range of employment was offered to York carpenters, smiths, tailors, ropers, bowyers and fletchers and to masons working not only on ecclesiastical, civic and domestic buildings but on the king's siege engines and the castle. Cloth, shoes and canvas were bought in York, and in 1304 arrows and the ingredients to make Greek fire. York's port, Hull, also seemed to be doing well. As the English share of wool exports increased, Hull merchants flourished, William de la Pole being, of course, the outstanding example. In 1329 he exported no less than 2,377 sacks of wool, mostly through his home port. Yet Hull's general economy does not seem to have been as buoyant. Edward I's plans for physical growth and for increased profits from rents were slow to be realized post-1300. Vacant plots proved difficult to let and at the general re-letting of 1317 the rents of 1293 could not always be achieved. The total valuation of the town in 1320 was £62.4s.2½d., excluding stallage and court profits, a reduction of £4.8s.1½d. since 1293. The decay of rents continued after 1320 and the underlying economic trend at Hull was stagnation, which the success of the wool trade cannot disguise.

If York, and to a lesser extent Hull, profited from the war in the North, Southampton was nearly ruined by the French wars. The raid of 1338 is usually taken as betokening the beginning of hard times; in fact they had begun some ten years before. In the 1320s men from Winchelsea, with the ostensible pretext of controlling the seas, were terrorizing the South Coast. They landed at Southampton and burnt 17 ships lying on the strand. This was not a unique incident, for the men of the Cinque Ports often seemed more interested in piracy than fishing or trading. As a result, on the king's instructions, the burgesses began the heavy burden of completing the town's defences. But the cost was great and the leading men in Southampton who held property by the sea were unwilling to have their access to it cut off. In 1338 they paid for their folly. Southampton was sacked by the French, with great destruction of wool, wine and property, much of which was still waste in 1340 and 1342. Edward III was so angry that he took the town into his own hands, garrisoned it and ordered the completion of the walls. The victory of Sluys removed the immediate threat of invasion, but there were renewed scares in 1340, 1342 and 1346, and the burgesses had to pay for their own defence. The Black Death therefore merely intensified an already deepening recession at Southampton. In sharp contrast, Salisbury enjoyed a period of prosperity. Its merchants were involved in the wool trade and it was rapidly becoming the centre of the Wiltshire cloth industry. Indeed, wherever we have information, the success of one town can be balanced by difficulties for a neighbour. In spite of the revival of cloth manufacturing at Norwich, the opening years of Edward III's reign saw the town in something like a depression compared with its rival Yarmouth. The earliest surviving list of contributors to the subsidy in 1332 shows 415 at Norwich and 281 at Yarmouth. But, two years later, when the contribution each should make to the subsidy was fixed, Norwich paid £94.12s.10d. and Yarmouth £100. With its control of the river, Yarmouth was putting a stranglehold on Norwich goods passing through the port, charging tolls on them to the detriment of Norwich's trade. Gloucester and Hereford suffered as their military importance declined with the conquest of Wales. But Gloucester remained an important iron-working centre and both towns gained from being centres of pilgrimage, to Edward II's tomb at Gloucester and Bishop Thomas Cantiloupe's at Hereford, at both of which miraculous cures were said to have occurred. At Hereford this allowed continued work on the cathedral and in both towns the 'tourist trade' provided employment for townsmen. Banbury had no saint, and its expansion ceased in the fourteenth century, whilst Chester began to suffer from the silting up of the River Dee and declined as a port.

It is much easier to catalogue these tales of success and failure than it is to provide a neat economic explanation for them. Obviously local factors were often important – the rivalry between Yarmouth and Norwich for instance, the French raid at Southampton, but they will not account for Leicester's decline and Coventry's rise, unless the region could not support two flourishing towns. Certainly this is no picture of uniform prosperity and in this sense the Black Death only accelerated existing trends in the urban sector, for the striking feature of the later medieval economy is the success of some towns and the stagnation of others. But, prosperity or no, there does not seem to have been any easing of the social friction which was such a marked feature of the late thirteenth-century town. There were the same complaints about the domination of urban government by the wealthy, its perversion to suit their own ends and of inequalities in taxation. Only in one town, or rather city, does there appear to have been continued economic success and some liberalization of government, and that is London. Edward II's reign was a stormy period in London's history. There were political and constitutional struggles on various levels, the most important being that between the old patrician oligarchs, whose power Edward I had tried to break, and the rising crafts, the fishmongers, cornmongers, vintners and those connected with the growing Baltic trade. Both groups also disliked power passing to professional administrators, as it did in the mid-1310s, and fought against them. At the same time, the *populares*, the bulk of London's population, were trying to secure a toehold in city government. There was thus a constant ebb and flow in London politics, which were often a microcosm of national struggles. London played an important part in the opposition to Edward II, siding with the Ordainers in 1310–11, with Thomas of Lancaster and finally with Mortimer and Isabella in 1326–7.

Eventually the city won its full independence from an unwilling Crown by the charters of 1319 and 1327. The power of the professional administrators was broken, for city government was to be under the control of an annually elected mayor. Professional servants were to be elected, not appointed, and their salaries were to be fixed by common consent of the citizens. City tallages were to be controlled by elected auditors and aldermen were to be taxed as other citizens. They were to be removable at will and were not to have an automatic second term, to prevent them establishing almost hereditary power. The attempt to secure their annual election was a failure, but the crafts won a considerable victory in two senses. First there was a fusion of citizenship and craft membership. Only those who were sponsored by a craft or were formally approved by the whole community could now become citizens. Secondly, no aliens were to be admitted to the franchise and non-citizens were not to be allowed to trade retail. Power in the city had now shifted decisively in favour of the crafts and participation in government thus widened, for the number of crafts increased rapidly in the early fourteenth century. Many of them were also obtaining royal charters granting them extensive privileges. Those of 1327 to the Goldsmiths, Skinners, Girdlers and Tailors granted them the right of search for defective workmanship throughout the realm. The charter granted to the city itself confirmed all its privileges and made it at last a full, self-governing entity.

The liberalization of government must not be overstated, however. To enter a craft a man had either to have served a long seven-year apprenticeship or have compounded by a money fine, and the majority of Londoners still had little say in city affairs. Moreover, the leading men in the crafts, the great merchants, the wealthy trader-manufacturers, were themselves to become in the course of time the new oligarchs. Yet perhaps the most striking feature of the new patriciate was that so many of its members were immigrants. The wealth of London – and its merchants were among the greatest in the realm, collectively undoubtedly the greatest – was beginning to act as a magnet to up-and-coming young men, especially from Norfolk and the East Midlands. There was such a flood of immigrants from these areas that a change in the city's dialect resulted. The new families did not found new dynasties and a pattern very evident in the later Middle

Ages was soon established. When the family had made its wealth in London, usually within three generations provided it survived the rigours of urban life, it moved out to join the ranks of the landed gentry. Their enterprise, however, and the presence of the royal household and the main organs of government made London into England's capital and its one great city in European terms. Whether or not its insatiable appetite for new blood was altogether beneficial for the English economy remains to be seen.

To strike a final balance sheet for the English economy in the first half of the fourteenth century is not an easy task. The trends are contradictory, even confusing. In spite of the shift away from demesne farming, most great estates carried on as they had done in the thirteenth century. Much of the peasantry remained impoverished and heavily burdened by taxation yet, in spite of a retreat in cultivation and settlement, their numbers do not appear to have fallen to any appreciable extent. The population appears to have replaced itself after the famines and villages were full, if not over-full, on the eve of the Black Death. In other, less important, sectors of the economy, change was under way, although it must be doubted whether contemporaries could have read the signs clearly. Nor could they have foreseen either the extent of the calamity that was about to fall on England in 1348 or the profound effects it was to have on the whole English economy.

7 Crisis and Change in the Agrarian Economy

'In this year 1348, in Melcombe in the county of Dorset, a little before the Feast of St John the Baptist, two ships, one of them from Bristol, came alongside. One of the sailors had brought with him from Gascony the seeds of the terrible pestilence and, through him, the men of that town of Melcombe were the first in England to be infected.' So, rather blandly, the chronicle of the Grey Friars at Lynn records the return to England, after nearly 700 years, of bubonic plague. From the West Country it was to spread by 1350 to all parts of Britain. It left in its wake a terrible trail of death, perhaps not as great as the 'nine parts in ten of them through England' the Eynsham Chronicler would have us believe, but still fearful enough. 'Nobody could be found who would bear corpses to the grave,' wrote the monk William Dene of Rochester. 'Men and women carried their own children on their shoulders to the church and threw them into a common pit.' The Louth Park (Lincolnshire) Chronicler best sums up the cataclysmic shock the Black Death brought. 'It slew', he said, 'Jew, Christian and Saracen alike; it carried off confessor and penitent alike . . . It filled the whole world with terror.'[1]

To later writers the advent of endemic plague has often seemed to usher in 150 years of misery for the whole of Europe. Not only plague became endemic, but so also did warfare. The longest conflict was that between England and France, which dominated the politics of western Europe between 1337 and 1453. There were many others, perhaps not as long but equally bitter. In fifteenth-century Italy city state fought city state whilst in western Germany, in the absence of strong imperial government, private warfare flourished. Bohemia was rent by the Hussite wars, in the lands beyond the Oder the expanding kingdom of Poland fought with the Teutonic knights, whilst south-eastern Europe saw the almost inexorable advance of the Turks. None of these can be equated with the 'total war' of modern times when the whole economy is directed to military ends. Yet, although armies were small, they still absorbed manpower and resources. The development of the national state made it possible for rulers to exploit their subjects to a far greater degree than had previously been possible. Taxation was constant and often heavy and at least one historian, Professor Postan, believes that the outflow of money from England to pay for the French campaigns was not balanced by the incoming profits of war in the shape of ransoms, booty and revenues from captured lands.[2] England was at least spared the destruction done in France by her own armies and the 'Free Companies', bands of mercenaries who fought on their own account when there were no official campaigns. More seriously for the English economy, the war interfered with both trade and traders. For example, embargoes on wool and cloth exports to Flanders could be used as diplomatic levers to force alliances. Each side preyed on the other's shipping and at times, especially in the fifteenth century, piracy flourished.

Taken together, endemic disease and endemic warfare are held to have caused for Europe as a whole 'the economic depression of the Renaissance' and for England in particular a century of 'stagnation tinged with gloom'.[3] As the population fell, it is argued, so did demand for food. Low prices for agrarian products were matched by high labour costs. Not only were there less people to do the work, but the labour force was further diminished by the movement of men from wage labour to vacant tenements. The ratio between resources and people was changed drastically. Landlords were faced with a combination of high costs, low profits from the sale of agricultural produce and the collapse of manorial discipline. Villeins could no longer be compelled to perform services or even stay on the manor when other lords could offer either higher wages or more favourable tenancies. Gradually, the landlords contracted out of demesne farming, opting for the administratively easier and cheaper policy of leasing which saved them the burden of hiring expensive labour to till their lands. From this, given the falling demand for land and low rents, they could but obtain a declining income. Lay lords sought relief in warfare or in the scramble for office which finally led to the civil wars of the 1450s and 1460s. Ecclesiastical lords had no such alternatives: they simply slid into genteel bankruptcy. The residual legatees of this collapse at the top were those at the bottom, the peasants. Now there was enough land for all: holdings could be enlarged and worked by family labour. Self-sufficiency was to be the keynote, for the peasant went to the market neither for food nor for other products. The resulting decline in demand led to a concomitant decline in towns, industry and trade, an overall decline which was not offset by the expansion of the cloth industry. Exports of broadcloths rose, but not until the end of the century did they equal in value the raw wool exports of the late thirteenth and early fourteenth centuries.

This is a gloomy picture of later medieval England. In some ways it is a hangover from Tudor propaganda which sought to exaggerate all the ills of the fifteenth century to show that the alternative to their strict rule was civil war and misery. Modern research has shown the reality to be far more complex. There was neither universal prosperity nor universal depression, nor did one class in society necessarily prosper whilst others went to the wall. But without doubt the Great Plague of 1348–9 gave both economy and society a severe jolt. Landlords were faced in 1349–50 with vacant holdings and a sharp if temporary rise in wage bills. Their immediate, panic, reaction was to try to control the labour market by first the Ordinance of Labourers in 1349 and then a specific statute in 1351. This sought to ensure a supply of cheap labour by pegging wages at pre-plague rates. Lords were given first claim on the services of their own men, skilled workers and others were not to leave one master to serve another before their contracts were completed, and masters were not to offer wages above the customary rates. Some attempt was made to control prices which had risen sharply if temporarily, but the specific regulations applied only to goods sold directly by the maker and thus affected only craftsmen and artisans. Food prices were simply to be 'reasonable', whatever that might mean. The statute was a clear piece of class legislation. It was passed by the Commons in parliament as the representatives of smaller employers in direct conflict with richer lords for fewer men and for a time it did succeed in holding back wage rises.

The panic did not last long. Within a few years the agrarian economy throughout the length and breadth of the country had recovered along traditional lines from the first onslaught of the plague. In Cornwall in 1349 the heavy mortality meant vacant lands and the cancellation of the fines and tallages due to the duchy from customary and villein tenants under the 1347 assession. The year 1350–1 was an awful one, bringing as it did a 40 per cent drop in income. But, by the end of that year, all holdings on its manors in south-east Cornwall had been re-let at their former annual rents, tenants were being tempted back on the north-east and central manors by reduced rents and only on the manors of Helston in Kirrier in the west and Liskeard in the east were long-term vacancies to be found. At Helston the problem of vacancies had existed before the plague arrived, and in 1350 over 3,000 acres of land were lying idle. Here, as at Liskeard, it was poor land that could not be let, however. Otherwise, recovery was rapid and near complete. The duchy benefited from the continued demand for land from previously landless men who had survived the plague and from its own wise policy, which saw that lower rents and full tenancies were preferable to the capital depreciation which the rapid deterioration of vacant lands and buildings would bring.

This same phenomenon of men waiting to take up land, to step into dead men's holdings, can be seen again and again. On the east Midland Ramsey estates the plague badly interrupted demesne cultivation, and to meet the decline in income the Abbey decided to switch from services to rents for its customary lands. Landless men and wage labourers were attracted to take up the holdings and the fall in revenue from demesne cultivation affected by the loss of labour services was offset by leases of parcels of the demesnes. On the neighbouring Crowland manors vacant holdings were soon taken up on pre-plague conditions by men from within the villages. The only land left vacant was on the margin of cultivation and no great loss to agriculture. Demesne cultivation was also maintained at Cuxham (S. Oxon) and all the holdings which had come into the lord's hands as a result of the plague were let again by 1355. Further west on Winchcombe Abbey's Cotswold manors the plague brought the disintegration and regrouping of holdings, but at both Bledington and Hawling (Gloucs) the lands were filled and at Sherborne heavy expenditure on labour for haymaking and harvesting between 1355 and 1358 shows the continuation of demesne cultivation. The plague seems to have hit particularly hard on the bishop of Winchester's estates which stretched from Taunton in the west to Witney in Oxfordshire, Crawley in Sussex and Farnham in Surrey. But on one manor only, Witney, where as many as two out of three people died, were there any long-term vacancies, 32 virgates being in the lord's hands in 1353 and 35 in 1376–7. Elsewhere the take-up of land was rapid. On the bishop's largest manor, Farnham, which coincided with the hundred and comprised land in ten villages, the plague raged from 1348 to 1351. Even three years of pestilence could not dislocate the workings of the manorial demesne and the lord could find tenants for all but the poorest land.

Across the whole of southern and central England the story is the same – after the heavy mortality from the first plague the lands were soon filled and there was no real dislocation of demesne farming. The great landlords showed a remarkable ability to weather the storm. On one or two estates only did the first plague mark the beginning or intensification of problems. Ramsey Abbey was heavily in debt before 1349 and in the decade after the Black Death there was a fall in money income in spite of the switch to rents. The abbey's cellarer received in cash from his manors less than half the pre-plague income from rents in kind of corn and other produce. In the 1350s and 1360s debts began to build up as rents from tenements, mills and customary holdings and entry fines remained unpaid. Some of the demesne was leased, but considerable amounts were just not used: the rest was farmed by hired labour, as services had been commuted. A thinner stream of profits, coupled with persistent manorial insolvency over two decades points to 'a fundamental malaise in manorial production, an underemployment of capital and labour',[4] the classic signs of depression due to depopulation. Battle Abbey's troubles, too, were just beginning. In the first decades after the Black Death long-term debts began to mount up, which forced the leasing of the demesne in the 1380s.

Ramsey and Battle are atypical, however. Elsewhere there was little interruption in the pattern of demesne farming in the 1350s and 1360s, profits were being made and seigneurial incomes were buoyant. The Winchester demesnes were still being farmed by labour services. Wage labour was only used on the Taunton group at harvest time or for skilled tasks such as thatching or masonry work. Labour costs rose by 25 to 35 per cent but since so much work was still done by customary labour, the lord could easily cope with such a rise, which in monetary terms might be only a few pounds for the whole group. On the bishop's Hampshire manors profits were higher in 1376–7 than they had been before the plague whilst there had been only a slight decline in receipts compared with pre-plague averages on the Somerset group; only in the mid-1370s was there any sign of a major shift from demesne cultivation to leasing. Much the same can be said of the Clare estates in East Anglia. The rent rolls gradually recovered after the Black Death although at the expense of labour services which, unlike those on the Winchester manors, were commuted. Theoretically this should have made demesne farming impossible: but it flourished, for by the 1360s wages had been regulated to not much above pre-plague rates. Elizabeth de Burgh, the lady of the estate, used the East Anglian manors as a home farm, whilst her cash income came from lands in the West and in Wales, from rents and the profits of justice. In Wales the fourteenth century was a period of stability in profits, although in the mid-1370s the proportion of income from rents declined whilst that from justice rose. Heavy fines were levied, in 1362 no less than £4,000 on the whole Denbigh lordship for the failure of men to attend courts, and that at a time when the total revenue from the Welsh estate was only £1,000. Such exploitation provoked deep resentment which was to burst forth in the Glyndwr rebellion in the early fifteenth century. Revenues from the lands in and around the borough of Bridgwater in Somerset were soon stabilized and vacancies filled. Indeed, it has been calculated that in the 1370s the income from the Clare estates was less than 10 per cent below a pre-plague average of about £2,000. Given the decline in population it probably meant that Elizabeth de Burgh was increasing her share of the total national income.

If the profitability of the Clare estate depended to some extent on the exploitation of judicial rights, the duchy of Cornwall's did not. It came from rents and by 1356 these had regained their pre-plague levels. For those who farmed the lands high labour costs were offset by high agricultural prices. Demand came from workers in the tin mining industry, from ships in west-country ports waiting to be victualled and from English garrisons in Gascony. Only poor lands could not be let and by the 1370s rising rents and court profits pushed ducal income to heights greater than those achieved before 1348. Nor was agriculture profitable only in 'free' areas. The Essex manor of Writtle was being farmed successfully by a mixture of hired and customary labour in 1360–1. The sale of corn and dairy produce brought in £109.10s.3½d., inclusive of supplies sent to the lord's household, rents, sales of work and perquisites of the court a further £79.6s.7d., making a total income of £188.16s.10½d. Against this was set expenditure on ploughs, carts and repairs to the park and watermill of £16.15s.3¼d. The manor was in fact working well below its potential, but at a fair profit. So was Winchcombe Abbey's manor of Sherborne, so were the Winchester estates and the archbishop of Canterbury's demesnes. Not until the 1380s did that shrewdest of all landlords begin permanently to lease the 40 demesnes, mills, marshes, meadows and parks scattered all over south-east England.

In the two decades after 1349, then, many great lords were more than holding their own. Not only did they continue to till their demesnes but they were able to use their coercive judicial powers to enforce their rights over their tenants – and make a handsome profit from it, too. This could be done on a national and a local level. Nationally, the Statute of Labourers was made to work. After the plague years of 1348–51 wages did not rise as sharply as might have been expected. They were held back partly by a continuing surplus of labour and partly by the rigorous enforcement of the statute. The hostility which met the justices of the labourers wherever they went, the rescue of offenders from their custody and attempts to kill the justices themselves are fair evidence of effective enforcement in some areas. Nor did it die down after the first shock of the plague was over: indeed, enforcement probably became more vigorous in the late 1370s when the shortage of labour really began to bite. Presentments in Lincolnshire in these years concerned the failure to fulfil contracts, the taking of higher wages than those allowed by statute and the enticement of a servant from his master by the offer of better terms.

Locally, the lords had a whole battery of weapons at their disposal to help them maintain their income. Labour services might be renewed or intensified to provide cheap labour. Money rents could be raised, as they were on the Durham Priory estates and on the Beauchamp manor of Elmley Castle (Warws), whilst the reorganization of the Eynsham Abbey (Oxon) lands after the first plague led to entry fines, new money rents and boon services greater than the old level of money rents plus commuted services. The unfree status of the villeins could be exploited in a number of ways. On the Evesham Abbey estates in 1368–9 a fine of 40s. was levied for permission to marry the widow tenant of a yardland, and merchet payments were as high as 20s. In many places tenants were forced to work vacant holdings or pay fines for the privilege of not doing so. Judicial powers were also there to be used. At Elmley Castle in 1356 the homage was collectively fined £20 for declaring a fugitive to be a free man when they had previously recognized his villeinage. But this was as nothing compared to the Black Prince's extortion in his county palatine of Cheshire, which provoked a rebellion in 1353. Hard pressed for money, he ordered a thorough investigation into all breaches of the forest laws in the Wirral which raised £3,928 in 1353–4 compared with an average annual income from the county of £1,300–1,800 in the early fourteenth century. What the Black Prince did in Cheshire, so did many another. There can be little doubt that the decades after the Black Death saw exploitation of the peasants in excess even of the bad days of the thirteenth century.

Some historians have interpreted the Peasants' Revolt of 1381 as the

213

inevitable reaction to this oppression. The lords, they argued, prevented the villeins taking advantage of the opportunities offered by a substantial reduction in the population and the peasants rebelled, letting loose the pent-up hostility of a hundred or more years. Such an explanation does not ring entirely true, for the fifteenth century was to show that manorial discipline could not be enforced when there was an acute shortage of labour and a large surplus of land. Oppression was not possible unless lands were full and there was competition for jobs, the situation that seems to have prevailed in England until the mid-1370s. After that signs of change really begin to appear as the relaxation of population pressure in the 1360s and 1370s altered the landlord's position. It was not until the years 1370–90 that the tide turned full against him. Rising labour costs and falling commodity prices drove him to the wholesale leasing of the demesne. On the Clare estates such leasing began in the 1360s and gathered pace until it was virtually completed by 1381. Writtle's demesne was partly in the hands of a tenant in 1376 and partly derelict, the Canterbury Priory manors were leased about 1370, the Abbey of Bec's in its bailiwick of Ogbourne (Wilts) by 1379. Coupled with this were the beginnings of long-term vacancies in peasant holdings and of flights from the manor. The depopulation of Hatton (Warws) began about this time. The unfree tenants, dissatisfied with their status and unwilling to pay the high rents demanded by the bishop of Worcester, started to leave the manor. At Forncett in Norfolk the turnover of land was high and an increasing number of tenants were waiving their lands and leaving the manor. As at Hatton, high rents were part of the reason, 2s. per acre for customary land where services had been commuted compared with 10¾d. on the open market. The peasants were not prepared to pay, and voted with their feet.

Only in the mid-1370s then did plague really begin to bite hard into the traditional manorial economy. From 1375, for the first time in the fourteenth century, money wages did not conform to the movement of prices, for low prices did not force down wages as they had in the 1340s.[5] Costs rose, rents fell, vacancies increased and the lords were clearly troubled. Petitions in the parliaments of 1376 and 1377 spoke wildly of servants fleeing from their masters, of confederations by the peasants to resist their lords, to try to prove that they were not liable to labour services, of attacks on seigneurial servants. The lords had lost much profit from their lordships, in many parts of the realm the corn lay unharvested and unless a speedy remedy was applied war might well break out within the kingdom. Hyperbolic language, perhaps, but also the complaints of worried men. They had reason to be. In the late 1370s conditions had changed and not in their favour. Resistance to overt seigneurial oppression was becoming widespread, unlike the isolated incidents of the late thirteenth and early fourteenth centuries, and all classes of the peasantry were involved in it. Wage labourers were resentful of the regulation imposed by the statute and in the areas where it was enforced rigorously the rising of 1381 seems to have been particularly bitter. The land-holding, unfree peasant, suffered in a number of ways. The more prosperous and enterprising saw their efforts to acquire now vacant land blocked by their lords' insistence that, as unfree men, they were liable to entry fines, services and other payments. Freedom was not to be established by the purchase of land. That had long been the case, but it now became an intolerable restriction. The steward of the St Alban's estates was instructed not to grant several holdings to one man, or where it had happened to split them up and to insist on the unfree nature of the tenures. There was bitter resistance to this and in 1381 the abbot was forced to grant a charter of liberties which included the freedom of alienation.

Just as important as the freedom to acquire land was freedom before the law, the right of access to the royal courts of justice for the protection of one's land instead of being answerable only in the lord's court. The prosperous peasant was also in competition with the lord for labour to till his larger holding. He had no reserves of servile labour to fall back on, nor the power to control the distribution of wage labour by judicial means. Ordinary customary tenants were equally resentful. They hated labour services, especially summer boon works which came at a time when peasant resources were thinly spread, and would refuse to do them. In 1379 conflict over the performance of labour services led to the general seizure of the goods and chattels of all servile tenants on the Worcester Cathedral Priory estates. And, as has been seen, the ruthless exploitation of other aspects of villeinage was to all unfree peasants' disadvantage. There was only one effective way to end the exploitation – end villeinage.

The kindling for a general peasant revolt was there in the 1370s, and the resistance was for the first time born of hope, not despair. The basic relationship between land and people had at last changed. Social and economic freedom now seemed a practical possibility and this is what the peasants demanded at Mile End in 1381, an end to villeinage, free rents at 4d. per acre and freely negotiable wage labour contracts.

Rebellion might have come in any year after about 1377 and to understand why it did not come until 1381 the Revolt has to be set firmly in its political background. By the 1370s English politics had turned sour. Edward III was in his dotage, his eldest son, Edward the Black Prince, was sick with the illness which was to kill him in 1376. The French war was going badly: it cost a great deal but the government appeared unable to protect even the South Coast. There had been outright attacks on the king's ministers in the Good Parliament of 1376 and discontent smouldered during the unpopular regency of John of Gaunt after Edward III's death in 1377. To general political unrest must be added anti-clericalism. The resentment of the Church's wealth permeates the works of Chaucer and Langland. An heretical movement, Lollardy, inspired partly by John Wyclif, was growing in strength. The Lollards demanded the disestablishment of the Church and the redistribution of its property. Such ideas had a wide popular appeal as can be seen in the fundamental cry of the rebel priest John Ball,

> When Adam delved and Eve span,
> Who was then the gentleman?

Yet what finally set the revolt off was the weight of taxation. Between 1377 and 1381 the government, in addition to the normal taxes on movable property, the subsidies of fifteenths and tenths, took three new levies, the poll or head taxes levied on all over the age of 14. An anonymous poem written after the revolt claimed, rightly, 'Tax hath tenet [ruined] us all'. The burden of old and new taxation was too much to bear. In 1379, for instance, a graduated poll tax ranging from £6.13s.4d. from the duke of Lancaster to 4d. for the single peasant man or woman was levied on top of other subsidies which between 1378 and 1380 were estimated to be likely to yield over £120,000. The third poll tax of 1380–1 was the final straw. Its collection was bungled so that it seemed as if another new tax was being taken without consent. In early June an attempt was made to arrest villagers near Brentwood (Essex) who had refused to pay. They resisted, and soon the whole of south-east England was in turmoil. The rebellion had begun.

The Peasants' Revolt is a subject worth studying in its own right, for it is one of the few genuinely popular uprisings in English history. Its most serious manifestation was the attack on London by the rebels from Kent, Sussex and Essex. The government was badly shaken and the young king, Richard II, had to make major concessions, promising the rebels personal and economic freedom. But the rebellion was not simply confined to London. There were serious outbreaks in East Anglia with particularly vicious risings in Cambridge and Bury St Edmunds. In both cases the burgesses settled old scores, in the one case against the university, in the other the abbey. Ecclesiastical landlords appear to have been the most hated, perhaps because manorialism was most developed on their estates. At St Alban's burgesses and peasants joined forces against a hated lord, there were attacks on Grace, Dunstable and Redbourne monasteries, along with a widespread destruction of manorial records, to remove all evidence of personal unfreedom. Outside southern and central England disorder was less common. Tension between the burgesses and the Augustinian hospital of St Thomas lay at the heart of the uprising in Bridgwater, and social conflicts unconnected with the Peasants' Revolt caused the northern riots at York, Scarborough and Beverley.

Obviously, this was something more than a peasant rebellion. Townsmen, artisans hit by the effects of the Statute of Labourers, poor parish priests little better off than most of their parishioners, lesser landlords who also found the labour legislation working to their disadvantage, all threw in their lot with the peasants. Yet what the rebels wanted, what they demanded at Mile End, was freedom for the peasantry and for much of the summer of 1381 they kept the south east of England in a turmoil in pursuit of that end. Eventually the government recovered its nerve, rallied its troops and went back on its promises: 'villeins you are and villeins you shall remain', Richard II is said to have told an Essex deputation demanding ratification of the promises made at Mile End. By autumn, in all parts of the country, relative peace had returned.

It is easy to dismiss the Peasants' Revolt as an interesting event of minor importance: 1381 saw neither the end of villeinage nor of peasant discontent. There were further complaints about disorder in the parliament of 1388, frequent renewals of the Statute of Labourers and even further general risings in Cheshire and Yorkshire in 1392–3. Rebellion only died down as economic trends began to move even more in the peasants' favour. Yet it is worth speculating what might have happened had the government not acted in the way it did. There was no wholesale persecution of the rebels. Some of the leaders, the most notorious like John Ball and Jack Straw and William Grindcobbe at St Alban's, were executed but the majority of the insurgents were left unharmed. The stories of ruthless suppression contained in the Chronicles are largely unjustified. A quite remarkable degree of clemency was shown which allowed villeinage in England to die a protracted but quiet death.

Die it had to, for in the long run there was nothing the lords could do to reverse the trends. The 1390s brought a short-lived prosperity based on wool and cloth exports and, presumably, the profits of arable agriculture, for even Ramsey Abbey was tempted back into demesne farming. But from the early fifteenth century the signs of change in the economy are all too obvious, the most apparent being the decline in the demand for land. Poor and good soils alike began to go out of cultivation on most manors. Between 1410 and 1450 on the Battle manors holdings became derelict as peasants refused to take them up. The arable on the Writtle demesne was further reduced, no more than 565 of the 1,300 acres being under crop in 1413. On the Ramsey estates there was an accelerating pattern of decline. Deserted and dilapidated holdings rose from one or two to six or more on most manors and then, between 1420 and 1440, to eight or nine. Even in Cornwall where tin mining and other trades and industries kept demand buoyant in the east there was further contraction in the west. Two thousand acres of land remained unleased within the conventionary system at the beginning of the fifteenth century. On manors like Tywarnhaile the situation had become even worse by the assession of 1420. Substantial areas of land were not taken up and there was a sharp decline in rents and fines from the rest.

The most extreme manifestation of the fall in demand for land was the desertion of villages. There were few parts of England where this did not occur, but depopulation seems to have been at its worst in Norfolk, in the North East and above all in the Midlands, especially in Warwickshire, Oxfordshire and Northamptonshire. Plague of itself had little to do with the desertion, except in general terms. Rather, it was a gradual process, beginning before the plague and continuing well on into the fifteenth century when depopulation was at its most intense. About 70 villages disappeared in Oxfordshire between 1350 and 1486, some 25 per cent of the whole, the comparable figure for Northamptonshire being 18 per cent. These villages lay in the heart of arable England and the traditional story is that the tenants were driven out by rapacious landlords who sought to offset the decline in income from the sale of corn by switching to sheep raising to supply wool to the home and export market.[6]

Such stories are untrue. In most cases the peasants left against their lord's wishes. The villages most likely to be deserted were usually small, on poor land and with an inadequate supply of pasture. Hatton in south Warwickshire is almost a classic example. It had grown rapidly in the thirteenth century and was peopled by unfree tenants. Tax figures suggest that it was richer than its neighbour, Hampton Lucy, since it contributed more to the subsidies of 1327 and 1332. But high taxes were matched by high rents, some 40 per cent more at Hatton than at Hampton. The ploughing-up campaign of the thirteenth century had brought much poor land into use, as well as cutting down the amount of manure available. Gradually, disliking both unfreedom and high rents the tenants began to drift away in the 1370s, and by 1427–28 the whole village was depopulated. The lord, the bishop of Worcester had been forced by rising costs and falling prices to abandon the cultivation of the demesne. Now he was losing his rent income as well and it was in desperation that he turned to pastoral farming for a few years. Eventually he decided to abandon demesne farming altogether and leased the pasture as well as the arable. There was no sudden eviction for sheep farming – especially when wool prices were so uncertain. Hatton, like many another village died a long slow death, whilst its neighbour Hampton survived. There the free tenants proved a stabilizing influence. They had a status and an inheritance worth keeping. Holdings were enlarged and often consolidated and enclosed and it was the peasants, not the lord, who took advantage of abundant pasture, increased their flocks and herds and engaged in the local cloth industry.

Hatton was not untypical. Other Warwickshire villages such as Kingston and Compton Verney were depopulated in the same way and on the same time scale. Only when wool prices rose above those for grain in the late fifteenth century did landlords seize upon these vacant lands and turn them into large and enclosed sheep runs. Before that they bear silent witness to the decline in demand for land. At the same time demand for labour outstripped supply, so that wages and therefore costs rose whilst, with a smaller population to feed and perhaps increased productivity, prices for agricultural produce fell. The realities of the situation can be seen on Battle Abbey's manor of Marley. It lay near the abbey and was used as a home farm. A professional manager was hired to run the estate after the plague. He used a much smaller labour force than before, but with a much higher proportion of skilled workers, and experimented with convertible husbandry to improve yields.[7] Efficiency and cost saving were the key notes at Marley in the 1350s but when at the end of the decade the abbey was unable to find another professional manager, the manor had to be leased. Profitability at Marley depended, as at Cuxham, on professional skills, careful management and low wages. When the manor came back into hand again in 1384 there was no longer any advantage in direct management. Wage costs, which had been about 3s. per acre in the first 60 years of the century now stood at 8s. an acre. That was too much. Corn would have had to have been continually at a premium price to cover costs: leasing offered a cheaper and administratively more convenient method of securing a regular income from one's estates, and Battle Abbey took it.

So did most other landlords, although the pace of change varies from estate to estate, region to region. All Battle's 28 manors were at farm by 1382–3, at Durham Priory the crucial years for leasing were between 1408 and 1416 and Westminster Abbey's demesnes were leased by 1420. On the other hand Winchcombe Abbey's manor of Sherborne was not finally leased out until 1464 and the bishop of Worcester did not abandon demesne lands and sheep flocks until 1450. Nor was leasing always continuous. A manor might pass back into hand if no tenant could be found for it, as Writtle did between 1450 and 1457. None the less, it remains broadly true that between 1380 and 1440 most landlords leased out both arable and pastoral demesnes and the customary peasant lands, the critical period probably falling between 1380 and 1420. Occasionally, as at Battle, the manors were leased out en bloc. For the most part, however, the demesne land or flock would be leased as a whole either to one man or partnerships of two, three or four men, or in small parcels to peasants or others willing to take them up. The peasants now paid money rents for their land and these, with the older fixed or assized rents, were paid directly to the lord. Every aspect of the manor's economy was thus geared to provide a rent income for the lord.

Ruin, according to the Postonian thesis, should have stared these men straight in the face. Their standard of living should have declined dramatically, unless they could find alternative sources of income. Yet many great lords lived in considerable estate, built extensively, fed many retainers and indulged in that most expensive of games, politics. Tales of woe there certainly are. Ramsey Abbey met with nothing but disaster in the fifteenth century. Reorganization of the manorial economy on a rentier basis was accompanied by the deepest and most prolonged recession in the Abbey's history. Tenants were unwilling or unable to pay their rents and debts grew until they had to be wiped out as uncollectable between 1460 and 1470. Leicester Abbey was in like case. In 1341 the value of tithe and demesne corn sold on the Abbey's Leicester lands was £573: in 1477 income from both rents and corn sales came to only £240, a fall in income of something over a half. But there is also ample evidence of adversity successfully faced. The archbishop of Canterbury's revenue of £3,466 in 1535 was over £1,000 higher than it had been in 1291. In part this was due to the acquisition of more land, and administrative costs had risen, but he was still better off in the fifteenth century. Durham Priory's income did decline, from about £2,000 per annum in the early fifteenth century to £1,572 at the time of the Dissolution, but the monks' standard of living did not decline with it and they, like Canterbury, were able to indulge in an extensive rebuilding programme. Richard Beauchamp, earl of Warwick (d.1439) was far better off at the end of his career than at its beginning. By 1435, thanks partly to an increase in his estate through inheritance, his landed income stood at £5,000 compared with £1,400 clear in 1401–7. No wonder he could order in his will that four gold images of him, each 20lb in weight, should be made and distributed to the four most fashionable shrines in England. Falling rents and narrowing horizons affected neither the house of Beauchamp nor the house of Stafford. The Countess Anne, who survived three husbands, held English and Welsh lands worth about £4,350 gross or £3,700 net in the late 1430s. Her son, who eventually acquired her lands, had an income of £6,000 per annum gross or £5,000 net, which made him a very wealthy man. But such stories of wealth and property have to be set against the more familiar tales of the Percy earls of Northumberland who, if they had not acquired more lands, would have seen their income fall by a quarter between 1400 and 1450, or the duke of York, potentially the wealthiest lay subject in the land, whose 270 manors brought him in about £3,500 per annum, only four times as much as Edmund Grey, lord of Ruthin, made from 34 manors and lordships.

How can such an apparently random pattern of success or failure be explained? In the first place it must be acknowledged that in any age there are fools who come to grief by political misfortune or sheer fecklessness or both. Playing politics in the fifteenth century was dangerous and expensive, no sure route to success at all. The Percy earls of Northumberland had a considerable landed patrimony in the North, in Yorkshire, Northumberland and Cumberland, as well as lands in Sussex. In 1399 they had benefited from supporting Henry IV in his seizure of the throne, but in 1403 they threw all their advantages

221

away by rebelling against him. After a protracted struggle they lost, their estates were confiscated and only partially restored in 1416. Between 1416 and 1461, determined but not altogether successful attempts were made to regain the lands but in 1461 the family again backed the wrong side in the struggle for the Crown and its estates were once more confiscated, until 1469. Discontinuity in management, disinvestment, lost revenues, all help to explain the Percys' fifteenth-century troubles. It is true, of course, that no great family could afford to stay completely aloof from either national or local affairs. In order to protect its own interests it needed a broad basis of support from the local gentry in its own area of influence. The services of such men were retained for a yearly fee. A lord with political pretensions or who lived in an area where royal authority was weak and local disorder prevalent had to face a heavy burden of fees. The Percys lived in the lawless North and were engaged in a running feud with their rivals, the Nevilles. In 1461 administrative overheads along with fees and annuities amounted to one-third or even one-half of gross revenues on both the northern and Sussex estates. The Percys were heavily in debt, since their landed income just did not meet their needs, and office holding was no answer to the problem. They were Wardens of the East March, responsible for border defence against the Scots. Their expenses from April 1440 to Michaelmas 1457 were £52,995 but the bankrupt Lancastrian monarchy could pay them only £36,000, leaving a debt of £16,995 as a very considerable burden on the earl's already stretched revenues.

Politics were no route to success for the Percys – quite the reverse. Some men, like Ralph, lord Cromwell, may have profited from office but others, such as the duke of Suffolk or William, lord Hastings, lost their heads, whilst the Herbert earls of Pembroke under Edward IV were to find that what had been given could as easily be taken away. It must also be remembered that the profits of office did not flow equally into all pockets. Only a select group at the centre and their clients did well: others had no share of the spoils at all, and the scramble for office will not explain the success of Tavistock Abbey nor the failure of Leicester and Ramsey. Nor can the profits of war be regarded as the panacea for all ills. Mr McFarlane has brilliantly shown that there certainly were profits to be made from ransoms, booty, pay, revenues of lands in France and of course, sheer peculation. Sir John Fastolf noted that he made 20,000 marks from the single Battle of Verneuil in 1424, whilst on the eve of the collapse of the English occupation in 1447–8

Humphrey, duke of Buckingham drew about 800 marks income from his French lands. Such profits were invested in building – Farleigh Castle in Somerset was built from the ransom of the duke of Orleans captured at Agincourt – or, and above all, in land. But there is a loss as well as profit side to the account. The heir to the Hungerford barony, Robert, lord Moleyns was captured in Gascony in 1453. His ransom was £6,000 but interest charges and the cost of keeping the prisoner in sufficient estate brought this sum up to nearly £10,000. The Moleyns and Hungerford estates had to be mortgaged and then, when Moleyns chose the wrong side in the civil wars, the lands were forfeited altogether. Command also brought its financial problems. The duke of York was owed £18,000 for wages paid to troops in France when he was principal commander there and he probably made neither profit nor loss from subsequent commands in France and Ireland. York did badly from both war and politics, for he was never properly repaid for the heavy loans he made to the Crown between 1442 and 1452. Others were more successful and it may be that the balance of profit did come to England, that the country was wealthier in 1450 than it had been in 1350, yet vast sums, some £8 million in all, were spent on the war and not all of it can have come back into the country.

Perhaps the most striking feature of both office holding and warfare is how often the profit was invested in or came in the shape of that supposedly worthless commodity, land. Estates were bought by successful warriors or given to royal servants like Ralph, lord Cromwell, sometime Lord Treasurer, on whose death lands worth £5,500 were returned to their lawful owners. The issue cannot be evaded: ultimately the key to success or failure in terms of income somehow lay in the land, and the problem still remains, why should one lord be able to maintain a high level of revenue from his estates whilst others found it difficult to make ends meet? One argument seeks to explain the difference by separating lay from ecclesiastical landlords. The former, it says, were better able to meet the difficulties of the age because they were able to acquire more and more land, so placing a greater share of national wealth in progressively fewer hands. This was possible because of a basic change in the land law which allowed the creation of trusts to hold the lands of tenants-in-chief (and sub-tenants), the tenant himself holding from them a life tenancy only. When he died his estate no longer escheated to the Crown, and the strict laws of inheritance were defeated. Provision could be made for younger sons or daughters, or women could be excluded from inheritance until all lineal male heirs were extinct. What before had been uncertain, how the lands would descend, was now made certain. Estates stayed together for long periods and the way was open for the acquisition of more lands for the family by dynastic marriages. So Ralph Neville, the first earl of Westmorland married his 22 children by two wives at tender ages into some of the most distinguished houses in England. One son married at 17 the 15-year-old Joan Fauconberg, an idiot since birth but heiress to the barony of Fauconberg, whilst another acquired the earldom of Salisbury through his wife. The result was that much more land came into family hands and whilst the Nevilles are an extreme case what they did was not exceptional. More land came into fewer hands. At the end of the thirteenth century the nobility consisted of some 12 or so earls along with some 3,000 gentlemen with incomes of £20 per annum and above. By the end of the fifteenth century a 'peerage' of some 50 or so had emerged, controlling large blocs of land. The lay estate had been given the homogeneity long since enjoyed by its ecclesiastical counterpart. Marriage made the Nevilles and saved the Percys. It might be argued that it saved the nobility generally.

The thesis is persuasive, but the fact remains that not all lay landlords prospered whilst some ecclesiastical corporations did, and they could scarcely play the marriage market. Nor did they continually receive fresh endowments since gifts from the laity had long since dried up. No, the factors which, combined, brought success for some and acute difficulties for others were good management and the location of one's estates. As in any age good administration was important. The leasing of the demesnes did not for the good lord mean abnegation of responsibility for the lands. No lord could afford to see his demesnes farmed to ruin by a tenant seeking quick profit or to let buildings and fences fall into decay. That would mean a considerable loss of capital invested in land and equipment and would require heavy expenditure to put matters right before a new lessee would be willing to take up the land. Competent management wrote into its leases a liability on the tenants to maintain the land in good heart and buildings and mills in good repair. The archbishop of Canterbury specified that the farmers must pay for the results of their own negligence and that the arable must be kept in good and seasonable tilth, on occasion defining the scale of manuring and marling to be carried out. Westminster Abbey insisted on the same conditions and often made its tenants enter into an indemnity bond to ensure that they were carried out. But it was not just a matter of protecting the land: the lord had to be prepared to put in his own money to help maintain the demesne lands and buildings. In the second half of the fifteenth century the archbishop of Canterbury allowed his farmers anything from 3-20 per cent of annual rents to pay for repairs they performed locally, whilst on the Beauchamp manor of Lighthorne (Warws) the figure was 4 per cent of total cash receipts between 1390 and 1436. Provision by the landlord of assistance in building and repairs, chiefly in the form of grants of timber, was in fact, quite normal. Some care has to be taken in using percentage figures of expenditure in this way, since a rising proportion of revenue spent on building and equipment could conceal a falling physical volume of this type of capital as the landlord's receipts and profits fell and labour costs rose. But the property that could be let was not allowed to run down. Capital investment had to be maintained if the lord was to attract and retain worthwhile tenants.

The second essential was the development or adaptation of estate administration to meet the new conditions of a rentier economy. No two estates were alike, in size or geographical distribution of holdings or administration, and the basic administrative structure outlined below is necessarily an idealized account. First, the manors would be grouped into units called receiverships, either on the basis of geographical contiguity or because they had formed a previous administrative or tenurial group. The official in charge of the unit, the receiver, as his name implies, received monies paid over by the lessees of the demesnes and the reeves and other administrative officers who collected the customary rents. He paid out locally wages, fees, money for repairs and other items, as directed. The receiver was something more than a mere rent collector, however: he had to oversee all the lord's property in his bailiwick and even act as a local cash depository, circumventing the central financial apparatus. The receivers, of course, gained considerably in local influence whilst, if they were efficient, the lord benefited from a regular or even an increased income.

As the receiver was the central point in the local administration, so the receiver general occupied a similar position in the system as a whole. There might be one for the whole estate or a receiver general for specific groups of receiverships. The receiver general was the chief financial and accounting officer, providing the essential link between local and household officers, receiving monies from the localities and distributing them to the treasurer of the household or in fees and wages to knights, esquires and other servants. In this way the lord obtained a

225

regular flow of cash from his estates for both his day-to-day and his long-term needs.

The function of the next group of officials, the auditors, is largely self-explanatory. They checked both central and local accounts, visiting the various receiverships to charge the officers with all the monies for which they had to account and then discharging them for all authorized payments and other expenditure for which good reason could be shown. They checked on repairs, inquired into debts and arrears and arranged for payment by instalments if necessary. Centrally the auditors drew up from the local and central records a valor and an arrears account. The valor was a digest of all the local accounts, showing the lord the potential receipts from and allowances made on his estates in any one year. Its essential complement was the arrears account which recorded monies not paid in that year and debts of long standing which were thought desperate or irrecoverable. Together, the two documents were important steps forward in estate accounting which came into general use by the end of the fourteenth century. They gave the lord a clearer idea than ever before of the actual cash surplus he could expect from his estate in any one year.

The two final essential components of estate administration were the steward and the council. There might be a steward for each receivership or, as in the thirteenth century, one for the whole estate. His most important duty was to hold the lord's courts, which had not been abandoned with the leasing of the demesnes. He also supervised all other officers and where, as on the vast duchy of Lancaster estates, there was a chief steward for all the lands, then he travelled far and wide on the lord's business. Difficult matters were reserved for his decision and he would be joined in his judgment by the local officers. If the receiver general was the chief financial officer, then the steward was the chief legal and administrative servant. Finally, at the heart of the whole estate lay the lord's council. Originally intended to advise, it now dealt with the whole administration of the estates acting as the supreme judicial body, hearing appeals from the local courts and the most difficult cases. So, one would expect to find lawyers and judges sitting on it, along with the lord's most trusted servants and councillors, with the lord himself as its head and driving force.

This was how administrations developed on lay estates in the fourteenth and fifteenth centuries. The church lands already had systems which could be adapted to new needs. But efficiency depended as much on the quality of leadership and servants as on sound administrative structures. Dishonest servants and poor leadership could spell disaster. Edward Stafford, third duke of Buckingham, suffered a decline in rent income from his English and Welsh estates in the late fifteenth century. In part this was due to growing arrearages of rent as tenants refused to pay them, a not uncommon problem in the fifteenth century. But there were also officials who would not hand over monies paid to them and like many another lord, Buckingham faced a dilemma. He wanted the money, but his local officers were men of standing whose influence he could not afford to lose and who could not, therefore, be distrained for non-payment. This attitude may well explain the well-known inefficiency of the duke of York's administration. He had a potential income from his English and Welsh lands of £8,000, which after expenses had been deducted ought to have yielded £4,500, but he received in cash only about £3,500. York failed to interfere in or improve his administration and he did not try to exploit the latent resources on his manors. The growing cloth industry on his estate at Bisley offered him the same opportunities as it did Sir John Fastolf at Castle Combe. Fastolf took his opportunities, charged high rents and entry fines, exploited water rights and took chevage for permission to remain on the manor from 60-70 workmen employed by the master clothiers. He made a fair profit, whilst on York's manor it was the tenants who reaped all the benefits. York probably did not see his estates so much as a source of income as of landed and political influence, but good management could undoubtedly have brought him a far greater monetary return. Durham Priory's troubles were also as much administrative as economic. Times were hard in the North East since endemic warfare was piled on top of economic recession, but the priory had largely come to terms with that. Its only period of real difficulty came in the 1430s when the office of bursar, always unpopular, was entrusted to an inexperienced monk who ran up huge debts and eventually fled the monastery. These were also years of harvest failures and high prices and the monastery, under a prior who had no interest in administration, was nearly ruined. But it fought its way out of the difficulties and could afford, in the first half of the fifteenth century, to invest a considerable amount of capital in an expensive rebuilding programme. Just how much difference a good administrator could make, when conditions were right, can be seen on the estates of Ewelme Hospital. It had been endowed by the duke of Suffolk with three manors, one in Wiltshire, one in Hampshire and one in Buckinghamshire. Administration costs and rents were high in the first half of the fifteenth century and yet arrears mounted. Not until the 1450s was a man found with enough sense to wipe out arrears, lower rents to what the market would bear and increase the Hospital's actual as opposed to its theoretical income.

So, a good administration which set fair and flexible rents, ensured that they were collected, that officials did not cheat and arrearages did not build up could help the lord to weather the storm. On the duchy of Lancaster's Welsh estates in the early fifteenth century such policies were followed: arrears of rent and corrupt officials were ruthlessly pursued and as a result, in the reigns of Henry IV and Henry V 98.8 per cent of potential revenue was actually collected. There were other, equally ruthless landlords in the fifteenth century, the bishop of Winchester for one, Joan Beauchamp, lady of Abergavenny, William Herbert, earl of Pembroke for others, just as there were fools like the sixth earl of Northumberland who in the early sixteenth century earned himself the sobriquet 'the Unthrifty'. But, good administration was not a cure-all. Sometimes it could make little or no difference. The bishops of Worcester were not lax administrators, for instance, but they could not cope with the simple refusal of tenants to pay rents or officials to hand them over. Nor could the Talbot family, for all their efforts, prevent the decline in the revenue from their large Shropshire estate at Whitchurch. This covered some 32,000 acres of mixed farming land in the Midland Gap. Revenue came mainly from rents for copyhold[8] land ($\frac{1}{3}$), land still in demesne and manorial issues ($\frac{1}{4}$) and the profits of controlling local justice, trade and industry ($\frac{1}{4}$). Between 1383 and 1422 the estate was managed directly by the lord, then from 1422 by John, earl of Shrewsbury's professional administrators, but neither could halt falling revenues. In the first half of the fifteenth century they went down from £321 in 1400 to £236 in 1437, as rent income fell, lands were left vacant, demesne farming proved increasingly unprofitable and the profits of justice, towns and trade declined. There was no local demand, no local cloth industry to stimulate it. The Shropshire economy had stagnated and there was nothing that aggressive management could do about it.

There was no salvation, either, in switching from arable to sheep farming. The hard facts are that for most of the fifteenth century grain prices stayed above those for wool except for the years 1462–86. Running demesne flocks of sheep was not cheap either. The sheep were cosseted and pampered, fed expensive pulses and housed in expensive buildings in winter. Between 1434 and 1439 the duchy of Lancaster actually made a net loss on its sheep farming operations on its three

Berkshire manors, providing capital depreciation is taken into account. Sales of wool and sheep brought in £245 but expenditure on buying sheep, wages and harvesting hay with estimated capital depreciation came to £252, a loss of £7. Gradually the duchy leased out its flocks to the local gentry and peasantry who spent much less on them and could accept lower prices. Even so, sheep farming was only economically attractive for short periods in the fifteenth century, a fact that was certainly reflected in the demand for pasture on the Derbyshire lands of the duchy of Lancaster. A sharp slump between 1448 and 1456 was followed by increased demand and rents from 1457 to 1465, stagnation up to 1475, rising demand again up to 1485 but from then to 1505 falling demand and rents. Sheep farming did not end the century on a booming note and for most great lords it was certainly not a viable alternative to leasing the demesnes.

The location of estates also provides a key to understanding why some lords prospered and others did not. A comparison between the subsidy returns for 1334 and 1514 shows that there had been a dramatic shift in the geographical distribution of wealth from the old Midland grain belt to London and the South East and the cloth producing and tin mining areas of the South West. Those with estates in these areas benefited accordingly. The archbishop of Canterbury's buoyant income was without doubt due to the pull of the London market. The rent rolls of his manors near the city were swollen by those who wanted houses outside the plague-ridden city and a peasantry anxious to farm for a still-growing market, whilst there was a much intenser exploitation of the rich arable and marshlands in the north and east of Kent. There was no slackening in the demand for good land, except for a brief period in mid-century, and clearly nearness to London and the availability of cheap waterborne transport were the key to the region's prosperity. Small ports like Faversham and Romney flourished in the fifteenth century off the London trade, the one acting as an outlet for the grain and wool of north Kent, the other for the produce of the rich marshlands behind it. Less is known of the lands north of London but it would be surprising if Ipswich, Colchester and other small ports did not act in the same way as Romney and Faversham and thus provide prosperity and a continuing demand for good land in their Essex and East Anglian hinterlands. London's tentacles spread far: they reached out to the Midlands for meat and to East Anglia for grain and fish. The very presence of the only English city of any size provided wealth for the South East of the country in the later Middle Ages.

229

Figure 7.1 Distribution of lay and clerical wealth per thousand acres in 38
counties of England in 1334. The numbers show the ranking of each county

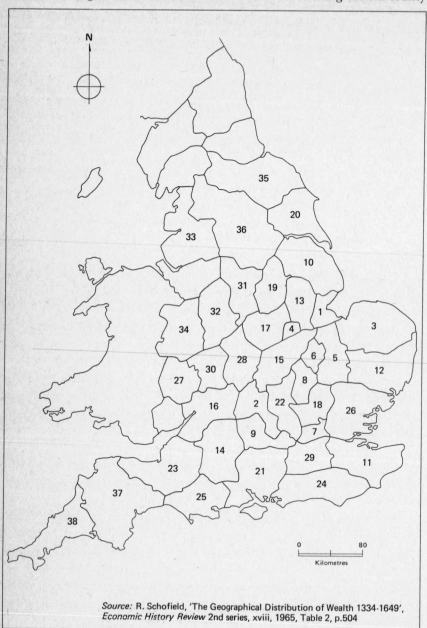

Source: R. Schofield, 'The Geographical Distribution of Wealth 1334-1649',
Economic History Review 2nd series, xviii, 1965, Table 2, p.504

Figure 7.2 Distribution of lay and clerical wealth per thousand acres in 38 counties of England in 1514. The numbers show the ranking of each county

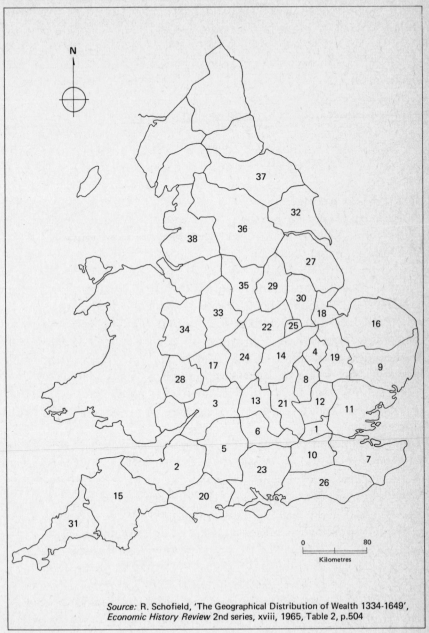

Source: R. Schofield, 'The Geographical Distribution of Wealth 1334-1649', *Economic History Review* 2nd series, xviii, 1965, Table 2, p.504

The other wealthy area was the South West with its cloth production and mining. The agrarian history of Devon and Cornwall illustrates well the importance of local demand. In Cornwall, the sharp contrast was between east and west. The land market in the west was depressed. After the second decade of the century there was a decline in both tin output and the demand for food. The soil was poor, land fell out of use and there was migration to the east. There, cloth making along the border with Devon was expanding and there were opportunities to supply food to the Devon Stannaries, less than a day's journey by cart from south-east Cornwall. Land was in demand for both arable and pastoral farming and the local economy thrived. If the duchy estate had been as efficiently managed in the fifteenth century as it had been in the fourteenth, then the duke's income would have benefited accordingly. Tavistock Abbey's did. Although some outlying demesnes were leased, the remainder were farmed – and farmed well. Grain was still produced for the market along with wool and dairy produce, and at a profit more often than not. Under three able abbots the monastery flourished in the fifteenth century, thanks again to local demand. Equally striking is the contrast between east and south Devon. East Devon in the late fourteenth and the fifteenth century transformed itself from an arable into a wood/pastoral economy due to the demands of the local cloth industry which needed both workers and raw materials. The economy was buoyant, local court and rent rolls show a countryside fully occupied, no shortage of tenants or lack of demand for land. By contrast south Devon was unsuited to pastoral farming and had no local industry. The result was depopulation, which allowed the tenants who remained to enclose and consolidate their arable holdings, but was of little benefit to local lords.

Outside the South East and South West there were other areas where local demand can clearly be seen to have affected rents and seigneurial incomes. There was demand for pasture on the duchy of Lancaster's Derby estates in the second half of the fifteenth century and expansion into the waste in the Forest of Blackburnshire by a rent-paying peasantry whose livelihood was stock raising. The rent income from Haslingdon and Accrington went up accordingly, at Haslingdon from £6.17s.2½d. in 1324 to £9.7s.4½d. in 1451 and at Accrington from £2.8s.2d. in 1296 to £12.9s.9½d. in 1451. This more than offset the decline in traditional revenues from the lordship of Clitheroe held by the duchy of Lancaster. But against this has to be set the tale of woe coming from the Midland 'grain belt', the counties stretching from

Gloucester and Worcester in the west to Cambridgeshire, Huntingdon-shire and parts of East Anglia in the east. There seemed to be nothing that landlords in this region could do to stave off disaster. The bishop of Worcester held 17 manors in three west Midland counties. Direct cultivation of the demesne was abandoned late in the fourteenth century, the lands being let out first for short terms which lengthened in the fifteenth century to 40 years or more. Demesne flocks were leased out by the 1450s and by that time the bishop's income came entirely from rent. It ought to have been about £850 to £1,000 per annum, a decline from a high point of £1,200 in the early fourteenth century, but due to arrears which in 1460 reached the staggering sum of £1,449 it was nothing like that. Some of the arrears were temporary only, but a great many were bad debts and in the long episcopate of John Carpenter (1444–71) some £60-150 of such debts were pardoned in any one year.

These arrears did not result from lack of tenants or desertion of villages or reduction of rents. These were already taken care of by the general decline in the value of the estate. Rather the bad debts arose from the refusal of both demesne lessees and peasants to pay their dues, secure in the knowledge that threats to abandon their holdings would prevent the bishop taking any action against them. At the other end of the Midland belt Ramsey was in such straits by mid-century that debts had to be written off. Penalties for dilapidations were unenforceable, for as on the Worcester estates the peasants would rather leave the land than pay the fine. Conditions were no better in Warwickshire. The 1480 accounts for the late duke of Clarence's estates show a high proportion of uncollectable rents for the non-demesne lands, ranging from 40 per cent of the total at Brailes to 8 per cent at Sutton Coldfield. Rents paid by the demesne lessees at Warwick and Morton had fallen by 36 per cent compared with earlier years and no one could be found to take up the demesne at Sutton Coldfield where the fulling mill was in ruins and the dovecote destroyed. If there was a landlord's purgatory in fifteenth-century England, then it lay in the Midlands. Local demand for grain had fallen sharply, plague and migration had caused the desertion of villages. There was no hope of supplying the rich South East with corn because of lack of good direct water routes. Sheep farming brought no salvation, although cattle raising seems to have been the saving of lesser men, and it is no wonder that there was a general shift of wealth to the South East and South West.[9]

Just as there was no general overpopulation in thirteenth-century England, so there was no general agrarian depression in the fifteenth

233

century. There was indeed no one English economy, but rather a whole series of regional economies. Some prospered, others suffered, and there could be wide variations within the regions themselves. Within prospering areas and even, paradoxically, within some depressed regions, there was a continuing demand for the core of good land being farmed. It came not simply from the upper ranks of the peasantry, seizing the opportunity to make for themselves small or even medium-sized farms, but from those who, for want of a better term, are called 'the middle class' or 'the gentry'. The fifteenth century was not simply a peasants' benefit: to farm a demesne you needed capital, to pay the rent, buy the seed, hire the labour and to cover expenses whilst waiting for the corn or other produce to be sold. Not surprisingly, everywhere one finds gentlemen, knights, esquires, yeomen, lawyers, richer merchants from the towns, either singly or together leasing demesnes from the greater landlords. In Cornwall it was the duchy officials – tin-mining entrepreneurs and burgesses – who took up the leases, in the North East yeomen and merchants from Newcastle upon Tyne. On the Battle estates, where whole manors were leased, burgesses from the town, with business interests and prosperous relatives spread over east Sussex and Kent, took them up, whilst in the Honor of Tutbury in Staffordshire and on the abbot of Westminster's demesnes the lessees included a fair number of former officials, bailiffs and sergeants who were essentially working farmers. Provided he had or could acquire some capital it was the man on the spot with local knowledge who was best placed to take up the land.

Occasionally it is possible to see how such men built up or expanded their estates. Bartholomew Bolney was a member of the administrative middle class and trained in the law. He served the abbot of Battle as his senschal, holding various courts for him from the 1440s onwards, he was a JP between 1450 and 1476 and a member of various commissions of oyer and terminer and dykes and sewers in the Pevensey levels. Bolney was admirably placed to acquire lands and his book of charters shows how he put together a small estate around the manor of Amyse in Firle (Sussex). He held land in many ways and of many men, working within a complex land market, and so had to keep a careful record of all his leases. What he and his neighbours were trying to do was consolidate scattered plots of land, especially downland and marshland pasture, into units that could be efficiently managed. His contemporary in the Midlands, John Brome, descendant of a Warwick tanner, had a similar administrative background and held posts in both national and local government in the reign of Henry VI. He had inherited the manor of Baddesley Clinton but it is some indication of the velocity of the local land market that it had changed hands no less than four times between 1394 and 1438. In addition to the main manor, he acquired various parcels of land in Warwickshire, the largest being 250 acres near Nuneaton in 1457. Brome, like Bolney, did not exist in a vacuum but in the midst of what appears to have been a thriving yeoman society much in competition for the pasture now available in the seemingly depressed Midlands.

Why were such men at best eager, at worst willing to take up and farm the demesnes? It should not be assumed that the lands handed over to them were in dire economic straits. Many were like Clyst near Exeter which the bishop of Exeter kept in hand until 1420. In the seven years before leasing the average clear income was £32, the largest element coming from rent and stock farming, with only £4.16s.0d. from the arable. As has already been seen, capital investment by the lords did not stop and to a certain extent the lessees used the lord's money to finance their own operations. Of course, not all lessees succeeded: several of Durham's tenant farmers in the fifteenth century found that the experience ruined them, rather than made their fortunes. A survey of 1446 leaves little doubt that at that time many villagers were reluctant to take up leases. But the mid-fifteenth century was a sticky period generally and it is quite clear that men like Bolney, Brome and their contemporaries did make a success of farming the demesnes. Not only did they take advantage of continued investment by the lord, but they had much lower overheads. Many were working farmers, employing the minimum of labour and using it wisely, as the professional manager of Battle Abbey's manor of Marley did in the 1350s. He cut down waste and in particular the amount of corn paid out in wages and perquisites, undertook to be responsible for a minimum harvest of three times the seed corn sown and made the manor more profitable than it had ever been. Profits could still be made in the mid-fifteenth century. John Brome had a large enclosed demesne of some 300 acres of pasture on his manor of Baddesley Clinton, along with some meadow and 200 acres of woodland. This land he used for fattening cattle bought nearby at Birmingham and Coventry, which had links with the Welsh Marches, and then sold to local butchers and on occasion to Londoners. From this trade, from a quarry and tile works (a not unusual combination of agriculture and industry in a wood-pasture district) and from some rents, he made a fair profit. Running costs were low after the initial capital investment had been made in clearing, fencing and stocking the land. He had few administrative overheads, because he farmed the estate himself. Cattle sales brought in about £10-15 a year and the total income from this manor was about £20 per annum. This was about the same as he might have made from leasing the estate but, because of the problem of arrears, potential and actual income were not the same. In all Brome made a comfortable income of about £40 per annum from his Warwickshire lands. Like many others, he had seen that what paid in the Midlands, and elsewhere, was cattle, which could be driven to the market cheaply, and not corn. It is this that helps to explain the continued demand for pasture in the Honor of Tutbury, the pressure on grazing in manors around London like Tottenham, the expansion in pastoral farming in Rossendale and Derbyshire.[10]

To achieve a balanced judgment on the prosperity of the middle classes is not yet possible. Not all could have fared as well as the Bromes, Bolneys and the Pastons or the Kentish gentry and yeomen of fifteenth-century Otford with their investments in building and property and in cloth, as well as cattle and malt. Yet the vigour of the class, their ability to use their own and their lord's capital, to enclose and invest in cattle and possibly improved forms of arable farming and to diversify into industrial operations is impressive. The days of king grain were over: farming was much more mixed, and the increased number of cattle cannot but have improved arable yields,[11] especially now that only the best lands were cultivated. These middle-class lessees of the demesne added an element of vitality to English society in the fifteenth century. If they managed to secure their lands freehold or on long leasehold – and leaseholds were lengthening as a return to demesne farming became more and more unlikely – then they would prosper in the sixteenth century. If knights, gentlemen and yeomen collectively held more land than the nobility, the peasantry farmed more than all other classes put together. Of all elements in late medieval society, they experienced the most change in the years after 1381. Most men in the pre-plague period had been tied to the land, but that was now no longer the case. Vacant holdings were to be had everywhere, there was a continuing demand for wage labour from demesne lessees and wealthier peasants. Death and migration could produce startling turnovers in holdings. Only five of the 27 families on the Ewelme Hospital manor of Marsh Gibbon (Bucks) were the same in 1492 as in 1408 and the most striking feature of a comparison between Bolton Priory rentals of 1473 and 1539 is the small proportion of names which appear in both.

Thaxted (Essex) with its cutlery industry seems to have been a magnet for outsiders. Less than a quarter of all holdings in it were in the same family's hands in 1393 as they had been in 1348, and nearly a quarter of those passing into other hands went to outsiders. Other industrial villages probably had the same experience, and the small market town of Leighton Buzzard (Beds) certainly did. Newcomers here were involved in 66½ per cent of 909 recorded transfers of customary lands between 1464 and 1508. In most cases the blocks of land being transferred were small, but by the late fifteenth century an increasing proportion, some 18 per cent of transfers, were of holdings over eight acres, some of them being of 40 acres or more. The active land market in Bedfordshire generally allowed the wealthy and the enterprising to enlarge their holdings into small farms, a phenomenon noticeable all over England.

So the bonds of manorial discipline were broken: customary tenants could not be forced to stay on the manor or work for the lord. The change was not sudden. Villeinage was not abolished at a stroke, nor did it die completely, for there were still a few serfs to be found in sixteenth-century England. But landlords could not prolong the custom when economic forces were against it. Land was readily available and at reasonable rates. Rents at Forncett were 6d. an acre in the mid-fifteenth century, half what they had been in the 1370s. Peasants could not be forced to take up holdings against their will: they would simply leave the manor if this happened. Unpopular exactions could not be levied. The recognition fine due from each man of the new bishop of Worcester in 1435 could not be collected because the peasants threatened to leave his manors. It was no bluff: a study of Ramsey's estates shows that whilst the majority of tenants stayed where they were after 1400, a substantial proportion moved away from their home manor. Most went relatively short distances in search of better land or better terms, even to other villages controlled by the Abbey. Others went to neighbouring towns, St Ives or Huntingdon, to take up a trade, whilst some inevitably were drawn to London and the South East. As they moved out, so incomers came into the Ramsey manors and there was nothing the lord could do to stop such movement.

It was not always the enterprising who migrated. At Compton Verney and Kingston (Warws) it was those poor in capital equipment and money resources who surrendered their holdings to the lord and left to seek their fortunes elsewhere in highly paid wage labour or in the cloth industry. So, in many parts of England, an active peasant land

237

market developed, both for parcels of the demesne and for customary lands. Lords leased, rather than sold the lands, on a variety of terms and conditions. Coventry Cathedral in the early fifteenth century leased 11 demesnes in Warwickshire and Leicestershire for terms ranging from 2 to 60 years and for rents in kind as well as cash. Lessees of demesne lands could often sublet, thus complicating matters even further, and they enjoyed greater security of tenure the longer the century wore on. Not all land became leasehold, however. The majority of the old villein tenures were converted into what became known as copyholds. But the variety of terms is bewildering and in some ways it is a mistake to look for patterns. Nevertheless, some generalizations can be drawn and the peasantry divided into three main groups.

At the top were the wealthy and enterprising, who had always been present in peasant society and who now exploited the land market to piece together holdings of 30 to 60 acres or so. Tilsworth, Bedfordshire, may be taken as fairly typical of what happened in a manorialized area. The majority of men there held between 10 and 39 acres, but three held substantially more than that, one 55 acres of arable and 4 of meadow, the second 92 acres of arable and 8 of meadow and the third 102 acres of arable and 7 of meadow. In pastoral areas herds and flocks were built up, a sign of capital accumulation by the peasantry. This was particularly common in the west Midlands and Derbyshire, where in the High Peak peasant flocks of over 400 were not unknown and of 250 quite common. So a peasant aristocracy emerged, leasing parts of the demesne, renting other lands, consolidating their position by marriage like their social betters and thriving into the ranks of the gentry. On Battle Abbey's manor of Marley two families, the Gunnes and the Hamonds, seized the opportunities offered and extended their lands. Both prospered and eventually, thanks to intermarriage, Simon Hamond became heir to both sets of property in the mid-fifteenth century. Even in Cornwall, where there had been no trace of a peasant aristocracy before 1347, one now emerged as working farmers built up their holdings.

The day of the yeoman farmer had arrived, of men holding 60 or so acres of land by a whole variety of tenures, freehold, leasehold, at will (that is, from year to year) or even copyhold. An upper limit to the size of farm does seem to have been imposed by the availability of capital and the cost of labour, especially in arable farming. The size of arable holdings suggests that these men were farming for the market, as their pastoral counterparts certainly were. The connection between the villagers of Hampton Lucy and butchers in neighbouring towns has already been seen, as has the continuing demand for pasture from Rossendale to Sussex. Pastoral farmers could serve more than the local market. Wool went from Derbyshire to the West Riding, whilst cattle from that county were sent to be fattened on the pastures of Leicestershire and Cambridgeshire and thence to the markets in the South East. With the possibility of improved arable yields, there is perhaps something to be said for the argument that the lowness of cereal prices bears witness to the tireless energy of the peasantry in producing for the market.[12]

This class of wealthy peasant was relatively small. A breakdown of the land-holding pattern on the Ewelme Hospital manors of Ramridge (Hants) and Marsh Gibbon (Bucks) (Table 7.1) is probably fairly typical. The largest holdings represent the lands of no more than 2-4 families and what is striking is the survival of the 'traditional' virgater and the high proportion of smallholders who probably worked for wage labour. It is the status and condition of this middle rank of the peasantry which is the most difficult to determine. They were neither aspiring to the ranks of the gentry nor enlarging their holdings. Nor did most of them seek to make themselves free men by the process of manumission, the grant of free status by a charter from the lord. That could be expensive: Ramsey villeins paid between £10 and £20 for the privilege in the early fifteenth century. No, the majority sought instead a fixed agreement with their lord, that they should hold their land by copy of court roll according to the custom of the manor. That varied from one village to the next, and one set of villagers might well be able to obtain

Table 7.1 Distribution of holdings on the Ewelme Hospital Manors of Ramridge (Hants) and Marsh Gibbon (Bucks)

Acreages	Ramridge 1433 % of population	Marsh Gibbon 1492 % of population
3 Virgates + (120 acres)	{ 3.5	4
2 Virgates + (60 acres)		8
1–2 Virgates (30–60 acres)	16.5	46
1 Virgate (30 acres)	33	23
½–1 Virgate (15–30 acres)	29.5	
Less than ½ Virgate	{ 16.5	{ 19
Less than 8 acres		

(J. P. Genet, 'Economie et Société Rurale en Angleterre au XV⁰ siècle, d' après les Comptes de l' Hôpital d'Ewelme,' *Annales (Economies, Sociétés, Civilisations)* 27, no. 6, p. 1465.)

more concessions from their lord than another, so generalization is again difficult. But basically most copyholds were like those found on Bedfordshire manors in the fifteenth century. When the customary holding was surrendered to the lord, the new tenant, the heir or an incomer, would, after payment of an entry fine, receive a copy of the entry on the court roll recording his admission to the holding at a fixed annual rent. The land was heritable, it could descend from father to son, but usually only for a term of lives, often three. After that, a new tenancy agreement would be made. The copyhold could be sold by the peasant, however, provided the transfer was recorded in the court and the appropriate entry fine was paid.

Thus the inalienable holding from which a whole series of services and payments were due had changed into a heritable and alienable holding, at a fixed rent, but still liable to entry fine and heriot. Obviously in the fifteenth century no lord could charge either excessive rents or excessive entry fines or indeed sometimes any fines at all. Yet, whilst servility by tenure had largely disappeared, nowhere in the copyhold did it say that the man was legally free and therefore able to claim protection for his land outside his lord's court, in the royal courts. It is said that by the mid-fifteenth century the common law was beginning to protect the security of tenure of the copyholder as were the courts of equitable jurisdiction, like the Chancery, on the grounds that many gentlemen held both free and copyhold land. These were very different men from the mass of the peasantry and it still has to be shown that all copyholders, or even a majority of them, did receive such royal protection. In the fifteenth century the problem was not crucial but in a less favourable economic climate the copyholder's position could become very vulnerable. Rents for copyholds may have been fixed but entry fines were not, and when demand for land grew again they could be raised. Even where the terms were fixed, if the copyhold was for three lives, then conditions could be reviewed at regular intervals, in practice about every 21 years. Every two decades accidents of death and succession might leave the peasant helpless before his lord. In the long run one cannot help feeling that the mass of peasantry may have exchanged the devil for the deep blue sea.

Nevertheless, villeinage had virtually disappeared, there was land enough for peasants to support their families in all but the worst years of harvest failure like the 1430s, and possibly have a surplus for sale. Income might be supplemented or even wholly earned by wage labour. In any village there seems to have been a core of men who farmed little land but lived by hiring out their labour and thus formed the third main class of the peasantry, the wage labourers. They were much in demand, even in the depressed Midland areas of England. John Brome[13] spent £20 on labour in 1444–5, the majority of it for the services of skilled craftsmen. One such earned a total of £3.19s.6d. which would have kept himself and his family in comfort. Some of Brome's workers were not in fact cottagers but substantial cultivators who used their own equipment when working for Brome. If agricultural labour was not attractive, then there was also employment to be found in the textile or other rural industries. For the wage labourer life was good in the fifteenth century, but again, as with the copyholder, only because of the prevailing balance between land and people.

The prosperity of all classes of the peasantry must not be exaggerated. There were poor men still, disease was rife, starvation possible, yet compared with the thirteenth century the fifteenth was one of quiet prosperity for the mass of the people. They had enough to eat, possibly money to spend on products other than food and the opportunity to acquire more land if they wished. A major question, however, is where the peasants (or, indeed, the middle classes) acquired the capital which allowed them to build up flocks and herds, where did they find the fixed and circulating capital which allowed them to engage in arable farming for the market, which needed ploughs, waggons, oxen and hired labour? The profits of trade would provide some of the money needed but prices were low and unless productivity could be increased, which may have been possible, such profits would have been slender. One way in which peasants and demesne farmers alike could accumulate or acquire capital was by exploiting the lord's resources. They could expect continued investment in their rented lands, and could refuse to pay rents or hand over monies they had collected. The problems such actions caused the bishop of Worcester have already been seen. He lost about one-twelfth of his income every year as a result of a refusal to pay rents and dues, a substantial downward redistribution of income which helped his tenants in the west Midlands to build up flocks and herds. The earl of Buckingham and other (but not all) lords faced similar problems, especially in the Midlands. On the manor of Lighthorne the villagers thwarted until at least 1480 attempts to collect their full rents. In the end the lord gave in and the tenants achieved a reduction of about 5s. of the 15s.6d. rent for a yardland. Like the bishop of Worcester's tenants the Lighthorne men pleaded poverty and the weight of taxation, but they were in fact well placed to serve local markets, being

241

some seven miles from Warwick at the junction of the Fosse Way and the Oxford to Warwick road. This was another effective redistribution of incomes, but the difficulty lies in applying this economic evidence to the South East and South West, where demand for land was still high.

Money, of course, could be borrowed, from relatives, wealthy villagers or even from outsiders. Little is known of this aspect of agricultural society. Cases of debt are frequently to be found in late medieval court rolls, since manorial courts could hear actions involving less than 40s. For the most part they concerned the sale of goods, especially of livestock, but sometimes they involved cash loans. Small sums, under 10s., may have been distress borrowing, but where amounts up to 40s. were involved, it is possible that one man was borrowing from another to invest. There were men in the fifteenth-century countryside willing to lend to those less fortunate or less able than themselves. One such was William Morton, almoner of Peterborough Abbey, who managed his own as well as the monastery's livestock. He 'lent' to 'borrowers' of cattle. Sometimes this was genuine: Morton would hire out cows at a yearly rent to peasants too poor to make the not inconsiderable capital investment themselves. At other times it was a device to cover up a little money lending. The loan was made for a period of years with the understanding that if the cow was not returned a specified sum of money would have to be repaid, which, understandably, was more than had been lent. Morton lent to all and sundry, to local merchants and butchers and farmers. Many borrowed to ward off creditors, yet this cannot disguise the fact that money was there and available in the fifteenth-century countryside. Peasants with skill enough both to accumulate and to farm holdings of up to 60 acres or more must also have had wit enough to know from whom and at what rates money for capital investment could be raised.

It now seems beyond doubt that there were significant improvements in English agriculture in the fifteenth century which raised productivity. How widespread they were is still not clear, but it does seem possible that one way capital could be acquired at a time of low prices and high costs was by producing more from the same or a smaller amount of land. This argument runs contrary to the idea that falling yields in the late Middle Ages, especially of barley and wheat, were only halted in the fifteenth century by concentration on the best land. But signs of technical improvement are clear on Battle Abbey's Sussex demesnes in the late fourteenth century. Farming practices were evolved from the three-course rotation which involved the suppression of fallow on the best lands, the extensive use of legumes and high seeding ratios. Up to a third or half the arable on manors such as Apuldram, with substantial meadow and pasture, were continuously cropped, using a three-year rotation of barley/oats, legumes and wheat or a variety of other combinations, but always involving legumes and high seeding ratios. Good seed beds were prepared using turn-wrest[14] ploughs, and the ground was maintained in good heart by the nightly folding of sheep on the arable, heavy use of manure and of nitrefying legumes whose properties were clearly understood. Seeding ratios were twice those recommended by the *Hosebonderie*, partly because germination was poor on dry light soils and partly to control weeds on chalk land where poppy and charlock were endemic. Dense sowing smothered weeds, kept the corn and legumes relatively clean and obviated the need for fallowing to clear the land.

Battle's reward was high net yields per acre. At Alciston, the home farm, cereal yields of sixfold were attained eight times out of 30 recorded harvests, representing net yields of 15, 20 and 20.97 bushels per acre for wheat, barley and oats respectively.[15] These far exceeded the returns advocated by the *Hosebonderie*, but so seldom attained. Yields of wheat and oats generally were also superior to those achieved on Lord Beveridge's sample of Winchester manors. Alciston's wheat yield per acre was 40 per cent higher than the mean of five Winchester manors and 25 per cent above the average yield of the most productive. Barley yields were also superior, Alciston exceeding the Winchester mean by 28 per cent. The achievement becomes all the more remarkable when the weather is taken into account, for the last quarter of the fourteenth century was a period of frequent storms and floods. But Battle was not alone in improving its agriculture. Further west, in Devon, on poorer soils Tavistock Abbey also achieved much higher than average yields. The key to productivity there was a combination of the use of manure, sea sand and beat burning. Emphasis was also placed on the growing of rye, which needs less nitrogen than wheat so that less has to be put back into the soil.

These results were obtained by working within the existing rotation courses. But at Battle and possibly at Tavistock an even more advanced form of husbandry was also being introduced in the late fourteenth century, convertible or up-and-down or leys farming. Instead of the permanent division between arable and grass, which undermined the fertility of both, the two were now alternated. When used as arable, corn, fodder crops (especially legumes) and grass would be grown to feed the increased number of animals kept on the temporary pasture. Running more animals produced more manure, which, with the legumes, added to the fertility of the soil generally. After a few years the arable would be turned over to grass to recuperate, whilst the grass would be ploughed up for arable. Essentially it was a system which benefited the dairy farmer, but convertible husbandry had a marked effect on arable productivity too. The increased production of fodder crops permitted an increase in livestock without a reduction in tillage, causing an ascending spiral of progress, more meat, more hides, more corn, less chance of soil exhaustion.

Battle used convertible husbandry, generally not held to have been widespread in England before the sixteenth century, on marshland manors where soils were too heavy to be amended by sheep folding and on the home manor of Marley, in the late fourteenth century. It is not hard to see why convertible husbandry should have been adopted there so early. The Abbey's estates lay along the coast, with good access to markets at home and abroad and good contacts with Flanders. As a wealthy monastery it had the capital for investment and to cover the increased labour costs which the system needed – but until the late fourteenth century at least higher profits were also generated. Tavistock similarly had markets to supply to generate the capital needed. The real question is not whether convertible husbandry was to be found in later medieval England, but whether it had spread beyond the south and west of the country. Indeed, could it spread when the major institutions with capital were going out of direct production for the market?

The answer to both questions seems to be yes, it did spread beyond the South and new methods were sustained when the demesnes were leased. It was, after all, often the manorial officials who took over what were still going concerns and 'men such as Marley's farmer, the abbey's steward who . . . kept the practice alive on leased land.'[16] If it could be done on one manor, why not another, and why could it not spread? The switch to pastoral agriculture which was accompanied by the widespread diffusion of leguminous crops was precisely the combination between pastoral and arable farming to which convertible husbandry was most suited. The Midlands, where there was pasture and arable a-plenty, were ripe for such a development and there are signs that it was being adopted before the end of the century. It has been postulated that convertible husbandry was practised on Brome's estate and also that in the Cotswolds it prevented the wholesale conversion to pasture whilst helping to accelerate it in the Yorkshire and Lincolnshire wolds. On Leicester Abbey lands the rapid increase of leguminous crops and the greater numbers of livestock, coupled with the break-up of old rotations, paved the way to leys farming. The new methods may even have reached the North, for it seems possible that convertible husbandry was used on the Bolton demesnes in the late fifteenth century.[17] The evidence is not overwhelming, but it should make one very wary of speaking of fundamental alterations between grass and grain in the Midlands or elsewhere. The concept has to be grasped that grass could benefit grain and that improvement could take place within the existing agrarian framework. Whether or not it made a significant difference to productivity in the fifteenth century remains to be proved – but the possibility cannot be ignored.

The fifteenth century, then, had seen considerable changes in the English countryside. Land had been deserted and enclosed, depopulation had occurred on a large scale in many areas, whilst in others good land was still in demand. Not all had prospered, but neither had all gone to the wall. There is no real sign that the agrarian economy had turned in on itself, even in the Midlands, where profits were to be made from the cattle trade by those able to exploit local circumstances to their own advantage. Those lords who were fortunate enough to hold estates in areas of demand and who managed them properly flourished: the less fortunately placed and the less able suffered. The middle classes everywhere seem to have been in quiet and prosperous estate and those who had secured their land freehold or on long leasehold were to benefit from rising prices in the next century. The top ranks of the peasantry seized the chances to consolidate and enclose small farms whilst the main bulk of the customary tenants saw the end of villeinage. Yet of all classes their prosperity, and that of the wage labourers, was the most transitory. It was based on a change in the balance between land and people consequent upon the high death rates due to continued disease in the fifteenth century. Once the population began to grow again and the balance changed, then the position of the peasantry once more became precarious. Of all the changes, however, the most interesting and perhaps the most important remains the most obscure, the introduction of new techniques which for the first time in the Middle Ages raised the productivity of the soil without bringing more and more of it under cultivation. Whilst it cannot yet be argued that they transformed English agriculture in the fifteenth century, they were of great importance for the future.

8 Freedom Versus Restriction: Town and Countryside in the Later Middle Ages

Town and countryside in medieval England were inextricably inter-
twined. The one served the other, providing both a market for agricultural produce, the most important function of the majority of towns,
and such goods and services as the countryside could not supply from
its own resources. It follows, therefore, that the profound changes in the
agrarian sector of the economy ought to be mirrored by equal changes
in the urban sector. Unfortunately, there is as much, if not more
controversy about the fate of English towns and their role in the
economy in the late Middle Ages as there is about conditions in rural
England. On the one hand a grim picture has been painted of extreme
urban decline. On all sides, it is argued, the foundations of prosperity
were undermined. Demand for goods and services fell as the countryside turned back in on itself. Foreign trade slumped after a brief
period of expansion at the end of the fourteenth and the beginning of the
fifteenth century. Wool exports were in sharp decline and do not seem
to have been offset in quantity or value by the growth in the cloth export
trade. Wine imports, another major element in English commerce,
were badly hit by the reverses in the Hundred Years War and the
eventual loss of Gascony. Plague became endemic in most towns and,
as economic troubles mounted, so oligarchic control of government,
trade and industry tightened. Corruption was rife and the few ruthlessly exploited the many. The consequence was that men of enterprise
or ambition were driven from the towns and the revival of the cloth
industry was therefore essentially a rural phenomenon. Decaying trade
and decaying industry brought financial problems, and towns in the
fifteenth century complained increasingly that they were unable to pay
either their fee farm or the taxation demanded of them because they
were so impoverished. With economic decline came physical decay.

Houses lay empty, parish churches fell out of use, suburbs contracted in size, grass, it was said, grew in the streets of Winchester.

Inevitably, such a thesis of gloom had to give rise to an antithesis, brilliantly propounded by Dr Bridbury.[1] He argues that towns remained in the late Middle Ages an indispensable and flourishing part of the economic system. They continued to serve a prosperous country-side, releasing farmers from the need to market their own produce and turn their own raw materials into finished goods. Relative to the declining population industry also flourished, as the statistics for tin production and cloth exports show. Industry had need of towns. There capital and labour came together with distributive and redistributive services and production was at its most efficient. Consequently towns were very much involved in the resurgence of the cloth industry – it was not simply a rural phenomenon. Not only was much country cloth bought and sold in their markets but towns such as York, Coventry and Salisbury remained major centres of production, whilst new towns like Lavenham (Suffolk) and Castle Combe (Wilts) developed in the main cloth-producing areas. Economic vitality, he argues, was matched by increasing democratization of government, not by growing oligarchy. Through the development and enlargement of the common council a growing proportion of the town population was represented in its government. Old rules which had prevented artisans, and especially those in the textile industry, becoming freemen of the borough and thus being able to participate fully in its trade were relaxed. Young men were prepared to serve long apprenticeships to gain freedom of the town, and if that was the case in an era when ordinary wage labour was an attractive alternative, then that freedom must have been worth having. The only conclusion that can be drawn, says Dr Bridbury, is that towns continued to flourish, so much so that a comparison between the taxation returns for 1334 and 1524 reveals that urban wealth comprised a far higher proportion of total wealth in the early sixteenth than in the early fourteenth century.

To hope to produce at this particular time an altogether satisfactory synthesis from two such diametrically opposed arguments would be presumptuous. Much more work needs to be done on the history of later medieval towns, particularly the smaller market towns, before firm conclusions can be reached. Nevertheless, as with the agrarian sector of the economy, neither argument would appear to be completely true. In spite of Dr Bridbury's persuasive thesis, the hard evidence for real decline in some towns, great and small, cannot be ignored. York

247

was England's second city, capital of the North, the seat of a great archiepiscopal see and frequently visited by great nobles and royal servants. Economically, it was the market town of the North, a major distributive and industrial centre. The textile industry flourished there in the late fourteenth century and York merchants were actively engaged in overseas trade through Hull. If one looks at the evidence from the last quarter of the fourteenth century on its own, then it would seem that York had weathered the plague successfully. But, by the early fifteenth century there are ominous signs of future troubles. The most obvious are the slump in wool exports through Hull and the flight of the textile industry into the countryside. The decline in wool exports was national but it was not offset at Hull by increasing trade in cloth. Hull merchants could not break into the Baltic, in the face of determined Hanseatic opposition, and could not face the overwhelming competition from London in the trade to the Low Countries. Waning commercial prosperity was intensified by the decline of the textile industry as it moved out to the West Riding villages. York might have found an alternative role as a redistributive and marketing centre for country cloth, but the West Riding clothiers began to deal directly with London, both as an outlet for their cloth and as a source of raw materials. Nor were textiles the only industry in decline. The number of leather workers seems to have shrunk by two-fifths and of metal workers by about one-third in the second half of the fifteenth century.

York was clearly less prosperous at the end of the fifteenth century than it had been in the late fourteenth. Its commercial horizon had narrowed considerably. The decline in prosperity had obvious economic consequences for the town as a corporate body as well as for individual citizens. By the mid-fifteenth century there was a crisis in civic finances which worsened as the century progressed. Income from all sources of revenue fell, whilst expenditure on the wages of city officials and the city MPs' expenses rose. There was usually a deficit on the year's working which by 1463 had risen to over £250. By 1484 it still stood at £160 and was only cleared off by the end of the century. This helps explain why York's citizens, like those of many another town, sought a reduction in their fee farm of £160 to the Crown. Eventually they succeeded; Richard III reduced it by £60 and Henry VII remitted it entirely. The farm was not the only problem, however. There were direct taxes to be paid, loans to be made to the king and to great men whose patronage was thought worth having, all from the basis of reduced prosperity. York's complaints of civic poverty were not

crocodile tears and corporate problems were matched by private difficulties. Property owners found that rents were falling rapidly in the
fifteenth century. There were derelict tenements in Hungate as early as
1409 and ruinous and vacant tenements elsewhere within the city by
the reign of Henry VII. The citizens were certainly exaggerating when
they told Henry in 1487 that York was not half as prosperous as it had
been, but immigration, which had helped to replace the population
after the plague, had slackened off considerably. The city was no longer
attractive to outsiders and its decline was absolute as well as relative to
the post-plague conditions. In 1377 it had stood second to London in its
tax assessment. By 1524 it had fallen behind Bristol, Norwich and
Newcastle, and probably Exeter and Salisbury as well.

York's decline as an economic centre affected the fortunes of its port,
Hull. The overall value of its trade fell by at least three-quarters in the
fifteenth century in the face of competition from Hansards and Londoners. The same pattern of a crisis in civic finances, decaying property
and declining rents can also be seen there, whilst support for the
Lancastrian cause in 1460–1 seriously depleted Hull's financial
resources and left heavy debts. Other towns were in worse case. Lincoln
did not even enjoy the brief prosperity of the late fourteenth century.
The town was badly hit by the plague and the limited revival of the
cloth industry was not sustained. The vital link to the Trent waterway
system, the Fossdyke, silted up and there were growing obstructions in
the River Witham leading to Boston. The city declined rapidly and
throughout the fifteenth century the citizens pleaded that the weight of
taxation and the fee farm were driving men from Lincoln. Their pleas
were heard. Taxation was cut first in part, then wholly, in the 1420s and
1440s, and then in 1445–6 Lincoln received remission from all tenths
and fifteenths for 40 years. It was to no avail. By 1466 the city was so
poor that more land from surrounding villages had to be added to it to
increase its potential taxable resources. The grant spoke of desolation
and decay, of the poverty and paucity of the inhabitants and this seems
to have been the truth. By 1500 the suburbs and back streets had few
inhabitants and Lincoln had become virtually the single-street city
depicted on eighteenth-century maps.

The catalogue of decline is impressive, listing towns great and small.
Leicester's heyday was over by the late fourteenth century. There was
no cloth industry to replace the declining wool trade and the fifteenth
century saw a depletion of its population and a sharp fall in its prosperity. Some parish churches lay in ruins, the value of property had fallen

and the town generally was in a sad state. A few townsmen were wealthy, perhaps like the Wyggestons very wealthy, but the remainder were impoverished. Nottingham suffered a like fate. By 1376 there were complaints of houses falling into decay because of a lack of population and by 1433–4 Nottingham was treated as an impoverished town and part of its farm remitted. The navigation of the Trent, and thus an outlet to the sea through Boston and Hull, was becoming increasingly precarious in the fifteenth century. Deprived of access to the sea, of diminishing importance as a local market in the depopulated Midlands and, again, with no cloth industry, Nottingham stagnated. Its neighbours Bedford and Warwick had similar problems, Warwick, with no manufactures save those of purely local importance, obtaining relief from taxation in 1444–5.

Decline was not confined to the Midlands, however. To the east Yarmouth, once a major fishing port, was in distress, with its harbour silting up and its fee farm falling into arrears. To the south the port of Southampton, which had apparently recovered from the effects of the plague and the burdens and interruptions of warfare also found it difficult to meet its fee farm of £200. By 1461 the debt had become so desperate that several prominent burgesses were imprisoned in London on account of it. The trouble was that most of the trade passing through the town was in the hands of London and Italian merchants. There was no industry to provide an alternative source of wealth, most townsmen, with the exception of a wealthy few, making a meagre living from providing services such as carting or supplying and repairing shipping using the port. Much more should have been charged for the use of harbour facilities and by way of tolls on goods leaving the town. Failure to do so, plus the increasing burden of maintaining the town's defences, meant that Southampton did not prosper in the fifteenth century. In Devon the situation was more serious for some seaports and market towns. Crediton, Okehampton and Tiverton which served nothing but local markets had their tax assessments reduced by 74, 61 and 50 per cent respectively in 1445 because of their poverty. Of the south-west ports, Plymouth and Dartmouth had suffered badly from French raids. Dartmouth, in particular, had been hard hit by decay of trade and had its tax assessment reduced by 40 per cent. Four towns only were relatively prosperous, Torrington, Ashburton, Plympton and Tavistock, the first because it had become the principal market centre of north Devon, the other three because they were stannary towns. The declining prosperity of the unincorporated town of

Whitchurch in Shropshire meant a substantial loss of revenue for the Talbot family, whilst in the North East the Scarborough fishing fleet, on which the town depended, dwindled in numbers in the fifteenth century. The reason seems to have been partly demographic. In the four years between 1414 and 1418 recorded deaths exceeded births once only, but in 1434–5 there were 117 deaths to 49 births and in 1438–9 161 deaths to 35 births. Scarborough's economy was transformed by the ravages of plague and other epidemics, a stark example of how seriously disease could affect urban life in the fifteenth century.

For some towns, then, the later Middle Ages brought declining prosperity. At the same time, others seemed to be able to cope with difficult economic circumstances until the last decades of the fifteenth century at least. Whilst regional centres like York, Leicester and Lincoln suffered, Gloucester did not. The town was hit severely by the Black Death and subsequent plagues but losses were made up by immigration. Cloth and metal working industries drew workers into Gloucester, which also benefited from the economic activity in its region, the Cotswolds, a major cloth-producing area. It was indeed connection with the cloth industry which provided one of the keys to survival for many late medieval towns. Coventry, for instance, reached the height of its prosperity in the late fourteenth and the first half of the fifteenth century. Unlike Leicester and Nottingham it had made a successful transition from the wool trade to cloth production with perhaps a quarter or a third of its inhabitants engaged in the textile industry. Coventry was admirably placed to act as a collecting point for cloth exports and as a distributive centre for raw materials. Its own cloth and that of the surrounding countryside could be exported through any one of four major ports, London, Bristol, Southampton or Boston. In return, large quantities of raw materials were sent back, especially from Southampton, both for Coventry's own industry and that of the surrounding countryside. But the town did not depend solely on textiles. There were metal- and leather-working industries as well. Coventry's was a diversified economy which served the surrounding countryside and benefited enormously from connection with the leading export trade.

The same pattern can be seen at Salisbury and Norwich. Salisbury played a leading role in the revival and expansion of the Wiltshire industry. Cloth production seems to have been at its zenith there at the turn of the fourteenth and fifteenth centuries. With its excellent communications to Southampton, the principal port for the import of raw materials for the cloth industry, Salisbury could supply the surrounding countryside with woad and other dyestuffs, alum, wool oil and soap and collect cloth and send it for export. Thus the town both contributed to and benefited from the wealth of its region and some measure of its success can be seen by comparing its contributions to the subsidies of 1334 and 1524, £75 to the former, £405 to the latter. Norwich had suffered badly from the plague. The rent roll of city property in 1357 lists tenements, shops and stalls vacant and in ruins. By 1377 the population had reached 5,000 again and doubled in the course of the fifteenth century. The textile trade and especially the worsted industry was the town's lifeblood. Worsted was made at Norwich and the town acted as the centre for the industry in the Norfolk countryside. Between 1350 and 1361 an average of about 12,000 single worsteds were exported from England annually, in some years more than 20,000, and of these about three-quarters were sent out through Norwich's port, Great Yarmouth. There was a slump in the trade in the mid-fifteenth century but its fortunes revived after 1465 and by the first two decades of the sixteenth century exports exceeded 10,000 pieces per annum, the majority by that time going by road to London. Norwich, therefore, like Coventry and Salisbury, acted both as a centre for production and for its locality which it could supply with a whole variety of goods either made in the town or imported, and it had a choice of ports for the export trade. Its prosperity can be seen in the rebuilding which took place in the fifteenth century, flimsy wooden structures being replaced by solid stone buildings, and the city paid eight times as much tax in 1524 as in 1334, £749 compared to £95.

Not only established towns benefited from the revival of the cloth industry. The great expansion of cloth production in the South West, East Anglia and the North East led to the development of some villages into unchartered towns – Lavenham and Hadleigh in Suffolk, Totnes in Devon, Castle Combe in Wiltshire and Minchinhampton and Bisley in the Stroudwater area of Gloucestershire, Halifax and Wakefield in Yorkshire. In the early fifteenth century Lavenham was only a small village. By the 1520s it was the thirteenth wealthiest town in England, paying over £180 in tax in 1524, more than Leicester, Northampton, Nottingham, Oxford, Southampton, Winchester and Worcester. Totnes and Hadleigh were only a little behind and there had been equally rapid growth in the South West. Castle Combe was a village with 55 inhabitants in the fourteenth century, whilst Stroudwater was not a village at all but a stretch of water between the upland settlements of Minchinhampton and Bisley. Again, comparison between the tax assessments of 1334 and 1524 shows the real shift of wealth. Winchcombe, an old town, paid less in 1524 than in 1334 whilst Bisley paid 13 times as much and more than Cirencester, formerly chief town of the Cotswolds, expected to pay. These cloth 'villages' deserve, in economic terms, to be treated more as towns than older boroughs such as Lincoln and Leicester. They may have had no charters, no formal government except through the manorial court, but that was a positive advantage. It meant that they were free of the trappings and expense of civic obligation and the regulation that surrounded urban industry.

One route to survival was plain, therefore: involvement in the cloth industry on both the productive and distributive sides. Another was to be a port on a major and thriving trade route. One such was Bristol, where cloth manufacturing was combined with international commerce. The town served as one of the outlets for the cloth industry in the South West, exporting particularly to Gascony where cloth could be exchanged for wine. There was a considerable expansion of exports in the 1350s and 1360s, averaging 2,500 cloths per annum in the latter decade and in one year exceeding 8,000 compared with only 3,500 through London. Bristol was England's second provincial town after York and its prosperity reached a peak in the late fourteenth and early fifteenth centuries. There was an active cloth industry in both town and surrounding countryside and new markets were found in the Iberian peninsula, Toulouse and Iceland. Later there were some setbacks with the decline of the Iceland trade, the loss of the Gascon market and the growing concentration of cloth exports through London to the Low Countries. But Bristol rebuilt her trade on traditional lines to Spain, Portugal, South-West France and Ireland, whilst local and national routes assumed greater importance as industrial growth in the hinterland created new demands. Cloth was sent by land to London or Southampton and raw materials were brought back. There were coasting links to Exeter and other West Country ports and wool for the local cloth industry came to Bristol from as far afield as Shropshire and Westmorland. Standing as it did at a nexus of road, sea and river routes, Bristol was well placed to serve a thriving hinterland, and, at least until the early sixteenth century, to prosper as a result. The results of that prosperity can be seen in the great church of St Mary Redcliffe, rebuilt by William Canynges, ship owner, ship builder and five times mayor of Bristol.

Head and shoulders above all other towns stood London. In spite of almost yearly outbreaks of plague, its population seems to have remained stable at somewhere between 30 and 40,000 and may even have grown slowly. Men were drawn to London for a whole variety of reasons. Some came because the city and its neighbour Westminster were the centre of royal and ecclesiastical government. A large, permanent body of officials lived in London and its population would be swollen during the law terms, as lawyers and litigants flocked to the courts, or when sessions of parliament or convocation were held there. To live in London was to be at the centre of power, which seems to have been an attraction for some men. Others came to the city from all parts of England, attracted by its wealth, for London was the greatest centre of trade and industry in the realm. That had been the case even in the thirteenth century, but London's economic predominance over other towns, especially in trade, became even more marked in the later Middle Ages. Its merchants gradually obtained a stranglehold on the English sector of foreign trade and especially on cloth exports to the Low Countries. To the port came ships from the Baltic and the Rhineland, to unload their wares at the Hanseatic Steelyard. Once a year the Venetian galleys came into the pool with cargoes of spices and raw materials to exchange for cloth. Dutch, Flemish and English ships went to Calais, Antwerp and Amsterdam, taking wool and cloth abroad, bringing back haberdashery, mercery, metal ware and foodstuffs. Coasting vessels brought tin from the West Country for the pewter industry and coals from Newcastle, and above all foodstuffs, corn from East Anglia, Kent and Sussex to feed a hungry population. So dependent was London on the countryside for its food that when the harvest failed in 1438–9 the mayor had to charter ships to go to Danzig in search of corn.

Supplying London with all its needs meant drawing on an ever-widening hinterland, on the West Country and the West Riding for cloth, on coal from Newcastle, on the Midlands for meat. London's merchants were everywhere, distributing the vast range of imports at the local fairs or selling them in other towns through their agents or country members of their particular gild. So London grocers sold fruit, wine and dyestuffs in Salisbury, Guildford, Newbury, Bristol, Northampton, Coventry, Reading, Oxford, Gloucester and Tewkesbury. Down these trade routes came migrants, to take the place of those killed by the plague or those who, fortunate enough to have amassed wealth, now wished to live the life of the country gentleman.[2] Employment was to be had in a whole range of industries – pewter making, cloth finishing, smithing, the manufacture of barrels, knives, pouches, furs, parchment – the list is almost endless. Nor did men only come from England. London and its suburbs had a growing population of aliens, Flemish beer brewers and domestic servants, Dutch and German goldsmiths, emphasizing the fact that this was a truly international city as no other town in England was. The importance of London's role, London's place in the English economy cannot be overestimated. By the mid-fifteenth century more than 60 per cent of all English foreign trade flowed through London and its outports Sandwich and Southampton. Its nearest rival, Bristol, handled only some 10 per cent of the whole. The measure of the pre-eminence, healthy or not, is obvious from a comparison of taxable capacity in 1334 and 1524. Whereas in 1334 London had been just over three times as wealthy as the richest provincial town, Bristol, in the 1520s the city was about ten times as wealthy as Norwich, by then the leading provincial town and 15 times as rich as Bristol. London's economic performance in the later Middle Ages is impressive, but at what cost to other English towns remains to be seen.

There was, then, no general pattern of success or failure and evidence from a few thriving towns in the late fourteenth century should not be taken as typical of the period as a whole. Nor are admissions to freedom a good indication of general urban prosperity. To be free of the borough meant acceptance of bearing one's share of taxation and public duty but conferred on the holder the various privileges granted to the community by charter. Freemen alone could exercise local political rights and were able to buy in the city or town with the intention of reselling and to keep shops for selling at retail. It was an important right, acquired either by inheritance, by serving an apprenticeship in a recognized craft or trade with a citizen or by purchase. Admissions to freedom might therefore be some guide to a town's economic importance, if the majority of applicants obtained their freedom by serving long and poorly paid apprenticeships. A recent study of such admissions at York throws considerable doubt on the validity of such evidence. For one thing entry to the urban franchise was rarely compulsory for every male craftsman; at York there was a large number of master weavers as well as apprentices whose names never appeared in the freemen's register. There was also a remarkable coincidence between high peaks in admissions to freedom and known outbreaks of plague, the absolute peak of 219 in 1364 coming two years after the general epidemic of 1361–2. The civic authorities, anxious to keep up

255

the numbers of freemen that the burden of taxation and office might be evenly borne, would tend to relax restrictions or might even force freedom on those unwilling to accept it, under threat of expulsion from the town. Most freedom at York was obtained by purchase not by apprenticeship, a pattern to be found in other towns. At Hull drives were made to enrol new burgesses at times of financial crisis, so that in 1445–6 and 1450–1 when 40 and 38 men were enfranchised, the honour was forced on them rather than being eagerly sought.

Taxation returns are no better evidence of general urban prosperity either. Comparison between the subsidies of 1334 and 1524 can be very useful. They can show relative changes in the geographical distribution of wealth, the shift from the Midlands to the South East and South West for instance. Whether they can be used to show, specifically, that urban wealth comprised a greater share of the national whole in 1524 than in 1334 and that towns as a whole were economically healthy is another matter. The basis of assessment differed radically in 1524 from that in 1334 and direct comparisons must be treated with some caution. But Dr Bridbury argues that we may look at the ratio of the earlier payment to the latter to show growth or decline. (For example, Boston, ruined by the collapse of the wool trade, thus has a negative ratio of 2:1 whilst Coventry paid in the ratio of 1:6.) Perhaps this is the case, although in certain towns one or two rich men dominated the community and the assessment reflects their wealth, not the town's. Coventry, for example, ranked nearly as high as Bristol, although only two-thirds of its size, thanks to three rich men, and at Lavenham the Springs, wealthy clothiers and landowners, paid 37 per cent of the town's contribution to the subsidy of 1524. More worrying is the attempt to show a movement of wealth from countryside to town. The exercise produces some very doubtful results. In Warwickshire, for instance, towns seem to have paid 9.6 per cent of the tax in 1334 but 69.9 per cent in 1524, or 6 per cent in Norfolk in 1334 but 41.8 in 1524. This would represent either urban growth or rural decline on an unprecedented scale. It might be accounted for by the expansion of Coventry and Norwich and the depopulation of the Warwickshire and Norfolk countryside, but that would run counter to the thesis which takes urban wealth as a sign of rural prosperity.

Given the positive evidence of decline in some towns and the dubious nature of some of the conclusions to be drawn from a comparison between the subsidies of 1334 and 1524, it is difficult to accept the argument for the general prosperity of towns. But, as in agriculture, regional variation might provide the key to the problem. It is not hard to see that there are common factors which explain the success of some towns. Involvement in England's chief export industry, the production of cloth, was most important. This might be direct, in the sense that cloth was made in the town, or indirect in that the industry lay in the town's hinterland. Urban labour and capital could be employed to the full in the productive and distributive roles and prosperity be maintained for much, if not all the fifteenth century. Failing cloth, some other industry might fulfil the same function as tin mining did for Tavistock and to a lesser extent metal working for Gloucester and Coventry, although that industry too was running into difficulties. Secondly, it was important to lie on a thriving trade route, be it national or international, even if that was no certain guarantee of success. Southampton did not benefit as a town from the trade of its port, but Ipswich's growth can be compared with Hull's decline, Exeter's expansion at the end of the century as the cross-Channel trade to France revived, with Boston's collapse. Reading had the best of both worlds. Favourably placed at the confluence of busy routes and with its own cloth industry, its population trebled between the early fourteenth and the early sixteenth century, in spite of the plague. Finally, the town might still prosper if its region's economy was buoyant. The contrast here is between the South East and the Midlands, between the stagnation and decline of Leicester and Warwick, the reversion of many villages which had received grants of markets and fairs in the thirteenth century to rural obscurity, whilst Romney and Faversham, Dorchester and Henley throve from supplying the capital with food.

Yet there are, again, difficulties in applying hard and fast rules attributing success or failure solely to regional variation. In the first place, the argument tends to suppose that all towns within the region would flourish. Such need not be the case. The large town might prosper at the smaller's expense. So Bristol's expansion killed off Bath's trade and Leominster could not stand the competition from Worcester and Hereford. Probably there were too many towns in late medieval England, and even within an economically active region not all could survive. Secondly, there are real problems involved in seeing the whole 150 years between 1350 and 1500 as a period of economic well-being for those towns which weathered the storms of the late fourteenth and early fifteenth centuries. Circumstances could and did change. Endemic plague led to population decline and in mid-century exports and trade generally slumped. Between 1450 and 1470 less than 40,000 cloths were exported annually and tin presented for coinage fell from 1,600,000 lb in 1414 to less than 800,000 lb in 1442. After 1470 the economy began to pick up. By 1489–90 60,000 cloths were being exported per annum, by 1509–10, 90,000. Tin production rose again, over 1,000,000 lb per annum being presented for coinage in the 1460s and 1,800,000 lb by the 1520s.

This ought to have provided the major towns with great opportunities, and yet by the end of the fifteenth century there are unmistakable signs that many of them were in deep trouble. York's fate has already been described but it was not alone in its plight. Bristol's prosperity did not last long beyond the turn of the century. From 1500 its cloth exports fell, to a level half that of the fifteenth century. Much West Country cloth now went through London and in 1518 there were complaints that about 800 houses were vacant and decayed, certainly an exaggeration but with a ring of truth in it. Most notable of all was the decline of Coventry which had appeared so buoyant in the earlier fifteenth century.[3] Its population *c*.1400 was about 10,000 but that represented a high point. A slow decline was accelerated by a virulent pestilence in 1479 in which, according to the city annals, some 3,300 inhabitants died within the town. By 1485–6 a rental of one of the largest property owners, the Trinity Gild, shows about one-third of its tenements empty, with rents down by about 20 per cent. Rents paid to the Corpus Christi Gild suggest a period of stability towards the end of the century, but then quickening decline. A census of Coventry in 1523 shows a minimum of 565 vacant houses, about 25 per cent of the whole. By the mid-sixteenth century the population was down to about 4,000, less than half what it had been a century earlier.

The causes of decline are not hard to find. It was not a case of being overtaken by a rival – there was none. Nor did London merchants carry away its trade as they did elsewhere. At the heart of Coventry's troubles lay demographic decline. Overall numbers fell, and there seems to have been a particular shortage of smaller masters in industry. The 1523 census shows that two-thirds of the domestic labour force (all-in servants) were female. Fewer than 20 per cent of all households had men servants. Even if all these were apprentices, then the city was failing to train up a sufficient reservoir of potential masters and journeymen for the future. This problem was compounded, even partly caused by, the growth of the cloth industry in the countryside. The mid-century trade depression hit Coventry badly and production of the traditional broadcloth never recovered. This was partly offset by the switch to cap making but by the 1540s that industry was also in trouble. The effects of industrial decline were exacerbated by involvement in the Wars of the Roses. Coventry was at the centre of hostilities and suffered financially, as did Leicester, York, Hull and Norwich. Fortifications and armour had to be paid for, the Lancastrian court entertained and since Coventry backed the wrong side it had to buy back its liberties. The worst years were 1469–71 when £600 had to be found to finance the earl of Warwick and pacify the king. Once under way, decay generated its own momentum. As population fell there were fewer men of sufficient standing to bear the considerable burdens and costs of office in gild and town government, the frequent and impressive ceremonial processions, the wearing of liveries, the feasts and banquets. A critical point was reached in the 1490s when there was an increasing reluctance to serve and difficulty in mounting the Corpus Christi plays. There is no doubt that the potential costs of office drove men from the town to live and work in the countryside and as rural industry spread, so Coventry's economy was further undermined. Finally in 1518–25 all the causes of decline came together. There was plague, dearth in 1520, local and national trade depressions and 40 times the annual tax levied in three years in loans, anticipations and subsidy payments. The result was crippling depopulation and widespread unemployment.

Not all the factors which caused Coventry's decline in the late fifteenth century can be found in other towns, but the most crucial probably can, demographic downturn, the high costs of office and the development of industry in the countryside. About the first, declining population, the towns could do little. Compared with the countryside they were unhealthy places, for plague and other diseases were endemic. But London could attract migrants because of its economic strength. If other towns could not, it presupposes that they were in difficulties and it is the growth of industry in the countryside which needs further examination for it seriously affected the economies of both Coventry and York. It was not the high costs of office alone which drove men out of towns, but the whole urban milieu which seemed to be hedged round with restrictions, to be ruled by the few to the disadvantage of the many, and to be inimical to enterprise. To understand this fully, it is necessary to look closely at the government of later medieval towns to see how oligarchic control was strengthened and how gilds emerged.

The paradox of later medieval town government is that whilst the representative element seemed to be enlarged, power in fact lay in the hands of a wealthy few. What happened at York is fairly typical of what happened to a greater or lesser degree in many other English towns. Powers of self-government were considerably strengthened towards the end of the fifteenth century when the town was made into a county in its own right. It was now completely separate from the surrounding shire administration. At the head of affairs and elected annually stood the mayor, the keeper of the city for the king, active in the various courts, the chief figure in the city council and recipient of all mandates from central government on all conceivable matters. The office was a great honour, but an expensive one. The mayor received a fee of £50, but the dignity of the office meant spending far more than that. Not surprisingly, the mayors were drawn from a select circle. Of the 85 men who held the office between 1399 and 1509, no less than 68 were merchants or mercers, a mercantile oligarchy. To assist him in his duties the mayor had the sheriffs, with important judicial and financial functions, and the chamberlains, in charge of civic finances. These officials were chosen yearly from amongst the citizens. The recorder, the chief legal officer, and the common clerk were professional officials, representatives of a new breed in the towns. Below them there was a whole series of lesser officials to administer law and order and the markets and fairs. The representative element was embodied in a whole series of councils who assisted the mayor in the government of the town. They are usually known by the number of their membership, the twelve, the twenty-four and the forty-eight. Representative is perhaps the wrong word to use, for they were no more than an ascending spiral of oligarchy. In York, the inner circle of twelve, called the aldermen by 1399, was a closed shop. Membership was for life and elections to the body were made by the mayor and the surviving aldermen who, naturally enough, preferred their own class. Qualification for membership of the twenty-four was previous service as sheriff, which meant a restricted body since only the wealthy could afford the burden of that office. Again, one served for life, unless elevated to the ranks of aldermen. Together, these two bodies with the appointed officers formed the city council which met at irregular but frequent intervals to run the town. The final element in city government, the forty-eight, had a very limited role indeed. They were representatives of the commonalty, the common council. Few if any had held municipal office, the majority being drawn from the manufacturing as distinct from the trading occupations. The forty-eight played a small part in choosing the mayor, approved the choice of other officials and assented to ordinances for the government of the city. They did little more than give formal approval to what had already been decided and the forty-eight was much more important as a political forum where all the internal stresses, the rising tensions in the city, could be aired.

Power in York was thus concentrated in the hands of a relatively small group of men, predominantly merchants. The same is true of many other towns, of Warwick, Lincoln, Leicester, Southampton, Norwich, and Lynn where oligarchic control was even tighter. The Gild of the Holy Trinity virtually ran Lynn. Its alderman automatically became deputy mayor of the town. He chose the first four of the committee of twelve whose duty it was to elect the mayor and other officials annually. The town was graded into three classes, the powerful, the middle and the low, and the Gild of the Holy Trinity and the twenty-four consisted entirely of the powerful. Even the common council was chosen from their ranks, and never had the semblance of a properly elected body. What was true of the larger centres was equally true of the smaller towns. At High Wycombe a close oligarchy of 15 men monopolized the mayoralty in Henry VIII's reign. Aylesbury was ruled by the optimates, 'the best men', and at Bridgwater (Soms) the new constitution of 1468 made no difference to the fact that those who governed the town were the rich.

Why should this have created an atmosphere inimical to industry? It need not have done so, for merchants and manufacturers should not have had opposed interests. In London oligarchy reigned supreme but trade and industry prospered. But, as in all things, London was the exception. In many towns oligarchic control acted against the enterprising and was thus one of the factors which helped drive them out of town. As government became more concentrated in the hands of the wealthy, so it became grander. Town officers were expected to maintain certain standards of living and display. Not all could afford it. In 1478 a young York merchant was excused election to the office of sheriff for eight years unless by the grace of God 'he may grow in goods and riches to have the said [office]'. Small wonder that men tried to avoid office, either by paying a fine or, as at Coventry, by leaving the town altogether. As the letters patent regulating the election of the mayor of Lincoln clearly put it in 1438, middling persons of the city have chosen that they would rather abide in the country than in the city, to avoid office holding – and manufacturers tended to be in the ranks of the middling rather than the great.

Oligarchy also bred social strife. Power could easily be abused for there were ample opportunities for fraud, manipulation of justice and inequitable distribution of taxation. There was nothing new in this, but the problems seem to have worsened in the fifteenth century. A commission was appointed at Lincoln in 1399 to find out what had happened to funds raised to pave the streets and rebuild the gild hall, but with no success. The chancellor, archbishop Arundel, was called upon in 1413 to act as an arbitrator at Lynn, to try to allay discords concerning alleged oppressions and extortions done by the wealthier citizens against the others in the town. Discontent everywhere focused on the power of the oligarchs and the right of the commons to a share in government. To take York as an example again, the late fourteenth century was a period of considerable strife. In part it was created by conflict between various factions striving to control the office of mayor, but between 1379 and 1381 there was a revolt of the commonalty against the oligarchs and extensive riots. Renewed prosperity brought quiet, but from the mid-fifteenth century onwards, as York's decline began, so troubles mounted. The 1470s, 1480s and 1490s were punctuated by riots, especially at the time of mayor-making. The commonalty presented petitions demanding more say in the city's government and complaining of financial mismanagement. The merchant oligarchy was under attack by a democratic movement which drew its strength from the crafts, but at the close of the Middle Ages its power was still supreme.

Borough government in the later Middle Ages, then, was oligarchic, bureaucratic, top heavy and expensive to maintain, which meant heavy local taxation. It also produced social discontent leading to violence not only at York, but at Lynn, Norwich, Southampton and even in the capital where between 1376 and 1384 John of Northampton sought unsuccessfully to break the power of the aldermen. The expense of living in a town was increased by the costs of office, pageantry and the loans or benevolences that many were called on to make to the king. Civil war brought added burdens for some towns and when all this is added up, it becomes clear that the overheads of living in a borough were far greater than those in the countryside. But the greatest advantage countryside had over town was the absence of regulation. Urban industry was hedged around with a whole mass of rules and regulations, promulgated by the town government either directly or through its agents of economic legislation, the gilds. Their emergence was essentially a phenomenon of the later Middle Ages and coincides with a period of economic difficulty and population decline. London, again, was the exception. As early as 1327 the Skinners, Merchant Tailors,

Goldsmiths and Girdlers were granted royal charters allowing them to regulate their trades within the capital and without, setting a precedent that other London companies were to follow. In other towns gilds emerged more slowly, in some not at all. Their most fertile breeding ground was the medium-sized town with a population of up to 10,000 and a varied range of industries producing mainly for the local market and some longer-range trade connections. There was more scope here for specialized skills than in the small market town. York had 57 gilds in 1415, Hereford, a smaller regional centre, 20 by the late fifteenth century. Here gilds flourished or even existed because they could control the supply of commodities for which demand was essentially inelastic. By contrast there was no craft structure at Hull, where everything was concentrated on foreign trade, or at Durham which had little in the way of manufacturing industries. Smaller towns might have one omnibus trading gild of mercers, haberdashers and grocers. Adequate machinery for the control of trade and industry already existed in the borough court and there was no need for specialized grouping where industry was on a small scale, serving only the very local market and using local raw materials.

As separate gilds evolved, so the power and influence of the gild merchant waned. That body had represented traders who, in the twelfth and thirteenth centuries, were unspecialized. They used their capital both to trade and to control the work of local craftsmen. As the thirteenth century wore on, however, large wholesale dealers who bought in bulk to distribute to the smaller retail shopkeepers began to concentrate on one particular branch of trade. So there emerged, above all in London, the wealthiest and most important gilds or misteries, groups of traders, not craftsmen or artisans, the mercers, tailors, drapers, grocers, fishmongers, vintners. Specialization was rarely complete. Most of the mercantile gilds dealt in cloth, and in any case citizens of London were free to sell any commodity within the city. But each gild did seek to regulate one main area of trade and was regarded by the urban authorities as responsible for it. This was a process of natural evolution from the gild merchant. Not so the emergence of craft gilds. Crafts ranged from tanners, who required a high degree of capital, to the weaver who bought in his yarn as needed, made it up into cloth which was sold to provide for his family and buy more yarn. Few craftsmen were sufficiently wealthy to hold large stocks of raw materials or employ other craftsmen. Often their landlord was the richer merchant who might also own the capital equipment, the loom

263

or, in London, the bakehouses used by the bakers, and would employ the craftsmen on piece rates. The emergence of the craft gilds was therefore initially a reaction against mercantile capital which had prevented their organization in the thirteenth century. They were not to be stopped in the later Middle Ages when economic circumstances had changed in the craftsmen's favour. For their organization they took the obvious model, the mercantile mistery, and so founded companies of plasterers, glaziers, weavers, fullers and so on.

So there were two types of gild, mercantile and craft or industrial. Both were essentially associations of masters who formed the freemen of the gild. Beneath them were the journeymen, qualified workers who had served their apprenticeship but lacked the capital to set up on their own and worked for day-wage rates, and the apprentices, bound by covenant to their masters, generally for a seven-year term, to be taught the trade or occupation. The purposes of the association were to regulate the trade or industry; to protect the interests of its members; to control standards of workmanship; to prevent anyone working as a master who was not free of the borough and of the gild; to watch carefully that members of an allied trade were not trespassing on their preserve; and to resolve disputes between members. To do all this the gilds needed a governmental structure and rules. These they achieved by modelling themselves on town governments, with elected officials, wardens or bailiffs in charge of the gild for a year and their own statutes and ordinances. An oligarchic hierarchy within the gild soon emerged too, to be found in its most advanced state in London. There gilds obtained royal charters allowing them to hold lands and draw rents. Within the general membership an exclusive group emerged, the livery, who were allowed to wear the distinctive dress of the freemen of the company. Others were allowed to wear only the hood and the rest were simply ordinary members of the gild. Gradually the two parts tended to draw apart and the wealthier came to dominate the gild as they did the town. Elsewhere gilds were not always as highly organized. Royal charters of self-government were rare. Indeed, towns were often wary of bodies with independent powers within their walls and regarded it as their right to control trade and industry. But they were prepared to devolve their rights to gilds as a means of enforcing legislation on quality control and illegal working. So gild ordinances were often approved by the town council and breaches of them were made enforceable in the mayor's court. Gilds were also brought fully into civic pageantry as well as organizing their own feasts and processions.

Gild powers could therefore be extensive, controlling as they did entry to the rank of the masters and ensuring proper training for the future masters through the apprenticeship system. The number of apprentices a master could take was often limited to restrict entry to the occupation and gilds also regulated wages and working hours. York coverlet weavers were allowed to weave only as long as the light of day permitted them to ply the shuttle, and work was forbidden on Sundays and Feast Days. Quality control was one of the most important aspects of all gild regulations. Regular searches were made to ensure that only good quality raw materials were used and that goods offered for sale were to the requisite standard. These were wide powers and the rules could be altered to suit the circumstances. It is generally noticeable in the fifteenth century that entry into the gild was more tightly controlled. Numbers of apprentices were kept down. Access to the freedom of the gild became more and more expensive and attempts to stop non-members trading or working within the franchise more vigorous. In these harder times, when competition was greater and demand quantitatively less, all proper precautions were taken to ensure that as much as possible of a town's trade and industry should be restricted to gild members. Consequently gilds have been accused of being monopolistic, inimical to competition and to the introduction of new and labour-saving methods. Indeed, it is alleged that their attitude was one of the prime factors which inhibited industrial development in later medieval England and drove industry from the town to exploit freer conditions in the countryside.

These are grave charges, but gilds must be seen in their proper perspective before coming to any judgment as to whether their influence was harmful. They controlled only the handicraft industries in the towns. Mining and smelting, building in stone and, increasingly, the cloth industry were beyond their grasp. Even within towns it was often difficult to maintain their monopolies in the face of cheaper goods made in the suburbs or the surrounding countryside or imported. Yet the existence of gilds and the way in which they functioned did tend to enshrine the small unit of industrial production, one master with a few servants and apprentices, working and selling from his home and concentrating on one branch of trade or industry. This may have prevented sensible rationalization of production – and even where there were no strong craft gilds, then town government showed the same attitude. So the Coventry Leet in 1435 put an end to the practice whereby various processes in metal working were being brought

265

together under one roof in the workshops of a few wealthy masters. No one henceforth was allowed to engage in more than two branches of the industry. That stopped practical reorganization which would have brought down costs and probably increased production. This was one way in which gild and urban attitudes were inimical to progress. Another was that gilds seemed to have little or no interest in helping develop their branch of trade or industry by the investment of corporate funds. The money was spent instead on building halls or buying land or on consumption, feasts and entertainment. It could be argued, and with some force, that in the industries which gilds controlled there was little or no need for innovation or large-scale capital investment. Such new technology as there was lay in the fields of mining and smelting, outside their purview, and that increased production would only have been justified by increased demand. At the quality end of the market there was probably more than enough capacity to meet potential demand. It was at the cheaper end that gilds may have damaged their own interests and hindered urban industry in England. Their insistence on high standards made the product more expensive. In an age of greater general prosperity the area where demand was growing was for cheaper goods and these could be supplied by less organized and less supervised country competitors or by cheaper imports. Merchants, by distributing such products within the towns, ironically hastened the industrial decline.

This, perhaps, is the key to understanding how town and gild attitudes drove industry, especially the cloth industry and maybe also metal working, into the countryside. There was too much regulation, too much control of the product and the conditions under which it was produced. The freedom of the small man to make and sell on his own account became more and more circumscribed. Gild membership fees could be heavy, especially for poor men, whilst fines for working not free of the gild were ever increasing. Penalties for poor work were harsh. Dyers at York who did faulty work were to be fined 40d. for the first offence, 6s.8d. for the second and were to be expelled from the city for the third. York fullers had to provide security in case cloths were damaged in the course of fulling, coverlet weavers were faced with confiscation for a first offence of bad workmanship but with expulsion from the occupation for repeated poor work. No such controls existed in the countryside. The only constraints were the national regulations concerning the size of cloths and their quality – and the latter were largely ineffective. There were no restrictions on working hours, no fixing of wage rates, no expense of gild or civic pageantry, no costly mounting of cycles of mystery plays. The attractions of the countryside were thus very considerable. The merchant capitalist might be tempted by the prospects of cheaper labour – and labour costs were half the value of cloth; he might bring country-made cloth into the town and undercut the urban industry. The poorer weaver, the journeyman with no hope of setting up on his own, the apprentice tired of working out his long term of training and providing his master with cheap labour might be tempted to migrate and set up on his own in the suburbs or the countryside and join the growing band of rural industrial workers.

English towns at the end of the fifteenth century present a rather sorry picture then. The success, the economic importance of London cannot be denied, but that success in itself was affecting the fortunes of York, Bristol, Hull, Boston and other towns. Exeter in the South West and Salisbury in the Wiltshire cloth-producing area managed to weather the storms of the plague and the troubled waters of the late fifteenth century when demographic decline, heavy taxation, the burdens of office and the growth of rural industry brought ruin to Coventry. The fate of smaller market towns remains to be explored. Many in the depopulated Midlands must have shared the fate of Warwick and stagnated. Conversely, in the South East, supplying the ravenous capital with food meant continued prosperity for those on good road and river routes to London – for Enfield, Henley, Dorchester, Faversham and Romney. The picture of decay and gloom must not be overdrawn. Even a town like Leicester had its rich families, like the Wyggestons, it still had some functions as a market, its depleted population still had to be fed. But, compared with the busy days of the thirteenth century it was, like many another provincial town, a sad place in the late fifteenth century.

The major industrial phenomenon of the later Middle Ages was the rapid expansion of the cloth industry. England gradually became the leading supplier of medium-priced and fine broadcloths in Europe, serving markets as far away as Italy and Poland. The first stages of the industry's recovery have already been described. Continued growth in the later fourteenth and fifteenth centuries had much the same causes, a high tariff-barrier, low wool prices at home and the autonomous decline of the Flemish industry. In the long run the European economy probably could not support more than one major cloth industry and it is very noticeable that distress and depopulation in the Flemish towns reached a peak as English cloth exports finally overtook wool exports in value in the 1430s. It is important to grasp that the expanding export trade allowed the industry to develop a productive capacity far above that required to supply the home market. When restrictions were placed on the credit purchase of cloth by aliens in 1429 much distress and unemployment was caused in the industry and the regulations had to be repealed two years later. It was the cloth workers of Gloucester-shire who petitioned the Crown on behalf of the German merchants in 1468 when a breach between England and the Hanseatic League seemed inevitable. They knew full well the consequences of interruptions in the export trade – unemployment at home. What also needs stressing is that this was essentially a native industry. Much attention has been paid to the supposed influx of Flemish weavers in the 1330s and 1340s, fleeing from unrest in Flanders and encouraged by grants of protection from Edward III, which is supposed to have stimulated cloth production in England. But the industry was expanding before then. Only favourable circumstances were needed for whole-scale revival and when they came, Englishmen grasped them. Detailed studies of the industry in York and the West Riding[4] suggest that Flemings played little part in it. The overwhelming majority of weavers were natives. The manor court rolls of Bradford cover the 45 years of Edward III's reign when immigration was supposed to be at its height. There are many entries concerning the textile industry, but not once is a Fleming or Brabanter mentioned. The poll tax of 1379 confirms this pattern for the district as a whole; Flemings are to be found, but not in any great numbers. The man power for the regeneration of the industry was provided by the English towns and the English countryside.

As has been seen, the towns played an important role in the initial expansion. In 1394–5, for instance, 5,039 cloths of assize were sealed at Salisbury, compared with 723 for the rest of the county. Some of these cloths were brought in from the surrounding countryside, but many had been made within the town. Then, as the fifteenth century wore on, there was a steady growth of cloth making in the Wiltshire countryside. The poll tax of 1379 suggests that the only centres of cloth production outside Salisbury were in the south west of the county in Heytesbury Hundred, in the Wylye valley and around Mere. By the end of the fifteenth century there had been major development around Mere, Heytesbury and Warminster in the south west, in and around Castle Combe and in the towns of the basin of the Bradford Avon from

Malmesbury in the north to Westbury in the south and especially in and around Trowbridge, Bradford, Westbury, Steeple Ashton and Devizes. By Edward IV's reign there were substantial clothiers in all these towns, responsible for all the manufacturing processes and selling the finished article in London or Bristol. Best chronicled is the rise of Castle Combe, from a small village with a fulling mill and a few weavers in the fourteenth century to a major cloth-producing centre in the mid-fifteenth century, attracting migrants from as far away as Ireland. An energetic landlord, Sir John Fastolf, helped the expansion of the industry there by ordering large quantities of cloth for the soldiers under his command in France between 1415 and 1440. Weavers, fullers, fulling mills multiplied, 50 new houses were built and all in the atmosphere of freedom from regulation. The manor court, the only regulating body in the village, dealt with cases of debt and breach of contract between clothiers but never a one concerning breaches of rules governing cloth manufacture, for there were none. The clothier was free to work as he liked, and might even introduce new methods like the gig mill which raised the nap on a cloth mechanically by the use of teasels fixed to a roller driven by water power.

What happened in Wiltshire also happened in other areas of the South West, in the West Riding of Yorkshire and in Kent. Why should the industry have been concentrated in these areas and not others? Two of the usual reasons given for the location of an industry are easy access to raw materials and to a distributive system, preferably a port. These do not seem to apply in later medieval England. The basic raw material, wool, was to be had everywhere. Other necessary materials could be moved over long distances – Southampton supplied Coventry with woad – and cloth could be shipped from distant ports. Even wool had to be moved to the major cloth-producing areas for they soon outran local supplies. The key factor seems to have been not supplies of raw materials but the availability of a workforce. Here the social structure of the local community and the ability to combine industry with agriculture were all-important, for the countryside had to supply the majority of the workers. In Wiltshire, the north west of the county was given over to small pastoral farms concentrating on cheese making, in the south west around Mere to small butter-making farms. These were the lands of family farmers and self-employed persons who had the spare time necessary to combine cloth manufacturing with farming. Similarly the Suffolk industry centred around Sudbury in the central southern part of the county. Farming in this district was typical of a wood/pasture area, with dairy farms exporting butter and cheese to London. It seems possible also that there was a surplus of population there even in the fifteenth century, thanks to partible inheritance, which could provide the cloth industry with its labour force. The Wealden area of Kent was a forest region with a whole range of industrial occupations, of which cloth making was only one. There were also narrow valleys with swift streams to drive the fulling mills. As for the North, both the West Riding and, later, the area around Kendal were pastoral regions, the lands of small farmers with spare time on their hands and the need for additional sources of income.

There had to be an adequate labour force available, for a considerable amount of man power was needed to produce one cloth. Apart from the introduction of the gig mill, no basic changes occurred in methods of production in the later Middle Ages. A sixteenth-century account of broadcloth manufacture shows that to make a dozen, or cloth of half length ($12 \times 1\frac{1}{2}$-2 yds), 15 persons were employed for a week, three to sort, clean and dye the wool, seven or eight to do the carding and spinning, two weavers, a shearman and odd labour employed taking the wool to the spinners and the cloth to the fulling mill. To produce a standard broadcloth would not mean twice as much labour, for no more than two weavers would be required for example, although more yarn meant more carding and spinning, but it would still tie down more people for a longer period. Labour had to be readily available. In arable areas the needs of agriculture meant that farmers had little spare time. The wood/pasture and forest regions could provide the labour, and the industry was largely located in these regions.

The workers once found had to be organized. There is a common assumption that the transfer of the industry to the countryside meant the simple transference of the putting-out or domestic system of production, dominated by the wealthy clothier. Such a man would concentrate his activities around a complex of wool sheds and fulling mills, which represent his fixed capital investment. He would buy in the wool from local farmers or middlemen, put it out to be made up into cloth by spinners and weavers working in their own homes, then have it fulled and finished either at his own mill or that of a specialist firm before he sold it. Certainly the entrepreneur, tying up considerable working capital in stocks of raw materials, cloth in production and waiting to be sold and using the domestic system, existed in the fifteenth-century countryside. Indeed the domestic system was well suited to rural production. The country craftsman did not have the easy access to the market his urban counterpart had and he certainly lacked the capital to purchase stocks of raw materials or hold them for many months until he sold his cloth. The entrepreneur bore the cost of the raw materials and connected the craftsman to the market. On the other hand the system was open to abuse. Rural craftsmen had no protection against the entrepreneur, for they were too widely dispersed to form gilds and fix high wage rates. They became almost his servants, relying on him for raw materials and for the sale of their cloth.

But it is wrong to assume that the industry was structured exclusively along these lines. In Salisbury there existed alongside the merchant clothiers a group of prospering and property-owning weavers, associated together in a craft organization and able to sell and deal in cloth as well as manufacture it. Similarly, although the industry had a capitalist structure at York, there were also small producers working on their own account. If this variety of modes of production could exist within the town, how much more so in the countryside where there was no regulation. In the Wiltshire industry no one pattern of organization prevailed. The capitalist entrepreneur is found alongside the clothier conducting his business in his own home, keeping one or two looms in continuous production and tying up considerable amounts of working capital in stocks of raw materials, cloth being made, finished and waiting to be sold. He was as much a capitalist as the entrepreneur using the putting-out system. At the other end of the scale there was still room for the small man. Not all weavers were poor men working for the larger clothier. Some were prosperous, property-owning folk, merging into the lower ranks of the clothiers. Smaller producers also seem to have predominated in the West Riding, if sixteenth-century conditions are to be taken as typical of the fifteenth. Their output was in the region of one half-broadcloth a week, buying in wool from middleman dealers, making it up into yarn to sell to other weavers or turning it into rough, unfinished cloth to sell to merchants or their agents. Profits were small, but added to those from pastoral agriculture a man could earn enough to support his family, and he still had his independence. There were also prosperous clothiers who worked by a combination of continuous production and the putting-out system for spinning and the finishing processes. These men were not unlike their Wiltshire counterparts, or the wealthy Paycockes of Coggeshall (Essex) or the Springs of Lavenham (Suffolk).

By these methods an unregulated industry produced a whole variety of broadcloths, dyed blue, black, russet, deep purple or in stripes

271

(rays). From Norfolk came worsted, from Sussex and Essex streits (half-size cloths), blankets were made near Bristol and a whole range of cheap cloths like friezes in the countryside generally. The clothiers sold their cloths to the exporters, the merchants of the principal ports, and especially to the Londoners. The market at Blackwell Hall in the city became the chief point of exchange for cloth in the realm. The industry clearly brought prosperity to the areas where it was located. William Heynes, a villein of Sir John Fastolf at Castle Combe, had goods and chattels valued by his lord at £2,000 when he died in 1436. That figure was challenged and later reduced to £200, this time probably an underestimate. His widow, Margery, was able to pay £27 towards his funeral, £40 as an entry fine for possession of William's moveables, including cloth and madder and woad for dyeing, and the house in which she was living. Later she paid another £100 for permission to remarry and for possession of all William's property, including fulling, gig and corn mills. Margery's brother, Ralph Hawley, was a combination of cloth maker, mill owner and farmer, with two fulling mills in the village. He had built nine new houses in Castle Combe and employed a number of craftsmen as apprentices and servants. Another wealthy man of humble origin was James Terumber of Bradford and Trowbridge. He seems to have come from Bristol and set himself up as a fuller, gradually becoming an entrepreneur clothier. By the late 1450s and early 1460s he was already selling cloth in London to Italian merchants and by that time must have been one of the most prominent clothiers in the Bradford region. The aulnager[5] in 1466 attributed to him half the cloth sealed in Bradford Hundred between April and Michaelmas, giving a somewhat artificial overall figure of 236 cloths. If this is anywhere near correct, and it may include cloth he bought in for finishing, then he must have employed a very considerable workforce. By 1468 Terumber was working in Trowbridge, helping to finance the rebuilding of the church there, investing in lands and houses in the town and surrounding districts, farming the fairs at Trowbridge from the Crown and founding an almshouse for six poor folk. There were many others like Heynes and Terumber, greater and smaller, who invested in mills, sheep pastures, farms and houses, who travelled to and fro managing their property, selling their cloth in London and buying in new stocks of raw materials.

The migration of cloth making to the countryside meant that a great deal of English industry was now rurally based. This was a European-wide phenomenon. Towns were left with the rump of cloth production, and also the handicraft industries – although their goods were increasingly being challenged by products made in the countryside. Town smiths, for example, faced the same problems as cloth producers. The price of bar iron went up as labour costs rose. Attempts at price fixing tended to diminish town supplies to the advantage of the countryside. Town smiths lost country business and cheaper country-made products came into the town, brought in by the same merchants who supplied the smiths with their iron. The inevitable result was that the town industry declined, to the benefit of the country workers. Obviously not all crafts and industries were forced out of the towns. Highly specialized craftsmen like goldsmiths or scriveners were still town based, but the challenge from the countryside was clearly a problem for all late medieval towns.

The location of industry was also, of course, dictated in part by its nature. Iron, tin and coal had to be mined where the deposits were found and smelting, where necessary, would be carried out nearby. Shipbuilding and shipping were based on the ports, as was fishing. There had been little technical advance or structural change since the thirteenth century and the main problems to be discussed are not concerned so much with the nature or location of industry as with whether production increased, remained static or declined and whether there were any factors holding back output. These are difficult questions to answer. Production has to be seen in relation to demand. The sheer fall in the number of people would have meant less overall demand and higher labour costs meant that the price of industrial products did not fall to anything like the extent of those for foodstuffs. One might therefore expect to see a downturn in production in relation to the level of the population. But this could have been offset by the increase in general wealth. The population as a whole might have had greater ability to buy cloth or cheap metalwares and other household goods. It is not possible to make a general judgment, however, when the only figures we have are for cloth exports and tin production. The former show a rapidly expanding industry which certainly supplied all home needs except for the expensive imported damasks and silks and overtook wool as England's chief export. Given the decline in population, cloth exports were worth more than wool exports had been in the thirteenth century, which gave more people more spending power.[6] The amount of tin presented for coinage gives no indication, unfortunately, of what went for export, what was made up into pewter or otherwise used in England. Without figures for the home consumption

273

of any product, it is necessary to look at each industry individually before assessing the relative health of the industrial sector of the economy.

The passion for building does not seem to have flagged in the later Middle Ages. Merchants in town and countryside built and rebuilt their parish churches and gild halls. St Mary Redcliffe is not the only monument to mercantile wealth. It stands alongside St Nicholas, Wells, St Thomas, Salisbury, Ludlow parish church, the churches at Thaxted and Saffron Walden in Essex, Lavenham in Suffolk and Northleach in Gloucestershire. Wealthy monasteries renewed their fabric. Durham Priory was rebuilt and Bell Harry Tower erected at Canterbury. Great secular buildings were probably more important now, however, and new materials like brick were being used at Eton College, Beverley Bar, Tattershall Castle and Lord Hastings's dwelling at Kirby Muxloe (Leics). Tattershall was a massive structure, built for Lord Cromwell between 1433 and 1446. It had a mighty tower 62 feet by 48 feet over the walls which were 12 feet thick at the base. Cromwell spent about £450 per annum on building this splendid edifice and as much again on his huge freestone house at South Wingfield (Derby) and another dwelling at Colly Weston. This was no more than other wealthy men were doing at Ampthill Castle, Sudeley Castle, Hurstmonceaux, Farleigh Castle, Raglan Castle or the duke of Suffolk's palace at Ewelme. There was no shortage of work which was often done by contractors operating on a large scale such as William Sharnhale, who in 1382 received £270.10s.4d. in part payment of £456 for work done for Sir John Cobham at Cooling Castle. Other building operations were organized in the manner described above (Chapter 5). Masons were well paid too, usually more than the rates laid down by the Statute of Labourers. Those working on London Bridge in the early fifteenth century received wages well above those fixed by national or municipal regulations. They were paid 3s.9d. a week all year round and on feast days and holidays as well. In terms of purchasing power their wages were worth far more in the later Middle Ages than in the thirteenth century. Such was the demand for labour that unskilled men's wages crept up to near the skilled men's rates.

The building trade, therefore, seems to have been buoyant. Considerable amounts of money were spent by the upper and middle classes on churches, colleges and on increasingly comfortable homes. They also invested their capital in shipping. Like clothiers, shipowners came from all ranks of society. They saw in shipping an attractive investment. There were great risks of course but the life of a merchantman was fairly long and there was a low rate of depreciation. In the best of circumstances the capital outlay may have been recoverable within a year. Moreover, investment seemed attractive to merchants since it gave them preferential freight rates and a say in where the ship went. Often it was a case of co-ownership, of groups of partners owning shares in the vessel, shares which were readily bought and sold. Surplus capital could thus be invested and realized quickly, as perhaps in no other field of commerce or industry. So merchants, clergymen and landowners great and small put their money into shipping. Great men like Sir John Howard, later duke of Norfolk, and the earl of Warwick saw the small fleets they owned both as a commercial investment and as an expression of their aristocratic power which could be used, as Warwick's fleet was at Calais in the 1450s, to further their own political ambitions. Investment could be considerable. It has been estimated that William Canynges of Bristol had in the 1460s shipping worth nearly £4,000 and that Warwick's ships were worth nearly £3,000. But whether or not there was sufficient investment to provide English trade with all the shipping it needed is another matter. The customs accounts show that in the fifteenth century much of English trade was carried in foreign bottoms, especially in Dutch and Flemish ships. Only half the ships using Hull in the late fourteenth and the fifteenth centuries, for instance, were English; the rest came mainly from the Low Countries. Nor did investment in shipping necessarily benefit the shipbuilding industry. There was a universality of design in North European shipping at this time. Considerable amounts of foreign tonnage were brought, from the Hanse and the Dutch, although Canynges had ships built at Bristol and there was an active industry at Southampton in the early fifteenth century. On balance, however, it seems doubtful whether the industry did expand sufficiently to meet the demands placed upon it as Englishmen came to take a larger share of their country's trade.

No comprehensive study of the allied industry, fishing, has yet been made. An intensive local examination of the industry at Scarborough,[7] a major North-East fishing port shows that it was in sharp decline in the first half of the fifteenth century, however. The fleet seems to have shrunk from about 70–100 vessels employed in both coastal and deep sea fishing, especially off Iceland, to some 50 boats in 1434–42, mainly engaged in North Sea fishing. Scarborough pulled out of the Iceland venture, and there is no clear reason why. The town was badly hit by the plague in these years and there may have been a lack of capital. Equipping a dogger with a crew of 40 for a four-month expedition to Iceland from Dunwich in 1545 cost £200. Even allowing for Tudor inflation, this was still a very considerable sum. Scarborough merchants, in the grip of demographic decline, may not have had the money to invest. Another theory is that London merchants, who had previously underwritten the costly venture, found it more convenient to deal with East Anglian fishermen. East coast boats were certainly active in the Iceland fisheries in the first half of the fifteenth century but, like those from Bristol and Hull, they suffered from Hanseatic competition in the second half of the century and in the North Sea from the challenge of the Dutch. It was not, as is commonly held, the migration of the Scanian herring which brought the North Sea fisheries to the fore. That did not happen. Rather it was the development of new methods of storing herrings, fatty fish which cannot easily be dried. In the late fourteenth century the Dutch began gutting the fish as soon as they were caught, salting them, placing them in barrels in layers, head to tail, each layer being separated by salt. The barrels were then tightly sealed. There were large imports of such fish and other varieties by aliens and especially by Dutchmen and Flemings. Yarmouth, which in the fourteenth century had been the centre of the herring industry with its great annual herring fair, was in distress in the fifteenth century, its harbour being allowed to silt up and its fee farm falling into arrears. It has been argued that this was the result of a fall in demand for salt herring, yet imports were very considerable and it is equally possible that the English fishing industry declined in the face of Dutch competition.

It is when one turns to the mining and metallurgical industries, which in Western Europe provided the main growth points for capitalism, that more obvious signs of trouble appear. Statistics for tin production show a sharp decline in the mid-fifteenth century; not until the early sixteenth century were the levels of the 1390s and 1400s again reached. It is very noticeable that the slump coincided with a sharp downturn in foreign trade and that as trade expanded, so production rose. There are, however, no signs of a scarcity of tin in the mid-century. Tin prices did not rise. Pewter prices show a U-shaped cycle, almost parallel to that for tin output. Decennial averages from 1421 to 1470 were less than the 4s. per dozen lb of 1411–20, falling as low as 3s. per dozen lb in some cases. This would seem to point to stagnant home demand, perhaps to demand for a durable product falling away once the initial stocking by households great and small had taken place. Pewter production certainly declined at London, although this was offset in part by the spread of the industry in the provinces. Nor did exports of pewter pick up when those for tin rose again as new centres in Europe expanded pewter production and England was threatened with low-grade foreign imports.

Was home production to blame? Stiff quality control was exercised by the Pewterers' Company in London, which did not allow the production of cheap goods, although they were increasingly in demand. There also seem to have been difficulties in the mining of the tin itself. The industry employed a substantial labour force, probably 6–8,000 men when production was at its height, who lived by mining alone, rather than combining it with agriculture as the lead miners of the Mendips and Derbyshire did. The life of the tinner was precarious. As has been seen, in the thirteenth and early fourteenth centuries he was forced to pledge his tin in advance of production, living almost perpetually in debt.[8] Labour only worked in the industry when no other alternatives were available. In the fifteenth century there was land to be had and the low level of production was consequent in part at least on a shortage of labour. There may also have been a shortage of capital. The grip that capital had on the industry in the late thirteenth and early fourteenth centuries has already been described.[9] A wealthy class of mine owners and middlemen employed wage labour and took shares in mines in which they could be sleeping as well as active partners. One man in 1357 employed 300 men in seven works. The unit of production was no longer the free tinner and further concentration into larger units might well have been expected as the Middle Ages wore on. Surface deposits were being exhausted, streaming had to go deeper and more and more men were required. But capitalism did not increase, quite the reverse.

Dr Hatcher has analysed ownership of tin presented for coinage in the fourteenth and fifteenth centuries.[10] In the fourteenth century it was the merchant entrepreneur not the working tinner who presented tin to be stamped and between a quarter and a half of the tin so presented was in the hands of persons having over 20 thousandweight. By mid-fifteenth century it was less than one-tenth, by 1519–20 less than one-fifteenth. Only one person presented over 20 thousandweight in 1519 compared with 23 and 19 in 1393–4 and 1395–6 respectively. Conversely the number of persons presenting less than three thousandweight rose rapidly. The trade was now in the hands of the small man and there had been a levelling downwards rather than upwards in the later Middle Ages. Dr Hatcher suggests that this was due to the greater availability of capital and credit. Wealth was no longer in a few hands. Similarly, opportunities were better for wage earners as rates for skilled and semi-skilled men rose and labour shortages were experienced. Working tinners were thus able to avoid the clutches of the tin dealers and could retain their tin until coinage-time to obtain a better price.

There is a certain inconsistency of argument here. On the one hand it is said that tinners were only too glad to leave the industry if other alternatives were available, on the other that wage rates were attractive, opportunities for profit greater. It might also be the case that there were fewer capitalists in the later Middle Ages because less capital was being invested in the industry. Did this, in the long run, hold back production? On the face of it, it did not, because output in the later fifteenth century was comparatively high. But that was the last flash in the pan. By the sixteenth century a crisis was approaching as surface deposits were exhausted and the need to exploit underground lodes, at heavy capital costs, grew. The mid-century downturn may have been caused by a combination of labour shortages and a slump in foreign trade, but problems of capital supply and the pewter industry's failure to develop cheap products also deserve attention. It is ironic that when tin production was stagnant there should have been substantial imports of cheap metal cooking utensils through London, worth between £300 and £1,000 a year. Production centred on Namur, Liège, Dinant and Cologne, the utensils being made from a mixture of copper and lead or tin. The copper came from the Harz mountains, the lead and tin often from England. There was no possibility of making such goods or brassware in England since English copper was not exploited. It is noticeable also that other pots and pans, new and old, sometimes of unspecified materials, sometimes of brass, were also imported. Tin production was tied to quality pewter and that was failing to satisfy the mass market.

Other extractive and related industries also seem to have faced problems. Iron mining and possibly working were in some sort of difficulty, the precise nature of which is not altogether clear. The trouble may have lain in the actual mining of the ore as surface deposits began to run out and there was a need to go deeper. Contemporary technology could cope with the necessary drainage and ventilation of the shafts, but at a price. It is again interesting to note that there were substantial imports of iron ore from the Basque regions of Spain in the fifteenth century. The Genoese in 1438–9 brought in 182 tuns of iron ore worth £455 through Southampton. That was the alien trade alone; there were substantial English imports from the same region. Why was it necessary to import such large quantities of ore? Certainly it produced better quality iron, which may have been the main reason behind the imports. But it must also have been profitable to do so, which meant it could challenge the home product on equal terms. If it could do this, given transport costs both to England and then to the smelting forge, customs duties, insurance and other charges, then either it was being produced very cheaply or locally mined ore was pricing itself out of the market, perhaps due to difficulties in the extractive industry.

That there were problems in the smelting industry which made the iron to be worked into the finished articles by the smiths seems beyond doubt. The possibility of a fuel shortage has already been discussed.[11] Supplies were being conserved by coppicing but that still pushed up the price of the smelting fuel, charcoal. The costs of converting wood into charcoal and carriage to the forge at an iron works at Tudeley, Kent, between 1350 and 1354 were half the total working expenses. They would have been even greater except that the wood came free of charge from the owner's estates. Labour costs at Tudeley formed about one-third of the whole, but of course the percentage would be higher after the Black Death as piece rates per bloom went up from $5\frac{1}{2}$d. to between $7\frac{1}{2}$d. and $9\frac{1}{2}$d. Inevitably this was reflected in the price of iron. Before the plague a bloom of iron cost about 1s.8d; afterwards it doubled. High prices could have been brought down by the application of new technology, especially by the use of water power and the indirect method of production. It has already been seen that the application of water power could improve output considerably.[12] The next development in iron making was most important.[13] At some time in the fifteenth century the blast furnace developed from the hearth. The size of the furnace was much increased and a more powerful blast was produced by the use of water power to drive the bellows. This led to higher temperatures within the furnace and a more complete fusion of the metal. Instead of a bloom a pool of liquid metal formed on the floor of the hearth. At first the sides were dismantled to reach it (this was the Stückofen). Then it was found that if a vent were built into the lower wall of the furnace and plugged with clay during smelting, the liquid iron could be run off. Production was vastly increased, but it was a different kind of iron with a higher carbon content, greater fluidity but

279

also greater hardness and brittleness. It was in fact cast iron which could be run off into moulds. To make it into cutting tools it had to be worked again on another hearth. A jet of air provided by water power oxidized the pigs of iron, removed the carbon and produced soft malleable iron or steel bars. This was the indirect method, involving the use of water power to provide the blast for both the furnace and the hearth. It was a profound change with great implications for the future since it so greatly increased the production of iron.

The blast furnace proper did not reach England until after 1500, but water power was used to provide an improved blast from the fourteenth century onwards. Not only were water-blown forges more productive but they also saved on labour costs. A works at Treeton with a water-driven bloomhearth and stringhearth employed only three men to work both hearths in 1507. At the bloomery of Llantrisant in Glamorgan, newly erected in 1530 but without water power, three times as many men were required to work the two hearths, of which as many as four were needed to operate the bellows. But the use of water power had its drawbacks. Such forges produced more iron but they also consumed more charcoal. Nor could they wander round the countryside, exploiting iron deposits until they were worked out. They were now fixed and iron making became concentrated in areas where there were plentiful supplies of both ore and fuel. Most important of all they required heavy investment in fixed capital equipment. To build the water wheel and construct the mill race was an expensive business. Whether that capital was readily available is open to question. Evidence of the size of the English industry and the extent of the application of water power in the later Middle Ages is admittedly scant, but there is no doubt that its output was small compared with that of the industries in Styria and the Palatinate. Import figures also suggest that it was not completely able to meet home demand. Steel imports were quite substantial. Hansards alone brought in 112 barrels of bar steel worth £422 through London in 1438–9 along with 187 stones and one bundle of wire and 37 barrels of nails. Other aliens imported a further 16 barrels of ordinary nails, three thousandweight of lath nails, one thousandweight and three small barrels of patten (clog) nails and 225 stones, 72 bundles, 20 dozen and five barrels of iron wire. European iron production as a whole was increasing slowly in the fifteenth century from $c.25$-30,000 tons in the 1400s to $c.40,000$ tons in 1500. It was able to supply England with what apparently she could not produce for herself. This may have been due to increased demand but it was more probably the consequence of inadequate production due to a combination of high costs and a low level of technology.

The other major extractive industry was coal mining, particularly important in the North East. The burgesses of Newcastle complained that they had no other commodity of trade and that ordinances prohibiting the export of coal made it impossible for them to pay their fee farm. There was a lively trade to London and the South East and to Europe where coal was used as a domestic fuel, for drying madder, smoking and drying fish and, in Holland, in the brewing industry. But output seems to have remained small in the fourteenth and fifteenth centuries compared with that in the Tudor period. It was hampered by the low level of industrial demand, since coal could not be used in metal working without being turned into coke, and by factors local to the North East. Most mines in the area were owned by ecclesiastical bodies and particularly by the bishops of Durham. They took a very restrictive attitude when leasing out their mines. In 1364 the bishop leased a mine in the Gateshead area on condition that only one shaft be worked at any one time whilst in 1399 the prior of Durham, when entering into an agreement for supplying coal to the monastery, agreed to cease production from his own mines. The burgesses of Newcastle were forced either to enter into these restrictive leases or to rely on the bishop of Durham and other ecclesiastical bodies for their supplies. There were also prolonged quarrels in the fourteenth century over freedom of trade on the Tyne as the bishop of Durham and the prior of Tynemouth attempted to gain a monopoly of coal exports. All this held back the development of the industry but there may also have been technical problems. Mines in the Duffield Frith in the Honor of Tutbury (Staffs) were gradually abandoned in the fourteenth century because of the flooding of the pits. As surface deposits were worked out there was a need to go deeper and at once problems of drainage and ventilation were encountered. The techniques of deep mining were not unknown in England. The Crown used them in its silver mines in Devon. At Bere Ferrers in the late fifteenth century large numbers of pumpmen and charcoal burners (fires were kept burning in the shafts to draw air through) were employed, as well as 79 miners, but that required money. Clearly deep mining was beyond the resources of the Duffield Frith miners; whether similar problems were encountered in the Newcastle area is not known, but it would be surprising if they were not.[14]

An interesting picture of English industry begins to emerge. There had been a tremendous expansion in cloth production, both to supply the home and export markets, but other industries seem to have been running into difficulties. The evidence is certainly inadequate. We have no figures for the output of the handicraft industries. Most of them worked in the upper end of the market, however, making goods to order. They were not mass producers. If there had been economic growth one would have expected to find greater emphasis on industrial production, particularly in the metallurgical industries. Clearly this did not happen. What then held back development? It was not lack of demand. On average, Englishmen were wealthier in the later Middle Ages. They had more surplus cash to spend on industrial products and the details of imports show how many cheap goods were being sucked in. Nor was it a case of inability to expand because of lack of new techniques. They were already there in mining and metal working but do not seem to have been fully applied. This raises the question of the extent to which a limited supply of capital affected the development of English industry in these years. There was a clear need for investment, not so much in the handicraft occupations where the unit of production was small and the master needed only his tools and a stock of raw materials, but in cloth, shipping and the mining and metal-working industries. Clearly a great deal of working capital was needed in cloth production. Investment in fixed equipment, fulling mills, could also be heavy, but it is surprising that there was no concentration of production, no use of the factory system in the fifteenth century. It was a more efficient method of manufacturing, avoiding both delays in the transfer of yarn and cloth from one group of workers to another and fraud which often occurred when workers used their master's materials to make their own cloth. One factor militating against its introduction was a lack of surplus labour willing or able to devote the whole of its time to industry rather than combining it with agriculture. Another, however, is that it would have needed a considerable amount of both fixed and working capital to gather a substantial number of men together under one roof and keep them in continuous employment. Circulating capital had always been necessary, too, in mining. The search for and extraction of ore was essentially a speculative business. The primitive level of prospecting and mining techniques meant that returns on invested capital were uncertain. Large sums had to be expended over long periods before any profits were realized. This was generally true but, as has been seen, the need for capital investment grew even greater in the later Middle Ages as surface deposits were exhausted and miners needed to go deep in search of ore. Capital was also essential for the shipping and fishing industries.

The need is clear – the supply more uncertain. There were, of course, no banks and whilst lack of working capital was partly solved by the use of credit, money for fixed capital investment was harder to find. England's was essentially an agrarian economy where much wealth was immobile, tied up in land which, even in difficult times, brought in a more certain return than industry or trade. Supply of capital was therefore limited and too much may have been absorbed by one or two industries, by cloth making and shipping, to the detriment of others. The most obvious sources of capital were the industrialists themselves, re-investing in their own enterprises, and merchants with liquid wealth from trade. The evidence suggests that in neither case was industrial investment made on a large scale. Leland, the sixteenth-century historian who travelled through Wiltshire in 1542, remarked on the wealth of some of the clothiers in the Bradford and Trowbridge areas. He singled out in particular three men, Thomas Horton, Thomas Bailey and Alexander Langford, each of whom ran cloth-manufacturing businesses which continued for at least three generations. They bequeathed going concerns to their sons but each also had substantial investments in land and houses and a collection of plate and treasure, as well as owning fulling mills, the central pivot of the clothier's business. These investments were intended to provide security for their wives and their old age as well as a patrimony for their children, and they conferred on the clothier a degree of respectability, for being a gentleman went with holding land, not producing cloth. William Stumpe of Malmesbury, one of the wealthiest of all early sixteenth-century clothiers followed precisely the same course of action. He invested in land and houses in Wiltshire and the Cotswolds, building up an immense estate. The bulk of it passed to his eldest son James, already knighted and established as a country gentleman in his father's lifetime.

These sixteenth-century examples may be taken as typical of what was happening in the fifteenth. The profits of industry were being invested in land, and the same is true of mercantile wealth. Some York merchants in the late fourteenth and early fifteenth century accumulated large cash fortunes. Thomas Alstanmore (d.1435) is said to have left wool, silver vessels and other goods and chattels worth £760, Richard Russell's cash legacies and dispositions amounted to over £700 and Nicholas Blackburn's to about £800. By mid-century more was invested in land in the city and the surrounding countryside. In part this was certainly the result of the decline in York's trade as merchants sought security in urban property and country estates. What this meant in the long run can be seen in the career of Richard York an immigrant to the city from Berwick on Tweed. He had houses in Hull, Newcastle and Berwick itself and land in about 11 Yorkshire villages. When his sons appeared in the sheriff's court at York in 1500 to claim a debt they were described as Richard York esquire, Thomas, William and John York, gentlemen, and Christopher York LL.D. The family had moved from commerce to gentility in one generation.

To a greater or lesser degree this was also true of merchants in other provincial towns. At Salisbury mercantile wealth was quite heavily invested in city property, at Leicester the Wyggestons, wealthy wool merchants, owned 22 per cent of the taxable property in the town in 1524, and the wealthiest citizens of Hull invested in both urban and rural property. It became almost a rule that three generations would see a family establish itself in trade and then move out to a substantial country estate. There were three generations of the Springs of Lavenham (*c.*1400–1523), of the Canynges at Bristol (*c.*1369–1474), the Marlers at Coventry (*c.*1469–1540) and the Wyggestons at Leicester (*c.*1430–1536). Of course, investment in land was not always to the detriment of trade and industry. Land could be, and was, used as security for loans and urban property produced income, both of which could be used to further commercial enterprise. But the fact remains that a substantial number of provincial merchants were more interested in investing their surplus wealth in land in order to secure an income for their families after their death, to provide masses for the good of their souls or to turn their sons into country gentlemen rather than using it to develop trade or industry.

This is all the more true of Londoners and here the problem was more serious. London was the only city of any size by Continental standards. It dominated the country's trade and drew to it new men from the provinces anxious to make their fortunes, often bringing with them substantial amounts of capital. For the poorer man the way forward was not easy but was by no means impossible. The level of wealth needed to open a business was modest: £40–50 would do in the Mercers' Company, although it must be said that this was quite beyond the reach of most Londoners. If a man prospered, then he might increase his fortune by a good marriage. The young merchant looked around carefully for a match, made business-like inquiries about his proposed bride's wealth and was willing to pay commission on her dowry to a marriage broker. Widows with young children were often a very good bargain, especially if the stepfather was allowed control of his stepchildren's inheritance. One fifteenth-century grocer, marrying as his second wife a widow with a dower of £764, was appointed guardian of her children and allowed to trade with their patrimony, another £764. Not all merchants acquired great fortunes, however. Analysis of their estates from the valuations given in the records of the Court of Orphans and the wills of grocers between 1350 and 1506 shows that there were plenty of men with only moderate wealth. Twenty-four per cent left less than £100, but the median value of estates was £300 and one or two left well over £1,000.

This wealth was spent on display and on acquiring urban and rural property, for the same reasons as provincial merchants. The man who was both successful and socially ambitious might, by the time of his death, have a third to a half or more of his fortune in lands. John Hedde, draper, estimated that his debts and merchandise would realize £4-5,000; his income from manors in Kent was £41; he had property in Essex including several manors, a mill and the reversion of a quay in Colchester probably bringing in as much again; and income from London property assessed in 1412, six years before his death, at £54.14s.7d. Sir Geoffrey Boleyn, who died in 1463, drew £115 a year in rents from lands in Kent, Sussex and Norfolk and London, which meant an investment of over £2,000. Citizens of London seem to have owned estates in every county of England except Worcester, Rutland, Lancashire and those in the extreme North. All types of property which would produce revenue were involved, mills, quays, fisheries and woodlands as well as sheep pastures and arable. Some of this might be termed industrial investment but they were buying existing installations rather than creating new ones. Neither, as far as one can tell, did they put money into mines or forges or, mills apart, into cloth making.

It is possible to overemphasize the extent of property ownership. Possibly only 900-1,000 households were backed by property in 1412. Some of the wealthy had no land at all, their ability to make advantageous marriages for their children making them less directly interested in property. But again and again the 'traditional' pattern can be seen of the rich merchant's son moving out of trade back into the countryside or into the law or the administration. This, coupled with the failure of the merchant class to replace itself made for even greater social mobility than in the provincial towns. There were few long-lasting dynasties, building up wealth from generation to generation, investing and re-investing in trade and industry. If capital on a large scale was not to come from London, then from where else in the kingdom? There are few signs that landowners, lay or ecclesiastical, invested in anything except a little trade and shipping. They may have owned the mines and forges but they leased them out for others to exploit. Income was for consumption not for creating more wealth.

The urban and industrial sectors of the English economy at the end of the Middle Ages, then, show distinct signs of malaise. Towns were in difficulties, if not in outright decline. Industry had moved out into the countryside but it seemed to suffer generally from a lack of capital investment and, with one or two honourable exceptions such as cloth, from an inability to produce cheap goods for the mass market. Did it matter? In one sense, no. What English industry could not supply, English and alien traders appear to have been able to make good. The popular market was catered for, the better off could still indulge their tastes for luxury, for good quality English cloth, fine imported damasks and silks, spices and wines, for pewter which an Italian visitor in the late fifteenth century likened to the best silverware. They could spend large sums on building, turning their draughty dwellings into comfortable houses. But if the proper purpose of this study is to look for signs of substantial change in the economy, for economic growth, then there had been none. Industry continued to occupy no more than 10–15 per cent of the workforce at the most. England was still overwhelmingly a semi-developed or even an underdeveloped agrarian economy with wealth immobilized in land. There had been no vast switch to manufacturing, which would have provided more wealth to take up the surplus labour beginning to appear again in the early sixteenth century. Cloth making is a good example of the benefits which accrued from adding to the value of the raw material, creating rural and mercantile wealth, especially in the ever-growing London. But London's strength may have been deleterious to other towns and traders – it took trade away from York, Bristol, Boston, Hull, it drew merchants to it to seek their fortune from all over the country. It is difficult to avoid the conclusion that some inland towns filled the same role that Southampton and Sandwich did as London's outports. The gloom must not be overstated. Demand was supplied; but there had been no real economic growth.

9 English Trade in the Late Middle Ages: the Triumph of the English?

In the framework of later medieval European trade, England was part of a North Sea – Eastern Atlantic economy which, from the fourteenth century, was linked to the Mediterranean world by direct sea routes. England's most important market in the period, both for wool and cloth, was Flanders and the Low Countries. At the Staple, at Calais, wool was sold to Flemish and Dutch clothiers, whilst cloth went directly to the markets and fairs at Antwerp, Bergen op Zoom and Utrecht. In return came either gold or silver in payment for wool, or a whole range of raw materials, foodstuffs, especially fish, and cheap manufactured goods, mercery and haberdashery, bought from the profits of the cloth trade. That was not the only market, however. There was a considerable amount of cross-Channel trade with Brittany and Normandy, whilst further west there were major trade routes to the English possessions in South-West France, Gascony/Guienne, where cloth and grain were exchanged for wine, and to Spain and Portugal which supplied England with iron ore, wool oil, soap for washing cloth, dyestuffs and citrus fruits. By the late fourteenth and early fifteenth century the sea route to the Mediterranean was in full use. Venetian and Florentine galleys and Genoese carracks brought raw materials vital for the cloth industry – woad, alum and dyestuffs – spices and drugs, precious cloth, and expensive sweet wines. In return they exported vast quantities of cloth, along with wool, tin and pewter.

Trade to the north was equally complex. Here the English were challenging the monopoly of the Hanse and trying to break into the Baltic. The Hansards' interest in England grew as the country became a leading supplier of broadcloths. They exchanged for cloth naval stores, hemp, pitch, tar, furs, flax and linen, mineral ores, potash (used in the cloth industry), and fish. Merchants from the Baltic towns of Lübeck, Danzig, Stralsund and Königsberg were not the only Han-

Figure 9.1 The principal commodities and routes of English foreign trade in the later Middle Ages

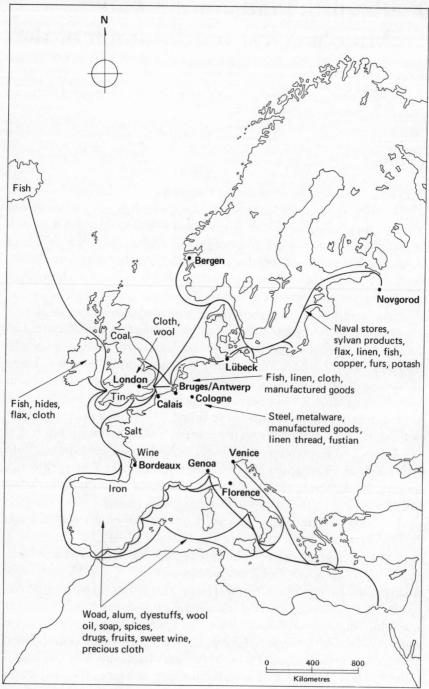

N

Fish

Bergen

Novgorod

Cloth, wool

Coal

Lübeck

London

Tin

Bruges/Antwerp

Calais

Cologne

Fish, hides, flax, cloth

Salt

Wine

Bordeaux

Genoa

Venice

Iron

Florence

Naval stores, sylvan products, flax, linen, fish, copper, furs, potash

Fish, linen, cloth, manufactured goods

Steel, metalware, manufactured goods, linen thread, fustian

Woad, alum, dyestuffs, wool oil, soap, spices, drugs, fruits, sweet wine, precious cloth

0   400   800
Kilometres

sards trading to England. Equally important were the Cologne merchants who distributed English cloth down the Rhine and imported cheap fabrics, steel and metalware and cheap manufactured goods. England's most remote market was probably Iceland. Ships from Bristol, Hull and London took foodstuffs, manufactured goods and cloth there, bringing back stockfish, a necessity, not a luxury in an age when Lent was strictly observed. Nearer at hand there was a flourishing trade between the west coast ports and Ireland in cloth, hides, fish and foodstuffs.

England was thus one of the nodal points in European trade, where north met south. Merchants from many lands came there; ships from many countries passed along her coasts, especially through the Channel, on their way to the Baltic or to Flanders, or to the Bay of Bourgneuf for salt. English merchants therefore traded in a European-wide market and that market was influenced by general economic circumstances and particularly by an absolute fall in demand consequent upon population decline. There were also other factors which affected trade. It had to operate in the political world and particularly within the sphere of northern European politics. For most of the period England was at war with France: actual hostilities may have ended in 1453, but there was no real peace, however shaky, until the Treaty of Picquigny in 1475. The war badly affected England's commercial relations with France and Gascony and, after 1449, with Normandy and Brittany. The problem became worse as the dukes of Burgundy sought to unite the Low Countries (Flanders, Holland, Zeeland and Brabant) and follow policies independent of the French Crown. Burgundy and England were at first allies, then enemies, then allies again, and neither king nor duke hesitated to wage economic warfare on the other in pursuit of diplomatic or fiscal ends. In the north the English and Dutch fought to break the Hanseatic monopoly of the Baltic. This trade war soon became political, since the Hansards traded to the Burgundian Netherlands as well, and were affected by interruptions in Anglo-Burgundian commerce. Quarrels between the Hanse towns and Denmark could lead to the closing of the Sound to all shipping, and the markets in the Baltic hinterland were badly disturbed by wars between Poland and the Teutonic Knights. To the south, the French war spilled over and damaged relations with Castile and Genoa, whilst the continual wars between city states in fifteenth century Italy interrupted trade to the Mediterranean. Within England the breakdown of law and order leading to civil war in the 1450s and 1460s allowed widespread piracy to flourish, to the detriment of trade, whilst both Lancaster and York tried to buy mercantile support by making concessions not always in England's best interests.

There is no better example of how politics exacerbated the effects of falling demand than the Gascon wine trade. Supplies of grain from England allowed Gascony to concentrate on viticulture. In the early fourteenth century, Gascony exported as many as 90–100,000 tuns (a tun = 252 gallons) of wine a year of which England absorbed some 20,000 tuns, imported chiefly through London, Hull (to serve the northern market), Bristol and Southampton by English rather than Gascon merchants. The land war which broke out in 1337 caused widespread destruction in Gascony whilst naval operations made the trade route dangerous and pushed up the costs of shipping. By the 1360s Bourdeaux's exports had declined to 30,000 tuns, and the price per tun in England had doubled from £3 to £5–6. There was a limited recovery in the later fourteenth century, but English imports ran at only 9–10,000 tuns per annum in the fifteenth century, half the volume of the early fourteenth century, a decline certainly greater than that resulting from falling demand due to declining population. These levels were maintained until the final loss of Gascony in 1453, which dealt a blow to the trade from which it did not recover until after the Treaty of Picquigny (1475). When recovery came, much of the shipping used was Breton or Spanish, not English, and only in 1498–9 and 1499–1500 did imports again reach 10,000 tuns. The trade, too, was now concentrated on London and the West Country ports, much to the detriment of Southampton and Hull, and the other East Coast ports.

Trade was the victim of falling demand and, above all, of warfare which destroyed areas of production and cut across sea routes. Elsewhere Englishmen tried, and failed, to break into the new markets on the Baltic and the Mediterranean. Eventually their trade was concentrated along one main route, to the Low Countries, and of course, wool was replaced by cloth as the principal export.[1] Good quality cloth was one of the great commodities of European trade because it could be produced on a relatively large scale, and be sold at a profit large enough to cover the high transport costs. In the later Middle Ages, England replaced Flanders as the leading supplier of quality broadcloths in Europe. Figures 9.2 and 9.3 show the rise in cloth exports from the mid-century when figures are first available and the comparable decline in wool exports. What it also shows is that the expansion was not steady. Rather there were phases of expansion and contraction,

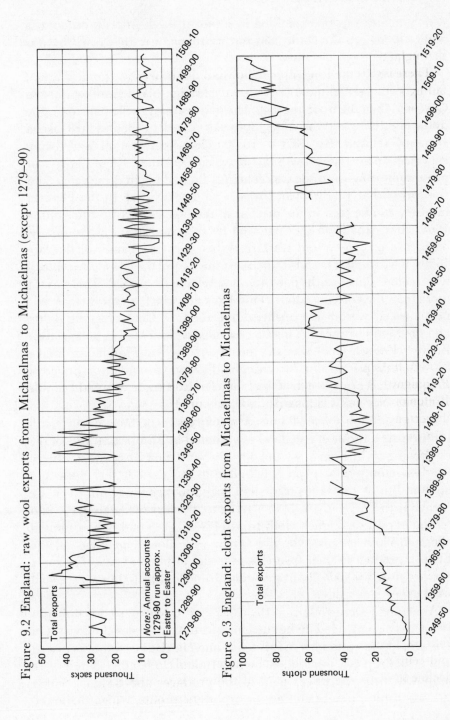

Figure 9.2 England: raw wool exports from Michaelmas to Michaelmas (except 1279–90)

Figure 9.3 England: cloth exports from Michaelmas to Michaelmas

Taken from E. M. Carus-Wilson and O. Coleman, *England's Export Trade 1275-1547* (Oxford, 1963), pp. 122-3, 138-9. Reproduced by permission of the Oxford University Press.

which, again, can be explained in terms of the European economy's ability to absorb the cloth, and interruptions in trade caused by war and politics.

By the 1350s the English industry had recaptured the home market, but exports were minimal due to the effects of plague and warfare in Gascony, then the main market. The first real stage of expansion came in the late 1350s and the early 1360s as food prices fell and the Gascon economy revived. By 1366–8, 16,000 cloths per annum were being exported, an average growth rate between 1350 and 1368 of 18 per cent per annum. English trade was generally flourishing in these years, and the threat that English cloth was beginning to pose to the Flemish industry can be seen in the distress in the Flemish textile cities in the 1360s. But expansion was followed by recession in the wake of new outbreaks of plague and warfare. When recovery came, in the late 1370s, it was at first hesitant, then sustained until the end of the century when some 40,000 cloths per annum were being exported. This was far more than the Gascons alone could have absorbed, and it is clear that new markets were being opened up in the Low Countries, the Baltic and the Mediterranean. This success must also be seen in perspective. Enough English wool was still being exported to Flanders to make 80,000 cloths per annum, twice England's exports – and until the end of the fifteenth century much of the English export trade was in the hands of aliens, especially Hansards and Italians.

Twenty troubled years followed the expansion of the late fourteenth century. As a result of a general contraction in European trade, of the re-opening of the French war, of disputes with the Hanse and a wave of Anglo-Breton piracy, exports fell often to less than 30,000 cloths per annum. But by the 1420s trade had begun to pick up again. Even the breach with Burgundy in 1435 leading to the siege of Calais and a ban on the import of English cloth from 1434 to 1439 had only a limited effect on cloth exports, for the Dutch were now dependent on the English product in their own export trade. From 1437 to 1447 export reached nearly 60,000 cloths per annum, and for the first time exceeded wool exports in value.

Attaching precise values to the cloth and wool exported is difficult. Wool was never valued in the customs accounts, whereas cloth was. On average, in the years 1421–61, English and Hanseatic cloth was priced at £1.15s. the piece, other alien, mainly Italian cloth, at £2. These were supposed to be the prices paid to the producer and do not include customs duties, freight charges or exporters' profits, which made the price charged to the foreign customer much higher. Using the same criterion, the price paid to the supplier, wool shipped by native merchants can be valued at £5.10s. the sack until 1450–1, and high quality wool shipped by alien merchants – almost exclusively Italians – at £8 the sack. These are lower figures than used by Gray[2] and are based on statistics recently produced by T. H. Lloyd who showed that there was a glut of wool and consequently low prices in mid-fifteenth century England.[3] The cloth valuations are also probably too low, and the following figures must be taken only as a rough-and-ready indicator of the comparative value of exports. Cloth had finally established itself as England's leading export. It was in demand because, as at Toulouse, where it supplanted Flemish cloth by the 1430s, it offered to men of middling wealth a medium quality, medium-priced product, dyed in a variety of shades.

Table 9.1 Decennial averages of cloth and wool exports, 1421–1451

Year	Cloth	Value	Wool	Value
Michaelmas to Michaelmas	Broadcloths	£	sacks	£
1421–2/1430–1	41,750	76,590	13,732	77,780
1431–2/1440–1	45,050	82,310	6,710	39,370
1441–2/1450–1	49,350	89,660	8,810	51,080

Totals calculated from E. M. Carus-Wilson and O. Coleman, *England's Export Trade 1275–1547* (Oxford, 1963). A broadcloth was 24 yards long by 1½–2 yards wide. Smaller cloths were exported, but were converted into broadcloth equivalents by the customers. A sack of wool weighed 364lb.

The expansion of exports could not be maintained in the third quarter of the century. A general depression in European trade, coupled with the outbreak of civil war at home, continuing disputes both with the Hansards, culminating in their expulsion from England from 1468 to 1474, and with Burgundy, resulting in bans on the import of English cloth from 1447 to 1452 and from 1464 to 1467, all hit exports hard. They fell to about 40,000 pieces per annum between 1447 and 1475, and in one year (1464–5), when the Burgundian cloth ban was introduced, to only 20,000 cloths. Peace with the Hanse (1474), with France (1475), and restoration of normal commercial relations with Burgundy, combined with an upturn in demand as the European population began to rise, brought relief and expansion in the last quarter of the century. By 1475–80 exports again averaged 60,000 cloths per annum. There was a slight downturn in the 1480s but then a steady rise. Even Henry VII's boycott on trade with Burgundy from 1493 to 1496, in retaliation for aid given to the pretender to the throne, Perkin Warbeck, could only halt progress temporarily. As soon as Anglo-Burgundian trade was restored, by the favourable commercial treaty known as the Magnus Intercursus (1496), cloth exports boomed. In 1499–1500 they reached over 70,000 and continued to rise.

Although cloth is not a story of unbroken success, the contrast with the fortunes of the wool trade could not be more striking. From the high point in the 1350s, when over 40,000 sacks were exported in some years, exports slumped to an average of 13,000 sacks per annum between 1401 and 1430. But the real disasters, from which the trade never recovered, came between 1429 and 1439. These years saw restrictions on the use of credit sales and open warfare with Burgundy, the main market, culminating in the siege of Calais (1436), by then the home of the wool Staple. This brought an almost complete cessation of the trade. After 1439 there was a partial recovery but for the rest of the century exports ran at only 8–9000 sacks per annum. The reasons for this decline are discussed more fully below, but it is obvious that the more English cloth exports grew, the less would be the demand for English wool in Flanders.

Cloth and wool dominated England's export trade. Our only other product of note was tin, sold either as rods or blocks of pure ore, or made up into pewter vessels. The opening up of new mines in central Europe reduced demand for English tin in Germany, but the Italians more than made up for any loss in that sector. From Southampton and later London, the Genoese and Venetians shipped large quantities of tin to the Mediterranean and beyond to Asia Minor. In a single year, 1380–1, the Genoese and Catalans shipped 350 thousandweight (350,000 lb), more than one-third of the average amount of tin presented for coinage in Cornwall and Devon at this time. From London, too, there were regular shipments of tin and pewter by Hansards, by merchants from Holland and Zeeland, and by Londoners trading to Calais or the Netherlands. From the south-western ports there was a direct route to France, which certainly expanded after peace was finally achieved in 1475. Even so, tin exports could scarcely have amounted to more than £10,000 per annum, perhaps less in some years, because it is likely that they declined steadily in the fifteenth century in line with the decline in tin production.

So, in the course of the later Middle Ages England became an exporter of a finished or semi-finished article rather than a raw material. This was of considerable benefit to the economy. It brought more employment and more wages to be spent. It meant more profit to the producer, to the exporter, and to the country generally, for cloth sold abroad would be worth more than its equivalent weight in raw wool. There is no single explanation for this important change; rather it resulted from the interaction of several complex factors. Firstly, the later fourteenth century saw the final emergence of the Staple, the one fixed point through which all wool exports had to be directed, and of a company of English merchants, the Fellowship of the Staple, who had a near-monopoly on exports. The Staple was the product of a comprom-ise between the Crown and the various other parties who had interests, often conflicting interests, in the wool trade. The earlier part of this story has been told above, and what happened between 1350 and 1400, by which time the Staple was firmly established at Calais, follows familiar themes. The Crown, above all, could not do without the high export duties levied on wool to finance its wars. It needed, too, finan-ciers, to replace the Italian bankers, the Bardi and Peruzzi, who had gone bankrupt, and the syndicates of English merchants, led by Mel-chebourne, Chiriton and Swanland, who had suffered the same fate. The custom and subsidy on wool provided a good security for loans, however, and if control of the trade was given to a more broadly based company of merchants, they they would be able to lend the Crown money from their monopoly profits which could be repaid from the export duties on wool. Finally, the Crown required a secure base for military operations in northern France. If that, too, could also be financed from the profits of the wool trade, an important burden would be lifted from the shoulders of a needy king. The wealthier English merchants, chiefly Londoners and men from eastern towns such as Lincoln and York, wanted a complete monopoly, of course. Failing that, they wanted to be in a position to dominate the trade, and keep out the alien merchants. The latter aspiration was shared by the mass of English wool merchants but they had an almost equal dislike of the monopolists who had in the past squeezed them out of the wool trade. The lesser merchants found an ally here in parliament, and particularly in the Commons who, as representatives of the wool-growers, had seen that monopolist control meant low prices for them. The Commons had grown increasingly resentful of Edward III's arbitrary levying of wool taxation as part of an agreement with the monopolists. The king, they argued, might have his subsidy on wool, but the Commons should grant it, there should be no monopoly control of the trade and the Staple should remain fixed at the place nominated by them. That left only the aliens. All they wanted was free trade, so that with their greater expertise and capital reserves they could dominate the market.

From this welter of interests there emerged the Company of the Staple at Calais. There were some extraordinary twists and turns in the course of its evolution. Sometimes there were home Staples as in the years after the Ordinance and Statute of the Staple in 1353. Wool was to pass through nominated towns but, in the hope that the power of the monopolists would be broken, only aliens were allowed to export. At other times, the Staple was at Calais, though the Crown would sell licences to export directly to the Netherlands, reaping thereby a double duty on the wool. All this enraged the Commons, who in 1372–3 demanded that a single staple should be adhered to and claimed that it had been established at Calais by authority of Parliament. In Richard II's reign (1377–99) the Staple was moved to Middelburg, in the 1380s and briefly, in 1391, there was a return to home Staples, but with the accession of Henry IV the liberties of the Staplers at Calais were guaranteed.

Most parties were satisfied with the compromise. The Crown had its broadly based company of about 200 merchants, though one dominated by a group of wealthy capitalists, mainly from London. These men were wealthy enough individually and corporately to make the Crown substantial loans, like that of £10,000 in 1377 which was to be repaid from the wool duties of 50s. per sack, collected at the leading ports. The Staplers were indeed to become a major prop of Crown finances in the fifteenth century. The wool merchants themselves were reasonably content. They were based in an English town on the Continent, roughly equidistant from all centres of production, so that no one group of merchants was favoured above others. The Company of the Staple, ruled over by the mayor and aldermen, had wide powers to regulate the trade, and a near-monopoly of it. From 1378 Italians and Spaniards were allowed to ship directly to the Mediterranean, but their share of the trade was now negligible, having fallen from 34 per cent in the 1370s to 10 per cent by the early 1400s. High alien export duties had discouraged them from buying English wool. The merchants of Newcastle were from time to time allowed to ship directly to Flanders, because their low-priced northern wools would not bear the additional cost of transport to Calais. But to preserve their monopoly the Staplers fought against this arrangement, and, indeed, against the granting of any licences to export wool other than through Calais. Parliament had won its battle for control of the wool subsidy; the important garrison town of Calais could be financed through the wool trade – every interest group seems to have benefited. Only wool exports themselves reaped no advantage from this arrangement.

The years which saw the development of the Staple also saw the rapid decline in the volume of exports. Whilst no one factor will explain that decline, it seems certain that the Staplers used their monopoly power to pass on the cost of high export duties to their foreign customers. That gave the English cloth producers a very considerable advantage. But what gave English cloth an even greater edge was that it carried an export duty of only about 3–5 per cent of its value, compared to 30–33 per cent for wool. The Staplers could not pass back the duty to the growers. Wool prices in England had collapsed in the 1380s and over-production ensured they remained low for the rest of the Middle Ages. The Crown and the Staplers had given the growing English cloth industry a considerable cost advantage, and the more cloth exports grew, the more wool exports declined. Fifteenth-century Europe could not afford more than one industry serving the same limited market.

But what delivered the finishing stroke to England's major cloth-producing competitors was the way in which the Staple was used as an instrument of fiscal policy in the search for bullion. Bullionism, the desire to maintain and increase a nation's supply and stocks of gold and silver, was common in both thought and practice in late medieval Europe.[4] Supplies of precious metals were, however, limited, and one nation's gain could often only be at another's expense. So it was with England and the duchy of Burgundy, whose economies were so closely interrelated. The dukes of Burgundy, anxious to build up their power and expand their territories, were in desperate need of revenue. One of the easiest and most lucrative ways of raising it was frequent debasements and recoinages, since in medieval Europe the prince had the right to take seignorage, a percentage of all bullion brought to his mints for recoining. Providing the dukes set an attractive price for bullion, so that the merchant came away with more coins of the same face value than he had taken to the mint, then specie and coin would flow to his mints and he would reap a handsome reward. So the dukes of Burgundy from the 1380s to the 1470s pursued aggressive mint policies, but obviously, they were not alone in this. Rulers in surrounding countries operated similar policies, and there was a constant struggle for bullion.

There was one country however, which did not practise frequent recoinages, and that country was England. English kings faced the same desperate need for money for their wars, but Edward III's interference with coinage in the opening stages of the Hundred Years War had raised such a storm that in the Statute of Purveyors of 1352 he had had to promise not to worsen in fineness or weight the current coinage. His promise was kept by subsequent rulers and there were only two major recoinages in fifteenth century England. The result was that the English coinage was of good quality and had a high metal content. It was much in demand abroad, and tended to be replaced in England itself by foreign imitations of inferior quality. Regular wear and tear had to be made good, so that England, too, needed a constant supply of bullion. But this could not be done by debasing the currency in regular recoinages. England therefore had to adopt a dual policy of prohibiting the export of specie, and of imposing controls on foreign trade designed to extract a proportion of export receipts in the form of bullion from the merchants.

It is this that explains the obsession with the balance of trade in late medieval England, and the attempts to force aliens to spend all they made on the sale of imports on exports. But the main vehicle for the acquisition of bullion was to be the wool trade, since, in the second half of the fourteenth century, it was still England's premier export. Regulations requiring the desposit of a certain amount of bullion at the mint for every sack of wool exported appeared soon after the opening stages of the Hundred Years War. They were repeated frequently, but were never very successful. It was soon seen (by 1363–4 in fact) that the best way of achieving England's ends was to make the customers at the Staple pay in whole or in part for their wool in bullion. This could then be struck into English coin at a mint especially established at Calais. These coins could be sent back to England, the coinage would be replenished, and inferior foreign imitations, accepted as payment for wool, would not pass into circulation.

In abstract the idea was excellent: in practice it infuriated the dukes of Burgundy whose merchants were the chief buyers of English wool. They were being forced to pay for it in bullion, which was thus being drained from Burgundy, denying the dukes' mints of vital supplies. Add to this the problems caused by denial of credit[5] to Flemish merchants at the Staple, the high cost of English wool, the growing competition from English cloth, and it is easy to see why the dukes of Burgundy were so often at odds with the kings of England and why retaliatory measure followed retaliatory measure.

The critical period for the wool trade was in the 1420s and 1430s, precisely the point at which cloth overtook wool as the principal export. The duke badly needed money to finance his wars of conquest against Holland and Zeeland, and faced stiff competition from surrounding mints in his attempts to accumulate bullion. Henry VI's government needed revenues from the Calais mint to pay its troops in France, whilst within the Staple itself a power struggle was developing with some 20–30 rich merchants trying to squeeze out the lesser men. This is the background to the passing in 1429–30 of what are known as the Bullion and Partition Ordinances. The Bullion Ordinance required that the entire price of wool bought at the Staple must be paid in gold or silver. No credit was allowed at all. To prevent fraud, the seller was not to hand back any money to the buyer by way of a loan, and one-third of the price was to be delivered by the seller, in bullion or in foreign coins, to the Calais mint. The Partition Ordinance introduced a scheme whereby the wool merchants divided or partitioned all their receipts, not according to the individual sales, but to the amount each had brought to the Staple. The wool was graded and pooled with other wool of the same quality. Only as and when the whole stock was sold did a merchant receive payment for his share.

The Ordinances were probably the product of collaboration between the Crown and the leading Staplers, the one wanting to finance the Calais garrison, which was virtually England's only standing army in France, the other desiring control of the wool trade. Whatever the reasons, the effects on the wool trade were catastrophic. Flemish and Dutch merchants were hard pressed to find the whole price of the wool, and their cloth industries suffered accordingly. The lesser English wool merchants were ruined. They received proportionately less for sales in the initial partitions than did the wealthy merchants, and they had insufficient working capital and credit for maintaining their trade over the long period of the several successive partitions necessary to produce their final sales receipts. The few surviving merchants were able to monopolize the trade and fix prices at higher levels. Most of all, the duke of Burgundy was outraged. Breaking his alliance with England in 1435, he launched an attack on Calais, which helped paralyse the wool trade until 1439.

Although the Ordinances were lifted in 1444, the wool trade never recovered. It was to be the victim of continuing bans on credit sales, and of bullionist regulations until the late 1470s. Only then were normal credit transactions allowed, and the picture of the organization of the wool trade obtained from reading the Cely Papers should not be taken as typical of the century as a whole. The English cloth producers, of course, reaped an enormous advantage, and, before the general mid-century slump in trade, exports leapt ahead. English cloth not only routed its foreign competitors, it also began to play a vital part in the Dutch economy. The Dutch finishing industry began to process semi-finished English cloth, Dutch merchants exported increasingly large amounts to the Baltic, Hanseatic and other merchants bought the cloth for export at the great fairs in the Netherlands.[6] Consequently, Burgundian cloth bans rarely worked for long, although they are responsible for some of the erratic movements in export figures in the fifteenth century.

So, as Eileen Power wrote, the Staplers killed the goose that laid the golden egg. A combination of high taxation, monopoly control and bullionist policies helped price England's cloth-producing competitors out of the market. They faced other problems, too. Civil War literally ruined Flanders between 1379 and 1385, there was continual social discontent in the towns, and the industry began to move out into the countryside to produce lighter, cheaper cloths using cheaper and inferior Scottish, Spanish and native wools. Much the same happened in Brabant, whilst the Florentine industry was dealt a severe blow by the revolt of the Ciompi in 1379.[7] In one sense, therefore, the expansion of the English industry helped fill the vacuum left by the decline of the great Continental industries, but the main agent of change must still be seen in the misfortunes of the wool trade.

Whatever the cause, the growth of a native cloth industry and the rise of a great export trade in cloth was beneficial to the economy. As has already been seen, it provided labour and brought new profits to manufacturer and merchant alike. It also meant that England's export trade did not decline to anything like the extent it might have done if wool had still been the only export. The existence of the customs accounts makes possible a comparison between the value of the English export trade in the late thirteenth and the mid-fifteenth centuries. In the decade 1280–90 an average 26,806 sacks of wool per annum were exported. Most of this was medium-quality wool which was bought from the grower at around £5.17s. per sack,[8] so it was worth in all about £157,107. In the decade 1441–51, 49,350 cloths per annum were exported, which, using the valuations given above (see page 293), were worth £89,660. In addition an average 8,810 sacks of wool went abroad, worth an estimated £51,080; so cloth and wool exports combined came to £140,734. The cloth exports were the equivalent of 11,408 sacks of wool (using the conversion rate of $4\frac{1}{3}$ cloths to a sack)[9] and would have been worth an estimated £65,596 compared to the £89,660 for the cloths actually exported. Cloth was then worth at least 37 per cent more than wool, probably much more, since as has been explained, the customs accounts probably undervalued cloth. It is clear from these estimated figures that cloth was worth very much more than wool, and that whilst in absolute terms there had been a decline in the value of England's main exports, in relation to a fall in the population of at least one-third, there had been no decline at all. If the comparison is made in terms of wool only, exports had sunk from 26,806 sacks to 20,218, a decline of far less than a third: if values are compared, £157,107 against £140,734, then there had been a decrease of only about 10 per cent. The English export trade was withstanding well the rigours of the later Middle Ages.

To deal solely in numbers and conditions of demand, however, is to ignore other important aspects of overseas trade. It could not, for example, have functioned without an adequate system of internal trade to deal with the redistribution of imports and the collection of exports. As has already been argued, road, river and coasting transport were capable of meeting current needs.[10] Later medieval evidence merely confirms this picture. To the main ports came large quantities of raw materials, especially woad, alum, wool oil, soap and dyestuffs for the cloth industry, of wine in 252 gallon barrels, of foodstuffs, manufactured and luxury goods. Outward bound went cloth, wool and tin, which in many cases travelled long distances. The tin came by coasting traffic to Southampton and then by road to London; wool came by river and road from the Cotswolds and the Welsh Marches, to London and Southampton. Cloth from the Cotswolds, East Anglia and the West Riding was despatched to all the main ports, but more and more to London. A great deal is known about the redistributive trade of one port, Southampton, in the mid-fifteenth century, thanks to records of a toll collected on carts leaving and entering the town. Apart from serving the surrounding villages with small quantities of imported goods in exchange for grain and meat, Southampton had important road links with Winchester and Romsey, the one an ecclesiastical centre, the other with a flourishing cloth finishing industry; with Salisbury which took large amounts of woad, about 800 bales or 80 tons per annum, for redistribution to the Wiltshire industry; with London, whence Italian and London merchants consigned large quantities of woad and alum and luxury goods; and with Coventry, over 100 miles away. Winter and summer the carts went out to this important Midland cloth centre, laden with woad, alum, madder and wine. Back they came, a week or ten days later, with wool and cloth to unload and start the journey all over again.

Southampton's trade is a telling commentary on the supposed inadequacies of the medieval road system. Nor should it be regarded as unique. A combination of road and river routes served Hull and Bristol, whilst London had to handle a large volume of Hanseatic and native as well as Italian trade. Gilbert Maghfeld, a London ironmonger, dealt not only in iron from Spain, but in woad and alum. One-third of his trade in alum was with customers as far afield as Suffolk and Salisbury. The debts of the London grocers, who dealt in both spices, and dyestuffs, metals (especially tin), and other raw materials, show them trading with spicers and apothecaries in Bristol, Gloucester, Leicester, Oxford and Maidstone, with dyers in York and Beverley, with merchants and chapmen from Westmorland to Exeter. Back to London came some 20–30,000 cloths per annum in the first half of the fifteenth century, along with 4–6,000 sacks of wool. Drapers and clothiers from all over the country sold directly at Blackwell Hall, or made contacts with exporters who bought by sample. In the wool trade, the fourteenth and fifteenth centuries saw the emergence of the middleman dealer, now that the days of the large-scale contracts were over. These men, like the famous William Midwinter of the Cely Papers, or the Forteys of Northleach, or the Grevell family of Chipping Camden, gathered in the wool from the mass of small producers, and sold by sample to the exporters. The wool then had to be appraised, to ensure that the seller was not deceiving the buyer, and then packed by the Fellowship of Wool Packers of London. They valued the wool as they packed it, and marked the grade on the bales or samples. Then it was sent to London or Southampton for export.

Thus there existed a system of transport and internal trade quite adequate for current needs of foreign commerce, and without which it could not have flourished. There also existed an adequate financial infrastructure, where the use of credit and loans was normal, where money could be transferred from one country to another easily, and where a form of paper money was being created by the practice of assignment of debts. Sale credits were vital to the workings of later medieval trade. If merchants had had to pay cash down for the goods they bought, it would have severely limited the scale of their operations.

All exports, for example, would have had to be sold in the Netherlands before any goods could be bought for import. Credit enabled the merchant to engage in several ventures at once, for not all his capital was tied up in any one of them. It allowed the smaller merchant, with limited capital resources, to enlarge the scope of his operations, since as well as selling he also bought on credit, and could afford to wait for payment from his own customers. Lastly, credit freed trade from the limitations of the money supply. There simply would not have been enough money available for all transactions to be conducted in cash.

By the later Middle Ages the use of credit was ubiquitous. The best-known example comes from the later fifteenth-century wool trade and the commercial dealings of the Cely family. Their chief agent bought on credit from the growers and sold on credit to the Celys, the normal terms being one-third of the price down, and the balance paid within a year in two or three instalments. The Celys then sold on credit at the Staple to Flemish and Dutch clothiers. Again, part of the money was paid in hand, the rest collected in instalments at the great seasonal fairs of the Netherlands, held in winter (Cold mart), at Easter (Pask mart), at Whitsun (Synxon mart) and in October (Balms mart). A whole chain of credits thus ran from the grower in the Cotswolds to the draper in the Netherlands. Precisely the same pattern existed in the cloth trade. A scrivener's book of 1458–9 shows two German merchants entering a bond with John Harding of Tidbury, Gloucs, clothman, in February 1459, agreeing to pay him £12 at the following Whitsun, £11 in November, and £11.6s.10d. in February the following year. Repayment could be made abroad as well. Another two German merchants agreed to pay a London mercer £50 in Flemish money at Antwerp in Holland at the next fair held there. Although it is not specified, these transactions almost certainly involved the purchase of cloth. The very rare survival of a London merchant's ledger from the late fourteenth century shows that Gilbert Maghfeld conducted at least 75 per cent of his business on credit. Like other merchants he probably charged interest by varying his price, trying, not always successfully, to keep the terms short, to five or six months at the most.

Credit sales could go wrong, of course. The merchant might find himself short of ready cash to pay his creditors. He would then have to borrow, either from another merchant with spare funds, or against the security of property, or in London from institutions such as the Court of Orphans (whose funds were held by the City). The Celys regularly borrowed when they were short of cash to pay their woolmen and lent when they had funds after payment at the fairs. The loans they made were usually short term, two to six months and at an interest rate of about $2\frac{1}{2}$ per cent per month. When they were caught really short of cash, like other merchants they would borrow by way of exchange. English trade ran along one main axis, to and from the Netherlands. Merchants needing money in one area and having funds in another could transfer them by way of exchange.[11] It could be a simple transfer, using perhaps an Italian or Spanish banker. So in September 1487 William Cely at Calais sent 100 nobles sterling (£33.6s.8d.) to George Cely at London, through an Italian firm. He paid for the sterling in Flemish money, getting slightly below the market rate for sterling to allow for interest, and on receipt of the bill of exchange the Italian, or his agent in London, would have honoured it in sterling. At other times bills of exchange were used to make loans. A merchant having funds in the Netherlands, from the sale of wool perhaps, but needing cash in England to buy more wool, would make exchange with another merchant, requiring money to buy imports in the Netherlands. So the first merchant would deliver his Flemish money to the second, receiving a bill of exchange payable at a future date in London and in English money. Interest was expressed, again, in the exchange rate, and would vary according to the size and length of the loan. It used to be argued that this was a simple case of exchange between Mercers and Staplers, the one having funds in England but needing money in Flanders to buy their imports, the other having funds in Flanders but needing cash in England to buy for export. This view, based largely on the late fifteenth-century evidence from the Cely Papers, is misleading. The Celys dealt only in wool. Other London merchants, especially the grocers, dealt in wool and cloth, and in any case the mercers sold their cloth in the Netherlands and would have had ample funds there. The use of exchange did not depend on any special relationship between Staplers and Mercers. It was simply a part of normal mercantile practice – and one in which the Italians and later the Spaniards played an important role.

Two other developments helped to oil the wheels of trade. Merchants regularly discounted or 'assigned' debts owed them in payment of debts they owed. This was a regular practice in all branches of trade at home and abroad. The records of Mayor's Court of the City of London abound with examples of this method of paying debts, whilst in the trade to the Netherlands obligations changed hands easily. Ade, a female merchant of Haarlem, in 1447 paid her debt to William Bruwel, an English merchant, by giving him an obligation she had from John Reynald, a London mercer, for £Fl.97.18s.4gr.[12] This sum was more than she owed Bruwel, so he gave Ade several obligations in which various merchants promised to pay him £Fl.78. In this way the debt of £Fl.19 was discharged, with the obligations being used as a sort of paper money. So were certificates of debts and warrants for payment of debts which the Staple issued to its members, who had lent the Company money. These were similar to the debentures issued by the royal wardrobe for its debts, and both were used as a form of money.

If the mercantile community was devising means to help it avoid the limiting effects of having to pay for everything in ready money at the time of purchase, it also had to develop more flexible methods of actual trading. Gone were the days when the merchant travelled with his goods, sold them and returned home with silver or foreign wares. Now he regularly received and despatched cargoes and had credit payments to make at home and abroad at regular intervals. Nor could large consignments of goods sent to him be sold all at once, for that might knock the bottom out of the market. Continuous action was necessary both at home and abroad, and since the merchant could not be in two places at one time, he had to employ others to represent him. Often he would have a factor, a young man learning the trade, a junior member of the family, resident abroad at Calais or Antwerp to handle his business, whilst he stayed at home. Or he could employ another merchant resident abroad to act as his attorney, or agent, on a commission basis, whilst merchants resident abroad would need factors or attorneys in England.

So English trade was infinitely more complex than it had been in the earlier Middle Ages, both in the markets it served and in the techniques it used. In relative terms, it had held up well in the face of general economic contraction, but there are dangers in being too euphoric. As well as successes, English overseas trade had its fair share of failures, which left English merchants too narrowly concentrated on one product along one main route, leaving aliens the more distant markets – although that does not mean that English trade overall was not well in balance, bringing money into the country. A mass of information from the royal customs accounts allows the economic historian to calculate some national figures of the value of imports and exports and to see what proportion was in native, and what proportion in alien hands.

These accounts take two main forms. The particulars of accounts were the working ledgers of the customs officials, in which they recorded ships entering and leaving the ports, the merchandise on them, whether it belonged to an English, a Hanseatic or an alien merchant, and sometimes its value. Where these have survived it is possible to build up a detailed picture of the trade of a port, and its value, and enough of them have survived for the period 1421–61 to construct some hypotheses which can be applied to the enrolled accounts, the overall totals calculated by the Exchequer from the particulars of numbers of cloth and sacks of wool exported, the tuns of wine imported, the value of general merchandise paying various dues. The values given above have been used for cloth and for wool until the 1450s when the clear fall in wool prices necessitates a drop to £5 per sack for native wool, £7 for alien. Wine has been valued at £5.10s. the tun until 1449, and then, owing to a sharp rise in prices, at £7 the tun.[13] General merchandise has been divided into imports and exports according to the pattern established by analysis of the particulars. Once again it must be stressed that these are customs valuations and can only be taken as a general guide. Because of the nature of the accounts the period cannot be divided by decades. The figures in brackets are incomplete (see Table 9.3).

The general fall in the value of English trade is immediately obvious, although the figures for the last nine years must be treated with caution, because of the effects of civil war. In only one period was any branch of the trade out of balance, and that was in 1431–42 when the denizen sector suffered from the effects of the siege of Calais. Otherwise exports more than paid for imports. It is interesting that only the Hansards managed to maintain their relative and absolute share in English trade, whilst that of other aliens, mainly Italians, had declined substantially by 1461. Even so the combined alien share of English foreign trade was very considerable (see Table 9.2).

Information after 1461 is less complete. There were major disputes with the Hanse and constant interruptions in the cloth trade in the 1460s and 1470s. By 1479–82, when Gray calculated his balance of trade, there had been a general recovery.[15] He noted the growing strength of the English Merchant Adventurers, major exporters of cloth and importers of general merchandise, who in his valuations handled one-third of the exports and half of the imports. Hanseatic trade had recovered, but that of the Italians had continued to decline. Trade was still well in balance, and as cloth exports boomed, one must assume it

Table 9.2 Percentage shares of Denizens, Hansards and other aliens in English foreign trade, 1421–61[14]

Year Mich.–Mich.	DENIZEN		HANSEATIC		OTHER ALIENS		ALL ALIENS	
	Imports	Exports	Imports	Exports	Imports	Exports	Imports	Exports
1421–31	(62)	68	9	7	29	25	38	32
1431–42	65	57	12	12	25	31	37	43
1442–52	61	62	13	14	26	24	39	38
1452–61	62	60	18	19	20	21	38	40

Table 9.3 Estimated value of English overseas trade, 1421–61[14]

Year Mich.–Mich.	DENIZEN		HANSEATIC		OTHER ALIENS		TOTALS	
	Imports £	Exports £	Imports £	Exports £	Imports £	Exports £	Imports £	Exports £
1421–31	(658,320)	1,128,960	97,940	123,180	(310,190)	414,730	(1,066,450)	1,666,870
1431–42	923,580	849,260	139,840	182,910	360,380	464,950	1,423,800	1,502,120
1442–52	850,160	975,960	182,210	212,300	359,170	384,300	1,391,540	1,572,560
1452–61	588,220	620,950	175,600	195,690	189,100	216,910	952,920	1,033,550

remained so. Yet analysis of the cloth export figures shows that the alien share of English trade was still substantial:

Table 9.4   Percentage shares of English cloth exports[16]

Year	Denizen	Hanseatic	Alien
1480–81	60	24	16
1490–91	54	19	27
1500–01	60	21	19

The continuing strength of alien participation in overseas trade must be seen as much in terms of English failure as of alien success. Whilst by the end of the century the English dominated the North Sea routes to Calais and the Netherlands, the Hansards retained their grip on trade to the Baltic and down the Rhine via Cologne. The Italians appear to have dropped out of direct trade to England – although this is as yet by no means proven – but the English had not broken into the Mediterranean to any great extent. There was no lack of hostility to aliens at home. During the late fourteenth and the fifteenth centuries an increasingly xenophobic campaign was mounted against them in parliament which had as its dual aims trading rights in the Baltic for the English equal to those enjoyed by the Hansards in England, and severe restrictions on Italians trading in England to put them at a disadvantage, the English at an advantage. It was a campaign which had little or no success. The English did not break into the Baltic nor did they take over trade to the Mediterranean. Why?

For the Hansards, England formed one end of their great route from the Baltic to the North Sea, exchanging raw materials for manufactured goods, especially cloth. They had Kontors or trading posts in the East Coast ports of Boston, Lynn and Hull, and, most important, in London, where the Steelyard was an enclosed, self-governing community. Successive charters from English kings, and especially Edward III's Carta Mercatoria of 1347, gave them valuable exemptions from customs duties, so much so that they paid lower rates even than English merchants. They were not universally unpopular. Even the jingoistic *Libelle of Englyshe Polycye*, written *c*.1435–6, which supported fully the idea that English trade should be in English hands, recognized that they imported essential raw materials, and other goods sold 'well cheap'. Increasingly, in the later fourteenth century, they turned to England for cloth exports, and that was when the trouble began. Inevitably, their interests clashed with those of a small group of merchants from Lynn, Hull and Boston, who wanted to handle the cloth trade to the Baltic themselves, and demanded reciprocity or equal rights there.

The Hanse, by this time a league of towns rather than of merchants, was determined to preserve its Baltic monopoly in the face of English and Dutch competition. Yet it was a body divided within itself. Danzig and Cologne were reluctant to take direct action against the English because of their reliance on the export trade in English cloth. Lübeck, the League's leader, saw its commercial supremacy threatened by English and Dutch shipping using the direct sea route to the Baltic and tried again and again to organize concerted resistance to the English, though with little success. Against opposition in such disarray the English ought to have had some success, and at first they did. Prussian resistance to penetration of the Baltic prompted English reprisals and attacks on Hanseatic shipping. A series of ephemeral treaties failed to resolve the problem and in the 1420s and early 1430s it was obvious that unless there was peace, a wholesale commercial war would break out, disastrous to both sides.

It was against this background that the great Hanseatic delegation, led by Hinrich Vorrath, burgomaster of Danzig, came to England in 1434–5 and negotiated the treaty of 1437 which bore his name. By this, the English were given equal rights in the Baltic, complete freedom to trade and sell in Prussia, while the Hanse had their privileges in England confirmed. But Prussia refused to ratify the treaty and from this point the tide began to turn against England. The breakdown of government allowed and even encouraged piracy to flourish, and there were irresponsible attacks on the Bay Fleet (an important annual convoy of Hanseatic and Dutch shipping going to the Bay of Bourgneuf in Brittany for salt) in 1449 and 1458. What finally united the Baltic Hanse against England was the seizure of Hanseatic goods in London in 1468. Edward IV's government, having secured the main channel of trade by making peace with Burgundy in 1467–8, thought it could take decisive action against the Hanse. The flimsy pretext of the seizure of English ships by Denmark was used as the excuse for the attack, but it turned out to be a disaster. Only Cologne retained normal trading relations with England. The Baltic towns began a vicious sea war which raged until the Treaty of Utrecht in 1474. The English were not without success in this war, but it was the Crown's interests that determined there should be peace. Edward IV was grateful to the Hanse for providing him with shipping in his successful invasion of

England to regain the throne he had lost in 1470. More than that, in 1474 he wanted to reopen the war with France in alliance with Burgundy. That would not have been possible if the Channel and the North Sea were not secure, and that meant there had to be peace with the Hanse. Their privileges in England were restored, Cologne was punished by exclusion from the Hanse for some years, and although in theory the English were promised equal rights in the Baltic, they never received them. Effectively they were excluded from the Baltic for the rest of the century, and because of Hanseatic hostility their trade to Scandinavia and Iceland was severely damaged.

Most historians have chosen to follow Professor Postan's lead and see this defeat in mainly political terms.[17] In the critical years of the mid-fifteenth century the English government failed to support the country's merchants as it should have done. Desperately reliant on customs revenue, and locked in combat with the main trading partner, Burgundy, the English Crown could not afford to close the other important trading route to the Baltic. Nor in the years of civil war could it prevent the irresponsible actions of some important subjects, such as the earl of Warwick, who relentlessly attacked Hanseatic shipping. This kept alive a conflict which might otherwise have been resolved in England's favour. Ultimately it was also political expediency which determined the peace of 1474. It was thus the English Crown that failed the English merchants. Yet this explanation is not altogether convincing, for where England failed, the Dutch, with no more constant support from their rulers, succeeded. Perhaps it was lack of economic as much as of political strength which led to the English failure. Only a limited number of East Coast merchants were interested in trading with the Baltic. The all-important Londoners concentrated on the Low Countries' trade. Had they been involved in the struggle economically, the English challenge would have been more powerful, the pressure on the government greater. Obsession with the Baltic may also have disguised the fact that the main route of Anglo-Hanseatic trade lay through Cologne. Merchants from that city, from Frankfurt, Dinant and the Zuider Zee controlled trade down the Rhine, to south Germany and as far east as the Danube valley and Galicia, with its great markets of Lemberg and Cracow. They had a strong interest in English cloth and in the mid-fifteenth century a tightly-knit group of these men, the Rincks, Questenbergs, Greverodes and Blitterswicks, with John Salmer and Lambert Josse from Dinant, were by far and away the most important Hansards trading to England. The London petty custom account of 1446 shows their imports to have been three times those of Baltic merchants, their exports twice as large. It was probably they who sustained the Hanse trade in the difficult years of the mid-fifteenth century. How important a part they played in the expansion of Hanseatic trade in the latter part of the century is not known, but it must have been substantial. Whether the English would have been any more successful in breaking into the Rhine trade than they were in the Baltic is a moot point. But it is important to see that failure against the Hanse meant the closing of not one, but of two great routes to them.

The English were no more successful against the Italians, who were in fact the chief butt of most of the anti-alien propaganda in the fifteenth century. They were accused of all manner of sins, of importing expensive, worthless luxuries and buying little or too cheaply for export; of cheating the English by buying on credit in England, selling for ready cash in Italy, transferring the monies back to Flanders and lending them to the English merchants at interest. But it was the balance of payments that was the greatest obsession, the idea that through trade and banking, the Italians were draining money from England, 'as the wafer sucketh honey from the bee'.[18] To remedy this, frequent demands were made for all aliens, but especially the Italians, to go host, to be under the supervision of an English merchant who would ensure that all monies obtained from the sale of imports should be spent on exports. This was actually put into practice in the seven years after 1440. Other regulations demanded that in banking operations a like sum of money must be spent on English goods for export as was sent abroad by letters of exchange and the deposit of bullion for wool exports.

To all the above-mentioned charges the Italians could plead 'not guilty', but it is not hard to see why they were the focus of so much ill-will. It was not any longer because they were the great Crown financiers and wool merchants – the bankruptcy of the Bardi and Peruzzi had taught them not to lend to princes, whilst they had been forced out of the wool trade. Now they were general traders linking the northern seas to the Mediterranean world. Here the vital development had been the opening of the direct sea-route to the Mediterranean in the fourteenth century, for sea transportation was at a quarter of the cost of land. Genoese carracks, large two- or three-masted vessels of up to 700 tons' burden, Venetian and Florentine galleys, smaller in size but more manoeuvrable in coastal or tidal waters, were now regular visitors to northern seas. At first they made Bruges their main centre,

311

with Flemish cloth their chief export, but as the English cloth industry expanded, so England became their main port of call. The Venetians favoured London, since the capital provided the best market for their spices and precious cloth. From the 1390s their state galleys became regular visitors, usually arriving in the autumn and staying in the port two or three months. The Genoese preferred Southampton as a better port for their heavier vessels to make. They were regular visitors from the late fourteenth century, except for a period in Henry V's reign when they were in league with the French. The Florentine state galleys, which first came to England in 1425, also chose Southampton and vessels which had unloaded their imports at Bruges would call there or at Sandwich to load cloth, wool and tin for export.

Whichever port the Italians used, London was their headquarters. There, in the mid-fifteenth century, lived a colony of some 50–60 resident merchants and their servants, the representatives of some 20–30 Venetian, Genoese, Florentine, Milanese and Lucchese companies. These Italian companies now had proper corporate structures, which long outlived their individual members. Their London representatives were but one part of a wider organization, which might have other branches in Bruges, Barcelona, Venice, Florence, Alexandria or Constantinople. Developments in book-keeping, and especially the use of arabic numerals and of bilateral and double-entry accounting, not widely used in northern Europe until the sixteenth century, allowed them to operate in a far more sophisticated way than their English or Hanseatic rivals. They were able to see easily what their financial position was at any moment. They acted as both merchants and bankers, accepting deposits from outsiders, at interest, which of course much increased their working capital. Ledger transfers were made from one customer's account to another's, or to merchants' accounts with another company with whom they did business, without a coin ever changing hands. Loans were easily raised and it was the Italians who had developed the bill of exchange which allowed them to move funds across Europe almost at will. Each company in London, of course, acted as agents for other Italian merchants who had no resident representatives there. Thus merchants of middling wealth and rank like Andrea Barbarigo of Venice could conduct a triangular trade between Spain, Italy and the Levant, paying for English cloth with the proceeds of the sale of Spanish wool and oil, transferring money to and from London by bills of exchange and yet not have to leave their home cities.

The scale on which the Italians operated was one of the reasons for English envy and hostility. Between them they controlled nearly a quarter of all overseas trade. Individually their turnover was substantial. The Venetian Marcuonovo brothers between Michaelmas and Michaelmas 1441–2 received from the Venetian galleys 58 bales of pepper and various other drugs and spices, as well as silk and other precious cloth and 174 balets of woad. From this and their stock they sold to London mercers and grocers goods worth £3,690. In return they bought for export cloth and wool valued at £6,290. The Views of Hosts[19] show them not to be untypical. The Contarini brothers traded on the same scale in 1440, and there is no reason to suppose that the Spinoli, Cattanei, Alberti or Medici operated at a lower level. Only the wealthiest Londoners could rival them, for most English merchants were men of moderate wealth. What is more, the Italians, especially the Florentine and Milanese companies, had a virtual monopoly of banking and exchange. How important this was for the English can be seen in the accounts of Filippo Borromei and Company, a London branch of a Milanese firm, for 1436–9. In the first year of its operations its turnover was £30,000 of which £9,500 was letters of exchange to Venice, Genoa, Avignon. In other years the bank also dealt with Antwerp, Middelburg, Bergen, Basle and Barcelona. Prominent London mercers, grocers and vintners regularly used its services to transfer money to and from the Low Countries, especially to the cloth marts at Middelburg and the head office of the bank at Bruges. Without the services of the Italian bankers, English foreign trade might well have ground to a halt.

The English may have had some grounds for disliking the Italians, but in fact they were of considerable benefit to the economy. Analysis of the London and Southampton particulars of customs accounts for the year 1438–9 shows that Italian trade was well in balance.

Table 9.5 Italian imports and exports through Southampton and London

	Imports £	Exports £
Florentines	1,395	7,329
Genoese	9,758	9,820
Milanese-Lucchese	1,019	1,984
Venetians	9,365	18,359
	22,347	37,987

On top of this there were some £8,000 of customs duties to be paid. Unless the Italians sold their imports at vastly inflated prices, making great profits (and the Views of Hosts suggest strongly that this was not possible) they would have had to move substantial amounts of money into England, probably from surpluses in Flanders, to cover the deficit. Nor was the trade all of worthless luxuries: 38 per cent of imports were of raw materials for the cloth industry especially, and 5,617 balets of woad were brought in by the Genoese alone. Venetian merchants did concentrate on the spice trade, but they produced the best surplus balance, whilst the Florentines had little to import, but were prepared to spend heavily on English wool for export. The year 1438–9 is slightly atypical, for the Venetian surplus was usually not as large, the Genoese trade usually worth more.

Even so, the figures given above (figures 9.2 and 9.3) clearly show that the Italian share of English trade was on the decline. It would be easy but wrong to interpret this as a victory for the English, who took over their trade. Certainly the Italians were hedged around with restrictions and penalized by having to pay far higher customs duties than most other merchants. There were outright attacks on them in the serious London riots of 1456–7, and in Southampton in 1460. Genoese goods were seized and their merchants imprisoned in 1458 as a reprisal for the pirating of Robert Sturmy's ship in 1457. Sturmy was a Bristol merchant who was trying to break into the Mediterranean trade, but his second voyage met with disaster. It cost the Genoese dear to obtain their freedom, and their trade was harmed by the affair. But these were pinpricks. What really hurt the Italians was conflict in the Mediterranean. Constant warfare interrupted both the Venetian and Florentine galley fleets in the 1430s, 1440s and 1450s; the Genoese were locked in struggle with Naples and lost their bases at Constantinople and Foglia, with the monopoly of the alum trade, to the Turks. Genoese trade to England gradually declined, the final blow coming in 1489, when the import of Toulouse woad in foreign bottoms was prohibited. Before then the Florentine galleys had ceased operating. Organized to secure wool supplies for the cloth industry, because of high costs they were never commercially viable. When in 1465 the Florentines opened the port of Pisa, competition from foreign shipping proved too strong, and the galleys had ceased trading by 1478. That left only the Venetians, who, though facing troubles in their main spice market, Alexandria, and beset by enemies, still managed to keep their galley fleets sailing to the north.

The English do not appear to have benefited by the Italian decline. Before 1460, one or two London and Southampton merchants were trading on the Italian galleys and carracks to the Mediterranean. After 1460 some English ships took wool to Porto Pisano, and there was an attempt to establish a wool staple there in 1489, but in 1494 Pisa revolted against Florence and destroyed the Florentine commercial system. In any case, in the first years of the Staple, Biscayan and other foreign shipping carried most of the wool to the Staple. Some English ships did voyage to Candia (Crete) for wine, but it was essentially the Spanish and the Dutch with cheaper shipping who filled the gap left by the Italian decline.

Failure to break into the Baltic was thus matched by failure to exploit opportunities in the Mediterranean. True, the English did make the most of the revival of the cross-Channel trade consequent upon peace with France and were active in the trade to Spain and Portugal and to Ireland. But the main route of English commerce was across the Channel and the North Sea to the Low Countries, and was controlled by two companies, the Staple for wool and the Merchant Adventurers for cloth. Although the Staple was fully fledged at the beginning of the fifteenth century, the Company of Merchant Adventurers was only gradually emerging. The term 'Adventurer' was originally applied to any merchant engaged in overseas trade in commodities other than wool. They concentrated mainly on the export of cloth and imported a whole variety of general merchandise, voyaging not to Calais but to the Baltic, to Norway, to Spain and above all to the Netherlands. In their home towns they formed themselves into trade associations, Companies of Merchant Adventurers like those of York and Newcastle, or the Gild of St George at Hull, whilst in London groups of Adventurers began to develop within the ranks of the already powerful mercantile companies, the Grocers, Skinners, Haberdashers and, above all, the Mercers. These merchants also felt the need for societies abroad, to settle disputes amongst themselves and generally to protect their interests. So, those trading to Prussia secured permission from the Crown to govern themselves according to privileges granted them by the Grand Master of the Teutonic Order. In 1407 the Adventurers to the Netherlands, to Holland, Zeeland, Brabant and Flanders, obtained authority to have their own assemblies and elect governors. This charter, confirmed by later kings and the Lord of Holland and Zeeland, gave the three or four governors, representing the interests of different English towns, full powers to administer justice to English merchants, to settle disputes between them and foreigners, to make regulations to govern English merchants under their jurisdiction and punish those who did not obey. By 1421 the meetings of this body were held at Antwerp, which became the chief centre of the English cloth traders in the Netherlands, supplanting Middelburg and Dordrecht.

Gradually as the English trade to the north collapsed, all attention became focused on the Netherlands. Almost inevitably friction occurred between merchants from provincial towns and the Londoners. By 1486 the latter had finally been granted their own organization with full franchises and liberties. Each year the mayor and aldermen were to elect two able persons, one a mercer, the other from another craft, to be lieutenants in London to the governor beyond the sea. These lieutenants were given authority to summon assemblies in which, subject to the mayor's approval, ordinances might be passed for levying imposts on trade, organizing shipping and fixing freight rates. But long before this the London merchants had been trying to gain control of the Company overseas, much to the annoyance of the provincial merchants. In 1478 they complained that the Londoners were trying to force the formation of a single organization with exclusive rights to keep out interlopers. The merchants from York and other northern towns had established themselves at the mart towns with their own shops, well away from the Londoners. The royal charters had empowered the merchants to choose not a governor but governors. Yet John Pykering, the London governor, was trying to run the Company alone. He had seized the contributions of the northern towns, raised the entrance fee for trading, levied imposts, and forced all to show their cloth in the same streets. For this he was rebuked and when a unified Company abroad was formed, it was essentially forced on the merchants by Henry VII. Relations with Burgundy were as difficult in his reign as they had been earlier. Henry, in particular, resented the aid given by the Burgundians to the pretenders to his throne, Simnel and Warbeck. He saw the need for a unified trade which he could use as a diplomatic weapon. So, after the signing of the Intercursus Magnus (1496), and in spite of the northerners' protests, John Pykering was sent out as the sole governor of the merchants while the right of the London Fellowship to compel all trading in cloth to join it was acknowledged. The Company of Adventurers was thus consolidated into a single gild-like group with royal authorization and given the right to levy fines from all engaging in their trade.

At home the Companies of Adventurers acted as regulated companies. The merchants traded individually, but the Fellowship chartered the ships, fixed freight rates, determined when the fleets sailed to the marts, or if they sailed at all. Convoys were necessary in the troubled waters of the North Sea, and the Adventurers often arranged for protection from the king's ships, at a price. So, conduct money was levied on goods going to and coming from the Netherlands. The Companies' function was also to formulate common policy and take common action to secure the most favourable conditions for the trade, where again the London Adventurers took the lead and acted on behalf of the whole. They were implacably opposed to the imposition of poundage (an ad valorem duty of 1s. in the £) on cloth exports, and negotiated with the Crown whenever there was a possibility of embargoes on trade with the Netherlands. When trade with the Low Countries was interrupted, the Adventurers sought to protect their interests against merchant rivals like the Hansards and the Staplers. They would ask for similar restrictions to be placed upon the aliens, so that the Hansards especially did not capture the whole trade to the Low Countries. Relations with the Staple were necessarily bitter as cloth exports rose, whilst wool exports fell. The Staplers harassed the Adventurers whenever they could, and vice versa, but by the end of the fifteenth century the Adventurers had displaced them as the senior partners in English overseas trade.

Yet in its own way the existence of the Companies was an admission of a failure to meet competitors on level terms. One of the main reasons why both came into being was the need to join together to keep the aliens out. Perhaps they were successful in trade to the Low Countries, but English merchants were not able to break into new markets. Comparison with Continental rivals, especially the Italians, does suggest that individually English merchants lacked both the capital and the business techniques essential for far-flung commercial enterprises. As has been seen,[20] merchant dynasties rarely lasted for more than three generations. Trade was still not quite respectable. It was land ownership that brought with it social status and, as an investment, an annual return of about 5 per cent, only a little less than that from trade with much less risk. The result was that there were no highly organized long-lasting mercantile companies with the ability to accept deposits at interest from outsiders, to use them to further their own trade and reinvest the profits. Partnerships were formed, but were usually ad hoc arrangements for a specific venture, and were used as a way of raising capital to finance that venture, one man providing the money, the other

317

the services. As far as one can tell, the sophisticated techniques of the Italians were as unknown to the English as they were to the Hansards. Lack of them severely restricted ability to engage in a number of separate ventures at the same time. Indeed, the English had to rely heavily on the Italians for the exchange service essential to the Netherlands trade.

That is not to say that there were no wealthy English merchants. Some Londoners were men of great substance. On his death in 1458 Simon Eyre had 7,000 marks (£4,666.13s.4d.) invested in his business, and in Bristol in the late fifteenth century the Canynges family had a fleet of 11 ships which brought them £10,000 per annum in freight charges alone. In Salisbury one can still see the houses of wealthy merchants like John à Port, but they scarcely compare with the palaces of the Italian mercantile families. In the main, English merchants were men of moderate wealth; the Cely brothers, for instance, may have made an annual profit of only £100 apiece. Failure to generate great wealth, difficulties of access to capital, which seems largely to have been raised on an ad hoc basis – these were possibly limiting factors on English mercantile enterprise, for trade was expensive. Rigging and victualling ships involved considerable outlay of funds in the first instance. Capital investment by a variety of shareholders helped finance the shipping but, since voyages were long and slow, the merchant had to anticipate a fairly long-term investment. In a sense one can understand why the English chose to concentrate on the short cross-Channel route. There was a quicker return on capital and less risk. But it might well also be that so much of the limited capital available was tied up in this trade that there was not enough left to finance ventures to the Baltic or to the Mediterranean. Indeed, lack of capital may explain why there were shortages of English shipping on certain routes in the later Middle Ages. The cross-Channel route could be served but there was an increasing reliance, for instance, on Spanish and Breton ships in the wine trade.

Lacking capital, backward in business techniques, English merchants were thus forced to concentrate on the North Sea route and to band together in Companies to obtain corporately the strength they did not have individually. Did this matter? After all, 60 per cent of all overseas trade was in English hands, but that left 40 per cent to aliens, who seem to have made a better profit from their trade than did the English themselves. The English were simply taking the cloth to the Netherlands where it was bought for re-export by the Hansards, the

Dutch and others. It was these alien merchants, along with those exporting directly from England, who supplied their customers all over Europe. By moving English goods further along the route to their final point of sale they made a better profit from them. Similarly, if the English had imported the woad or alum they needed directly, they would have reaped a substantial reward. A consignment of 3,880 cantares of alum bought at the Papal mines at Tolfa for c.£4,187 and sent to Southampton in 1466 was finally sold for £5,844, a net profit of slightly over 26 per cent – which went to Genoese merchants. The same story can be told for export. In May 1444, Andrea Barbarigo received in Venice cloth and tin from England worth in all £900. Some of the cloth he consigned to Constantinople, the rest he disposed of in Italy, whilst the tin was sold either in Venice or sent to Alexandria. On the whole series of related transactions his profit amounted to about a third of his original investment (on the cloth alone it came to about 38 per cent, on tin 51 per cent). A Venetian merchant in the second half of the fifteenth century reckoned to make a profit of £5.10s.0d., or 37 per cent of his total investment, per sack of wool exported to the Mediterranean, compared to the £1–£2 per sack a Stapler selling at Calais might expect. Prices in the Mediterranean were generally higher than those in the north-west of Europe and failure to break into that market was costing the English merchant and the English economy dearly. In the same way it was probably the Dutch and the Hansards who were reaping the greatest benefit from the northern trade. The English themselves were no more than cross-Channel carriers.

The sixteenth century would show the dangers of concentrating too much on one product along the main route, the export of cloth through London to the marts of the Low Countries. This was unhealthy and to the detriment of other English ports. If the market collapsed, as it did in the mid-sixteenth century, then the repercussions would be severe, for, wool and tin apart, there was nothing else for the English to export. Indeed, the nature of English overseas trade throws new light on the economy as a whole. Cloth had to pay not only for the raw materials and the luxuries, but for all the cheap consumer goods the English seemed unable to produce for themselves, feather beds, lamps, copper kettles, drinking glasses, tankards, pepper-grinders, knives, scissors, playing tables and counters, market baskets and straw hats, all items that came in through Lynn in the year 1503–4, and presumably through most other ports during the course of the fifteenth century.

10 Economic Ideas

So far this study of the workings of the medieval English economy has been mainly empirical. It has sought to explain economic development in a practical way, in relation to demographic change or the limitations of techniques or availability of capital. Only indirectly has it been suggested that there could be intellectual or ideological stimuli to or restraints upon economic growth, that medieval man could formulate ideas and pursue economic policies with sustained and defined aims. It has been seen that this could happen on a limited level. Towns had their own attitudes towards the defence of their trading and manufacturing interests. They could pass and enforce laws which, at the least, influenced their economic performance. Far from drifting helplessly in uncharted seas, they steered a certain course which, while it did not necessarily bring them safely to harbour, did help determine the general direction in which they were heading. Many would argue that this represents the limit of the interaction between theory and practice. The town was a relatively compact, self-governing entity, ruled by groups of merchants, property owners and craftsmen who would necessarily seek to foster their own wellbeing. They had at their disposal the institutional means to accomplish their ends, assemblies to pass laws, courts to enforce them. Agrarian society by contrast is usually seen as much more diffuse and diverse, much more at the mercy of patterns of demand, and ruled by a landlord class interested only in consumption and not the sustained economic development of its estates. National government was either too weak, or too much wrapped up in its own dynastic and martial ends, to pay too much attention to the workings of the economy.

This seems an excessively pessimistic view of both the intellectual capacity of medieval man and of the influence that ideas had generally on the workings of the economy. In the first place, the whole of the medieval economy was affected by the basic medieval conception of the structure of society. From what we might call the feudal idea that the broad mass of the peasantry should support the fighting élite came the fundamental notion of a pyramidal society, with the many supporting the few. This applied to the agrarian sector, where the landlords creamed off the surplus income of their peasants. It applied to towns, where the few, whether oligarchs or not, exploited the many. A man's status in this social pyramid affected his economic condition quite profoundly. In many thirteenth-century towns an artisan might not become a member of the merchant gild unless he foreswore his occupation. Working with one's hands was beneath the dignity of the mercantile class. Sumptuary legislation sought not only to control the excesses of the rich, but to ensure that the humble did not get above themselves in aping the modes of their betters. A statute of 1337 expressed the extreme view that the wearing of furs of any kind was the privilege of those of gentle birth. Only the royal family, prelates, earls, barons, knights and clerks with at least £100 per annum could wear them. By 1363 more egalitarian times were on the way, and only peasants or those with less than 40s. worth of goods were entirely excluded. But there was still a scale – only the richest might wear ermine, whilst at the bottom end the humble were allowed only lamb, coney, cat or fox skins. Movement from one class to another was not impossible but respectability still lay chiefly in control over land. In medieval England, unlike the Italian city states, trade was not the occupation of a gentleman, a fact which had quite profound consequences for English commercial development.

Strictly speaking this is a concept of society with considerable economic implications, rather than an economic idea with economic consequences. Nevertheless, it helps give the lie to the notion that medieval man could not formulate broad concepts and implement them. Ideas and policies could be more than purely local. This became increasingly true as the Middle Ages wore on. In the early period, as the economy emerged from the Dark Ages, production was strictly on a subsistence and local basis. Political authority was also weak: power rested in the localities, economic legislation, such as there was, tended to be local. But from the ninth century onwards, political unity grew in England in the face of the Danish invasions as the West Saxon monarchy extended its control over the whole country. Kings of the tenth century could codify laws for the whole realm. They could try to control internal trade by confining it to recognized market towns. Standardization of weights and measures was attempted, minting became more or less a royal prerogative. Foreign merchants were encouraged to come to the country under royal protection. King Cnut on a pilgrimage to Rome, negotiated rights for Englishmen trading to North Italy.

Quite clearly, even before the Conquest, royal government thought itself able to intervene in matters economic. In the twelfth and thirteenth centuries its powers grew apace. A national system of royal justice developed and central departments of state emerged, staffed by trained officials who could pursue consistent aims. The Crown began to declare not what the law was (that is, what was the custom of the people) but what the law should be, widening further the scope for interfering in the economy. Representative institutions also began to emerge, providing a forum in which pressure groups from the landowning and mercantile classes could seek to exert influence on the government. Government capacity to influence the workings of the economy was now far greater than it had been before. At the same time, since the twelfth and thirteenth centuries were an age of economic expansion and inflation, new problems had to be faced, with the growth of urban communities, the development of long-distance trade and the increasing costs of government, and especially of warfare. And the problems only multiplied in the later Middle Ages. England became enmeshed in prolonged warfare, and demands for protection grew from the upper classes for the maintenance of their economic position in the countryside, from the merchants for restrictions on their competitors in international trade. Clearly, from the twelfth century onwards government could and did act in matters economic. The question is, can anything other than expediency be discerned in the policies it followed, did there lie behind its actions ideals wider than mere self-interest?

The second body which had the capacity to influence economic life was the Church. In an age of unfaith it is difficult for us to conceptualize the power of the Church. It touched on men's lives at all points from birth to death. In a grim, hard world it promised eternal salvation, and the prospect of eternal damnation was enough to make most men pay more than lip-service to its teachings. What is more it had its own laws and its own courts which dealt with far more than matters merely spiritual. Like royal government, it had to face new problems in the twelfth and thirteenth centuries. Its earlier ideas and doctrines had been related to a static agrarian economy. Now it had to deal with towns and traders, and important questions were raised as to the status of the merchant and the nature of profit. Again, it faced these problems with an increased ability to formulate ideas and carry them into action. The Church stood at the height of its international power in the twelfth and thirteenth centuries. Its scholars (indeed, there were no others) led the intellectual renaissance of the period which saw the reintroduction of the works of the great classical writers, and especially of Aristotle, to the western world. There may have been no direct teaching on matters economic, no direct economy theory. But what the Church had to say on the Just Price and particularly on usury rightly falls under the heading of economic ideas and had considerable repercussions on the workings of the economy.

The most obvious way in which royal government could intervene in the English economy was through its fiscal policies. Government cost money, if only to maintain the royal household in a suitable state of magnificence. As the administration grew more sophisticated, so it cost a great deal more – although that has to be balanced against increased revenues from the profits of justice, the exploitation of feudal tenures and attempts at taxation. Despite increased expenses royal revenues were adequate in time of peace: in time of war they were not, and from the Conquest onwards England was frequently involved in foreign campaigns, from 1066 to 1135 to retain or regain control over the duchy of Normandy, and then from 1154 to 1214 in defence of the Angevin lands in France, and in Richard I's crusade. Henry III (1216–72) spent intermittently but foolishly on campaigns in Gascony and on trying to win Sicily for the papacy. His son, Edward I, was one of England's great martial kings. His reign saw the conquest of Wales, the attempted conquest of Scotland and a war with France over Gascony. The legacy he bequeathed his successors was in many ways a bitter one – continued war with Scotland and disputes with France which led in the end to the outbreak of the Hundred Years War in 1337. Warfare dominated English society in the later Middle Ages. It grew more and more expensive as equipment became more complicated and troops at all levels came to expect payment for their service, rather than performing it as part of their feudal or national obligation to the Crown.

There is no question but that military expenditure was one of, if not the most important, incentives to the creation of a public revenue system. Until the end of the twelfth century and the rapid inflation of the years 1180 to 1220, rulers seemed able to cope from their traditional or 'ordinary' revenues. These came from the royal demesne, mainly let out for money rents, rather than the older rents in kind, the farms of the borough, the proceeds of feudalism, the profits of justice and the issues of ecclesiastical estates in royal hands during vacancies. In addition the Crown could tallage (tax) the Jews and the royal boroughs. All this brought John about £20,000 per annum in the early thirteenth century, but this was not enough. From Henry II's reign rulers had been casting around for new ways of augmenting their revenue. The most obvious was increasing the size of the royal demesne but there were serious obstacles to that. Any policy of territorial aggrandizement would lead to opposition from the baronage who would see it as a threat to their own landed patrimony. Edward I found that out when he deprived some leading families of their estates by less than legal means and stirred up considerable opposition. Besides that, the royal demesne was essentially a wasting asset. It was continuously used for patronage as the Crown sought to reward its followers for past service or to secure their future loyalty. As a result, it slowly shrank in size, to reach its nadir in the mid-fifteenth century when it provided a negligible part of royal revenues. All kings in the twelfth century exploited feudalism as ruthlessly as they could, demanding high reliefs or inheritance duties, selling wardship over the lands of minors to the highest bidder, taking regular scutages or money payments in lieu of personal military service. But, again, the greater the exploitation, the fiercer the opposition. The feudal baronage had their own firm ideas on the limits of Crown intervention in the workings of the feudal contract, and those limits were clearly stated in the Great Charter. The Church objected to the abuse of the royal right to enjoy the revenues of vacant sees and there was widespread opposition to the selling of royal justice at too high a price. Probably the only method of raising money to which there was no objection was the sale of charters of freedom to the royal boroughs.

The way forward did not lie ultimately in the more intense exploitation of the ordinary revenues of the Crown. All the same, thirteenth-century rulers did try to maximize their income from this source as much as they could, which explains, for instance, Henry III's reform of the exchequer in the 1230s. All the Crown's resources were surveyed, new rents or farms were set, inquiry was made into all rights held of the Crown to see if any were being exercised illegally. In view of the opposition aroused, it is questionable whether this was worth the financial return. No, the Crown had to find other ways of tapping England's wealth, and it found them through taxation. As early as 1203 John was experimenting with taxation (the subsidy) on movable property, which for most people in an agrarian society meant a fraction of the value of their agricultural crops or livestock. At first this was variable, but by the fourteenth century it had become fixed at one-fifteenth. Townsmen, who were held to be wealthier, paid at a higher rate, which was eventually fixed at one-tenth. In 1207 John's taxation of movables yielded no less than £57,000, compared with the normal revenue of £20,000, so the attractions of taxation are obvious. The experiment in his reign soon hardened into normal practice. Henry III asked for, but did not always receive, grants of subsidies. Edward I relied on them heavily during the crisis years 1294–7 when he faced wars with Scotland and France and rebellion in Wales. By 1334, however, the amount of subsidy produced was fixed at £38,170 and the contributions of each shire, borough and township were assessed proportionately. This was far below the real value of the fifteenth and tenth, and rulers later in the fourteenth and fifteenth centuries experimented, largely unsuccessfully, with new forms of lay taxation, poll taxes[1] and income taxes.

But, even when at their best, lay subsidies alone could not provide all the Crown's needs. So kings sought to tap the wealth of the greatest institutional landowners in the country, the clergy, by taxing their income. That, too, had its problems, for it raised the very vexed question of whether the lay ruler had the right to do this. Edward I was ruthless enough to override opposition, so that in his reign taxation of the clergy raised £200,000 compared with £500,000 from the laity. Later rulers were perhaps less successful and in the fourteenth and fifteenth centuries the most lucrative source of Crown revenues came from the taxation of trade. John had grasped how lucrative it might be and in the reign of Edward I it developed into the prop of Crown finances. First (in 1275) a fixed customs duty of 6s.8d. was levied on every sack of wool exported. Then in the 1290s the Crown imposed a high additional duty of 40s. or more a sack (the *maltote*) and a battle was joined which lasted for the next half century or more until the subsidy on wool became a permanent fixture. In the meantime other duties were imposed: the petty custom of 3d. in the £ on all alien and Hanseatic general merchandise imported and exported; poundage, an ad valorem tax of 1s. in the £ on all native and alien general merchandise and on the value of alien cloth exports; tunnage, an impost of so much per tun on wine imports; the cloth duty on each broadcloth exported, varying in incidence according to the exporter. By the late fourteenth century nothing entered or left the country but it was taxed in some way. And, when even taxation failed to raise the monies required, then the Crown had to resort to borrowing, from the Italians, from English syndicates and from the Company of the Staple. How important the extraordinary revenues of the Crown had become can be seen from the receipts of the Exchequer in 1374–5. They totalled £112,000, of which only £22,000 came from the hereditary revenues, £82,000 from direct and indirect taxation and the balance from borrowing. By Henry VI's reign, when government finances were in a parlous state, the customs alone produced about £30,000 of a total revenue of £57,000.

The economic consequences of the Crown's increasing demands for revenue have already been discussed in detail – the effects on the money supply and thus wages and prices in Chapter 2, on the economy in the early fourteenth century in Chapter 6 and on the wool trade and the cloth industry in Chapter 9. The question that has to be asked is, did the fiscal policies pursued by the Crown represent the conscious application of current economic ideas? or did they themselves result in the creation of new ideas and economic theories about the right to exploit the country's wealth? The answer in both cases seems to be no. Taxation did raise grave questions concerning the extent of the subject's political obligation to the Crown. Was it every man's duty to aid the prince in his necessity? If so, who was to be the judge of that necessity? Could assent be withheld, could the king take taxation arbitrarily? All these were questions of prime constitutional importance and there can be no doubt that the way in which they were answered affected the course of English political and constitutional history. Some thought was given to the ability of the subject to pay, since the poorest were excused. Otherwise the economic consequences were accidental. No grand design can be seen in Edward III's wool taxation. He had no intentions of damaging the Flemish industry by heavy duties on English wool exports or embargoes on trade with the Low Countries. All that concerned him was the money to wage his wars and the political uses to which trade could be put. If aliens were forced to pay higher customs duties than Englishmen, then it must be said that the government's prime aim was to screw as much out of them as it could, not to protect and foster the interests of English merchants by creating favourable tariff barriers. As will be seen, there were ideas that it was part of the prince's duty to pursue policies of plenty, to encourage trade to bring essential supplies to their dominions. These may have motivated some of the government's other actions, but fiscal policies were fiscal policies pure and simple. They represent the outcome of no lofty ideas but the government's hand-to-mouth scramble to finance its wars in pursuit either of its dynastic aims or its territorial ambitions, or, in a martial age, simply La Gloire.

Yet government did not exist purely to raise money; but to govern, to manage the affairs of the realm. Its chief duty was to maintain peace and order within the country and to protect it from its foes by both defensive and offensive warfare. But, increasingly, from the twelfth century onwards the government saw as part of its task the regulation of matters economic, adding a new aspect to the practice of statecraft. The first steps were tentative and perhaps not deliberately economic in intent. The charters of liberties granted to towns in the twelfth century which often conferred on them monopolies in local trade or industry were probably no more than a fund-raising exercise. The Crown had no long-term plan for fostering urban growth to strengthen the economy – indeed the whole concept of economic management as we know it today was alien to the Middle Ages. Gradually government intervention became more overt. By the Assize of Cloth in 1197 the Crown sought to confine the manufacture of dyed cloths to towns and laid down comprehensive regulations for size and quality. It may have suffered the fate of much medieval legislation in the sense that no sooner was it passed than men purchased exemptions from the Assize, but it is symptomatic of growing government involvement in the workings of the economy.

From then, intervention grew apace. Trade was fostered by granting protection to alien merchants. German merchants who by Henry II's reign had their own gild hall in London, were progressively given complete freedom to trade in England. Flemish, Norwegian, French, Florentine, Brabantine and other merchants came under royal protection in the thirteenth century; and at the beginning of the fourteenth century Edward I recognized the importance of alien traders in the Carta Mercatoria of 1303. All alien merchants in England were taken into the king's protection, freed from certain local charges, permitted to sell wholesale to anyone and mercery by retail, and promised speedy justice in their law suits. The Crown sought to regulate tin mining in Devon and Cornwall and lead mining in Derbyshire. It tried to enforce its rules on the size and quality of cloth through local officers called the aulnagers who were supposed to inspect and approve all cloth offered for sale. For trade to flow smoothly it was essential that merchants should easily be able to recover debts, especially when credit sales were so ubiquitous. Edward I laid down new procedures for recovery in the Statute of Merchants (1283) and of Acton Burnell (1285). Debts could now be acknowledged before judicial tribunals and entered upon their rolls, making it difficult for one of the parties to deny all knowledge of his obligations.

In the post-plague era government intervention became even more intense. The Ordinance and Statute of Labourers were only the first in a long line of enactments which tried to control the workings of the labour market. The wool trade and the Staple, cloth manufacture and its export, bullion supplies, alien traders were all the subject of frequent legislation. From Richard II's reign onward navigation acts sought to confine English overseas trade to English ships whilst a series of statutes tried to enforce standard weights and measures, even to the extent of prescribing the capacity of barrels for eels and butts for salmon. There was scarcely any aspect of the economy which did not come under the government's purview in the later Middle Ages.

Taken at face value, simply the scope of the legislation would seem to be impressive evidence of the Crown's ability to influence the workings of the economy. Moreover, they appear to have been influenced by current ideas. In the thirteenth century perhaps the greatest of the medieval philosophers, St Thomas Aquinas, stated that it was the duty of the prince to ensure that the community was supplied with all that was necessary for its sustenance and the proper equipment of the crafts and professions. English kings seem to have obeyed that precept. It could be argued that they encouraged trade and then, when it flowed freely, tried to protect the interests of native merchants. They sought to ensure adequate supplies for the community. Grain exports were forbidden in the era of high prices and scarcity in the fourteenth century; free export was only allowed in the fifteenth century when production could fully meet domestic needs. Royal legislation often echoed more specific urban ordinances against monopolists in the food trades. Edward III at one point empowered anyone to sell foodstuffs by retail in London, to break the monopoly of the victualling trades, whilst merchants importing fish in the fifteenth century were exempted from the laws prohibiting the export of bullion. The native cloth industry flourished behind discriminatory tariffs and in the fifteenth century specific protection was given to the makers of caps and the London silk workers. All this would seem to be a coherent policy of 'plenty' inspired by Aquinas' theory of the prince's obligation.

The truth is more prosaic. Royal legislation was often motivated not by high principles but by the exigencies of the moment, the need to placate powerful pressure groups or to raise money. It is very noticeable that as parliament developed and provided a forum for political discussion more purely economic laws were passed. The Crown was forced to listen to its subjects' complaints, which often disguised self-interest with loud protests about the national interest, and to act upon them if it wished to placate this or that particular group. The labour legislation, for instance, was entirely the result of pressure by the landed classes whose interests were threatened by excessive wage demands. What looks like the high-minded pursuit of the policy of plenty, could also conceal baser motives. Throughout much of the fifteenth century the Crown refused to take effective action against alien merchants. It did so not in pursuit of Aquinas' ideas of their public utility, as bringing necessary goods to the land, but because interfering with their trade would have diminished the customs revenues on which Crown finances so much depended. Government legislation was merely piecemeal. There was no well thought-out plan. Statutes were often ineffective, unenforced or unenforceable. The very frequency with which many of them, such as the labour laws or the navigation acts, were repeated is a fair indication that they were either not working or not being enforced. Cloth manufacture, for instance, was the subject of much regulation but most of it was totally fruitless. The elaborate aulnage system for the inspection of cloth simply did not work in the fifteenth century because the network of officials needed to enforce it properly did not exist. The Crown chose rather to farm it out for a fixed income and the impression is that for most of the fifteenth century inspection was purely perfunctory. The government's ability to influence the workings of the economy by legislation was indeed minimal. Nor is there much evidence that when it did intervene it was motivated by anything other than self-interest. Economic ideas did not fill the heads of medieval English kings.

But, from the welter of debate and polemic about the economy in the later Middle Ages certain themes do emerge which were later to develop into the theory of mercantilism. This was an age of nationalism, of national wars of the English against the French, an age when the English were demanding preference in trade over their alien rivals. The literature of the period abounds with expressions of nationalism. *The Libelle of Englyshe Polycye*, a rhyming tract of the 1430s, is almost jingoistic in its desire to see the English first. It urged naval dominance of the Channel to bring other nations to heel by controlling their trade through the narrow seas. Other pieces echoed such sentiments. The author of a rhymed memorandum on English commercial policy in

Edward IV's reign thought that all nations should pay respect to England on account of her ships and her wool. Through all this literature, and through the preambles to petitions in parliament, seeking redress of grievances, run certain common themes, the first of which was the idea of national prosperity. It was not a question of an individual or a group benefiting from this or that action, but that the country's wealth might be increased. Statutes speak of the universal good of increasing the prosperity of the realm of England, whilst the Staplers in 1429 went to the other extreme and spoke of the destruction of the realm which they thought would result from allowing aliens freedom of trade. In most cases the prosperity of the realm was equated with the prosperity of the merchant and wealth with an ample stock of gold and silver. Bullionism and the balance of trade were two major obsessions in the later Middle Ages, the two being closely linked. There was a widely held idea that unless English trade was in the balance gold and silver would be sucked from the country. A favourable balance could be achieved, it was held, by close restrictions on aliens at home and by furthering the interests of English merchants abroad. So the *Libelle of Englyshe Polycye* put it:

> For yef marchaundes were cherysshede to here spede
> We were not lykelye to fayle in ony nede;
> Yff they bee riche, thane in prosperité
> Schalbe our lordé, lordes and comonté.

Hence the continued demands for hosting laws to ensure that alien merchants spent all their profits from the sale of imports on English goods for export, the continual agitation for trading privileges for English merchants in Prussia or Flanders; and for restrictions on Italian banking and exchange operations which were held to drain money from the country.

Also strongly held was the idea that English trade should be carried in English ships, protected by a strong navy. Navigation acts tried (unsuccessfully, it must be added) to force English goods into English bottoms. The need for a powerful navy was recognized by the first two Lancastrians and its dismantling under Henry VI brought forth the agonized cry from the author of the *Libelle*:

> Cheryshe marchandyse, kepe thamyralté
> That we bee maysteres of the narowe see.

These words were echoed in a Commons petition in 1439. When the merchants of England might go in their ships, it said, and bring all manner of merchandise to England, then was all such merchandise in greater abundance, at better and cheaper price within the realm, and the merchants in a better state than they are now. All the ideas of latter-day mercantilism were there, and it is hardly surprising that they were being expressed mainly by the mercantile classes. Self-interest and the inability to compete on equal terms with their rivals forced them to develop theories about trade and the nation's wealth. But they were thinking in national terms at a time when the Crown still in many ways viewed the realm simply as an estate of which it was the chief lord. And, if their ideas were, fortunately, never effectively put into practice, that too was more to do with the Crown's weakness, than for want of trying.

With the Church it was a different matter. As has been said, it had no coherent economic doctrine, only ideas and teachings on many subjects which were morally binding upon the faithful. The chief of these concerned charity and private property, the Just Price and usury. In the first place, the Church recognized and accepted individual rights in private property. Thus by implication it also accepted the existing structure of society, since at every stage the tenure of land involved economic and social obligations. In a sense the Church was obliged to accept the situation. By the twelfth century it had become collectively the greatest landlord in Europe and could not afford to undermine its own position. Unfortunately, there was an obvious conflict here with the teachings of the early fathers. 'The common life, bretheren', St Clement is supposed to have written to the Christians of Jerusalem 'the use of all things that are in the world ought to be common to all men . . . And just as the air cannot be divided, nor the splendour of the sun, so the other things of the world which were given to be held in common by all ought not to be divided.'

That put the canonists who wrote on Church law and the scholastics, the philosophers and theologians who played such a leading part in the intellectual renaissance of the twelfth and thirteenth centuries in something of a quandary. They were concerned about the suggestion that private property was contrary to divine will. God created earth for all men and all should share its fruits. This was the law of nature, the idea that God had implanted in the nature of things and the nature of man norms of conduct more binding than any human laws. As Gratian, the first great canonist of the twelfth century, wrote in his *Decretum* (*c.*1140), natural law was common to all nations, and it involved common possession of all things. He tried to argue that although private property was against the natural law, nevertheless it was a precept of human law, distributed by God to the human race through emperors and kings. This was a logical absurdity, since natural law had to be superior to human law. Later canonists sought a solution to the problem by defining natural law in a different way. They argued that the term could be used to describe both man's primitive condition and the quality appropriate in a creature of man's peculiar intellectual and spiritual nature. One usage referred to man's origins, the other to his destiny. Common property was part of the first definition of natural law, which was merely a description of a former state of society, not forever binding. The abandonment of primitive communism had been made necessary by human sin; private property had come into being as a consequence of man's Fall. It was also argued by St Thomas Aquinas that private property was an invention of human reason, justified because people took better care of their own possessions than of what belongs to all. They exerted themselves more strenuously on their own account, than for others and, he said, the social order was better preserved if possessions were distinct. Aquinas' task was made easier by the re-emergence of the teachings of Aristotle. He had distinguished between the power of occupation and administration. There was a right to acquire and hold property for the maintenance of the family. Thereafter, the use to which it was put determined whether private property was good or evil. If it was being used simply to support the family then it was being properly used, but the unrestrained pursuit of profit was immoral.

So the Church came to terms with the realities of medieval society, but it was not as entirely cynical in its approach as one might expect. The doctrine that the end to which something was used made the action licit or illicit had important ramifications. The most obvious from the point of view of private property is that ownership carried social obligations, particularly towards the poor. The Church's attitude towards the poor was curiously and almost anachronistically modern. Poverty was not to be seen as a vice which had to be stamped out by punitive measures. Certainly the Church had not time for the idle who were able to work but chose not to do so, but it did recognize that poverty could be involuntary. Men might be willing to work but unable to do so, because of sickness or accident or lack of land. They should be given aid, and it was the obligation of the property owner to use his surplus wealth to that end. That was the right use of property. Super-fluities should be given away as an act of justice, the poor had a right to be supported from the surplus wealth of the community. In that sense, and that sense alone was property, and particularly Church property, common. In the early Church the duty of providing revenue for poor relief had been placed upon the bishop. He was to divide the revenues from his see into four parts, one of which was to be devoted to poor relief. By the thirteenth century the main burden had been shifted to the individual parish. The canonists believed that the holders of parochial benefices acquired, along with the income, responsibility to the poor. Difficulties arose when parochial revenues had been appropriated by a monastery and a poor priest left in charge. That applied to only one-third of English parishes, however, and the monasteries themselves provided some relief to the poor by distributing left-over food to them. Nothing like a third or a quarter of ecclesiastical income was spent on poor relief, though. Professor Tierney estimates that no more than 3–5 per cent was used to this end in the thirteenth century, but thinks that this was probably enough, since most people had land to support their families and poverty was not rife.[2] In addition, of course, private relief was provided to the sick and needy by the establishment of hospitals, for private property had as much of a duty to support the poor as ecclesiastical. There were some 600 hospitals in later medieval England, varying in size from St Peter's at York with permanent provision for the upkeep of 200 poor men, to numerous small houses caring for the sick, the lepers and the poor.

Was this sufficient to cope with poverty and did it divert funds from more economically useful sources? Tierney argues that it was sufficient in the thirteenth century but that the system broke down in the fifteenth century in the face of increasing vagrancy and the dissipation of parish revenues by appropriations and absentee priests. This seems doubtful. The real problem in the thirteenth century was not the destitute but willing worker, but small holders living on the edge of subsistence. They would not qualify for relief, since they had land, but they were the most in need. In the later Middle Ages poverty was far less acute. Increased mobility does not necessarily equal increased vagrancy. There was plenty of land and work to be had, and in spite of its diminished resources, the Church probably provided as adequately as it could, for those really in need. As to the suggestion that poor relief diverted money from more useful ends, it can be countered on two grounds. In however limited a way, it was socially desirable to care for the poor, and there is no evidence to suggest that the money would have been spent by the Church to more useful purpose. Most likely it would have been squandered on conspicuous consumption.

Just as the Church had to adapt its doctrines on property to fit the realities of medieval society, so did it have to face up to the problem of the merchant and his profits. The early Church looked on trade with as much distaste as it looked on private property, for trade was in a sense a form of property. Tertullian (*c.*155–222) argued that to remove covetousness was to remove the reason for gain and therefore the need for trade. St Augustine feared that trade would turn men from the search for God, whilst St John Chrysostom felt that merchants were men who wished to be rich at any price. Consequently, the doctrine that no Christian should want to be a merchant was common in the early Middle Ages. In a primitive agrarian economy that did not have serious consequences. Trade was mainly in luxuries which could yield great profits – and give rise to great temptations to become rich without limit. So, commerce was to be avoided. By the twelfth century the whole situation had changed. Towns and the numbers of merchants increased enormously. Trade was no longer simply in luxuries for the few. It now touched on the lives of many, and not least the Church, both as a consumer and, in England, as a producer of vast quantities of grain and wool.

Somehow, merchants had to be brought into the fold; but there were difficulties. Gratian still condemned all commercial profits and brought the charge of usury against certain forms of investment and partnerships. Fortunately, subsequent canonists did not follow his arguments. They still frowned on commerce. Aquinas still saw something base in trade, but he and others argued that commercial gain was justified by the necessity of making one's living; by the wish to acquire the means for charitable purposes; and by the wish to serve the public utility. Trade clearly could not exist without a profit and profit could be justified on three grounds: if the merchant increased the value of the goods by the addition of labour or capital; if there was a risk that the merchant might lose his goods; or where there existed intertemporal or interlocal differences in value. The distinction was again drawn between trade itself and the ends to which its profits were put. Supporting one's family was quite permissible, but the pursuit of gain for itself was not. In practice, the merchant was allowed pretty wide latitude. Labour and capital were normally employed in trade, and returns were quite modest. The estimate for the earning rate for capital employed in the Florentine wool trade is 7–15 per cent, and for merchant bankers 6–10 per cent. If the highly organized Italians made such modest gains, it is unlikely that the English earned more. And who could say whether a merchant was pursuing profit for its own sake? Most probably he did, which is why so many merchants made restitution for the good of their souls in their wills. The Church had come to terms with the trader, and no significant restrictions had been placed on his operations.

The Church also developed in the twelfth and thirteenth centuries distinct teachings on prices, and a doctrine of the Just Price which, it has been argued, held back economic development. Goods can be valued in two ways, by their utility to their owner, and by their value as a medium of exchange, for barter or, more important, for money. The question the Church asked was what determined the price – pure utility, the added value of labour and capital sufficient to give the manufacturer a reasonable profit, or the free workings of the market? There is a widespread belief that the Just Price was fixed by the second of these criteria, that the producer should be allowed a reasonable profit to support his family on a scale suited to their station in life. This idea comes from the writings of a minor figure in the fourteenth century, Henry von Langenstein who argued that where public authority failed to fix a price, the producer could fix it himself on the terms outlined above. But other authorities disagreed. Their writings are somewhat confused, but from Aquinas and Albertus Magnus in the thirteenth century and from the later scholastics, a positive line of thought does emerge, that the Just Price was the normal competitive price when fraud, collusion and monopoly were absent. Aquinas has a famous story of a merchant on his way to market with a load of grain. There is famine in the area and prices are high. Is the merchant obliged to tell his customers that ample supplies are on their way, which will lower prices? If he tells they will probably cease to buy and his profits will fall. Aquinas says he is not obliged to tell, but can take the competitive market price. Later scholastics developed further the utility theory of value. The utility to the buyer, they argued, was relative to the abundance or scarcity of goods. Thus they equated the Just Price with any competitive price, and were on their way to a fully fledged theory of supply and demand. The Just Price therefore reflected the free workings of the market, and free is the key word. All writers were firmly against artificially created prices brought about by monopoly or price agreement, forestalling, regrating or engrossing.

It is not difficult to find examples of the theory of the Just Price in action. Implementation rested chiefly with the towns. It was in their best interests to see that foodstuffs in particular flowed freely to the market and in urban regulations is to be found the most consistent opposition to monopolists. Given the parlous conditions of medieval food supply, that made sense. But, at the same time, towns were only too keen to offer protection to manufactured goods made within their walls.[3] Monopoly, too, lay at the heart of the gild system, despite the view often put forward that the Just Price found its most practical application in the gilds. They have been presented as welfare agencies which prevented unfair competition and protected consumers against deceit and exploitation. By creating equal opportunities for their members, they are said to have secured for them a modest but decent living in accordance with Langenstein's concept of the Just Price. In practice, their actions were far more selfish. They strove to keep imported goods from the market to limit competition and, where they could, to fix wages and prices in their own interests. Authorities may have frowned on the latter but it certainly went on. Thus it was hardly the free working of the market, and self-interest certainly overcame the Church's teachings. Had gild power been absolute, it would have held back economic development far more than the doctrine of the Just Price which offered no protection to the inefficient merchant or craftsman.

The one economic theory, for it can and must be called that, which did have wide-reaching implications was the Church's doctrine on usury. Throughout the Middle Ages its voice rang loud and clear – to lend money at interest was both legally and morally wrong. Christ's teaching on the matter is unmistakable. There may be only one slightly ambiguous reference to the subject in the New Testament, 'Lend hoping for nothing again' (Luke 6:35), but enrichment by lending at interest was regarded as the worst form of profit. The Old Testament was more explicit: 'If thou lend money to any of my people that is poor by thee, thou shalt not be to him as an usurer, neither shalt thou lay upon him usury' (Exodus 22:25). At first, in the early Church, the prohibition seems to have applied only to the clergy. Not till after 800 was the ban gradually applied to the laity, until by the Second Lateran Council of 1139 it was extended to the whole body of the Church. Gratian was quite specific – whatever is added to the principal is usury – and the Third Lateran Council of 1179 promoted a series of stringent prohibitions against taking interest.

By the thirteenth century scholastics were able to find a new and more rational basis for their opposition to lending at interest. They took their ideas from Aristotle and the precepts of Roman Law. Aristotle's views on usury were conditioned by his theories of natural and unnatural exchange and the quality of money. The only mode of exchange he regarded as natural was that which was required to provide the necessities of life for the household. Money arose as a means of facilitating that exchange and should be used for that end only and for no other. It was essentially barren and ought not to be made to bear fruit. Usury 'which makes a gain out of money itself and not for the natural use of it' was to be abhorred. To this Aquinas added the distinction in Roman Law between fungibles and consumptibles. Money for the scholastics was a consumptible: it was consumed in the act of being used like wine or food. Therefore it had no use which could be separated from its substance as had a house which was a fungible. To charge for the use of something which did not exist was illegitimate or usurious. These ideas persisted through the Middle Ages. Only perhaps in the fifteenth century did St Antonine of Florence see that money was not sterile. Circulating coin might be, but money capital was not because command of it was an essential condition for entering upon business.

The implications of this doctrine are wide. Had it been rigorously applied it would obviously have severely restricted economic development. Of course, it could not be. Again, it was suited to a static agrarian economy, not a society in which towns and trade flourished, where merchants needed access to capital, to extend credit and charge interest for it, to borrow to finance their operations. Bankers emerged who could transmit monies across Europe and the Church needed their services to gather its taxes and finance its wars. There had to be a modus vivendi and, as with the merchant, one slowly emerged. The canonists recognized that it was licit to charge damnum or interesse for reasons which were not inherent in the loan itself. The chief of these were when the borrower failed to repay the loan on time; when the lender deprived himself of the legitimate use of his money, and therefore of gain, over a period of time; and when there was a risk that the lender might lose his principal. It was also recognized as legitimate for the borrower to make a genuine and gratuitous 'gift' to the lender after the repayment of the loan. But the straight mutuum, the loan at interest, was forbidden.

This, again, left the mercantile classes a considerable amount of leeway. Credit for instance was quite licit. It involved both some risk and deprived the merchant of the legitimate use of his money over a period of time. Interest could be levied, and usually took the form of charging a higher price for goods bought on credit than for cash. One of the members in a partnership could also lend to the other at interest

337

because he faced the loss of his money and could not use it for his own purposes. Ostensibly, therefore the Church's teaching on usury in no way hampered the development of trade. Nor did it prevent an extensive but unquantifiable amount of borrowing and lending at all levels in society. Kings needed to borrow cash to anticipate revenues slow in coming in, and to finance their household expenses and especially their wars. Great nobles, lay and ecclesiastical, borrowed to pay taxes, to meet military expenses, to erect expensive buildings, or simply to meet their current expenses. Lesser men with inadequate means borrowed to maintain their standard of living, and the peasants in bad years to ward off starvation.

Up to the mid-thirteenth century in England the single most important source of loans was the Jews. It is wrong to think that they were the only source of credit: Christians were involved in the money-lending business as well. In the late twelfth century Henry II borrowed heavily from William Trentegeruns of Rouen and William Cade of St Omer. Cade was particularly wealthy and had many agents in Western Europe. Between 1155 and 1165 he lent the king at least £5,600 besides other loans to earls, bishops and abbots, as well as to lesser folk. Flemish financiers were very important in this period. They acted as the Italians did later, as international bankers, transferring funds from one country to another. Ecclesiastical houses used them to transmit money to the papal curia, thus avoiding the dangerous and costly business of sending specie. Another important source of loans, for a great monastic house like Canterbury Cathedral Priory, was its private friends, its lay and ecclesiastical neighbours. In one sense the priory acted as a deposit banker, accepting money with a promise to repay at a specific time. Kings of course borrowed from whom they could, Henry III turned for loans not only to Italian bankers, but to his brother Richard, earl of Cornwall, to religious houses, and in particular to the crusading orders the Templars and the Hospitallers.

But the Jews played the most important role in the money market until the mid-thirteenth century. Since they were not Christians, at first they lay outside the Church's laws on usury. They had become money lenders in the early Middle Ages when, debarred from trading associations with Christians, the only way in which they could employ their capital was to lend it out at interest. Their permanent settlement in England came after the Conquest, and they were taken under royal protection by Henry I. His charter gave them liberty of movement within the realm, freedom from toll, free access to royal justice and permission to retain land taken in pledge as security. The price of protection was to be high. Debts to Jews passed to the Crown on their death, and special registers called Archa were set up to record loans so that the royal treasury would not lose money after a Jew's death. Jews were also liable to tallage, arbitrary taxation, something that was to cost them dear in the thirteenth century. Most were men of moderate substance. Jews like Aaron of Lincoln or Jurnet of Norwich were relatively rare. Aaron (d.1180) could afford to lend nine Cistercian abbeys 6,400 marks (£4,266.13s.4d.) and 1,800 marks to one man in Yorkshire. All his loans were at interest. His bond with Count Aubrey of Dammartin for £118 shows that the sum to be repaid was greater than the sum lent, and this was common practice. But for the most part Jews lent small amounts, mainly to the rural middle classes. As has been seen, they played an important part in the land market in the twelfth and thirteenth centuries.[4] When debtors failed to repay their loans, their land was taken. The Jews had no interest in farming it. Instead they sold it to recover their debts, to religious houses or to up-and-coming men of the ministerial classes like the Braybrookes who built up a substantial estate in the twelfth and thirteenth centuries by buying land from the Jews.

In the thirteenth century the Jews were gradually forced out of England until in 1290 they were expelled altogether. The reasons for this were partly financial, partly religious. During this century the Crown sought to take its percentage of the profits of their money-lending by imposing tallages on the Jews. Henry III was particularly hard on them. Between 1227 and 1237 tallages to the combined value of 65,000 marks (£43,333.6s.8d.) were levied on them, forcing many Jews to leave England. Down to 1255 over 250,000 marks (£166,666.13s.4d.) were exacted from the English Jewry, a vast sum from a very limited community settled in some 20 or so towns. Increasingly impoverished, they were of less and less use to the Crown, whilst the whole spirit of the age turned against them. Jews had never been popular in England, and it was always easy to rouse the mob against them. In 1190, at the time of Richard I's coronation when crusading fever was at its height, a whole series of attacks on the Jews began in London with a massacre of the London Jewry. In the provinces the worst outrage was at York where some 150 Jews who had taken refuge in the Castle died either by their own hands or at those of the local populace. In the thirteenth century the Church's attitude to the Jews hardened considerably. The Fourth Lateran Council railed against Jewish usurers and Jews generally and in 1234 Pope Gregory IX promulgated his decretals which included the demands of the Third Lateran Council. Perhaps it was this which made Henry III order in 1240 that all foreign merchants practising usury were to leave the country within one month, although he later allowed certain Italian societies to stay provided they lent no further money at usury. This did not specifically include the Jews, but they were the most obvious usurers. The period of the barons' wars in the mid-century saw great hostility to the Jews and renewed attacks on them. Increasingly impoverished by heavy tallages they tried to cash in their debts. The result was the provisions of Jewry of 1269 which forbade the contracting of debts with the Jews on security of land held in fee. All such obligations were to be cancelled and the transfer of such a debt to a Christian was to be treated as a capital offence. Debts of any other kind could only be disposed of to a third party by special licence and on condition that the principal only without interest was to be exacted. This considerably limited the Jews' ability to make loans against land, or to sell land to recover their debts. A further mandate of 1271 restricted their ability to hold land, whilst in 1275 the Statute of Jews forbade them to lend at interest. Attempts to direct them into trading were a failure and the Jews were left impoverished by tallages and with no useful occupation to follow. By the time of their expulsion they were already a broken community.

At the upper end of the market, their place was taken by the Italians. The process was well under way by the early thirteenth century. The Italians' main advantage was their great liquid wealth based on the profits of both trade and money-lending. Their role as papal bankers and tax collectors brought them into contact with great monastic houses, who found them ideal agents for the transfer of monies to Rome. Heavy investment in the wool trade involved them with the lay and ecclesiastical nobility and their usefulness to the Crown was soon obvious. Henry III, whose financial position was precarious, borrowed from them, but Italian participation in royal finances really developed under Edward I. He found fresh revenues against which to borrow in the duties on wool. From the 1290s onwards war also made successive kings desperate for loans.

Although there were some 69 Italian firms in later thirteenth century England, the Crown usually relied on one or two major companies – Edward I on the Riccardi of Lucca and the Frescobaldi of Florence, Edward II on the Frescobaldi and the Bardi of Florence, whose assets in 1318 were *c.*£130,000 when Edward's ordinary revenues did not exceed £30,000 per annum, and Edward III on the Bardi and Peruzzi. Nor were these bankers simply the sources of loans. The Bardi and Peruzzi in the early fourteenth century accepted deposits from great men. Hugh Despenser the younger had no less than £5,886 on deposit with them at the beginning of September 1324. It freed him from the need to store large sums of money, and the bankers acted as his central treasury into which his officials paid revenues and from which payments could be effected quickly and without risk. He received no interest on his deposits – but others did. The Italians' fall was nearly as swift as their rise, however. Edward III's huge borrowings – no less than £125,000 in 1338–9 alone – brought them to their knees. Thereafter they concentrated, in England, mainly on exchange and trading operations. Indeed, the extent and functioning of the money market in the later Middle Ages is obscure. The Crown came to rely heavily on London merchants and the Staple, as well as borrowing heavily from the lay and ecclesiastical nobility and the landed gentry. It must be assumed that the pattern of lending and borrowing in the country generally was one of private individuals lending to other private individuals.

Two problems arise here – were these various loans at interest? and why did no English banking institutions emerge, to encourage lending and make capital more readily available for investment? There is no question that in the first half of the thirteenth century all loans were at interest. Canterbury Cathedral Priory borrowed extensively from Italians and Jews. Up to the 1240s they recorded the payment of interest, often at high rates. On a loan of 420 marks (£280) from Roman and Sienese merchants in 1221 they had to pay 117½ marks (£78.6s.8d.) interest, whilst typical Jewish rates ranged from 22 to 43 per cent per annum according to the security the borrower could offer. But one recent writer[5] has suggested that the progressive tightening and more rigorous application of the usury laws from 1240 onwards meant that first the usury was concealed, then no longer charged. By the 1280s, when Canterbury Cathedral Priory borrowed from both Italians and private friends, provided the money was paid back in time, no interest appears to have been charged.

From this evidence it is suggested that much private lending, probably the main source of finance, was undertaken with no expectation of profit. But profit can be taken in various ways. Those who lent to Canterbury Cathedral Priory may have done so for the favour a powerful landlord could show them. Certainly, the Crown still had to pay interest to the Italians in the fourteenth century. At the completion of the Frescobaldi's last account with the Crown in 1310 they were owed £21,635 of which interest and compensation accounted for £12,000, whilst in 1348 Edward III owed the Bardi £63,000 for advances made to him and a further £40,000 for interest. It is highly likely, therefore, that interest simply went underground. In the later Middle Ages the chief instrument for recording debts was the bond obligatory. In this no mention was made of interest because the sum it was made out for comprised both principal and interest, or in other words more was repaid than was borrowed. As with lending to great ecclesiastics, so with the Crown in the later fourteenth and the fifteenth centuries. Interest could be paid in a whole variety of ways, by 'gifts', by grants or favours, licences to export wool duty free, keeperships of royal manors or, as with the chief lender to Henry V and VI, Cardinal Beaufort, virtual control of the customs revenues of a great port over a number of years. In one way or another interest was paid on loans, credit flourished and it was not in this sense that the usury laws hindered the development of banking and an adequate money market in medieval England.

But hinder it they did. To understand how and why it is necessary to look at the way in which banking developed in medieval Italy, where there was the greatest concentration of urban wealth and liquid capital in Europe. Deposit banking grew out of money changing, the exchange of one currency for another. In the early thirteenth century the money changers began to form partnerships, accept time and demand deposits and make local payments from one customer to another by book transfers. Banking was soon combined with trade and credit extended to overseas customers. It was never difficult to pay interest on deposits from Italian nobles, clerics and businessmen who wished to share in the bankers' financial and commercial profits. The bankers simply made 'gifts' to their clients, usually in Florence at about 7–15 per cent annual rate of interest. There was no contract, so the banker was not obliged to pay the gift. If he did not, of course, his clients would soon go elsewhere. Lending was a different matter. Some way had to be found round the usury laws so that interest could be charged, legitimately, and that way was found by linking banking to exchange. As international trade developed there was an obvious need to move money around from one country to another. A merchant might have funds in Italy but need them, say, in Flanders, another merchant might find himself precisely in the opposite situation. The first would therefore lend the money to the second in Italy with the promise of repayment of an equivalent in Flanders in Flemish currency. From this basic transaction there developed by the fourteenth century the bill of exchange which involved four parties. First there was the remitter, the banker or merchant supplying the payee or beneficiary, with money in Italy (or elsewhere); secondly, there was the taker or drawer of the money; thirdly there was the agent of the remitter in a city abroad where the money was to be repaid; and fourthly there was the correspondent of the taker who was to pay the bill.

To see this in action we can take the widely quoted example from R. de Roover's *The Rise and Decline of the Medici Bank*.[6] On 20 July 1463 Bartolomeo Zorzi and Geronimo Michiel (the takers or drawers) took up a bill of exchange for 500 ducats from the Medici Company in Venice, the remitter. By the bill they agreed to repay the 500 ducats through their correspondents in London, Francesco Giorgio and Petro Morozino, at the rate of 47 sterlings (pennies) per ducat to the Medici's agent in London, Gherardo Caniziani, at usance, that is after a period allowed for the movement of bills between cities. In the case of Venice to London this was three months. Now this could have been a simple commercial transaction, with Zorzi and Michiel borrowing 500 ducats in Venice to finance their trading operations and repaying through their credit balances in London. They would be charged interest on the transaction, through the rate of exchange offered. In fact the ducat stood at 44 sterlings in London, so Zorzi and Michiel were paying back more than they borrowed. The money would then be transmitted back to the Medici in Venice by another bill of exchange. This was licit. The merchants argued and the theologians agreed that an exchange transaction was not a loan. Rather it was a commutation of monies or a buying and selling of foreign currency. A risk was also involved. The exchange rate might change against the remitter and there was a period of time in which the banker was 'deprived' of the use of his money. In fact the risks were minimal. The exchange rates were well known, and usually stood in favour of Italy. But the exchange between Zorzi and Michiel and the Medici Bank was not a commercial transaction but a straight loan at interest. When the usance of three months was up Zorzi and Michiel's agents in London refused to honour the bill. According to custom the payee (Caniziani) could then rewrite the bill, making it repayable by the taker to the remitter, by Zorzi and Michiel to the Medici. The bill's face value was 500 ducats or £97.18s.4d. at 47 sterlings to the ducat, and to this was added a 4s. handling charge. So a bill for £98.2s.4d. was sent back to Italy at 44 sterlings to the ducat, and Zorzi and Michiel had to repay 535 ducats in Venice. They repaid 35 more ducats than they borrowed and for the loan over six months they were charged an annual rate of interest of 14 per cent. This operation is known as Dry Exchange. The borrower was repaying the loan in the same currency, not abroad in a foreign currency. It was the standard way of making loans in Italy and was forced on the bankers by the usury laws.

The whole exchange operation was, to say the least, clumsy. To work properly it needed merchant bankers with substantial reserves of liquid capital, complicated book-keeping techniques and a network of companies with branches abroad in the principal cities of Western Europe. Only the Italians had such techniques, only Italian trade was based on long-range international exchange using agents or branches of their companies in many countries. Consequently banking was essentially an Italian monopoly in the Middle Ages. Englishmen had neither the extensive capital nor the accounting techniques, nor the pattern of trade to sustain banking operations. Nor were there even any money-changers from whom such bankers might possibly have developed. Private money-changing in England was prohibited. Merchants had to take foreign coins to the Royal Exchange at the Tower and the Royal Exchanger also had tables set up at Dover and other ports for the convenience of traders, soldiers, pilgrims and other travellers entering or leaving the country. The consequence was that although, as has been seen, English traders were able to use Italian bankers to transfer monies and raise short-term loans, there were no banking institutions in which surplus money could be invested and then used, by Englishmen, to finance trade more extensively or invest in other sectors of the economy. Thanks to the deposits of wealthy clients, the resources of the Medici Bank were several times larger than its invested capital. It used its money to extend its trading operations in general merchandise, alum and iron and to invest in the cloth and silk industries. In England surplus wealth went into land or gold and silver plate, and not productively into banks. It has been suggested that lack of capital was holding back some parts of the economy, shipping, mining, trade and even agriculture. It could be that in this way the Church's teaching on usury had quite a profound effect on the English economy in the Middle Ages.

Conclusion

During the 400 years which encompass the span of this book the English economy experienced considerable changes of fortune. Rapid population growth brought expansion in the later twelfth and thirteenth centuries. The area under cultivation was enlarged and farming organized to produce for the market as never before. Old towns grew, new ones were founded and wool exports boomed. But for substantial numbers of Englishmen the thirteenth century brought nothing but misery. Many peasants lived on the very edge of subsistence, burdened by increasingly heavy taxation and tied to the land by harsh manorial discipline which denied them personal freedom. Prosperity was enjoyed by the few, by the landlords and the merchants in the towns. Yet for many historians, dazzled by the glories of Salisbury Cathedral and Westminster Abbey, this has seemed the high point of the Middle Ages. By contrast, England from the 1380s to 1500 would seem at first sight a very unattractive place in which to have lived. Apart from the brief martial glories of Henry V's reign and until Edward IV and Henry VII restored stability, it was a politically embittered period. One king was deposed and murdered. His successor was threatened by a major rebellion and then, in the reign of the feeble, child-like Henry VI, government broke down. Quarrels were no longer settled in the law courts but by armed force. The Paston letters provide us with a picture – albeit a slightly exaggerated picture – of a countryside terrorized by the retainers of great lords. Eventually private quarrels became public and England was plunged into civil war. As if that was not enough, plague and other diseases were ever present. Small wonder that fifteenth century man was so obsessed with the good of his soul after death, for death was never far away.

Yet for those who survived or did not become involved in the political squabbles the fifteenth century had much to offer. For one thing, and most important of all, except in years of harvest failure there was enough to eat. There was enough land for families to grow all their own grain or it could be bought cheaply on a well-supplied market. The consumption of meat and dairy products also seems to have increased, a sure sign of a rising standard of living. More cattle were being kept by peasants and middle-class landlords alike. In Worcestershire over-stocking of the commons was becoming a problem in the fifteenth century, as manorial tenants built up flocks and herds and butchers themselves were attempting to step up supplies by increasing the amount of their own stock. The same was true in many other parts of the country and it would seem that diet generally improved in the later Middle Ages. Certainly contemporaries remarked on how well fed the English peasants were. Langland in *Piers Plowman* was shocked by their ample diet of ale, fish, bacon and other dishes whilst Chief Justice Fortescue wrote in the 1460s of the comfort and well-being of the English peasantry compared with the French.

Society, too, was much more mobile. In the countryside there were opportunities for men of ambition in all walks of life to improve their lot. The leasing of demesnes by the great landlords allowed knights, esquires, gentlemen, yeomen, even peasants to build up their own lands. For a peasant the breakdown of manorial control finally allowed the ambitious to participate freely in the land market. Almost every-where they can be seen enlarging their holdings and their houses. Wealthy peasants in Worcestershire, holding up to 60 acres or so, lived in houses with three, four or even more bays (rooms), a vast improve-ment on the one-room hovels of the poor. Indeed, men now built for comfort not for defence or mere shelter. Great lords tried to make their castles into homes rather than fortresses. The keep of Lord Cromwell's castle at Tattershall (Lincs) contains fine rooms with handsome fire-places, lit by wide windows. They give 'a remarkable impression of spaciousness, dignity and fine proportion' and were planned to be the home of a highly civilized people of noble birth.[1] Rich merchants, clothiers and craftsmen built themselves substantial and comfortable houses. The contract for the erection of a shop premises in Bucklers-bury in London in 1405 specifies that it was to have three storeys. The ground floor was to be a great shop 22ft 4in. by 18ft. The first storey contained a chamber and a parlour 11ft high, and the second two chambers 9ft high. Behind the house, over the great cellar a warehouse was to be built and over that a hall, 33ft by 20ft and 16ft high, with a bay window and two others. A gallery full of windows was to lead from the hall to the first-floor rooms over the shop. In addition there were to be a kitchen, buttery and pantry, making in all a comfortable dwelling for a citizen and carpenter of London.[2]

Such houses would be well furnished with benches, stools, chairs (although these were expensive) and tables and the bedrooms would have had joined beds. There might even have been imported carpets on the floors or tapestries on the walls. What there certainly would have been was a show of plate, of silver and gold. The Venetian ambassador coming to London in the late fifteenth century remarked on the extraordinary quality of the plate offered for sale in the 55 goldsmiths' shops in Cheapside. The court and the rich displayed it upon their cupboards to impress their friends or their betters. The wealthy – and even the not-so-wealthy – would also have been able to afford the luxury goods which came into the country in increasing quantities as the sea route to the Mediterranean opened up. In 1438–9 the Venetian galleys brought to London almonds, currents, dates, figs, oranges, pomegranates, raisins, sugar, cinnamon, green ginger, no less than $1,046\frac{1}{2}$ hundredweights of pepper, sweet wine and a host of other drugs and spices. The Lucchese firm of Felice da Fagnano and Company which traded in London in the 1440s imported rich damasks, satins, velvets and gold cloths and sold them to the royal wardrobe, to great lords like Suffolk and Fauconberg, to knights and esquires and to London mercers who resold them to their clients. The quality of life was better in the later Middle Ages simply because more goods were available at more moderate prices thanks to the development of international trade.

The population, or at least its upper ranks, was also better educated. It is difficult to quantify the extent of literacy. Sir Thomas More, writing in the early sixteenth century, thought that three out of every five people in the country could read. This seems rather unlikely. It might have been true in London where it has been estimated that 40 per cent of households could read Latin, but we have no way of knowing how many peasants could read and write. There is no doubt that merchants and middle-class landowners were interested in educating their sons. The number of grammar schools was expanding in the fifteenth century. Some were attached to religious foundations, to collegiate churches and chantries. The chantry priest often had to sing masses for the benefactor's soul and to keep a school. Gilds also employed chantry priests for this purpose or maintained separate grammar schools. Much training was also carried out in households. The sons of the nobility and the gentry would be sent to a great household where they would be taught not only the social graces but reading and writing. Merchants and craftsmen would teach their apprentices: indeed it was vital for any merchant to be able to reckon up and read letters perhaps sent to him from abroad. Mere chance has preserved the Cely letters, the correspondence of a wool-exporting family firm in the late fifteenth century. Their business could not have been conducted without a regular flow of letters between London and Calais or the Low Countries and to their middleman dealer, William Midwinter, in the Cotswolds. Many other merchants must have been in the same position. The written word would have been vital to them.

Nor was higher education neglected. Six new colleges were founded at Oxford and nine at Cambridge between the middle of the fourteenth century and the Reformation. The Schools at the universities taught a heavy diet of theology and philosophy and that was not what many young men wanted. Rather they were taught in the informal schools which existed alongside the regular faculties. Here they learnt to write letters in Latin and French, the practices of conveyancing and the holding of courts and other legal matters. This was essential training for any prospective landowner or manager who had to be conversant with all the niceties of the law. Such training might also be had at the Inns of Court. But education was not simply for vocational purposes. There is increasing evidence of the ownership and presumably the readership of books. Noblemen, knights and gentlemen were building up small collections. Many of the volumes were devotional works but the laity was also interested in history, especially in the Trojan legend, the *Brut* chronicle and the various deeds of kings, and in genealogy and topography. Legends like Malory's *Le Morte d'Arthur* were popular as was the poet Lydgate's *Fall of Princes*. Books were borrowed and lent readily so that although collections were small the reader had access to a wider range of material than would otherwise have been possible. The level of literacy and the reading of books must not be exaggerated. Merchants seem to have been little interested in books and English as a written language was still in its formative stages. The town chronicles of the fifteenth century written in the vernacular and kept by local citizens compare very unfavourably with the great Latin chronicles written by the monks in the twelfth and thirteenth centuries.

It is easy to be carried away by the virtues of the fifteenth century and to forget that economic well-being for the majority of the population still depended on the delicate balance between land and people. There had been no real economic growth, no major increase in productivity as a result of the introduction of new techniques or methods of production. The urban, industrial and commercial sectors of the economy remained small compared with the agrarian. Wealth, social status and political power all depended on the ownership of land which remained the chief target for investment to the detriment of trade and industry. True, there had been some improvements in agriculture with the introduction of convertible husbandry. How widely this system of farming was practised is not known, but in any case it was suited to an age when there was sufficient general wealth to buy the increased output of meat and dairy products which were more expensive than cereals. As the population rose again in the sixteenth century the emphasis swung back to grain, perhaps halting the rapid spread of these new methods.[3] Population rise also meant that pressure on land grew again. Only those with security of tenure, holding by freehold or long leasehold would be able to face the harsh conditions of the sixteenth century with any certainty that they would be able to hold on to their fifteenth-century acquisitions.

In the other sectors of the economy the expansion of the cloth industry was to be welcomed since it spread more wealth around the countryside, but it was the only industry of any size. No large-scale mining or metal-working complexes emerged to rival those in other areas in Europe. There seemed to be a shortage of English shipping and the most profitable markets for English exports were served by alien merchants. Indeed, compared not only with modern industrialized countries but also in relation to the standards of the 'developed' countries of that time – Italy, the Low Countries and South Germany – England was an underdeveloped country. It had not broken out of the medieval straitjacket. The implications of that for the sixteenth century, when population expanded again, were considerable. Would the country be able to produce enough food or earn enough to import substantial quantities of grain to feed everyone adequately? Could industry and trade absorb the surplus population? Unless there were substantial changes in the structure and workings of the economy then the answer to both questions would be 'No'.

Notes

1. INTRODUCTION: SETTLEMENT AND SOCIETY

1 For population totals see below, Chapter 2 *passim*.
2 See below, pp. 14–17.
3 See below, p. 17.
4 H. L. Gray, *English Field Systems* (Cambridge, Mass., 1915).
5 See below, p. 40ff.
6 See below, pp. 20–1.
7 E. Miller, *The Abbey and Bishopric of Ely* (Cambridge, 1951), pp. 89–90.
8 See below, p. 165ff.
9 A. R. Bridbury, 'Sixteenth-Century Farming', *Economic History Review* 2nd series, xxvii, 1974, p. 545.
10 Cited by J. Z. Titow, *Winchester Yields* (Cambridge, 1972), p. 149.
11 M. M. Postan, 'The Chronology of Labour Services', *Transactions of the Royal Historical Society* 4th series, xx, 1937.

2. PATTERNS OF DEMAND

1 See above, pp. 32–6.
2 See below, pp. 11–13.
3 See below, p. 174ff.
4 See below, pp. 236, 349.
5 See below, p. 319.
6 J. Hatcher, *Plague, Population and the English Economy 1348–1530* (London, 1977) p. 68.
7 See below, pp. 57–80.
8 J. Z. Titow, *English Rural Society 1200–1350* (London, 1969), introduction, *passim*.
9 G. C. Homans, *English Villagers of the Thirteenth Century* (Cambridge, Mass., 1942), pp. 209–12; H. E. Hallam, 'Some Thirteenth-Century Censuses', *Economic History Review* 2nd series, x, 1957–8, pp. 340, 352–3.
10 J. Z. Titow, *English Rural Society 1200–1350*, op. cit., p. 85.

11 H. E. Hallam, op. cit., p. 340.

12 See below, p. 62ff.

13 H. E. Hallam, op. cit., p. 361.

14 See below, pp. 110–11.

15 See below, pp. 78–9.

16 J. D. Shrewsbury, *The History of Bubonic Plague in England* (Cambridge, 1970).

17 See below, pp. 248–9.

18 J. Hatcher, op. cit., particularly pp. 17–19, 57–8.

19 Replacement rates are usually calculated from mothers but can only be calculated from fathers in the Middle Ages because of the nature of the evidence.

20 Ibid., p. 61.

21 A wapentake was the administrative subdivision of the county in the Danelaw areas

22 See below, Chapter 3 *passim*.

23 See below, p. 297ff.

24 P. D. A. Harvey, 'The English Inflation 1180–1220', *Past and Present*, 61, 1973.

25 See below, pp. 297ff., 329–30.

3. THE OVERCROWDED ISLAND

1 See above, p. 15.

2 For previous clearing from the forest see above, pp. 11–12.

3 See above, p. 11.

4 The Hundred, and in the Danelaw the wapentake, were the administrative subdivisions of the county.

5 See above, pp. 11–12.

6 Vaccaries were for cattle, bercaries for sheep.

7 See above, p. 24.

8 See above, p. 23.

9 It was also due to a rise in those rents themselves; see below, p. 110.

10 See above, pp. 72, 76.

11 See below, pp. 109–10.

12 For alternative methods of exploiting estates see above, p. 40ff.

13 F. R. H. Du Boulay, *The Lordship of Canterbury* (London, 1966), p. 204.

14 See above, pp. 72, 76.

15 P. D. A. Harvey, 'The Pipe Rolls and the Adoption of Demesne Farming in England', *Economic History Review* 2nd series, xxvii, 1974, p. 353.

16 These new procedures of the later twelfth century tended to protect tenants from arbitrary dispossession by lords.

17 See above, pp. 38–9.

18 See above, p. 37.
19 See above, pp. 13–14.
20 See above, pp. 18–19.
21 See above, p. 22ff.
22 See above, p. 17.
23 See below, p. 97.
24 See below, p. 97.
25 See below, p. 323ff.
26 See above, p. 75.
27 See below, pp. 165–6.
28 See above, p. 20.
29 See below, p. 122.
30 E. A. Kosminsky, *Studies in the Agrarian History of England in the Thirteenth Century* (Blackwell, Oxford, 1956), Chapter 3 and especially p. 194.
31 See above, p. 25.
32 See above, p. 32ff.
33 See above, p. 81 for a fuller definition of capital formation.
34 See above, p. 34.
35 Payments.
36 See below, pp. 341–2.
37 i.e. by other than military service.
38 For Professor Postan's argument see M. M. Postan (ed.), *Cambridge Economic History of Europe*, vol. i, *The Agrarian Life of the Middle Ages* (2nd edn., Cambridge, 1966), pp. 593–5.
39 See below, pp. 222–3.
40 E. A. Kosminsky, op. cit., p. 277.
41 See above, p. 88, n. 16.
42 F. R. H. Du Boulay, op. cit., p. 134
43 See above, pp. 49–50.
44 See above, pp. 51–2.
45 See above, Table 2.2, p. 71.
46 See above, p. 16.
47 R. H. Hilton, *A Medieval Society: the West Midlands at the End of the Thirteenth Century* (London, 1966), pp. 122–3.
48 J. Z. Titow, *English Rural Society 1200–1350*, op. cit., pp. 78–96.
49 See below, p. 159.
50 i.e. from year to year, the lease being terminable at the will of the lord.

4. THE GROWTH OF THE MARKET

1 For further discussion of internal dissension at London and Lincoln, and its causes, see below, pp. 145–6.

2 That did not make him free of the town. This right was reserved to burgesses or gildsmen; see below, p. 129.
3 These matters, and the motives behind them, are discussed more fully below, pp. 147–8.
4 G. Williams, *Medieval London: from Commune to Capital* (London, 1970), p. 2.
5 A league or three miles.
6 See below, p. 148, for a fuller discussion of this problem and its consequences.
7 See below, p. 171.
8 There were also other, more selfish economic motives in the later thirteenth century; see below, p. 158.
9 See below, pp. 158–9.

5. SUPPLYING THE MARKET

1 See below, p. 271
2 E. M. Carus-Wilson, 'An Industrial Revolution of the Thirteenth Century', *Economic History Review* 1st series, xi, 1941.
3 See above, p. 148.
4 See below, p. 166.
5 See below, p. 168.

6. TOWARDS A CRISIS

1 E. Miller, 'War, Taxation and the English Economy in the Late Thirteenth and Early Fourteenth Centuries', in J. M. Winter (ed.), *War and Economic Development* (Cambridge, 1975), p. 22.
2 See below, p. 214.
3 See below, p. 192.
4 See below, p. 214.
5 Full accounts are given in T. H. Lloyd, *The English Wool Trade in the Middle Ages* (Cambridge, 1977); E. Power, *The Wool Trade in English Medieval History* (Oxford, 1941); E. B. and M. M. Fryde, 'Public Credit, with Special Reference to North West Europe', in *The Cambridge Economic History of Europe* vol. iii, eds. M. M. Postan, E. E. Rich and E. Miller (Cambridge, 1963).
6 There was also a problem regarding the overvaluation of the Florentine gold coins for which they sold their wool in the Low Countries. The wool merchants alleged that these coins were overvalued by a third in terms of sterling silver and that this was detrimental to their trade. The problem was solved by the issue of an English gold coinage between 1344 and 1346; see above, p. 75.

7. CRISIS AND CHANGE IN THE AGRARIAN ECONOMY

1 P. Ziegler, *The Black Death* (Penguin, 1970), p. 122.

2 M. M. Postan, 'The Costs of the Hundred Years' War', *Past and Present*, 27, 1964.

3 See in particular M. M. Postan, 'The Fifteenth Century', *Economic History Review* 1st series, ix, 1938.

4 J. A. Raftis, *The Estates of Ramsey Abbey* (Toronto, Pontifical Institute 1957), p. 256.

5 See above, p. 78.

6 See below, pp. 228–9 for the economics of sheep farming.

7 See below, p. 243ff.

8 For copyhold, see below, p. 240.

9 This was a general shift in wealth, consequent partly upon population movements. It was possible that those who remained in the Midlands prospered.

10 The increased production of meat may also be an indication of rising standards of living; see below, p. 346.

11 A recent article has shown that improved yields on the Winchester demesnes in the second half of the fourteenth century came on manors with the highest ratio of livestock to arable; D. L. Farmer, 'Grain Yields on the Winchester Manors in the Later Middle Ages', *Economic History Review* 2nd series, xxx, 1977.

12 A. R. Bridbury, *Economic Growth: England in the Later Middle Ages* (London, 1962), p. 92.

13 See above, pp. 234–5.

14 A plough in which the mould board may be shifted from one side to the other at the end of each furrow so that the furrow-slice is always thrown the same way.

15 For modern yields see above, p. 36.

16 E. Searle, *Lordship and Community. Battle Abbey and its Banlieu, 1066–1538* (Toronto, Pontifical Institute 1974), p. 277.

17 C. Dyer, 'A Small Landowner in the Fifteenth Century', *Midland History* i, 1972, p. 6; M. Beresford and J. G. Hurst, *Deserted Medieval Villages* (Lutterworth, 1972), p. 16; R. Hilton, *The Economic Development of Some Leicestershire Estates in the Fourteenth and Fifteenth Centuries* (Oxford, 1947), pp. 65–6; I. Kershaw, *Bolton Priory Rentals and Ministers' Accounts, 1473–1539*, Yorkshire Archaeological Society Record, Series cxxii, 1970, p. xviii.

8. FREEDOM VERSUS RESTRICTION: TOWN AND COUNTRYSIDE IN THE LATER MIDDLE AGES

1 A. R. Bridbury, *Economic Growth: England in the Later Middle Ages* (London, 1962).

2 See below, p. 283ff.
3 What follows is based on C. Phythian-Adams, 'Coventry and the Problem of Urban Decay in the Late Middle Ages' (unpublished paper submitted to the 1971 Urban History Conference). Dr Phythian-Adams's views on Coventry have been expressed in general in *Towns in Societies*, ed. P. Abrams and E. A. Wrigley (Cambridge, 1978) and appear in particular in his *Desolation of a City* (Cambridge, 1979).
4 H. Heaton, *The Yorkshire Woollen and Worsted Industries* (Oxford, 1920); E. Miller, *Victoria County of Yorkshire: City of York* (London, 1961), p. 87.
5 The aulnager collected a tax on cloth produced for sale.
6 See below, pp. 300–1.
7 P. Heath, 'North Sea Fishing in the Fifteenth Century: the Scarborough Fleet', *Northern History* iii, pp. 57–66.
8 See above, pp. 166–7.
9 See above, pp. 166–7.
10 J. Hatcher, *English Tin Production and Trade before 1550* (Oxford, 1973), pp. 68–75.
11 See above, p. 193.
12 See above, p. 168.
13 The best general account of the development of the European iron industry in the later Middle Ages, on which what follows is based, is given in N. Pounds, *An Economic History of Medieval Europe* (London, 1974) p. 320ff.
14 Since this chapter was written I. Blanchard has shown that lead production actually rose in the fifteenth century. The article also contains a valuable study of labour productivity in the mining industry; 'Labour Productivity and Work Psychology in the English Mining Industry, 1400–1600', *Economic History Review* 2nd series, xxxi, 1978.

9. ENGLISH TRADE IN THE LATE MIDDLE AGES: THE TRIUMPH OF THE ENGLISH?

1 See below, p. 292ff.
2 H. L. Gray, 'English Foreign Trade from 1446 to 1482', in E. Power and M. M. Postan, eds., *Studies in English Trade in the Fifteenth Century* (London, 1933) pp. 6–7, 12–13.
3 T. H. Lloyd, *The Movement of Wool Prices in Medieval England* (*Economic History Review Supplement* no. 6, Cambridge, 1973).
4 See above, p. 74ff and below, p. 330.
5 For the importance of credit, see below, pp. 303ff.
6 See below, p. 303.
7 A rebellion of the lowest class of day labourers which caused three years of economic chaos in Florence.
8 T. H. Lloyd, op. cit., pp. 38–9.

9 See E. M. Carus-Wilson, *Medieval Merchant Adventurers* (2nd edn London, 1967) p. 250, n. 2.
10 See above, pp. 151–2.
11 For a fuller discussion of exchange transactions, see below, pp. 342–4.
12 That is, £Flemish, shillings and groats.
13 Values were not given in the customs accounts for wool and wine; see above, pp. 292–3.
14 Based on calculations in my unpublished Oxford B.Litt. thesis, 'Alien Merchants in England in the Reign of Henry VI, 1422–61'.
15 H. L. Gray, op. cit., pp. 36–8.
16 Calculated from the export figures in E. M. Carus-Wilson and O. Coleman, *England's Export Trade 1275–1547* (Oxford, 1963).
17 M. M. Postan, 'The Economic and Political Relations of England and the Hanse', in E. Power and M. M. Postan, op. cit., pp. 91–154.
18 *Libelle of Englyshe Polycye*, ed. Sir G. Warner (Oxford, 1926), line 398.
19 The Views of Hosts were the records kept by English merchants of the trade of alien merchants put in their charge by virtue of the Hosting Statute of 1439–40.
20 See above, pp. 283–4.

10. ECONOMIC IDEAS

1 That is, a tax of so much per head on the population over the age of 14.
2 B. Tierney, *Medieval Poor Law* (California, 1959), pp. 80–1; see also J. Gilchrist, *The Church and Economic Activity in the Middle Ages* (London, 1969), pp. 78–81.
3 See above, pp. 138, 265.
4 See above, p. 106.
5 M. Mate, 'The Indebtedness of Canterbury Cathedral Priory, 1215–95', *Economic History Review* 2nd series, xxvi, 1973, pp. 183–197.
6 R. de Roover, *The Rise and Decline of the Medici Bank* (New York, 1966), pp. 111–13.

CONCLUSION

1 J. Evans, *English Art 1307–1461* (Oxford, 1949), pp. 128–9, cited in E. Jacob, *The Fifteenth Century* (Oxford, 1961), pp. 651–2.
2 Quoted in E. Jacob, op. cit., pp. 653–4.
3 This problem is discussed fully by A. R. Bridbury, 'Sixteenth-Century Farming', op. cit.

Bibliography

Abbreviations

A.H.R.   Agricultural History Review
E.H.R.   English Historical Review
Ec.H.R.   Economic History Review
P. and P.   Past and Present
T.R.H.S.   Transactions of the Royal Historical Society
U.B.H.J.   University of Birmingham Historical Journal

GENERAL WORKS

R. BUTLIN and R. A. DODGSHON (eds.), An Historical Geography of England and
    Wales (London, 1978)
The Cambridge Economic History of Europe: vol. i., M. M. Postan (ed.), The Agrarian
    Life of the Middle Ages (2nd edn, Cambridge, 1966); vol. ii, M. M. Postan
    and E. E. Rich (eds.), Trade and Industry in the Middle Ages (Cambridge,
    1952); vol. iii, M. M. Postan, E. E. Rich and E. Miller (eds.), Economic
    Organization and Policies in the Middle Ages (Cambridge, 1963)
C. CIPOLLA, Before the Industrial Revolution. European Society and Economy
    1000—1700 (London, 1976)
SIR J. CLAPHAM, A Concise Economic History of Great Britain from the Earliest Times to
    1700 (Cambridge, 1949)
H. C. DARBY (ed.) A New Historical Geography of England (Cambridge, 1973)
J. HATCHER and E. MILLER, Medieval England: Rural Society and Economic Changes
    1086–1348 (London, 1978)
E. KING, England 1175—1425 (London, 1979)
E. LIPSON, An Economic History of England, vol. i, The Middle Ages (12th edn,
    London, 1959)
C. PLATT, Medieval England, A Social History and Archaeological from the Conquest
    to 1600 A.D. (London, 1978)
M. M. POSTAN, The Medieval Economy and Society (London, 1972)

357

1. INTRODUCTION: SETTLEMENT AND SOCIETY

W. O. AULT, *Open-field farming in England* (London, 1972)

—— By-laws of gleaning and problems of harvest, *Ec.H.R.* 2nd series, xiv, 1961–2

A. H. BAKER, Open fields and partible inheritance on a Kent manor, *Ec.H.R.* 2nd series, xvii, 1964–5

A. H. BAKER and R. BUTLIN (eds.), *Studies of Field Systems in the British Isles* (Cambridge, 1973)

G. S. BARROW, Northern English society in the twelfth and thirteenth centuries, *Northern History*, iv, 1969

M. L. BAZELEY, The extent of the English forest in the thirteenth century, *T.R.H.S.* 4th series, iv, 1921

M. BERESFORD, Ridge and furrow in the open fields, *Ec.H.R.* 2nd series, i, 1948–9

T. A. M. BISHOP, Assarting and the growth of the open fields, *Ec.H.R.* 1st series, vi, 1935–6

—— The rotation of crops at Westerham 1297–1350, *Ec.H.R.* 1st series, ix, 1938–9

A. R. BRIDBURY, The farming out of manors, *Ec.H.R.* 2nd series, xxxi, 1978

L. M. CANTOR, Medieval parks in Leicestershire, *Transactions of the Leicestershire Archaeological Society*, xlvi, 1971

H. C. DARBY, *The Medieval Fenland* (Cambridge, 1940)

B. DODWELL, Holdings and inheritance in medieval East Anglia, *Ec.H.R.* 2nd series, xx, 1967, 1–18

D. C. DOUGLAS, *The Social Structure of Medieval East Anglia* (Oxford, 1927)

F. R. H. DU BOULAY, *The Lordship of Canterbury* (London, 1966)

H. P. R. FINBERG, *Tavistock Abbey* (Cambridge, 1951)

H. L. GRAY, *English Field Systems* (Cambridge, Mass., 1915)

W. GREENWELL (ed.), *The Boldon Buke*, Surtees Society, xxv, 1852

J. GODBER, *The History of Bedfordshire 1066–1888* (Bedfordshire County Council, 1969)

W. HALE (ed.), *The Domesday of St Paul's*, Camden Society, 1858

H. HALLAM, *Settlement and Society: a Study of the Early Agrarian History of South Lincolnshire* (Cambridge, 1965)

R. H. HILTON, Freedom and villeinage in England, *P. and P.*, 31, 1965

—— *A Medieval Society: the West Midlands at the End of the Thirteenth Century* (London, 1966)

G. C. HOMANS, Partible inheritance of villagers' holdings, *Ec.H.R.* 1st series, viii, 1937–8

—— The rural sociology of medieval England, *P. and P.*, 4, 1953

—— The Frisians in East Anglia, *Ec.H.R.* 2nd series, x, 1957–8

P. HYAMS, Proof of villein status in the Common Law, *E.H.R.*, lxxxix, 1974

J. JOLIFFE, Northumbrian institutions, *E.H.R.*, xli, 1926

E. KERRIDGE, Ridge and furrow, *Ec.H.R.* 2nd series, iv, 1951–2

E. KOSMINSKY, *Studies in the Agrarian History of England in the Thirteenth Century* (Oxford, 1959)

B. A. LEES (ed.), *Records of the Templars in England. The Inquest of 1185* (London, 1935)

R. V. LENNARD, The demesnes of Glastonbury Abbey in the eleventh and twelfth centuries, *Ec.H.R.* 2nd series, vii, 1955–6

—— *Rural England, 1086–1135* (Oxford, 1959)

F. W. MAITLAND, *Domesday Book and Beyond* (Cambridge, 1907)

E. MILLER, *The Abbey and Bishopric of Ely* (Cambridge, 1951)

—— England in the twelfth and thirteenth centuries–an economic contrast? *Ec.H.R.* 2nd series, xxiv, 1971

—— The farming of manors and direct management, *Ec.H.R.* 2nd series, xxvi, 1973

C. S. and C. S. ORWIN, *The Open Fields* (2nd edn, Oxford, 1967)

M. M. POSTAN, The chronology of labour services, *T.R.H.S.* 4th series, xx, 1937

—— The Glastonbury estates in the twelfth century, *Ec.H.R.* 2nd series, v, 1952–3; ibid., ix, 1956–7

M. R. POSTGATE, The field systems of Breckland, *A.H.R.*, 10, 1962

J. A. RAFTIS, Social structures in five East Midland villages, *Ec.H.R.* 2nd series, xxvi, 1973

R. R. RAWSON, The open fields in Flintshire, Devon and Cornwall, *Ec.H.R.* 2nd series, vi, 1953–4

C. G. REED and T. L. ANDERSON, An economic explanation of English agricultural organization in the twelfth and thirteenth centuries, *Ec.H.R.* 2nd series, xxvi, 1973

E. J. RUSSELL, *The World of the Soil* (London, 1957)

F. M. STENTON, *Types of Manorial Structure in the Northern Danelaw* (Oxford, 1910)

—— *Documents Illustrative of the Social and Economic History of the Northern Danelaw* (London, 1920)

J. Z. TITOW, *Winchester Yields. A Study in Medieval Agricultural Productivity* (Cambridge, 1972)

R. TROW SMITH, *A History of British Livestock Husbandry to 1700* (London, 1957)

2. PATTERNS OF DEMAND

A. R. H. BAKER, Evidence in the 'Nonarum Inquisitiones' of contracting arable lands in England during the early fourteenth century, *Ec.H.R.* 2nd series, xix, 1966

J. M. W. BEAN, Plague, population and economic decline, *Ec.H.R.* 2nd series, xv, 1962

W. BEVERIDGE, Wages on the Winchester manors in the manorial era, *Ec.H.R.* 1st series, vii, 1936–7

—— Westminster wages, *Ec.H.R.* 2nd series, viii, 1955–6

A. R. BRIDBURY, The Black Death, *Ec.H.R.* 2nd series, xxvi, 1973

C. CIPOLLA, Currency depreciation in medieval Europe, *Ec.H.R.* 2nd series, xv, 1962–3

SIR J. CRAIG, *The Mint* (Cambridge, 1953)

J. DAY, The great bullion famine of the fifteenth century, *P. and P.*, 79, 1978

D. L. FARMER, Some price fluctuations in Angevin England, *Ec.H.R.* 2nd series, ix, 1956–7

—— Some grain price movements in thirteenth-century England, *Ec.H.R.* 2nd series, x, 1957–8

—— Some livestock price movements in thirteenth-century England, *Ec.H.R.* 2nd series, xxii, 1969

A. FEAVERYEAR, *The Pound Sterling* (2nd edn, Oxford, 1963)

H. HALLAM, Some thirteenth-century censuses, *Ec.H.R.* 2nd series, x, 1957–8

—— Population density in the medieval fenlands, *Ec.H.R.* 2nd series, xiv, 1961–2

B. HARVEY, The population trend in England, 1300–1348, *T.R.H.S.* 5th series, 16, 1966

P. D. A. HARVEY, The English inflation of 1180–1220, *P. and P.*, 61, 1973

S. HARVEY, The knight and the knight's fee, *P. and P.*, 49, 1970

J. HATCHER, *Plague, Population and the English Economy, 1348–1530* (London, 1977)

K. HELLEINER, 'The population of Europe from the Black Death to the eve of the Vital Revolution' in E. E. Rich and C. H. Wilson (eds.), *The Cambridge Economic History of Europe*, vol. iv (Cambridge, 1967)

W. G. HOSKINS, 'The population of Wigston Magna' in *Provincial England* (London, 1963)

I. KERSHAW, The great famine and agrarian crisis in England 1315–22, *P. and P.*, 59, 1973

J. T. KRAUSE, The medieval household – large or small? *Ec.H.R.* 2nd series, ix, 1956–7

A. LEVETT, 'The Black Death on the St Alban's manors' in H. Cam, M. Coate and L. S. Sutherland (eds.), *Studies in Manorial History* (Oxford, 1938)

A. LEVETT and A. BALLARD, *The Black Death on the Estates of the See of Winchester* (Oxford, 1916)

H. S. LUCAS, The great European famine of 1315–17, *Speculum*, v, 1930

M. MATE, High prices in the early fourteenth century – causes and consequences, *Ec.H.R.* 2nd series, xxviii, 1975

N. MAYHEW, Numismatic evidence of falling prices in the fourteenth century, *Ec.H.R.* 2nd series, xxvii, 1974

J. H. MUNRO, *Wool, Cloth and Gold: the Struggle for Bullion in the Anglo-Burgundian Trade 1340–1478* (Toronto, 1973)

E. H. PHELPHS BROWN and S. V. HOPKINS, Seven centuries of building wages, *Economica*, xxii, 1955

—— Seven centuries of the prices of consumables compared with builders' wage rates, *Economica*, xxiii, 1956

M. M. POSTAN, The rise of a money economy, *Ec.H.R.* 1st series, xiv, 1944

—— Evidence of declining population in the later Middle Ages, *Ec.H.R.* 2nd series, ii, 1949–50

M. M. POSTAN and J. Z. TITOW, Heriots and prices on Winchester manors, *Ec.H.R.* 2nd series xi, 1958–9

M. PRESTWICH, Edward I's monetary policies and their consequences, *Ec.H.R.* 2nd series, xxii, 1969

T. F. REDDAWAY, The king's mint and exchange in London, 1343–1543, *E.H.R.*, lxxxii, 1967

W. ROBINSON, Money, population and economic change in later medieval Europe, *Ec.H.R.* 2nd series, xii, 1959–60

J. C. RUSSELL, *British Medieval Population* (Albuquerque, 1948)

—— The effects of pestilence and plague, 1315–85, *Comparative Studies in Society and History*, 8, 1965–6

J. THOROLD ROGERS, *Six Centuries of Work and Wages* (London, 1884)

—— *A History of Agriculture and Prices in England*, 7 vols. (Oxford, 1866–1902)

S. THRUPP, The problem of replacement rates in late medieval English population, *Ec.H.R.* 2nd series, xviii, 1965

—— Plague effects in medieval Europe, *Comparative Studies in Society and History*, 8, 1965–6

J. Z. TITOW, Some evidence of the thirteenth-century population increase, *Ec.H.R.* 2nd series, xiv, 1961–2

—— *English Rural Society 1200–1350* (London, 1969)

A. WATSON, Back to gold – and silver, *Ec.H.R.* 2nd series, xx, 1967

3. THE OVERCROWDED ISLAND

M. BAZELEY, The extent of the English forest in the thirteenth century, *T.R.H.S.* 4th series, iv, 1921

J. BIRRELL, Peasant craftsmen in the medieval forest, *A.H.R.*, 17, 1969

C. BROOKE and M. M. POSTAN (eds.), *Carte Nativorum: a Peterborough Abbey Cartulary of the Fourteenth Century*, Northamptonshire Record Society, xx, 1960

L. M. CANTOR, Medieval parks in Leicestershire, *Transactions of the Leicestershire Archaeological Society*, xlvi, 1971

P. COSS, Sir Geoffrey de Langley and the crisis of the knightly class in thirteenth-century England, *P. and P.*, 68, 1975

E. B. DE WINDT, *Land and People in Holywell-cum-Needingworth* (Toronto, 1972)

N. DENHOLM YOUNG, *Seignorial Administration in England* (Oxford, 1937)

B. DODWELL, The free tenantry of the Hundred Rolls, *Ec.H.R.* 1st series, xiv, 1944

R. A. DONKIN, Cistercian sheep farming and wool sales in the thirteenth century, *A.H.R.*, vi, 1958

——Settlement and depopulation on Cistercian estates during the twelfth and thirteenth centuries, *Bulletin of the Institute of Historical Research*, xxxiii, 1960

—— Cattle on the estates of medieval Cistercian monasteries in England and Wales, *Ec.H.R.* 2nd series, xv, 1962–3

J. S. DREW, The manorial accounts of St Swithun's Priory, Winchester, *E.H.R.*, lxii, 1947

F. R. H. DU BOULAY, *The Lordship of Canterbury* (London, 1966)

H. P. R. FINBERG, *Tavistock Abbey* (Cambridge, 1951)

H. HALLAM, Some thirteenth-century censuses, *Ec.H.R.* 2nd series, x, 1957–8

—— Population density in the medieval fenlands, *Ec.H.R.* 2nd series, xiv, 1961–2

——*Settlement and Society: a Study of the Early Agrarian History of South Lincolnshire* (Cambridge, 1965)

J. HARLAND (ed.), *The De Lacy Inquisitions of 1311*, Chetham Society, lxxiv, 1868

J. B. HARLEY, Population trends and agricultural developments from the Warwickshire Hundred Rolls of 1279, *Ec.H.R.* 2nd series, xi, 1958–9

B. HARVEY, The population trend in England, 1300–1348, *T.R.H.S.* 5th series, 16, 1966

P. D. A. HARVEY, *A Medieval Oxfordshire Village: Cuxham 1240–1400* (Oxford, 1965)

—— The Pipe Rolls and the adoption of demesne farming in England, *Ec.H.R.* 2nd series, xxvii, 1974

R. H. HILTON, Peasant movements in England before 1381, *Ec.H.R.* 2nd series, ii, 1949–50

—— Freedom and villeinage in England, *P. and P.*, 31, 1965

—— *A Medieval Society: the West Midlands at the End of the Thirteenth Century* (London, 1966)

—— 'Rent and capital formation in feudal society' in *The English Peasantry in the Later Middle Ages* (Oxford, 1975)

G. HOMANS, *English Villagers in the Thirteenth Century* (New York, 1960)

W. G. HOSKINS, 'The making of the agrarian landscape' in W. G. Hoskins and H. P. R. Finberg, *Devonshire Studies* (London, 1952)

—— 'Wigston Magna: the medieval manor, 1066–1509' in *The Midland Peasant* (London, 1957)

P. HYAMS, The origins of a peasant land market in medieval England, *Ec.H.R.* 2nd series, xxiii, 1970

I. KERSHAW, *Bolton Priory: the Economy of a Northern Monastery, 1286–1325* (Oxford, 1973)

E. KING, Large and small landowners in thirteenth-century England. The case of Peterborough Abbey, *P. and P.*, 43, 1965

—— *Peterborough Abbey 1086–1310: a Study in the Land Market* (Cambridge, 1973)

T. H. LLOYD, *The English Wool Trade in the Middle Ages* (Cambridge, 1977)

P. A. LYONS (ed.), *Compotii of Henry de Lacy, Earl of Lincoln*, Chetham Society, cxii, 1886

M. MATE, The indebtedness of Canterbury Cathedral Priory, *Ec.H.R.* 2nd series, xxvi, 1973

A. MAY, An index of thirteenth-century peasant impoverishment – manor court fines, *Ec.H.R.* 2nd series, xxvi, 1973

L. M. MIDGLEY (ed.), *Ministers' Accounts of the Earldom of Cornwall, 1296–7*, Camden Society 3rd series, lxvi, 1942

E. MILLER, *The Abbey and Bishopric of Ely* (Cambridge, 1951)

—— The English economy in the thirteenth century, *P. and P.*, 28, 1964

—— England in the twelfth and thirteenth centuries – an economic contrast?, *Ec.H.R.* 2nd series, xxiv, 1971

—— Farming in Northern England during the twelfth and thirteenth centuries, *Northern History*, xi, 1975

M. MORGAN, *The English Lands of the Abbey of Bec* (Oxford, 1946)

D. OSCHINSKY, *Walter of Henley and Other Treatises on Estate Management and Accounting* (Oxford, 1971)

F. M. PAGE, *The Estates of Crowland Abbey* (Cambridge, 1934)

—— *Wellingborough Manorial Accounts 1258–1323*, Northamptonshire Record Society, viii, 1936

M. M. POSTAN, The chronology of labour services, *T.R.H.S.* 4th series, xx, 1937

—— Village livestock in the thirteenth century, *Ec.H.R.* 2nd series, xv, 1962–3

—— 'Medieval agrarian society in its prime: England' in *Cambridge Economic History of Europe*, vol. iii (2nd edn, Cambridge, 1966)

—— Investment in medieval agriculture, *Journal of Economic History*, xxvii, 1967

M. M. POSTAN and J. Z. TITOW, Heriots and prices on Winchester manors, *Ec.H.R.* 2nd series, xi, 1958–9

E. POWER, *The Wool Trade in English Medieval History* (Oxford, 1941)

S. RABAN, *The Estates of Thorney and Crowland. A Study in Medieval Monastic Land Tenure* (Cambridge, 1977)

J. A. RAFTIS, *The Estates of Ramsey Abbey* (Toronto, 1957)

—— *Tenure and Mobility. Studies in the Social History of the Medieval English Village* (Toronto, 1964)

B. K. ROBERTS, Medieval colonization in the Forest of Arden, *A.H.R.*, 16, 1968

E. SEARLE, *Lordship and Community: Battle Abbey and Its Banlieu, 1066–1538* (Toronto, 1974)

R. A. L. SMITH, *Canterbury Cathedral Priory: a Study in Monastic Administration* (Cambridge, 1943)

—— 'The central financial system of Christ Church, Canterbury' in *Collected Papers* (London, 1947)

E. STONE, Profit and loss accountancy at Norwich Cathedral Priory, *T.R.H.S.* 5th series, 12, 1962

J. Z. TITOW, *English Rural Society 1200–1350* (London, 1969)

—— *Winchester Yields. A Study in Medieval Agricultural Productivity* (Cambridge, 1972)

—— Some differences between manors and their effects on the condition of the peasantry in the thirteenth century, *A.H.R.*, x, 1962

G. H. TUPLING, *The Economic History of Rossendale*, Chetham Society new series, lxxxvi, 1927

4. THE GROWTH OF THE MARKET

M. BATESON, *Records of the Borough of Leicester*, vol i, *1103–1327* (Cambridge, 1899)

—— *Borough Customs*, Selden Society, 18, 21, 1904, 1906

R. P. BECKINSALE and J. M. HOUSTON, *Urbanization and Its Problems* (Oxford, 1968)

M. BERESFORD, *New Towns of the Middle Ages* (London, 1967)

J. B. BLAKE, The medieval coal trade of North East England: some fourteenth-century evidence, *Northern History*, ii, 1967

F. BRADSHAW, The lay subsidy of 1296. Northumberland at the end of the thirteenth century, *Archaeologia Aeliana* 3rd series, xii, 1916

C. BROOKE and G. KEIR, *London 800–1216: the Shaping of a City* (London, 1975)

E. M. CARUS-WILSON, The first half-century of the borough of Stratford-on-Avon, *Ec.H.R.* 2nd series, xviii, 1965

—— An industrial revolution of the thirteenth century, *Ec.H.R.* 1st series, xi, 1941

—— The English cloth industry in the late twelfth and early thirteenth century, *Ec.H.R.* 1st series, xiv, 1944

B. E. COATES, The origin and distribution of markets and fairs in medieval Derbyshire, *Derbyshire Archaeological Journal*, lxxxv, 1965

M. H. DODDS, The Bishop's boroughs, *Archaeologia Aeliana* 3rd series, xii, 1915

H. P. R. FINBERG, *Tavistock Abbey* (Cambridge, 1951)

C. M. FRASER, The pattern of trade in the North East of England, 1265–1350, *Northern History*, iv, 1969

A. T. GAYDON, *The Taxation of 1297*, Bedfordshire Historical Records Society, xxxix, 1959

J. GODBER, *The History of Bedfordshire 1066–1888* (Bedfordshire County Council, 1969)

S. H. A. HARVEY, *Suffolk in 1327*, Suffolk Green Books, ix, vol. ii, 1906

H. J. HEWITT, *Cheshire under the Three Edwards*, Chetham Society new series, lxxxviii, 1929

A. B. HIBBERT, 'The economic policies of towns' in *Cambridge Economic History of Europe* vol. iii (Cambridge, 1963)

J. W. F. HILL, *Medieval Lincoln* (Cambridge, 1948)

R. H. HILTON, *A Medieval Society: the West Midlands at the End of the Thirteenth Century* (London, 1966)

W. G. HOSKINS, The origins and rise of Market Harborough, *Transactions of the Leicestershire Archaeological Society*, xxv, 1949

—— 'The wealth of medieval Devon' in W. G. Hoskins and H. P. R. Finberg, *Devonshire Studies* (London, 1952)

W. HUDSON, *Leet Jurisdiction in the City of Norwich in the Thirteenth and Fourteenth Centuries*, Selden Society, 5, 1891

A. M. JACKSON, Medieval Exeter, the Exe and the Earldom of Devon, *Transactions of the Devonshire Association*, civ, 1972

M. D. LOBEL, *The Borough of Bury St Edmunds* (Oxford, 1935)

—— (ed.), *Atlas of Medieval Towns*, vol. i (London, 1969); vol. ii (London, 1975)

G. H. MARTIN, The English borough in the thirteenth century, *T.R.H.S.* 5th series, 13, 1963

——*Ipswich Recognizance Rolls 1294–1327*, Suffolk Record Society, 16, 1973

E. MILLER, The fortunes of the English textile industry in the thirteenth century, *Ec.H.R.* 2nd series, xviii, 1965

V. PARKER, *The Making of King's Lynn* (Sussex, 1971)

C. PLATT, *Medieval Southampton* (London, 1973)

S. REYNOLDS, *An Introduction to the History of English Medieval Towns* (Oxford, 1977)

E. L. SABINE, City cleaning in medieval London, *Speculum*, xii, 1937

J. TAIT, *The Medieval English Borough* (Manchester, 1936)

G. H. TUPLING, 'Markets and fairs in medieval Lancashire' in J. G. Edwards, V. H. Galbraith and E. F. Jacob (eds.), *Studies Presented to James Tait* (Manchester, 1933)

K. UGARA, The economic development of some Devonshire manors, *Transactions of the Devonshire Association*, lxxxxiv, 1962

W. URRY, *Canterbury under the Angevin Kings* (London, 1967)

Victoria County Histories:

    K. J. ALLISON (ed.), *Yorkshire, East Riding*, vol. i, *City of Kingston upon Hull* (Oxford, 1969)

    E. CRITTALL (ed.), *Wiltshire*, vol. vi, *City of Salisbury* (Oxford, 1962)

    R. A. MCKINLEY (ed.), *Leicestershire*, vol. iv, *City of Leicester* (Oxford, 1958)

W. B. STEPHENSON (ed.), *Warwickshire*, vol. iii, *City of Coventry* (Oxford, 1969); vol. viii, *Borough of Warwick*

P. M. TILLOTT (ed.), *Yorkshire, City of York* (Oxford, 1961)

G. WILLIAMS, *Medieval London: from Commune to Capital* (London, 1963)

5. SUPPLYING THE MARKET

E. K. BERRY, The borough of Droitwich and its salt industry, 1215–1700, *U.B.H.J.*, vi, 1957–8

J. BIRRELL, Peasant craftsmen in the medieval forest, *A.H.R.*, 17, 1969

J. B. BLAKE, The medieval coal trade of North East England: some fourteenth-century evidence, *Northern History*, ii, 1967

E. M. CARUS-WILSON, An industrial revolution of the thirteenth century, *Ec.H.R.* 1st series, xi, 1941

—— The English cloth industry in the late twelfth and early thirteenth century, *Ec.H.R.* 1st series, xiv, 1944

—— 'The woollen industry in Wiltshire before 1550' in E. Crittall (ed.), *Victoria County History of Wiltshire*, vol. iv (Oxford, 1959)

—— The medieval trade of the ports of the Wash, *Medieval Archaeology*, 6–7, 1962–3

E. M. CARUS-WILSON and O. COLEMAN, *England's Export Trade 1275–1547* (Oxford, 1963)

B. E. COATES, The origin and distribution of markets and fairs in medieval Derbyshire, *Derbyshire Archaeological Journal*, lxxxv, 1965

D. C. COLEMAN, *The Domestic System in Industry*, Historical Association Aids for Teachers (London, 1960)

H. COLVIN, R. A. BROWN and A. J. TAYLOR, *A History of the King's Works*, vol i, *The Middle Ages* (London, 1963)

T. K. DERRY and T. I WILLIAMS, *A Short History of Technology from the Earliest Times to 1900* (Oxford, 1960)

J. C. DAVIS, Shipping and trade at Newcastle 1294–6, *Archaeologia Aeliana*, 4th series, xxxi, 1953

—— The wool customs for Newcastle for the reign of Edward I, ibid., xxxii, 1954

J. G. EWARDS, Edward I's castle building in Wales, *British Academy*, xxxii, 1946

C. M. FRASER, Medieval trading restrictions in the North East, *Archaeologia Aeliana*, 4th series, xxxix, 1961

—— The pattern of trade in North East England, 1265–1350, *Northern History*, iv, 1969

E. B. FRYDE, The deposits of the Despensers with Italian bankers, *Ec.H.R.* 2nd series, iii, 1950–51

J. W. GOUGH, *The Mines of Mendip* (2nd edn, Oxford, 1967)

N. S. B. GRAS, *The Evolution of the English Corn Market from the Twelfth to the Early Eighteenth Century* (Cambridge, Mass. 1926)

P. D. A. HARVEY, *A Medieval Oxfordshire Village: Cuxham 1240–1400* (Oxford, 1965)

J. HATCHER, *English Tin Production and Trade before 1550* (Oxford, 1973)

J. HATCHER and T. C. BARKER, *A History of British Pewter* (London, 1974)

H. J. HEWITT, *Cheshire under the Three Edwards*, Chetham Society new series, lxxxviii, 1929

R. H. HILTON, *A Medieval Society: the West Midlands at the End of the Thirteenth Century* (London, 1966)

A. M. JACKSON, Medieval Exeter, the Exe and the Earldom of Devon, *Transactions of the Devonshire Association*, civ, 1972

R. JENKINS, The rise and fall of the Sussex iron industry, *Transactions of the Newcomen Society*, i, 1920–21

N. KERLING, *The Commercial Relations of Holland and Zealand with England* (Leiden, 1954)

D. KNOOP and G. P. JONES, *The Medieval Mason* (3rd edn, Manchester, 1967)

G. LEWIS, *The Stannaries* (Cambridge, Mass., 1907)

T. H. LLOYD, *The English Wool Trade in the Middle Ages* (Cambridge, 1977)

E. MILLER, The fortunes of the English textile industry in the thirteenth century, *Ec.H.R.* 2nd series, xviii, 1965

J. NEF, 'Mining' in *Cambridge Economic History of Europe* vol. ii (Cambridge, 1952)

E. POWER, *The Wool Trade in English Medieval History* (Oxford, 1941)

M. PRESTWICH, *War, Finance and Politics in the Reign of Edward I* (London, 1972)

A. A. RUDDOCK, *Italian Merchants and Shipping at Southampton, 1270–1600* (Southampton, 1951)

L. SALZMAN, *English Industries of the Middle Ages* (2nd edn, Oxford, 1923)

—— *Building in England to 1540* (Oxford, 1952)

H. SCHUBERT, *A History of the British Iron and Steel Industry, 450 BC to AD 1755* (London, 1951)

F. M. STENTON, The road system of medieval England, *Ec.H.R.* 1st series, vii, 1936

W. S. THOMSON (ed.), *A Lincolnshire Assize Roll for 1298*, Lincolnshire Record Society, 36, 1944

G. H. TUPLING, 'Markets and fairs in medieval Lancashire' in J. G. Edwards, V. H. Galbraith and E. F. Jacob (eds.), *Studies Presented to James Tait* (Manchester, 1933)

Victoria County Histories:

    W. FARRER and J. BROWNBILL (eds.), *Lancashire*, vol. ii (London, 1908)

    W. PAGE (ed.), *Derbyshire*, vol. ii (London, 1907); *Durham*, vol ii (London, 1907); *Gloucestershire*, vol. ii (London, 1907); *Nottinghamshire*, vol. ii

(London, 1910); *Sussex*, vol. ii (London, 1905); *Yorkshire*, vol. ii (London, 1912)

R. M. SERJEANTSON and R. D. ADKINS (eds), *Northamptonshire*, vol. ii (London, 1906)

J. WILSON (ed.), *Cumberland*, vol. ii (London, 1905)

J. WILLARD, Inland transport in the fifteenth century, *Speculum*, i, 1926

—— The use of carts in the fourteenth century, *History* new series, xvii, 1932

The reader should also consult the various monographs and articles on thirteenth-century towns listed in the bibliography for Chapter 4 which contain accounts of their local, national and international trade.

6. TOWARDS A CRISIS

A. R. H. BAKER, Evidence in the 'Nonarum Inquisitiones' of contracting arable lands in England during the early fourteenth century, *Ec.H.R.* 2nd series, xix, 1966

M. BERESFORD, *The Lost Villages of England* (Lutterworth, 1965)

M. BERESFORD and J. G. HURST, *Deserted Medieval Villages* (Guildford and London, 1972)

A. R. BRIDBURY, Before the Black Death, *Ec.H.R.* 2nd series, xxx, 1977

R. H. BRITNELL, Production for the market on a small fourteenth-century estate, *Ec.H.R.* 2nd series, xix, 1966

—— Agricultural technology and the margin of cultivation in the fourteenth century, *Ec.H.R.* 2nd series, xxx, 1977

E. B. FRYDE, Edward III's wool monopoly of 1337; a fourteenth century royal trading venture, *History* new series, xxxvii, 1952

—— *The Wool Accounts of William de la Pole*, St Anthony's Hall Publications, xxv (York, 1964)

—— *Business Activities of York Merchants 1330–1349*, Borthwick Papers, xxix, (York, 1966)

E. B. and M. M. FRYDE, 'Public credit with special reference to North West Europe' in *Cambridge Economic History of Europe* vol. iii (Cambridge, 1963)

J. GODBER, *The History of Bedfordshire 1066–1888* (Bedfordshire County Council, 1969)

E. C. and N. S. B. GRAS, *The Economic and Social History of an English Village* (Cambridge, Mass., 1930)

B. HARVEY, The population trend in England 1300–48, *T.R.H.S.* 5th series, 16, 1966

J. HATCHER, *Rural Economy and Society in the Duchy of Cornwall 1300–1500* (Cambridge, 1970)

—— *English Tin Production and Trade before 1550* (Oxford, 1973)

H. J. HEWITT, *Cheshire under the Three Edwards*, Chetham Society new series, lxxxviii, 1929

R. H. HILTON, *The Economic Development of Some Leicestershire Estates in the XIVth and XVth Centuries* (Oxford, 1947)

I. KERSHAW, The Great Famine and agrarian crisis in England 1315–22, *P. and P.*, 59, 1973

T. H. LLOYD, *The English Wool Trade in the Middle Ages* (Cambridge, 1977)

J. R. MADDICOTT, *Thomas of Lancaster* (Oxford, 1970)

—— *The English Peasantry and the Demands of the Crown, 1294–1341*, Past and Present Supplement no. 1, 1975

M. MATE, High prices in the early fourteenth century – causes and consequences, *Ec.H.R.* 2nd series, xxviii, 1975

E. MILLER, 'War taxation and the English economy in the late thirteenth and early fourteenth centuries' in J. M. Winter (ed.), *War and Economic Development* (Cambridge, 1975)

K. NEWTON, *Thaxted in the Fourteenth Century*, Essex Record Office Publications no. 33 (Chelmsford, 1960)

J. F. NICHOLS, An early fourteenth-century petition from the tenants of Bocking to their manorial lord, *Ec.H.R.* 1st series, ii, 1929–30

F. M. PAGE, *Wellingborough Manorial Accounts, 1258–1325*, Northamptonshire Record Society, viii, 1936

E. POWER, *The Wool Trade in English Medieval History* (Oxford, 1941)

R. SOMERVILLE, *The Duchy of Lancaster 1265–1603* (London, 1953)

J. Z. TITOW, *English Rural Society 1200–1350* (London, 1969)

—— *Winchester Yields. A Study in Medieval Agricultural Productivity* (Cambridge, 1972)

G. TUPLING, *The Economic History of Rossendale*, Chetham Society new series, lxxxvi, 1927

D. WILLIS (ed.), *The Estate Book of Henry de Bray c.1289–1340*, Camden Society 3rd series, xxvii, 1916

D. WATTS, A model for the early fourteenth century, *Ec.H.R.* 2nd series, xx, 1967

The reader should also consult the relevant sections of monographs and articles on towns, trade and industry listed in the bibliographies for Chapters 4 and 5.

7. CRISIS AND CHANGE IN THE AGRARIAN ECONOMY

N. W. ALCOCK, An East Devon manor in the later Middle Ages, *Transactions of the Devonshire Association*, cii, 1970

K. J. ALLISON and others, *The Deserted Villages of Oxfordshire* (Leicester, 1965)

—— *The Deserted Villages of Northamptonshire* (Leicester, 1966)

C. T. ALLMAND, The Lancastrian land settlement in Normandy 1417–50, *Ec.H.R.* 2nd series, xxi, 1968

J. M. W. BEAN, *The Estates of the Percy Family, 1416–1537* (Oxford, 1958)

M. BERESFORD, *The Lost Villages of England* (Lutterworth, 1965)

M. BERESFORD and J. G. HURST, *Deserted Medieval Villages* (Guildford and London, 1972)

J. BIRRELL, The forest economy of the honour of Tutbury in the fourteenth and fifteenth centuries, *U.B.H.J.*, viii, 1962

I. W. S. BLANCHARD, *The Duchy of Lancaster Estates in Derbyshire, 1485–1540*, Derbyshire Archaeological Record Series, iii, 1971

P. BRANDON, Demesne arable farming in coastal Sussex in the late Middle Ages, *A.H.R.*, 19, 1971

—— Cereal yields on the Sussex estates of Battle Abbey, *Ec.H.R.* 2nd series, xxv, 1972

A. R. BRIDBURY, *Economic Growth. England in the Later Middle Ages* (2nd edn, Sussex, 1975)

—— The Black Death, *Ec.H.R.* 2nd series, xxvi, 1973

—— Sixteenth-century farming, *Ec.H.R.* 2nd series, xxvii, 1974

—— 'The Hundred Years' War: costs and profits' in D. C. Coleman and A. H. John (eds.), *Trade, Government and Economy in Pre-Industrial England. Essays Presented to F. J. Fisher* (London, 1976)

R. H. BRITNELL, Agricultural technology and the margin of cultivation in the fourteenth century, *Ec.H.R.* 2nd series, xxx, 1977

C. N. L. BROOKE, Introduction to W. T. Mellows and P. I. King (eds.), *The Book of William Morton, Almoner of Peterborough Monastery, 1448–67*, Northamptonshire Record Society, xvi, 1954

M. CLOUGH (ed.), *The Book of Bartholomew Bolney*, Sussex Record Society, lxiii, 1964

N. DAVIS (ed.), *The Paston Letters* vols. i and ii (Oxford, 1971, 1976)

R. R. DAVIES, Baronial incomes, accounts and arrears, *Ec.H.R.* 2nd series, xxi, 1968

R. B. DOBSON, *The Peasants' Revolt of 1381* (London, 1970)

—— *Durham Priory, 1400–50* (Cambridge, 1973)

F. R. H. DU BOULAY A rentier economy in the later Middle Ages: the Archbishopric of Canterbury, *Ec.H.R.* 2nd series, xvi, 1963–4

—— Who were farming the English demesnes at the end of the fifteenth century, *Ec.H.R.* 2nd series, xviii, 1964–5

—— *The Lordship of Canterbury* (London, 1966)

C. C. DYER, A redistribution of incomes in fifteenth-century England? *P. and P.*, 39, 1968

—— Population and agriculture on a Warwickshire manor in the late Middle Ages, *U.B.H.J.*, xi, 1968

—— A small landowner in the fifteenth century, *Midland History*, i, 1972

D. FARMER, Grain yields on Winchester manors in the later Middle Ages, *Ec.H.R.* 2nd series, xxx, 1977

H. P. R. FINBERG, *Tavistock Abbey* (Cambridge, 1951)

H. S. FOX, The chronology of enclosure and economic development in medieval Devon, *Ec.H.R.* 2nd series, xxviii, 1975

J. P. GENET, Economie et société rurale en Angleterre au xve siècle, d'après les comptes de l'hôpital d'Ewelme, *Annales (Economies, Sociétés, Civilisations)*, 27, no. 6, 1972

J. GODBER, *The History of Bedfordshire 1066–1888* (Bedfordshire County Council, 1969)

B. HARRIS, Landlords and tenants in the later Middle Ages: the Buckingham estates, *P. and P.*, 43, 1969

B. HARVEY, Draft letters of manumission for the men of Somerset, *E.H.R.*, lxxx, 1965

—— The leasing of the Abbot of Westminster's demesnes, *Ec.H.R.* 2nd series, xxii, 1969

—— *Westminster Abbey and Its Estates in the Middle Ages* (Oxford, 1977)

P. D. A. HARVEY, *A Medieval Oxfordshire Village: Cuxham, 1240–1400* (Oxford, 1965)

J. HATCHER, A diversified economy: late medieval Cornwall, *Ec.H.R.* 2nd series, xxii, 1969

—— *Rural Economy and Society in the Duchy of Cornwall, 1300–1500* (Cambridge, 1970)

—— *Plague, Population and the English Economy 1348–1530* (London, 1977)

H. J. HEWITT, *Cheshire under the Three Edwards*, Chetham Society new series, lxxxviii, 1929

R. H. HILTON, *The Economic Development of Some Leicestershire Estates in the XIVth and XVth Centuries* (Oxford, 1947)

—— Peasant movements in England before 1381, *Ec.H.R.* 2nd series, ii, 1949–50

—— Winchcombe Abbey and the manor of Sherborne, *U.B.H.J.*, ii, 1949–1950

—— *Ministers' Accounts of the Warwickshire Estates of the Duke of Clarence 1479–80*, Dugdale Society, xxi, 1952

—— *The Decline of Serfdom in Medieval England* (London, 1969)

—— *Bondmen Made Free* (London, 1973)

—— *The English Peasantry in the Later Middle Ages* (Oxford, 1975)

R. H. HILTON and H. FAGAN, *The English Rising of 1381* (London, 1950)

G. A. HOLMES, *The Estates of the Higher Nobility in the XIVth Century* (Cambridge, 1957)

N. KENYON, Labour conditions in Essex in the reign of Richard II, *Ec.H.R.* 1st series, iv, 1932–4

I. KERSHAW, *Bolton Priory Rentals and Ministers' Accounts 1473–1539*, Yorkshire Archaeological Society Record Series, cxxxii, 1970

A. JONES, Land and people at Leighton Buzzard in the later fifteenth century, *Ec.H.R.* 2nd series, xxv, 1972

J. R. LANDER, *Conflict and Stability in Fifteenth-Century England*, chapter i (3rd edn, London, 1977)

A. E. LEVETT, 'The Black Death on the St Alban's manors' in H. Cam, M. Coate and L. Sutherland (eds.), *Studies in Manorial History* (Oxford, 1938)

A. E. LEVETT and A. BALLARD, *The Black Death on the Estates of the See of Winchester* (Oxford, 1916)

T. H. LLOYD, *The Movement of Wool Prices in Medieval England*, *Ec.H.R.* supplement no. 6 (Cambridge, 1973)

R. A. LOMAS, The Priory of Durham and its demesnes in the fourteenth and fifteenth centuries, *Ec.H.R.* 2nd series, xxxi, 1978

K. B. MCFARLANE, The investment of Sir John Fastolf's profits of war, *T.R.H.S.* 5th series, 7, 1957

—— England and the Hundred Years' War, *P. and P.*, 22, 1962

—— *The Nobility of Late Medieval England* (Oxford, 1973)

M. MOLLAT and P. WOLFF, *Popular Revolutions of the Late Middle Ages* (London, 1973)

K. NEWTON, *Thaxted in the Fourteenth Century*, Essex Record Office Publications no. 33 (Chelmsford, 1960)

—— *The Manor of Writtle* (Sussex, 1970)

F. M. PAGE, *The Estates of Crowland Abbey* (Cambridge, 1934)

A. POLLARD, Estates management: the Talbots and Whitchurch 1383–1525, *Ec.H.R.* 2nd series, xxv, 1972

M. M. POSTAN, The fifteenth century, *Ec.H.R.* 1st series, ix, 1939

—— Some social consequences of the Hundred Years' War, *Ec.H.R.* 1st series, xii, 1942

—— The costs of the Hundred Years' War, *P. and P.*, 27, 1964

T. B. PUGH and C. D. ROSS, Materials for the study of baronial incomes, *Ec.H.R.* 2nd series, vi, 1953–4

B. PUTNAM, *The Enforcement of the Statute of Labourers* (New York, 1908)

J. A. RAFTIS, *The Estates of Ramsey Abbey* (Toronto, 1957)

—— *Tenure and Mobility: Studies in the Social History of the Medieval English Village* (Toronto, 1964)

J. T. ROSENTHAL, The estates and finances of Richard, duke of York, *Studies in Medieval and Renaissance History*, ii (Nebraska, 1965)

A. SABIN (ed.), *Some Manorial Accounts of St Augustine's Abbey, Bristol*, Bristol Record Society, xxii, 1960

E. SEARLE, *Lordship and Community: Battle Abbey and its Banlieu, 1066–1538* (Toronto, 1974)

R. A. L. SMITH, *Canterbury Cathedral Priory: a Study in Monastic Administration* (Cambridge, 1943)

R. SOMERVILLE, *The Duchy of Lancaster 1265–1603* (London, 1953)

J. Z. TITOW, Weather on the Winchester estates, 1350–1450, *Annales (Economies, Sociétés, Civilisations)* 25, no. 2, 1970

G. TUPLING, *The Economic History of Rossendale*, Chetham Society new series, lxxxvi, 1927

B. P. WOLFFE, *The Crown Lands 1461–1536* (London, 1970)

8. FREEDOM VERSUS RESTRICTION: TOWN AND COUNTRY-SIDE IN THE LATER MIDDLE AGES

B. W. E. ALFORD and T. C. BARKER, *A History of the Carpenters' Company* (London, 1968)

J. N. BARTLETT, The expansion and decline of York in the later Middle Ages, *Ec.H.R.* 2nd series, xii, 1959–60

M. BATESON, *Records of the Borough of Leicester*, vol. ii, *1327–1509* (London, 1901)

R. BIRD, *The Turbulent London of Richard II* (London, 1949)

J. BIRRELL, The forest economy of the honour of Tutbury in the fourteenth and fifteenth centuries, *U.B.H.J.*, viii, 1962

—— Peasant craftsmen in the medieval forest, *A.H.R.*, 17, 1969

I. W. S. BLANCHARD, The miner and the agricultural community in later medieval England, *A.H.R.*, 20, 1972

—— Stannator Fabulosus, *A.H.R.*, 22, 1974

—— Labour productivity and work psychology in the English mining industry 1400–1600, *Ec.H.R.* 2nd series, xxxi, 1978

A. R. BRIDBURY, *Economic Growth. England in the Later Middle Ages* (2nd edn, Sussex, 1975)

A. E. BUTCHER, The origins of Romney freemen, 1432–1532, *Ec.H.R.* 2nd series, xxvii, 1974

—— Rent, population and economic change in late medieval Newcastle, *Northern History*, xiv, 1978

E. M. CARUS-WILSON, Evidences of industrial growth on some fifteenth-century manors, *Ec.H.R.* 2nd series, xii, 1959–60

—— 'The woollen industry in Wiltshire before 1550' in E. Crittall (ed.), *Victoria County History of Wiltshire*, vol. iv (Oxford, 1959)

O. COLEMAN, Trade and prosperity in the fifteenth century: some aspects of the trade of Southampton, *Ec.H.R.* 2nd series, xvi, 1963–4

F. CONSITT, *The London Weavers' Company from the Twelfth to the Close of the Sixteenth Century* (Oxford, 1935)

J. CORNWALL, English country towns in the 1520's, *Ec.H.R.* 2nd series, xv, 1962–3

H. A. CRONNE, *The Borough of Warwick in the Late Middle Ages*, Dugdale Society Occasional Papers, x, 1951

R. B. DOBSON, Admissions to the freedom of the City of York in the later Middle Ages, *Ec.H.R.* 2nd series, xxvi, 1973

—— Urban decline in late medieval England, *T.R.H.S.* 5th series, 27, 1977

M. DORMER HARRIS (ed.), *The Coventry Leet Book*, Early English Text Society, original series, 134, 135, 138, 146 (London, 1907–13)

R. DUNNING and D. G. TREMBLETT (eds.), *Bridgwater Borough Archives*, Somerset Record Society, lxx, 1972

A. D. DYER, *The City of Worcester in the Sixteenth Century* (Leicester 1973)

F. J. FISHER, The development of London as a centre of conspicuous consumption in the sixteenth and seventeenth centuries, *T.R.H.S.* 4th series, xxxi, 1948

H. S. FOX, The chronology of enclosure and economic development in medieval Devon, *Ec.H.R.* 2nd series, xxviii, 1975

T. GIRTIN, *The Triple Crowns. A Narrative History of the Drapers' Company, 1364–1964* (London, 1964)

—— *The Mark of the Sword. A Narrative History of the Cutler's Company 1189–1975* (London, 1975)

J. GODBER, *The History of Bedfordshire 1066–1888* (Bedfordshire County Council, 1969)

A. S. GREEN, *Town Life in the Fifteenth Century* (London, 1894)

G. HADLEY, *Citizens and Founders. A Short History of the Worshipful Company of Founders, London* (Sussex, 1976)

J. HATCHER, Myths, miners and agricultural communities, *A.H.R.*, 22, 1974

J. HATCHER and T. C. BARKER, *A History of British Pewter* (London, 1974)

P. HEATH, North Sea fishing in the fifteenth century: the Scarborough fleet, *Northern History*, iii, 1968

H. HEATON, *The Yorkshire Worsted and Woollen Industry* (Oxford, 1920)

H. J. HEWITT, *Cheshire under the Three Edwards*, Chetham Society new series, lxxxviii, 1929

A. HIBBERT, 'The economic policies of towns' in *Cambridge Economic History of Europe* vol. iii (Cambridge, 1963)

W. G. HOSKINS, *Essays in Leicestershire History* (Liverpool, 1958)

—— *Provincial England* (London, 1963)

W. G. HOSKINS and H. P. R. FINBERG, *Devonshire Studies* (London, 1952)

P. E. JONES, *The Butchers of London* (London, 1976)

S. KRAMER, The amalgamation of English mercantile crafts, *E.H.R.*, xxiii, 1908

E. LIPSON, *A History of the Woollen and Worsted Industries* (London, reprinted 1965)

E. MAYER, *The Curriers and the City of London* (London, 1968)

K. NEWTON, *Thaxted in the Fourteenth Century*, Essex Record Office Publications no. 33 (Chelmsford, 1960)

J. W. PERCY (ed.), *The York Memorandum Book*, Surtees Society, clxxxvi, 1973

C. PHYTHIAN-ADAMS, 'Urban decay in late medieval England' in P. Abrams and E. A. Wrigley (eds.), *Towns in Societies. Essays in Economic History and Historical Sociology* (Cambridge, 1978)

E. POWER, English craft gilds in the Middle Ages, *History* new series, iv, 1920

G. D. RAMSAY, *The Wiltshire Woollen Industry in the Sixteenth Century* (2nd edn, London, 1964)

T. REDDAWAY and L. WALKER, *The Early History of the Goldsmiths' Company, 1327–1509* (London, 1976)

J. C. RUSSELL, *Medieval Regions and Their Cities* (Devon, 1972)

G. SCAMMELL, English merchant shipping at the end of the Middle Ages, *Ec.H.R.* 2nd series, xiii, 1960–1

—— Shipowning in England *c.*1450–1550, *T.R.H.S.* 5th series, 12, 1962

W. D. SIMPSON (ed.), *The Building Accounts of Tattershall Castle, 1434–72*, Lincoln Record Society, lv, 1960

R. SPRANDEL, Le production de fer au Moyen Age, *Annales (Economies, Sociétés, Civilisations)* 24, no. 2, 1969

J. THIRSK, 'Industry in the countryside' in F. J. Fisher (ed.), *Essays in the Economic and Social History of Tudor and Stuart England* (Cambridge, 1961)

S. THRUPP, *A Short History of the Worshipful Company of Bakers of London* (London, 1933)

—— *The Merchant Class of Medieval London, 1300–1500* (Chicago, 1948)

—— 'The Gilds' in *Cambridge Economic History of Europe* vol. iii (Cambridge, 1963)

G. UNWIN, *The Gilds and Companies of London* (London, 1925)

E. M. VEALE, *The English Fur Trade in the Later Middle Ages* (Oxford, 1966)

—— 'Craftsmen in the economy of London in the fourteenth century' in A. Hollaender and W. Kellaway (eds.), *Studies in London History Presented to P. E. Jones* (London, 1969)

Other works on specific English towns and industries covering the later as well as the earlier Middle Ages are listed in the bibliography for Chapter 5.

9. ENGLISH TRADE IN THE LATER MIDDLE AGES: THE TRIUMPH OF THE ENGLISH?

A. BEARDWOOD, *Alien Merchants in England 1300–77* (Cambridge, Mass., 1931)

J. B. BLAKE, The medieval coal trade of North East England: some fifteenth-century evidence, *Northern History*, ii, 1967

A. R. BRIDBURY, *England and the Salt Trade in the Later Middle Ages* (Oxford, 1955)

—— *Economic Growth. England in the Later Middle Ages* (2nd edn, Sussex, 1975)

E. M. CARUS-WILSON, *Medieval Merchant Venturers* (2nd edn, London, 1967). This includes articles on the Overseas Trade of Bristol in the fifteenth century, the Iceland Venture and the origins and early development of the Merchant Adventurers' organization in London.

—— Trends in the export of English woollens in the fourteenth century, *Ec.H.R.* 2nd series, iii, 1950

E. M. CARUS-WILSON and O. COLEMAN, *England's Export Trade 1275–1547* (Oxford, 1963)

W. CHILDS, *Anglo-Castilian Trade in the Later Middle Ages* (Manchester, 1978)

O. COLEMAN, Trade and prosperity in the fifteenth century: some aspects of the trade of Southampton, *Ec.H.R.* 2nd series, xvi, 1963–4

O. COLEMAN (ed.), *The Brokage Book of Southampton 1443–4*, part i, Southampton Record Series, iv, 1960

P. DOLLINGER, *The German Hansa* (London, 1970)

R. FLENLEY, London and foreign merchants in the reign of Henry VI, *E.H.R.*, xxv, 1910

E. B. FRYDE, Anglo-Italian commerce in the fifteenth century: some evidence about profits and the balance of trade, *Revue Belge de Philologie et d'Histoire*, 1, 1972

N. S. B. GRAS, *The Early English Customs' System* (Cambridge, Mass., 1918)

H. L. GRAY, 'English foreign trade 1446–82' in E. Power and M. M. Postan (eds.), *Studies in English Trade in the Fifteenth Century* (London, 1933)

M. GUISEPPI, Alien merchants in England in the fifteenth century, *T.R.H.S.* new series, ix, 1895

A. HANHAM, Foreign Exchange and the English wool merchant in the late fifteenth century, *Bulletin of the Institute of Historical Research*, xlvi, 1973

A. HANHAM (ed.), *The Cely Letters 1472–88*, Early English Text Society 273 (Oxford, 1975)

J. HATCHER, *English Tin Production and Trade before 1550* (Oxford, 1973)

W. I. HAWARD, 'The financial transactions between the Lancastrian government and the merchants of the Staple from 1449 to 1461' in E. Power and M. M. Postan (eds.), *Studies in English Trade in the Fifteenth Century* (London, 1933)

J. HEERS, *Genes aux xve siècle* (Paris, 1961)

G. A. HOLMES, Florentine merchants in England 1346–1436, *Ec.H.R.* 2nd series, xiii, 1960–61

—— The 'Libel of English Policy', *E.H.R.*, lxxvi, 1961

W. G. HOSKINS, 'The wealth of medieval Devon' in W. G. Hoskins and H. P. R. Finberg, *Devonshire Studies* (London, 1952)

M. K. JAMES, 'Gilbert Maghfeld, a London merchant of the fourteenth century' *Ec.H.R.* 2nd series, viii, 1955–6

—— *Studies in the Medieval Wine Trade* (Oxford, 1971)

N. KERLING, *The Commercial Relations of Holland and Zealand with England* (Leiden, 1954)

F. C. LANE, *Andrea Barbarigo, Merchant of Venice* (Baltimore, 1944)

T. H. LLOYD, *The English Wool Trade in the Middle Ages* (Cambridge, 1977)

F. MACE, Devonshire ports in the fourteenth and fifteenth centuries, *T.R.H.S.*, 4th series, viii, 1925

M. MALLETT, Anglo-Florentine commercial relations 1465–91, *Ec.H.R.* 2nd series, xv, 1962–3

—— *The Florentine Galleys* (Oxford, 1967)

J. H. MUNRO, Economic aspects of the collapse of the Anglo-Burgundian alliance, *E.H.R.*, lxxxv, 1970

—— *Wool, Cloth and Gold: the Struggle for Bullion in the Anglo-Burgundian Trade 1340–1478* (Toronto, 1972)

M. M. POSTAN, Credit in medieval trade, *Ec.H.R.* 1st series, i, 1927–8

—— 'The economic and political relations of England and the Hanse from 1400 to 1475' in E. Power and M. M. Postan (eds.) *Studies in English Trade in the Fifteenth Century* (London, 1933)

E. POWER, *The Wool Trade in English Medieval History* (Oxford, 1941)

—— 'The wool trade in the fifteenth century' in E. Power and M. M. Postan (eds.), *Studies in English Trade in the Fifteenth Century* (London, 1933)

E. POWER and M. M. POSTAN (eds.), *Studies in English Trade in the Fifteenth Century* (London, 1933)

R. DE ROOVER, *The Rise and Decline of the Medici Bank, 1397–1494* (Cambridge, Mass., 1963)

A. RUDDOCK, *Italian Merchants and Shipping at Southampton 1270–1600* (Southampton, 1951)

F. R. SALTER, The Hanse, Cologne and the crisis of 1468, *Ec.H.R.* 1st series, iii, 1931–2

G. V. SCAMMELL, English merchant shipping at the end of the Middle Ages, *Ec.H.R.* 2nd series, xiii, 1960–61

—— Shipowning in England *c.*1450–1550, *T.R.H.S.*, 5th series, 12, 1962

S. THRUPP, 'The Grocers of London: a study of the distributive trade' in E. Power and M. M. Postan (eds.), *Studies in English Trade in the Fifteenth Century* (London, 1933)

—— *The Merchant Class of Medieval London, 1300–1500* (Chicago, 1948)

E. M. VEALE, *The English Fur Trade in the Later Middle Ages* (Oxford, 1966)

W. B. WATSON, The structure of the Florentine galley trade with Flanders and England in the fifteenth century, *Revue Belge de Philologie et d'Histoire*, xxxix, 1961; xl, 1962

P. WOLFF, English cloth in Toulouse 1380–1450, *Ec.H.R.* 2nd series, ii, 1949–50

The reader should also consult the various monographs and articles on towns and industries in the bibliography for Chapter 8 which contain accounts of local, national and international trade.

10. ECONOMIC IDEAS

SIR J. CRAIG, *The Mint* (Cambridge, 1953)

A. FEAVERYEAR, *The Pound Sterling* (2nd edn, Oxford, 1963)

P. ELMAN, The economic causes of the expulsion of the Jews, *Ec.H.R.* 1st series, vii, 1936–7

E. B. FRYDE, The deposits of the Despensers with Italian bankers, *Ec.H.R.* 2nd series, iii, 1950–51

E. B. and M. M. FRYDE, 'Public credit with special reference to North West Europe' in *Cambridge Economic History of Europe* vol. iii (Cambridge, 1963)

J. GILCHRIST, *The Church and Economic Activity in the Middle Ages* (London, 1969)

A. HANHAM, Foreign exchange and the English wool merchant in the late fifteenth century, *Bulletin of the Institute of Historical Research*, xlvi, 1973

T. H. LLOYD, *The English Wool Trade in the Middle Ages* (Cambridge, 1977)

M. MATE, The indebtedness of Canterbury Cathedral Priory, *Ec.H.R.* 2nd series, xxvi, 1973

E. MILLER, 'The economic policies of government: France and England' in *Cambridge Economic History of Europe* vol. iii (Cambridge, 1963)

J. H. MUNRO, *Wool, Cloth and Gold: the Struggle for Bullion in the Anglo-Burgundian Trade 1340–1478* (Toronto, 1972)

B. NELSON, *The Idea of Usury* (Princeton, 1949)

J. NOONAN, *The Scholastic Analysis of Usury* (Cambridge, Mass., 1957)

M. M. POSTAN, Credit in medieval trade, *Ec.H.R.* 1st series, i, 1927–8

E. POWER, *The Wool Trade in English Medieval History* (Oxford, 1941)

—— 'The wool trade in the fifteenth century' in E. Power and M. M. Postan (eds.), *Studies in English Trade in the Fifteenth Century* (London, 1933)

M. PRESTWICH, *War, Finance and Politics in the Reign of Edward I* (London, 1972)

H. G. RICHARDSON, *The English Jewry under the Angevin Kings* (London, 1960)

R. DE ROOVER, *The Rise and Decline of the Medici Bank, 1397–1494* (Cambridge, Mass., 1963)

—— *Banking, Business and Economic Thought in Later Medieval and Early Modern Europe* (Chicago, 1974)

C. ROTH, *The History of the Jews in England* (Oxford, 1949)

B. TIERNEY, *The Medieval Poor Law* (California, 1959)

CONCLUSION

Full bibliographies on social, religious, intellectual and art history can be found in D. J. Guth's bibliographical handbook *Late Medieval England, 1377–1485* (Cambridge, 1976)

Index

379